# PREVENTION AND THE LIMITS OF THE CRIMINAL LAW

# Prevention and the Limits of the Criminal Law

Edited by
ANDREW ASHWORTH
LUCIA ZEDNER
and
PATRICK TOMLIN

OXFORD
UNIVERSITY PRESS

**OXFORD**
**UNIVERSITY PRESS**

Great Clarendon Street, Oxford, OX2 6DP,
United Kingdom

Oxford University Press is a department of the University of Oxford.
It furthers the University's objective of excellence in research, scholarship,
and education by publishing worldwide. Oxford is a registered trade mark of
Oxford University Press in the UK and in certain other countries



First Edition published in 2013



Published in the United States of America by Oxford University Press
198 Madison Avenue, New York, NY 10016, United States of America

British Library Cataloguing in Publication Data
Data available

Library of Congress Cataloging in Publication Data
Data available

ISBN 978–0–19–965676–9

# *Acknowledgements*

The editors wish to express their thanks to the Arts and Humanities Research Council for generously funding the three-year 'Preventive Justice' Project (AHRC Project Number AH/H015655/1) from which this volume arose. We also thank Dr Ambrose Lee, Post-Doctoral Research Officer on the project for his excellent research and organizational help; Gabrielle Watson for her superb editorial assistance; and Alex Flach, Natasha Flemming, and colleagues at OUP for seeing this volume through to production. We are grateful to all those who participated in the two Preventive Justice seminars held at All Souls College, Oxford in September 2011 and January 2012. Particular thanks go to those who acted as formal respondents to the papers upon which these chapters were based: James Edwards, Cécile Fabre, Andreas von Hirsch, Murray Hunt, Nicola Lacey, Ian Loader, Laurence Lustgarten, and Shlomit Wallerstein. Last but certainly not least, we thank all the authors whose chapters appear here for devoting their very considerable acumen and insight to the questions of preventive justice that we posed to them and, in so doing, helping to further the aims of our Preventive Justice Project.

# *Contents*

# *List of Contributors*

**Andrew Ashworth** is Vinerian Professor of English Law in the University of Oxford and a Fellow of All Souls College.

**Petter Asp** is Professor of Criminal Law at Stockholm University and the holder of the Torsten and Ragnar Söderberg Chair of Legal Science.

**Markus D Dubber** is Professor of Law, University of Toronto.

**R A Duff** is a Professor in the Law School, University of Minnesota and Professor Emeritus in the Department of Philosophy, University of Stirling.

**David Dyzenhaus** is Professor of Law and Philosophy at the University of Toronto.

**Klaus Günther** is Professor of Legal Theory, Criminal Law and Criminal Procedure at the Faculty of Law, Goethe University of Frankfurt.

**Bernard E Harcourt** is the Julius Kreeger Professor of Law and Criminology and Professor and Chairman of the Department of Political Science at the University of Chicago.

**Douglas Husak** is a Professor of Philosophy, Rutgers University.

**Matt Matravers** is Director of the Morrell Centre for Toleration and of the School of Politics, Economics and Philosophy, both at the University of York.

**James W Nickel** is Professor of Philosophy and Law at the University of Miami.

**Pat O'Malley** is Professorial Research Fellow in Law at the University of Sydney and Visiting Professor in the Department of Sociology, Social Policy and Criminology, University of Liverpool.

**Peter Ramsay** is a Senior Lecturer in Law at the London School of Economics.

**Frederick Schauer** is David and Mary Harrison Distinguished Professor of Law at the University of Virginia and Visiting Professor of Law at Columbia University.

**Carol S Steiker** is the Henry J. Friendly Professor of Law at Harvard Law School.

**Victor Tadros** is Professor of Criminal Law and Legal Theory at the University of Warwick.

**Patrick Tomlin** is a Lecturer in Political Theory at the University of Reading.

**Lucia Zedner** is Professor of Criminal Justice in the Faculty of Law at the University of Oxford and Conjoint Professor in the Faculty of Law at the University of New South Wales.

# Introduction

*Andrew Ashworth, Lucia Zedner, and Patrick Tomlin*

This book arises from a three-year study of Preventive Justice, generously funded by the Arts and Humanities Research Council. The project's main objective is to develop an account of the principles and values that should guide and limit the state's use of coercive preventive techniques. Central to the project is an interdisciplinary and cross-jurisdictional approach, developed with the collaboration of scholars from a variety of disciplinary backgrounds, jurisdictions, and legal cultures. This book is the product of two seminars held at All Souls College, Oxford, at which 14 leading international scholars in the fields of criminal law, public law, legal theory, criminology, philosophy, and political theory presented and discussed early drafts of what were to become the chapters collected in this volume. Each draft paper was subject to detailed commentary by a designated respondent and then subject to searching analysis by the invited seminar participants. Their collective contributions advanced the debate and undoubtedly enriched the final chapters in this volume. The contributing authors are all world-renowned scholars in their respective fields. They include leading academics from the US, Canada, Australia, South Africa, the UK, and continental Europe.

Understood simply, the criminal law is a backward-looking institution. Whatever its overarching rationale or justification, in its implementation the core of the criminal law punishes persons for their past behaviour. However, this simple backward-looking story has never fully captured what the criminal law is or seeks to achieve, and increasingly states use the criminal law or criminal law-like tools to try to prevent or reduce the risk of (anticipated) future harm. Such measures include the criminalization of ordinarily harmless and seemingly innocent behaviour in order to allow authorities to intervene at an early stage; the incapacitation of suspected future wrongdoers; and extended sentences for past wrongdoers on the basis of their predicted future conduct.

There are good reasons to justify state use of coercion to protect the public from harm. And yet, although the rationales for and justifications of state punishment have been explored extensively, the scope, limits, and principles of what we term preventive justice—the use of the criminal law and related coercive measures in a directly preventive way—have attracted little doctrinal or conceptual analysis (save in respect of counterterrorist measures). The chapters in this book seek to reassess the foundations for the range of coercive measures that states now take in the name of prevention and public protection. Among the recent legal developments discussed below are the extension of criminal liability to merely preparatory and pre-inchoate acts, technologies of prevention relating to road traffic offences, specially restrictive measures against suspected terrorists, restraining measures that make use of civil procedures, expanding pre-trial detention, preventive detention of 'dangerous' offenders, and so on. In this Introduction, we outline the main contributions made by each chapter, and then explore some core themes.

The first five chapters examine the nature and historical antecedents of preventive justice and its relationship with criminal law and punishment. In the first chapter, **Schauer** questions the dichotomy assumed to exist between *ex ante* and *ex post* punishment. He argues that all judgements of guilt and all punishments have a probabilistic component and that, by accepting proof beyond reasonable doubt rather than requiring certainty, we place a probabilistic assessment at the heart of criminal justice. Given that we accept an error rate in respect of conviction, objections to preventive measures arise only if the error rate in respect of prediction of future crimes is higher. What is different about, and wrong with, preventive measures is less that they are preventive, than that they are often based on lower probabilities than the criminal law would demand. There are also non-probabilistic differences between *ex ante* and *ex post* measures. However, to the extent that they are relevant, Schauer argues, there may be a greater wrong in restricting someone on account of doing something they did not in fact do, than in denying someone who will probably offend in the future the chance to do wrong. His message is that preventive justice and probabilistic assessments are all around us, and when we object to them we must be precise about the nature of our objection.

**Asp** identifies a general trend toward 'preventionism', by which he means the criminalization of nonconsummate offences. Asp recognizes that prevention and criminalization are closely linked conceptually but argues that prevention poses difficulties for the distribution of punishment because it departs from the ordinary requirements and limits of deservedness. His particular concern is with the risks associated with preventionism and, in particular, in respect of complex nonconsummate offences, namely those that require ulterior intent. Although Husak has argued that a high culpability requirement helps justify criminalization of nonconsummate offences,[1] Asp regards this requirement as problematic because it holds the actor 'partially responsible for something that he or she has not done yet' and, in so doing, alters the scope and gravity of the offence for which an offender will face punishment.

**Dubber**'s chapter contends that much contemporary scholarship on preventive justice pays insufficient heed to the historical antecedents of preventive endeavour and consequently overplays the novelty of present developments. It follows, he argues, that scholars are misguided in attempting to evaluate preventive endeavours by reference to the principles of penal justice without first seeking to understand the historical origins of the penal state. Dubber's argument builds upon the contention,

[1] D Husak, 'The Nature and Justifiability of Nonconsummate Offences' (1995) 37 Arizona Law Review 151–83; D Husak, *Overcriminalization. The Limits of the Criminal Law* (2008) 159 ff.

developed in his earlier works (most notably *The Police Power*)[2] that the ideal of the *Rechsstaat* or 'law state' must be set against the historical exercise of the police power, which, insofar as it is concerned with the maintenance of peace and good order, is largely synonymous with prevention. From the perspective of the police power, ideas of justice and legitimacy have no purchase, argues Dubber, because the exercise of the police power is unconstrained by principles of any kind. He concludes that measures of preventive justice are less departures or deviations from justice, rather they result from a distinction 'between law and police as basic modes of governance'. Dubber thus offers an intriguing historical explanation for the relative ease with which states have developed preventive measures in a seemingly untrammelled manner.

**Günther**, building on the work of David Garland,[3] among others, claims that there has been a 'paradigm change' in criminal justice. Governments are increasingly focused on the protection of innocent citizens, who see such protection as a right, whereas constitutional and human rights documents traditionally seek to limit the state's power to punish by protecting the rights of suspected, accused, and convicted offenders. In investigating the significance of this shift, Günther explores the relationship between the Responsibility to Protect (RTP), an influential norm in international public law, and preventive justice. He takes RTP out of its international context and uses it, instead, as a lens through which to explore the preventive state. He traces the normative foundations of RTP to the contractualist justifications of the state found in Hobbes and Locke. In such theories, citizens give up their duty of self-protection to the state, which must then protect them, but, Günther argues, in democratic societies, this responsibility is passed back to the citizens. One danger of the preventive state is that, in tension with a democratically founded RTP, it encourages us to view ourselves as the 'good' in need of protection from the 'dangerous' and to seize human rights as a tool with which to do so. This responsibility to protect the majority against the minority of criminal offenders, argues Günther, 'changes the anti-majoritarian meaning and direction of human rights into a majoritarian right to protection'.

In his contribution, **Dyzenhaus** explores the implications of preventive justice for the larger 'rule-of-law project', namely the attempt to ensure that the decisions of public officials comply with values and principles that should be exhibited by a legal order. Key to his analysis is an insistence that legitimacy is achieved not merely by meeting formal or procedural conditions but that it also requires compliance with substantive or moral conditions. Dyzenhaus argues that legitimacy is attained when legislatures determine appropriate legal resolutions to contemporary problems and officials implement those resolutions according to law and principles of legality. There is, says Dyzenhaus, a 'surplus value created by the conversion of public policy into law'. He goes on, however, to identify a series of hazards particularly germane to preventive endeavours that range from the creation of legal black holes, such as Guantanamo Bay; legal 'grey' holes that give the appearance

[2] MD Dubber, *The Police Power: Patriarchy and the Foundations of American Government* (2005).
[3] D Garland, *The Culture of Control: Crime and Social Order in Contemporary Society* (2001).

of legality but mask substantive black holes and are, therefore, even more dangerous; and, perhaps most dangerous, the 'veneer of legality' that conceals questionable executive decision-making. Avoiding these hazards requires a high degree of vigilance by the legislature, judiciary, and other public officials if the 'virtuous cycle of legality' is to be maintained even in the most security-sensitive cases.

The next three chapters focus upon particular exemplars of preventive endeavour. **Duff**'s chapter examines the pre-trial detention of those denied bail, a long-existing facet of the criminal justice system that has received little attention from normative theorists. Pre-trial detention is problematic, argues Duff, because it treats the defendant as guilty ahead of trial, fails to treat the individual as a responsible agent, and seems to be inconsistent with the presumption of innocence. Duff regards the neglect of this category as odd, observing 'why should the detention of those suspected of involvement in something as seriously threatening as terrorism provoke so much louder protest than the far more frequent detention of those charged with, but not convicted of, far less serious crimes?' His chapter examines the 'instrumental, consequentialist rationale' for pre-trial detention; it explores whether it is possible to provide principled justifications; and, in particular, whether it is possible to reconcile pre-trial detention with the presumption of innocence. While acknowledging that becoming a defendant in the criminal process attracts 'certain new duties or responsibilities' that, in turn, justify different kinds of restriction of which detention is only the most onerous, Duff concludes that pre-trial detention is morally problematic in ways we rarely acknowledge.

In **Tadros**' chapter the related issues of preventive detention and the justification of intervention on grounds of risk coalesce around the problem of Control Orders, now Terrorism Prevention and Investigation Measures (TPIMs), used to detain those suspected terrorists deemed to pose a risk to national security. Tadros contends that there has been insufficient 'systematic evaluation of the moral significance of risk' and that the consequentialist approach to risk, which underpins these measures, has not been countered by a sufficient non-consequentialist account. Tadros demonstrates persuasively that risk underpins the Control Order/TPIM regime, yet the level of risk required is poorly specified and the requirement that the order be 'necessary' is ambiguous. He goes on to explore questions relating to the 'moral significance of risk prevention', positing that a distinction between 'open' and 'closed' risks may be able to explain why we should be more troubled by harmful preventive measures which eliminate a very small risk of a great harm than those that prevent a certain small harm. Like many other contributors to this volume, Tadros concludes that the philosophical groundwork for evaluating preventive measures is underdeveloped.

**Nickel**'s chapter offers a critical examination of the features of restraining orders and their growing use particularly in the USA and the UK. It explores the concept of restraint, its impact on the liberty of the individual, and the sorts of procedural protections that ought to apply. His analysis spans the most coercive exemplars, such as quarantine orders, through to less invasive examples such as domestic and workplace restraining orders. It considers their impact on liberty, deploying Pettit's conception of freedom as nondomination[4] to tease out the variety and degree of coercion entailed. Nickel goes on to explore the compatibility of restraining orders with human rights protections and concludes that not only do rights violations occur only rarely but that, at best, such orders 'redistribute freedom from the restrainee to the protectee(s) in ways that can increase freedom overall'.

The chapters by Husak and Steiker each address in different ways questions of how preventive measures should be conceived, justified, and restrained. Against those who have robustly objected to the 'cloaking' of preventive detention as punishment,[5] **Husak** has challenged the idea that preventive detention is conceptually distinct. Rather, he has argued that detention for preventive ends should be understood as punishment and the conduct or traits of persons that lead to detention should be constructed as crimes. By bringing preventive detention within criminal law and criminal justice, Husak claims, it can be justified as retributive punishment and be subject to the principled constraints that apply to such punishment.[6] In his chapter, Husak is primarily concerned to explore the conceptual and normative obstacles to doing this. By exploring and seeking to overcome these obstacles, Husak seeks to show that preventive detention can be both conceived of and justified as punishment. The most difficult element is that preventive logic requires the punishment to be tailored to danger, not desert. However, given the seriousness of crimes in view, Husak argues that in practice the proportional sentence and that required for preventive purposes are unlikely to differ.

**Steiker**'s focus is on the concept of proportionality, developed in respect of punishment. She explores the possibility that proportionality might be adapted for use in respect of prevention by focusing on the seriousness of the harm to be averted and the probability of its occurrence in the absence of prevention. Steiker contends that proportionality is not a justificatory theory of prevention any more than it is a justificatory theory of punishment but that it may have a role to play as a constraint. Thus conceived, proportionality might go some way to resolving questions of duration, conditions of confinement, discriminatory operation, and perhaps questions of procedural form. Steiker also recognizes that there are limits to its reach and its ability to provide clear guidance as to what may justly be done in the name of prevention. She recognizes also that there are obvious pitfalls—not least, how to measure the probability of future harm and, in particular, how to calibrate proportionality in the case of low probability but high harm risks; resort to the precautionary principle and its problems; the hazards of pretextual uses of preventive measures (for example the use of immigration detention and 'material witness' statutes in the USA immediately after 9/11); and the possibility of perverse interactions with the criminal law. Steiker reveals herself to be sceptical about the

[4] P Pettit, *Republicanism: A Theory of Freedom and Government* (1997).

[5] PH Robinson, 'Punishing Dangerousness: Cloaking Preventive Detention as Criminal Justice' (2001) 114 Harvard Law Review 1429–55.

[6] D Husak, 'Lifting the Cloak: Preventive Detention as Punishment' (2011) 48 San Diego Law Review 1173.

uses of proportionality in respect of punishment and she concludes that proportionality is unlikely to function as a robust constraint in respect of preventive measures.

The remaining chapters address very different aspects of the politics of preventive endeavour. Critiques of the expansion of the scope of the criminal law beyond the core of harmful behaviour, or behaviour closely related to harm, typically seek to show them to be inconsistent with liberalism. Instead, **Ramsay** seeks to develop an alternative political theory of preventive criminal law by exploring the extent to which pre-inchoate criminal laws can be rendered consistent with representative democracy. His chapter examines the grounds for and legal features of pre-inchoate offences and it examines the application of liberal principles, and in particular the harm principle, as a legitimating ground for pre-inchoate laws. Ramsay suggests that the articulation of a 'richer account of democracy', which includes 'a concept of political self-government' and respect for 'the institutions of formal trust among citizens', might more effectively inform and limit the scope of the criminal law.

**Matravers**' chapter provides a normative account of preventive justice that seeks to overcome the assumed antinomy between prevention and justice. It does so not by adopting a consequentialist account of prevention but by addressing the questions what is due to people and on what conditions can prevention be justified? Following Scanlon, he articulates an account in which, rather than thinking of prevention as a goal that must be constrained by concern for individual liberty or justice, it should rather be regarded as both motivated by *and* properly pursued through policies that respect the status of persons. Such an account places heavy normative weight on seeing individuals as agents who make choices in accordance with reasons. However, Matravers also contends that we are in the midst of a 'crisis in our understanding of agency' in which we are more and more aware of 'the degree to which our fates are not fully our own or determined by our choices'. Viewed from this perspective, Matravers argues, preventive policies may be seen in a different light: instead of regarding preventive justice as a means of protecting the public from those who threaten, it might better be thought of as protecting us all from ourselves in circumstances that risk harm.

**Harcourt**'s chapter identifies the origins of contemporary preventive endeavour in the work of the RAND Corporation in America, which developed highly technical studies of crime prevention based upon systems analysis. Harcourt suggests that RAND promoted a decidedly punitive style of prevention based upon policing and punishment that is replicated in modern 'punitive preventive measures'. Harcourt subjects these measures to searching criticism, focusing on the perils they pose and the weakness of their empirical foundations. Most worryingly, for Harcourt, these measures typically claim an apolitical, neutral emphasis on efficiency that fails to engage with the political values underlying them. In so doing, it tends to displace much needed political debate about their justifiability.

**O'Malley**'s chapter builds upon his extensive writings on risk and its management to examine the domain of traffic regulation, one in which, O'Malley observes, 'preventive justice has made rapid and far-reaching advances'. His chapter addresses the ways in which emerging technologies of prevention, risk assessment, and risk-based laws relating to traffic offences form the basis for what he calls 'mass preventive justice'. The scale and volume of mass regulation requires a shift away from individual defendants to 'coded identifiers' and 'risk pools' and away from individualized punishment to fixed monetized sanctions. O'Malley's contention is that 'the rise of mass preventive justice is part of the monetization of justice more generally': money sanctions make possible what O'Malley terms 'massification' and the revenues derived are drivers of expansion. O'Malley explores forms of resistance to mass preventive justice, including challenges to its claim to prevent harm and concerns about the invasion of privacy entailed by new technologies of surveillance. His chapter reveals the pervasive spread of preventive technologies; their 'embeddedness in everyday life'; and how little opposition they have provoked.

As can be seen from these summaries, the chapters discuss a wide range of preventive measures from a variety of theoretical perspectives. A volume of this kind cannot present an integrated theoretical framework, but what it can do is to raise and explore a number of central issues. Thus several themes emerge strongly from this collection, themes that must be taken seriously by those wishing to advance the study of preventive justice.

First, there is no doubt among the contributors that the state has a duty to protect people from harm, a duty that may provide the justification for a wide range of preventive measures (eg Matravers, Nickel, Günther). The precise contours of the duty to protect are contestable, both in terms of what risks should be protected against and in terms of what measures may properly be taken (Günther). In particular, this raises further questions of two kinds—whether there are intelligible distinctions between punishment and prevention, and what limits might properly be placed on the pursuit of prevention.

The definitional question of how preventive measures can be distinguished from punitive measures underlies several contributions. A preliminary task is that of identifying how much prevention there is within conventional criminal law and criminal justice and how far, therefore, preventive endeavours can be said to constitute a departure from the norm (Schauer, Dubber). Related to this is the question of how far prevention informs the substantive criminal law (Asp, Ramsay), and whether and to what extent 'preventionism' is altering the scope of the criminal law. The reverse question is how much punishment there is within measures formally labelled preventive (Harcourt). These enquiries are essential if the definitional question is to be placed in its full context. Indeed, they lead to a reconsideration of whether prevention and punishment are really distinguishable at all, particularly in respect of those measures at the most coercive end of the spectrum such as preventive detention of the 'dangerous' (Husak). In view of the contemporary prevalence of preventive rationales for compulsory measures (Asp, Schauer), are there convincing reasons for keeping the concepts separate?

The criminal law and punishment are certainly the paradigm forms of compulsory measure, and they typically carry with them a number of substantive limitations and procedural safeguards, some deriving from human rights instruments. Those particular limitations and safeguards tend not to apply to preventive measures outside the criminal law and yet such measures also impose significant detriments on those subject to them. This raises the question whether the legitimacy of preventive endeavour is principally a question of procedure, a substantive issue, or a matter of democratic mandate (Dyzenhaus). One concept that does duty as a restraining principle in punishment theory is proportionality and Steiker's contribution assesses the extent to which it can be mobilized to perform the same function effectively for preventive measures. There may be other restraining principles, such as requiring a preventive measure to be properly tailored to its objective (Dyzenhaus) and to be the least restrictive of the appropriate alternatives. Nonetheless, the difficulty of identifying restraining principles may result from the different logic of prevention, which in its pure form insists that measures are selected for their preventive efficacy rather than by any other metric, thereby focusing the choice of measure purely on empirical questions rather than normative ones (Asp, Harcourt). Indeed, some contributors identify the difficulties of constructing realistic limits (Duff, Tadros), although others suggest that within existing human rights parameters certain forms of preventive measure may be supported in a largely unmodified form (Nickel). These are important lines of enquiry: the predominant critique has consisted of liberal reservations about coercive preventive measures in and outside the criminal law, whereas there may be situations in which reasonable preventive endeavours are bound to reduce liberty if they are to exist at all.

To the extent that preventive measures can be justified, they will often depend on a form of risk assessment and often on an estimation of probability (Schauer). Dealing with probabilities is not alien to the criminal law—after all, a verdict of guilty requires not certainty but proof 'beyond reasonable doubt'—but the important questions concern the degree of probability required for the imposition of a particular preventive measure, the robustness of the supporting evidence, and whether or not it is consistent with the standards of the criminal process (Duff). The general evidence in favour of the reductive effect of some 'preventive' strategies in the road traffic sphere is doubtful (O'Malley), and the fragility of the evidential basis for strategies such as 'broken windows' theory, profiling, and selective and mass incarceration can be demonstrated (Harcourt). If the evidential foundations are unconvincing, the case for preventive measures is weakened.

This gives good grounds for reconsidering the preventive uses of the criminal law itself. It is accepted that many offences now impose criminal liability at an earlier stage than the law of attempts, for conduct that is remote from the harm-to-be-prevented. One argument is that this can be justified in view of the known frailty of human nature and imperfect resistance to temptation: by imposing liability well before harm is done (as in offences of possession, or the offence of 'engaging in any conduct in preparation for' giving effect to an intention to commit an act of terrorism), the law not only protects the general public but also protects defendants from the 'catastrophic consequences of their own behaviour' (Matravers). This is an argument that goes against the prevailing liberal theory and conception of the person as an autonomous agent, which objects to the criminal law holding someone liable for something that he or she has not done yet (Asp). But then it should not be assumed that we are confined to or by the liberal critique. Ramsay urges us to look beyond liberalism to other political theories, notably to the concept of representative democracy, arguing that the concept of the citizen found therein clashes with the way that some preventive measures require the state to see us, and us to see each other, and therefore offers a platform for resisting certain aspects of preventionism. Matravers, meanwhile, welcomes a questioning of the liberal view of the person as a fully responsible autonomous chooser. Thus, as many of the contributions suggest, the challenges posed by preventive justice are not to be found on the fringes of legal or political theory but rather go to the very core of the role of the state and the proper conception of the citizen.

# 1

# The Ubiquity of Prevention

*Frederick Schauer**

## A. Introduction

There can be little doubt that the universal incarceration of all males between the ages of fifteen and twenty-nine would bring about a dramatic reduction in crime, and especially violent crime. Indeed, the crime-reducing effect of such a strategy is not limited to the way in which it would simply produce a reduction in the number of crimes or criminals proportionate to the percentage of the population represented by the incarcerated group. Rather, the data plainly indicate that this group commits a disproportionate percentage of crimes in general, and an even more disproportionate percentage of violent crimes.[1] And thus the mass incarceration of the entire cohort of young males would almost certainly bring about a substantial decrease in the overall societal crime rate.

Plainly such a course of action would be politically, culturally, legally, economically, and, most importantly, morally, unacceptable. And equally plainly much of the modern aversion to preventive detention[2] is based on fear of milder versions of the strategy I have just sketched, or perhaps caricatured.[3] But the extreme example

* This chapter was prepared for the Oxford University seminar on Preventive Justice. I have benefited from the comments of the participants when the paper was presented in Oxford in January 2012, and especially from the formal commentary by Lucia Zedner and the written comments provided by Andrew Ashworth and Ambrose Lee.

[1] See United States Federal Bureau of Investigation, *Crime in the United States, 2010* (2011) Table 38.

[2] See, for example, ML Corrado, 'Sex Offenders, Unlawful Combatants, and Preventive Detention' (2005) 84 North Carolina Law Review 77; B Netter, 'Using Group Statistics to Sentence Individual Criminals: An Ethical and Statistical Critique of the Virginia Risk Assessment Program' (2007) 97 Journal of Criminal Law and Criminology 699; L Zedner, 'Preventive Justice or Pre-Punishment? The Case of Control Orders' (2007) 59 Current Legal Problems 174. Objections to preventive detention in any form should be distinguished from objections to treating preventive detention as an appropriate dimension of criminal punishment. See PH Robinson, 'Punishing Dangerousness: Cloaking Preventive Detention as Criminal Justice' (2001) 114 Harvard Law Review 1429. Douglas Husak observes, correctly, that '[m]ost of the scholarly reaction to systems of preventive detention has been hostile': D Husak, 'Lifting the Cloak: Preventive Detention as Punishment' (2011) 48 San Diego Law Review 1173. See also D Husak, this volume.

[3] The phrase 'preventive detention' has been used to encompass a host of different forms of prevention, as well as a huge number of different conditions for its application. See SB Elias, 'Rethinking "Preventive Detention" from a Comparative Perspective: Three Frameworks for

illustrates the basic issue. If there is a social group whose aggregate characteristics probabilistically indicate a proclivity to commit crimes, or to commit crimes of a particular type, then incapacitating or otherwise controlling the entire group would appear to be a way to reduce the number of crimes of that type. Such a strategy, however, conflicts with the strong objection on the part of many people to disabling people on account of the crimes they are statistically more prone to commit than the population at large, but which they have yet to commit. By punishing those who have already committed crimes, it is often argued,[4] we avoid the problems associated with disabling people on account of their characteristics, as opposed to the more desirable strategy of disabling them on account of the unlawful actions they have already taken. Preventive detention, it is thus said, strikes at the very heart of the idea of justice, for it involves punishing people for the harmful acts in which they might engage rather than for the harmful acts in which they have already engaged.[5] And a related argument stresses the basis for such predictions. Because any attempt to assess the risk that a given individual will commit a crime involves a prediction that necessarily relies on group characteristics, the harm of preventive disablement is thought to reside not only in restricting people on account of acts they might but have yet to commit, but also in evaluating people on the basis of group characteristics. More precisely, it is thought wrong to disable people not on the basis of their own unique characteristics, but on account of the characteristics of any of a number of groups of which they might be a member, but whose group characteristics the individual might not share.[6]

Beneath this stark dichotomy between *ex ante* prevention and *ex post* punishment lie numerous complications and qualifications, but in this chapter I bracket many of these often-important subtleties in order to examine the central claim that disabling people on account of their future-crime-indicating characteristics is different in kind from how the criminal law routinely operates. In important ways, I shall argue, there is more prevention in the ordinary operation of the criminal law than is often acknowledged. Recognizing that this is so should not, of course, be taken as an endorsement of mass preventive detention, or even as approval of any of the milder forms of preventive deprivations of liberty that are so controversial these days. But by seeing how much the standard dichotomy between *ex ante* detention and *ex post* punishment obscures, we may be able to focus more effectively on which aspects of prevention we do and should tolerate, and which aspects we do and should resist.

Detaining Terrorist Suspects' (2009) 41 Columbia Human Rights Law Review 99. For purposes of this chapter I lump many of these different forms and conditions together, and lump many of the critiques together as well, even as I recognize that in other contexts the differences may be crucially important.

4 See D Cole, 'Out of the Shadows: Preventive Detention, Suspected Terrorists, and War' (2009) 97 California Law Review 693; PH Robinson (cited in n 2).

5 See KF Arthur, 'Preventive Detention: Liberty in the Balance' (1986) 46 Maryland Law Review 378; L Tribe, 'An Ounce of Detention: Preventive Justice in the World of John Mitchell' (1970) 56 Virginia Law Review 371.

6 See, for example, V Tadros, this volume.

## B. Probability all the way down

In (at least) one important respect, using the criminal law in order to achieve preventive goals is a pervasive dimension of our long-standing practices of punishment. Thus, although scholars debate the relative importance of deterrence (specific and general), retribution, and rehabilitation in explaining and justifying punishment, there is moderately wide recognition that some role, albeit not the exclusive role, is to be played by incapacitation,[7] where by 'incapacitation' I mean not simply incarceration, but, rather, the full range of restrictions that make it more difficult for an agent to engage in some act with the restriction than without.[8] Whatever functions incarceration and other forms of restrictive remedies (such as transportation, in earlier times, and at-home confinement, post-conviction curfews and restrictions on travel, and disqualification from driving or holding office, in modern times) are designed to prevent, the individual subject to those remedies is at least partially disabled[9] from committing further crimes during the period of incapacitation. This common dimension of the criminal law, albeit controversial at the extremes,[10] and although questioned by, for example, those who see retribution (or desert) as the only legitimate goal of the criminal law,[11] is therefore a form of preventive justice, for it is concerned not with the crimes the defendant has already committed, but rather with the crimes the defendant might commit in the future. By restricting him, we make it more difficult for him to commit those crimes during the period of incapacitation, and society in general and potential victims in particular are better off because of it, or so the defenders of incapacitation maintain.[12]

[7] See FE Zimring and G Hawkins, *Incapacitation: Penal Confinement and the Restraint of Crime* (1995). Important economic analyses include I Ehrlich, 'On the Usefulness of Controlling Individuals: An Economic Analysis of Rehabilitation, Incapacitation, and Deterrence' (1981) 71 *American Economic Review* 307, and S Shavell, 'A Model of Optimal Incapacitation' (1987) 77 *American Economic Review* 107. On the non-economic and non-consequentialist arguments for incapacitation, see RS Frase, 'Can Above-Desert Penalties Be Justified by Competing Deontological Theories?' in M Tonry (ed), *Retributivism Has a Past: Has It a Future?* (2011) 169. See also LS Beres and TD Griffith, 'Do Three Strikes Laws Make Sense? Habitual Offender Statutes and Criminal Incapacitation' (1998) 87 Georgetown Law Journal 103, 113.

[8] Thus, a person who must report to the authorities for a weekly drug test, or a person who is required to wear a monitoring ankle bracelet, or (perhaps) even a person who is facing a higher penalty for a subsequent offence because of a prior offence, are all incapacitated in this broader sense.

[9] Few of these disabilities or restrictions are absolute, but they nevertheless serve the purpose of making it more difficult for the individuals who are restricted to commit a crime than it would be for individuals operating without the restriction. And it is in this sense that many non-custodial punishments are still incapacitative.

[10] As with increased, indeterminate, or extremely long sentences for multiple offenders. See LS Beres and TD Griffith (cited in n 7).

[11] Typically, retributivists see incapacitation as a fortunate side-effect of criminal punishment, but not as a goal. See M Moore, *Placing Blame: A General Theory of the Criminal Law* (1997). And see the various essays in M Tonry (cited in n 7).

[12] See RJ Allen and L Laudan, 'Some Kind Words for Preventive Detention' (2011) 101 Journal of Criminal Law & Criminology 781; RA Posner, 'An Economic Theory of the Criminal Law' (1985) 85 Columbia Law Review 1193; S Shavell (cited in n 7).

Incapacitation is widely accepted and widely practised, such that its very existence is rarely seen as a problem, or at least as a problem of a different and lesser order than the *ex ante* restrictions that are at the heart of the modern debates about preventive detention. And the implicit acceptance of incapacitation even by those who object to *ex ante* restrictions seems to be based on the belief that those who are incapacitated, and thus temporarily impeded from committing crimes, are only those who have already been convicted of committing a crime, ordinarily with the defendant-protective trappings of criminal prosecution in modern liberal states. But although there is indeed a difference between an incapacitation-motivated sentence after a criminal trial and an administrative detention without trial, it is important to bear in mind that sentencing even after the determination of guilt in a fully fledged criminal trial nevertheless remains probabilistic rather than certain, and in two ways. First, even with respect to crimes that have high rates of recidivism, it is very far from certain, and for some crimes even very far from likely, that those who have been convicted of one crime will then commit other crimes.[13] It is true that those who have committed particular crimes are, probabilistically, more likely to engage in repetitions of that type of crime than are those who have not committed those particular crimes, or even than the population at large.[14] And it is also true that those who have committed crimes in general are probabilistically more likely to commit other crimes, even if not the same crimes, than the aggregate of the population at large.[15] But these probabilities are some distance from certainties. And as a result, some proportion of the individuals who are incapacitated by incarceration are those for whom incapacitation would not have been necessary. They are individuals who are incapacitated—detained or otherwise controlled (and their liberty restricted) for reasons of prevention—where the prevention is in reality unnecessary. Consider the case of convicted criminal Charles, who is sentenced to five years in prison for having committed some crime, and convicted criminal David, who is sentenced to one year for the same type of crime but is then subject, as a convicted criminal, to various severely incapacitating conditions for four subsequent years. The crimes are, by hypothesis, the same, and the penalty seems greater for Charles than for David, yet concerns about preventive restrictions seem, curiously, to surface far more commonly with respect to cases like David's than with cases like Charles's.

13 See United States Department of Justice, Bureau of Justice Statistics, 'Recidivism', available at <http://www.bjs.gov/index.cfm?ty=tp&tid=17>; Pew Center on the States, *The State of Recidivism: The Revolving Door of America's Prisons* (2011).

14 See AJ Beck, United States Department of Justice, *Special Report: Recidivism of Prisoners Released in 1983* (1989) (31.9 per cent recidivism rate for burglary, 33.5 per cent for larceny, 21.8 per cent for drug offences); J Monahan, 'A Jurisprudence of Risk Assessment: Forecasting Harm Among Prisoners, Predators, and Patients' (2006) 92 Virginia Law Review 391.

15 See D Glaser, *The Effectiveness of a Prison and Parole System* (35 per cent general recidivism rate in US) (1984); United States General Accounting Office, *Report to Congressional Committees, Prisoner Releases* (June 2001), available at <http://www.gao.gov/new.items/do1483.pdf> (39 per cent); J Kinzig, *Schrankenlose Sicherheit? Das Bundesverfassungsgericht vor der Entscheidung über die Geltung des Rückvirkungsverbots im Massregelrecht*, (2000) 20(6) StV (Strafverteidigen) 330 (25 per cent in Germany); RK Hanson and KM Bourgon, Department of the Solicitor General of Canada, *Predictors of Sexual Recidivism: An Updated Meta-Analysis*, available at <http://ww2.psepc-sppec.gc.ca/publications/corrections/pdf/200402e.pdf> (2004) (36.3 per cent in Canada).

There may, to be sure, be concerns about the length of the sentence in the case of Charles, but the point of the example is only to show that *ex ante* preventive punishment is a more common—and often less noted and less criticized—dimension of ordinary *ex post* punishment than is typically appreciated.

Insofar as cases like either that of Charles or that of David are perceived as not problematic on moral or policy grounds, this lack of concern over the incapacitation of those convicted of crimes likely stems from the fact that those so incapacitated—those subject to preventive restrictions—have already committed crimes. It may appear, that is, that those who are prevented from committing crimes they might not have in any event committed have less cause for complaint, precisely because they have at least committed the precipitating crime in the first place.

Even this conclusion, however, is incessantly probabilistic, and this is the second probabilistic dimension of incapacitative restrictions imposed after a finding of guilt. By requiring proof beyond reasonable doubt for conviction, as opposed to absolute certainty, and by knowingly admitting evidence that itself may be flawed, we intentionally operate a system of punishment that can be expected to, and in fact does, convict some number of individuals who are in fact innocent. This is, of course, an inevitable feature of a criminal justice system that operates in a world of uncertainty. In such a world, as Blackstone and countless others have reminded us,[16] we balance, with an appropriately heavy thumb on one side of the scales, the expected costs of mistaken convictions against the expected costs of mistaken acquittals. But although we justifiably treat the former as far more grave than the latter, the *ratio* is not infinite. Recognizing that we could totally eliminate convicting the innocent only by convicting none of the guilty, we knowingly accept a system in which it is a virtual certainty that some number of innocent people will wind up being punished.

The implications of the fact that the criminal justice system accepts false positives as well as false negatives—both Type I and Type II errors—should be apparent. Suppose we assign a number to the probability of convicting the innocent, say 0.05.[17] And then suppose we assume, almost certainly counterfactually in most cases, that we are able to identify the characteristics of those who would commit future crimes of some type with a 0.95 probability. Under these circumstances, the likelihood of mistakenly punishing (and thus incarcerating or otherwise disabling) an innocent person by the standard system of *ex post* punishment is equivalent to the likelihood of mistakenly disabling an innocent person by a system of so-called preventive detention.

[16] With respect to conviction and punishment, Blackstone famously observed that 'it is better that ten guilty persons escape, than that one innocent suffer': W Blackstone, *Commentaries on the Laws of England*, vol 4 (1769) 358.

[17] This is very roughly where most of the empirical studies of burdens of proof would locate the 'beyond a reasonable doubt' standard. See HR Arkes and BA Mellers, 'Do Juries Meet Our Expectations?' (2002) 26 *Law & Human Behavior* 625; CMA McCauliff, 'Burdens of Proof: Degrees of Belief, Quanta of Evidence, or Constitutional Guarantees?' (1982) 35 Vanderbilt Law Review 1293, 1325, 1332.

Plainly most efforts to engage in preventive disablement do so with a 'hit rate' very far below 0.95. Thus, many of the forms of preventive detention and preventive incapacitation are morally and legally problematic for precisely this reason. But it is the fact of a low probability rather than the reliance on probability itself that is doing the work. Accordingly, once we recognize that the types of probabilistic errors that produce legitimate concerns in the standard contexts of preventive detention exist, and inevitably and knowingly so, in the normal criminal process, we can see that the question is not a question about fundamentally different approaches, but rather one of relative probabilities. So although the distinction between acceptable and unacceptable detention is often couched in terms of prior and subsequent, *ex ante* and *ex post*, it is not necessarily the case that the *ex ante*/*ex post* distinction tracks the difference between inaccurate and accurate. Insofar as we are concerned about mistakes (and while recognizing that there might be other concerns), and about detaining the innocent, it might be better to examine the aspects of different procedures for their tendency towards error rather than to assume, not necessarily correctly, that mistakes are exclusively or even largely the province of *ex ante* prediction as opposed to *ex post* factual assessment.

Thus, a person who is convicted of a crime is often deprived of some of his liberty, because, in part, of the probability that he or she might commit other crimes in the future. But once we recognize both that the initial conviction is probabilistic rather than certain, and also that the assessment that someone who has committed one crime will likely commit another is probabilistic as well, we can see the typical imposition of criminal punishment not only as a form of preventive restriction, but also as a form of prevention sharing at least some of the characteristics of those forms of preventive restriction that are commonly criticized. There are differences, to be sure, but those differences cannot reside in the fundamental wrongness or unfairness of probabilistic assessments of future dangerousness, for such assessments pervade even some of the least controversial dimensions of the criminal justice system.[18]

The question remains whether there are still relevant differences between *ex ante* and *ex post* probabilistic assessments. The differences are not statistical ones. A one in four chance of being wrong about what happened in the past is statistically the same thing as there being a one in four chance that one's prediction of the future may not come to pass. But there is a non-statistical difference, and that is that actions in the past cannot be changed, but that people might in the future act contrary to even the accurate probabilistic predictions of their future actions. But if this is morally significant, it is because there seems to be something wrong with restricting someone for $\phi$'ing who might not actually $\phi$. But in the case of assessments of the past, the risk is that we will restrict someone on account of

[18] For the argument that all such probabilistic assessments in the criminal justice system should be eliminated, or at least considered suspect, see BE Harcourt, *Against Prediction: Profiling, Policing, and Punishing in an Actuarial Age* (2007). And for the argument that such probabilistic assessments, even in the criminal law, are an inevitable part of human cognition and an often desirable component of institutional design, see F Schauer, *Profiles, Probabilities, and Stereotypes* (2003).

their having $\phi$'ed when in fact they did not $\phi$ at all. If anything, this is even a greater wrong than not giving someone who will probably $\phi$ in the future a chance to not-$\phi$. And if, as is the case, we accept the inevitability of some wrongs of this type by virtue of tolerating an imperfect system for assessing guilt, then it is hard to see why the wrong is greater in the case of not giving people a chance to act against the probabilities. If anything, it seems as if it should be less.[19]

## C. The preventive dimensions of the chilling effect

In the cases and commentary on freedom of speech and freedom of the press, and especially (but not only) in the United States, there is frequent reference to the phenomenon known as the 'chilling effect'.[20] The chilling effect is the phenomenon of excess deterrence, and the label comes from the fact that lawful conduct may be deterred, or chilled, insofar as rational (and, especially, risk-averse) actors under conditions of uncertainty will often refrain from engaging in legal conduct for fear of liability, and will do so because of the possibility that lawful conduct will produce legal liability despite its lawfulness in a world of legal uncertainty and imperfect legal institutions. If newspapers, for example, are subject to paying civil damages when they are found to have committed actionable libel, then a newspaper contemplating publication will take into account the possibility of its own mistake—that an article that it believes to be true or non-libellous may in fact be libellous and false.[21] And the newspaper will also take into account the possibility of legal error—the possibility that a newspaper article that is in fact either true or non-libellous will be considered otherwise by a judge or jury. And thus if the penalties for libel are serious enough, a risk-averse publisher will refrain from publishing at least some things that it believes are legally safe, and which are in fact legally safe. Insofar as the non-publication of legally permissible material ensues from the existence of legal penalties in a world of imperfect institutions and epistemic uncertainty, publication of some legally permissible and potentially valuable information and opinion is said to be 'chilled'.

With respect to freedom of expression, there is presumed social value in the unpublished information and opinion lying in the zone of excess deterrence. When a risk-averse publisher refrains from publishing legally permissible and often accurate information or often valuable opinion, society is the worse for it. And that is precisely why the chilling effect has figured so prominently in the development of legal

[19] It might be argued that there is an epistemic difference between *ex ante* prevention, where the false positives are undiscoverable, and *ex post* punishment, where the false positives can, in theory, be identified, but the argument is in some tension with the probabilistic assessments that are part of rational thinking. It is true that I cannot be absolutely sure that the bottle I do not drop would have broken upon hitting a hard floor, but I handle the bottle carefully precisely because of an *ex ante* assessment of the probability of some occurrence whose actual occurrence I will never perceive.

[20] See F Schauer, 'Fear, Risk, and the First Amendment: Unraveling the "Chilling Effect"' (1978) 58 Boston University Law Review 685.

[21] *New York Times Co v Sullivan* 376 US 254 (1964).

doctrine within cultures with especially (and maybe even excessively) strong commitments to freedom of expression. Yet despite the common association of the chilling effect with freedom of expression, the phenomenon exists throughout the sanction-applying domains of the law.[22] At times the excess deterrence is problematic in ways that resemble the example of freedom of expression. Excess deterrence of pharmaceutical innovation, for example, would have plainly negative consequences, as would the excess deterrence of 'Good Samaritan' behaviour.[23] In all of these instances there are reasons to be concerned about the abuses, and thus we can understand why the law sanctions defamation, the sale of untested and dangerous pharmaceuticals, and intrusive and unwanted medical care that produces negative outcomes. But every time a properly (assuming ideal application) crafted rule produces excess deterrence of socially beneficial conduct, the negative dimensions of the chilling effect are realized.

Not all excess deterrence is equally (or at all) socially harmful, of course. Insofar as the law against sexual assault deters some number of unwanted but legal sexual advances by risk-averse actors, there is a social benefit, even though the deterrence of wanted sexual advances may well be a cost. And so too when highway safety laws produce excess caution (while admitting that too much caution can be transportation- and trade-inhibiting), when laws against embezzlement produce meticulous accounting, and (possibly) when tax penalties produce excessively careful taxpayers.[24] Yet even when the conduct deterred is not as likely socially beneficial as it is in the case of freedom of expression and the development of pharmaceuticals, the conduct deterred is nevertheless lawful conduct that does not take place, and the rational agent who refrains from engaging in the lawful conduct is someone who is, rationally, restricting her own legal liberty. We can understand incarceration and other court-imposed penalties as particularly disabling deprivations of liberty, but if legal liberty, broadly conceived, includes, almost tautologically, the freedom to engage in lawful conduct, then the rational auto-deterrence engaged in by rationally risk-averse actors can be understood as a deprivation of liberty, albeit of a typically milder form.[25]

[22] See L Kaplow, 'Optimal Proof Burdens, Deterrence, and the Chilling of Desirable Behavior' (2011) 101 *American Economic Review Papers and Proceedings* 277.

[23] This is not to say that decreasing the risk-aversion of pharmaceutical companies or interventions intended to be helpful would be without cost. We can appreciate the social costs of under-innovation of pharmaceuticals while at the same time understanding the costs of over-innovation as well. And so too with those Good Samaritan interventions that the intervening party thinks, sometimes correctly and sometimes not, will be of benefit to the individual receiving the assistance.

[24] Thus, excess compliance with the tax laws produces more revenue for the government but less money available to consumers and investors, and the trade-off between the two is a complex financial, economic, and political issue. Similarly, excess compliance with environmental, consumer protection, and workplace safety laws brings benefits to those who are primary objects of the protection of those laws, but often less income to the regulated industries, a trade-off that implicates deep philosophical questions about commensurability, among others. And much the same could be said about highway safety laws, where excess compliance increases safety at the cost of decreased efficiency of transportation. Still, for current purposes all that is necessary is the basic point that excess deterrence sometimes brings social costs, and sometimes it does not.

[25] Thus, I agree with Tadros, this volume, that a liberty is restricted whenever one's (lawful) options are limited, even if they are options that one might not choose.

Thus, the excess deterrence of the criminal law can be understood as a form of prevention. Whenever someone refrains from engaging in lawful conduct for fear that their lawful conduct will be found to be otherwise by judge or jury, they have been prevented by the law, without trial, from engaging in conduct that they are legally entitled to pursue. It is true, of course, that this scenario does not involve preventive *detention*, but it does involve prevention, and indeed it involves prevention by restriction of the liberty to engage in lawful conduct, and it does involve people, for fear of sanctions, being prevented from engaging in conduct *ex ante*, as opposed to being punished *ex post* for behaviour they have already committed.

Indeed, although the negative dimensions of *excess* deterrence are particularly salient, even accurate deterrence is aimed at preventing conduct that is yet to occur. So perhaps it is better to say, more directly, that deterrence is itself a form of prevention. Putting aside questions about the particular goals of criminal law *qua* criminal law, we might reasonably think that the law, or the state more generally, would, as Bentham argued, have a preference for threatening sanctions rather than administering them. Surely a society with no harmful behaviour is better than one with some harmful behaviour that winds up being sanctioned. And thus by threatening sanctions the law substantially outsources the determination of guilt or innocence to the primary actor, who is accordingly given rein to decide whether his proposed conduct does or does not violate the law. This is almost certainly as it should be, and it is rather distant from the principal concerns surrounding the topic of preventive sanctions. But once we see that prevention is arguably a substantial policy goal, with law through the criminal law playing a major role in its implementation, and with punishment as the alternative when prevention fails, we can clarify the area of concern. It is not prevention that worries us, but rather poorly targeted prevention. But what is it for prevention to be poorly targeted? It is to that that I now turn.

## D. The inevitable imprecision of the criminal law

Let us leave the question of prevention by deterrence, and turn to punishment for acts already committed. And let us set aside as well the question of mistaken conviction, and thus of mistaken incapacitation, as discussed earlier, in section B. But after we put these issues aside, we see that even the accurate punishment of an individual for having (certainly) engaged in some act that violates the criminal law implicates many of the concerns that motivate the worry about preventive detention or other forms of preventive punishment.

Consider as a trivial example the prohibition on driving in excess of an officially designated and posted speed limit. Thus, it is a crime, albeit not a very serious one, to drive at 80 miles per hour on the M1 Motorway. But the prohibition on driving in excess of 70 miles per hour is not based on there being something intrinsically wrong about driving at such a speed. Rather, driving too quickly is thought to be unsafe, and the speed limit can be understood as a rule instantiating the background justification of prohibiting unsafe driving.

Like all rules, however, this rule is under- and over-inclusive with respect to its background justification.[26] It is under-inclusive insofar as some instances of unsafe driving do not violate the speed limit rule, and, more relevantly here, it is over-inclusive insofar as the rule prohibits some instances of driving that are not in fact unsafe. An experienced and careful driver in a well-maintained automobile on a clear, dry, and lightly-trafficked Sunday morning can generally drive safely somewhat in excess of the posted speed limit, which is, after all, designed for average drivers in average cars under average conditions. And thus the careful driver under safe conditions is, because of the probabilistic assessment about which driving will be unsafe, prevented from engaging in behaviour that in theory is not a concern of the law. Or, to put it differently, the driver is prohibited from engaging in behaviour that is not intrinsically wrong, but only probabilistically indicates the likelihood of wrong behaviour, that is, unsafe driving.

Indeed, much the same can be said at one remove, for even to prohibit unsafe driving is to prohibit conduct that creates a risk of accidents, rather than the certainty of accidents. Issues of the chilling effect aside, we could, after all, simply impose liability on those who have caused accidents, and do so only after those accidents have actually occurred. That we choose to sanction the risky behaviour rather than (or in addition to) the consequences that such risky behaviour may but will not necessarily produce is once again an example of the law's frequent preference for imprecise prediction and consequently imprecise prevention.

Once we see things this way, we can understand that there is little—maybe no—difference between a prohibition on teenage boys congregating after 10 p.m. and a prohibition on driving in excess of the speed limit, even though the former would almost certainly raise alarms about preventive disablement or preventive punishment, and the latter would almost certainly not. Yet in both cases the law prohibits intrinsically non-harmful behaviour because of its indicative or causal, but nevertheless probabilistic, tendencies vis-à-vis intrinsically harmful behaviour. There may be differences between the two cases, but the presence of prevention based on probabilistic characteristics is not one of those differences.

This last point is worth underscoring. Many criminal prohibitions are themselves preventive in the sense that they sanction intrinsically non-harmful conduct because of the tendency of such conduct to cause harmful conduct. That is, they regulate risk, a focus of many of the chapters in this volume.[27] Jeremy Bentham discussed such crimes as part of his larger category of 'accessory offences', and he included the crimes of gaming, prodigality, and idleness, which were, for him, crimes not because they were intrinsically harmful, but because they were likely to cause other and intrinsically harmful consequences.[28] These days we might think of this category in terms of arguments that the use or possession of so-called soft drugs

[26] See F Schauer, *Playing By the Rules: A Philosophical Examination of Rule-Based Decision-Making in Law and in Life* (1991). See also L Alexander and E Sherwin, *The Rule of Rules: Morality, Rules, and the Dilemmas of Law* (2000).

[27] See P O'Malley, this volume; and V Tadros, this volume.

[28] J Bentham, *Principles of the Penal Code*, book 4, ch 15 in *The Theory of Legislation*, trans R Hildreth from E Dumont (CK Ogden (ed)), (1931) 425–7.

is criminalized because of its tendency to lead to the use of hard drugs, or that we criminalize the use of child pornography because of a fear that it will lead to the abuse of children in addition to the children abused in the process of producing the material.[29] And Bentham also treated the criminalization of some sales of poison and gunpowder in the same way, arguing that the wrong in such cases was not in the conduct itself, but in the consequences that the conduct would likely but not inevitably produce. Even more broadly, the entire panoply of so-called inchoate crimes, including criminal solicitation, aiding and abetting the commission of a crime, incitement to crime, conspiracy to commit a crime, and attempts to commit a crime are all substantially preventive, and to the extent that they are preventive (as opposed simply to punishing certain states of mind for non-preventive reasons), they are preventive in an inextricably probabilistic fashion.[30]

Slightly less obviously, much the same applies to those offences that are indicative rather than causal.[31] When we prohibit the repackaging of legally obtained pharmaceuticals, for example,[32] we prohibit intrinsically benign conduct not (only) because of the harmful conduct that such benign conduct might cause in the future, but also, and more commonly, because of the way in which the intrinsically benign conduct is a probabilistic indicator of non-benign conduct that has existed in the past.[33] Thus, although less directly, a large number of such indicative offences seek to prevent or deter in an indirect way certain primary offences, but in every case the relationship between the indicative offence and the primary offence is probabilistic rather than certain.

## E. Implications

The important topic of preventive detention—putting people behind bars without the protections of the criminal justice process, to emphasize bluntly what is at stake—has, over time, morphed into the topic of preventive justice more generally. But the transformation may have been more distracting than useful. Preventive

[29] Indeed, the point would apply to virtually all possession offences. On possession offences more broadly, see MD Dubber, 'Policing Possession: The War on Crime and the End of Criminal Law' (2002) 91 Journal of Criminal Law and Criminology 829.

[30] See WR LaFave, *Criminal Law* (4th edn, 2003) 568–723.

[31] See F Schauer, 'Bentham on Presumed Offenses' (2011) 23 *Utilitas* 363.

[32] See *State v Walker* 333 So 2d 1137 (Fla App. 2nd Dist 1984).

[33] In some contexts, there are commentators who are worried that indicative (or evidentiary, or presumed, as Bentham labelled them) offences do not permit the person charged with such a crime to establish that he or she has not committed the deeper wrong that such laws are designed to combat. See J Edwards, 'Justice Denied: The Criminal Law and the Ouster of the Courts' (2010) 30 OJLS 725–48; V Tadros, 'Crimes and Security' (2008) 71 MLR 940. But such an objection would seem to apply to every *malum prohibitum* crime. Indeed, at the extreme the objection, at least under utilitarian premises, would seem to apply to every specifically-designated offence, for the argument, taken to its logical extreme, should create a right in every defendant to be able to attempt to prove that his conduct was not utility-detracting. Obviously this *reductio* is not conclusive, but it is designed to underscore the inevitably rule-based nature of almost all offences, and the way in which such offences rest on ultimately probabilistic assumptions.

justice, or simply the use of the coercive force of the state to prevent crime *ex ante* rather than simply to punish it *ex post*, is a widespread and widely accepted goal of the criminal justice system,[34] even as thoroughgoing retributivists might treat it as an incidental benefit, rather than a primary goal of, the criminal law.[35] And thus by examining the ways in which the goals of *ex ante* prevention of crime pervade numerous aspects of any regime of punishment and incarceration, we can see just how ubiquitous prevention is, and why it might well be folly to think that we can or even should substantially reduce it.

That said, however, there is definitely a difference between imprisoning someone who has been found beyond a reasonable doubt, under conditions of due process, to have committed crime *C*, on the one hand, and imprisoning someone, on the basis of a lower standard of proof and a proceeding with truncated procedures, whose characteristics indicate that he or she might commit crime *C* in the future. But what the analysis here has attempted to show is that the difference lies not in the existence or not of prevention, but rather in differences in degree, in differences in the burden of proof, and in differences in procedure, or in differences among the officials or other agents who might make the relevant determinations, differences that are no less important just because they are scalar rather than bimodal—questions of degree rather than simply one or the other.[36]

Thus, the flaw in most schemes of preventive detention lies in precisely the way in which most of the predictive probabilities involved in the typical preventive detention scheme are far lower than the probabilities we typically require for *ex post* punishment. But if we were 0.96 certain that someone would commit a crime of a certain type in the future, and if, in some system, people can be convicted of having committed that crime when there is a 0.95 probability of their guilt, it is not entirely clear that the preventive approach is deficient, and it may, depending on the probabilities, at times be better.[37]

[34] See L Alexander and KK Ferzan, *Crime and Culpability: A Theory of Criminal Law* (2009) 3 ('The criminal law's goal is not to compensate, to rehabilitate, or to inculcate virtue. Rather, the criminal law aims at preventing harm.').

[35] Michael Moore refers to deterrence as a 'happy surplus' from a retributivist perspective: MS Moore, 'The Moral Worth of Retributivism' in F Schoeman (ed), *Responsibility, Character, and the Emotions* (1989) 179, 180. See also MS Moore, *Placing Blame: A General Theory of the Criminal Law* (1997). Earlier, Moore had expressed sympathy with a mixed or hybrid view: MS Moore, *Law and Philosophy: Rethinking the Relationship* (1984) 238–43, and even a mixed or hybrid view of the goals of punishment would be entirely compatible with my claims here.

[36] A more sophisticated version of this argument is in RJ Allen and L Laudan, 'Deadly Dilemmas III: Some Kind Words for Preventive Detention' (2011) 11–24 Northwestern University School of Law Public Law and Legal Theory Series.

[37] I take this conclusion to be compatible with the arguments in D Husak, this volume; n 2. See also C Slobogin, 'Prevention as the Primary Goal of Sentencing: The Modern Case for Indeterminate Dispositions in Criminal Cases' (2011) 48 San Diego Law Review (forthcoming). It is also worth noting that under some circumstances a well-crafted prevention scheme might be more liberty-promoting than some ex post punishment schemes. Bearing in mind the discussion of the chilling effect in section C, some preventive approaches—imagine, as a fantasy and a mind experiment, a regime in which a licence was required before engaging in any behaviour whatsoever—might give agents guidance as to what they could and could not do, and would thus obviate the necessity for risk-averse agents to err on the side of caution. That is, the chilling effect might be largely a function of the

Much the same applies to the procedures that are adopted in order to determine who is—and who is not—to be detained or punished. Preventive detention typically involves identifying those who are to be subject to detention by the use of procedures more likely to be error-prone than those used to determine *ex post* guilt, including determinations by law enforcement officers rather than judges. But if the procedures employed to identify those to be preventively detained were as rigorous as those used to identify those who have committed crimes in the past, and if the agents making the determination were the same, it becomes less obvious what the exact nature of the problem is.

For many people, of course, the problem of preventive detention, and the problem of prevention in general, is that *ex ante* prevention fails to treat people as individuals, and instead assesses them on the basis of the characteristics of various groups of which they may be a member. But the notion that there is even the possibility of a non-probabilistic assessment of individuals is a mistake. All of our assessments are probabilistic, and all probabilistic assessments involve drawing on aggregate probabilities to make estimates in individual cases.[38] When we allow the use of evidence of flight as relevant (although not, of course, dispositive) to guilt, for example, we do so because in human experience people who flee are more likely than randomly selected members of the population to have done something wrong. When we allow the use of evidence of motive in determining the question of guilt, we draw on the fact that motive is probabilistically probative of guilt, even though many—probably most—people with a motive to commit a crime refrain from committing it.

Factual assessment is inevitably probabilistic, and thus the probabilistic assessments in determining *ex post* guilt involve risks of mistaken deprivations of liberty. And so too do the probabilistic assessments involved in preventing crime rather than punishing it. When liberty is at stake, there are sound reasons to try to minimize the mistakes of faulty deprivations of liberty. In many instances the probabilities and the procedures involved in prediction and prevention are weaker than those that are normally part of the criminal law, and so the presence of prediction and prevention may be a useful proxy for the low probabilities and coarse procedures that we properly want to avoid. But there is a difference between a proxy and what the proxy is a proxy for, and thus it is a mistake to assume that preventive justice is a problem in itself. Preventive justice is all around us, and it is hard to imagine a functioning society that could avoid it.

threat of *ex post* punishment, and the effect could be eliminated or lessened under a properly designed preventive approach.

[38] Note that I am making only the simple claim that if 50 out of 100 balls in an urn are striped, then the probability of any one randomly chosen ball being striped is 0.5. If 10 out of 100 adult males are bald, then the probability of a given adult male being bald, *absent any other information*, is 0.1. This simple use of group probabilities to make probabilistic estimates with respect to individual attributes (and not causal mechanisms) does not implicate the widely discussed ecological inference problem (see G King, *A Solution to the Ecological Inference Problem* (1997)). There is a different debate about the reliability of clinical versus actuarial risk assessments (see J Monahan, 'A Jurisprudence of Risk Assessment: Forecasting Harm among Prisoners, Predators, and Patients' (2006) 92 Virginia Law Review 391), which is somewhat more relevant here, but the existing evidence is substantially in favour of the actuarial assessments.

# 2

# Preventionism and Criminalization of Nonconsummate Offences

*Petter Asp*

One important aspect of criminalization concerns the relation between the act that is prohibited and the harm the occurrence of which one is trying to avoid (by criminalizing the act in question). If one paints with a very broad brush, one could say that the standard proscription in earlier times covered acts which themselves were harmful, but that there is (and has been) an ever-increasing inclination, on the part of legislators, to proscribe conduct which in itself does not cause any harm—ie, by introducing *nonconsummate offences*. This tendency raises both dogmatic questions[1] and questions about the justification of these offences.[2]

In this chapter[3] I contribute to the analysis of this development (1) by suggesting that this tendency is part of a larger trend which I have labelled *preventionism*, and (2) by highlighting some special problems connected to the justification of the criminalization of acts which are not in themselves harmful but which are undertaken with the ulterior intent[4] of committing a harmful act. Typical examples of such crimes are the offences of attempt, conspiracy, and grooming.

All these offences share the same structure: doing *X* with (some sort of) intent to do *Y* (shooting with the intent to kill a person, agreeing with someone to commit a crime with the intent of actually committing it, having contact with a child in a certain way with the intent of having sex with the child, etc).

[1] See, eg, D Frände, 'Faredeliktens allmänna läror' (1994) Oikeustide Jurisprudentia 5–100.

[2] See, eg, A von Hirsch and W Wohlers, 'Rechtsgutstheorie und Deliktsstruktur—zu den Kriterien fairer Zurechnung' in R Hefendehl, A von Hirsch, and W Wohlers (eds), *Die Rechtsgutstheorie. Legitimationsbasis des Strafrechts oder dogmatisches Glasperlenspiel?* (2003) 196–214; D Husak, 'The Nature and Justifiability of Nonconsummate Offences' (1995) 37 Arizona Law Review 151–83; and D Husak, *Overcriminalization. The Limits of the Criminal Law* (2008) 159 ff.

[3] The text builds upon ideas developed in P Asp, *Från tanke till gärning. Del I. Legitimationsfrågor rörande förfältsdelikt* (2005) and P Asp, 'Går det att se en internationell trend—om preventionismen i den moderna straffrätten' (2007) Svensk Juristtidning 69–82. See also P Asp, 'On the Justification of Non-consummate Offences' in H Müller-Dietz et al. (eds) *Festschrift für Heike Jung* (2007).

[4] By ulterior intent I mean (see AP Simester and GR Sullivan, *Criminal Law: Theory and Doctrine* (4th edn, 2010) 138) 'an intent to do something that is not part of the actus reus', ie, an intent that goes beyond the *actus reus*.

In the first part of the chapter I will argue that the increased interest in criminalizing such nonconsummate conduct reflects a *general tendency towards preventionism* (ie, towards an ideology according to which the prevention of harm is the primary focus) and I will sketch the risks connected to preventionism in crime control. In the second part of the chapter I will examine the use of nonconsummate offences which are qualified with an ulterior intent requirement from a justificatory perspective. My conclusion is that such offences are not necessarily preferable from a justificatory perspective to nonconsummate offences that do not require such an intent. In this regard I argue, to a certain extent, against a suggestion by Douglas Husak, that we should incorporate a (high) culpability requirement when criminalizing nonconsummate conduct. My conclusion is that it is too simple to say that it is always better—from a justificatory perspective—to include an ulterior intent requirement, and this is due to the fact that such a requirement also adds to that for which the person is being held responsible.

## A. Preventionism

### Preventionism as a general tendency

Preventionism is changing the way we think and argue about criminal law, and serves also as a yardstick for measuring the results of the criminal law system. Thus preventionism has the following characteristics:

- The general perception of the problem of criminality, including the fear of being the subject of an offence, is excessive (ie, not reasonable given the empirical evidence). People in general have an understanding that society today is very dangerous in comparison with society some twenty, forty, or sixty years ago and they look upon crime and criminality as one of the main social problems.
- The absence of harm and crime is seen as a normal state of affairs, ie, the starting point is that harm actually can be, and always could have been, avoided. Thus, if harm actually occurs, then something has gone wrong. This means that harm occurrence is, at the micro level, followed not only by a search for a responsible person (ie, by a search for a perpetrator), but also by a search for political responsibility: harm has occurred despite the fact that it should not have occurred; thus there must be something wrong with the system.

This type of thinking is often fuelled by political rhetoric. For politicians it can, of course, be tempting to argue that things could have been different ('if we had had the power this would not have occurred'), ie, to imply that they have the means to prevent disastrous things from happening. In a way one can say that this trait of preventionism reflects an overly optimistic view of the ability of mankind to steer and control the world.

- Prevention by the means of criminal law and procedure is seen as the primary form of prevention. When discussing harm prevention, the criminal law system has a prominent place (despite the fact that the most general lesson to be learned from modern criminology is that changes in the criminal law system have little or no impact on harmful behaviour).
- The yardstick for measuring the success of the criminal law is empirical in character, ie, the central criterion for success is whether crime—or rather harm (crime as such is, of course, a direct consequence of criminalization)—is reduced or not. Thus, the main question when evaluating the criminal law is not whether the law deals with cases in a just and reasonable way, but rather whether it prevents harm effectively. Another way of expressing this is to say that criminal law is very much seen as an instrument which can be used for achieving results, rather than as a system of fundamental norms upon which the rest of society is built.

The tendency which I describe and label as preventionism has strong connections to other diagnostic labels that have been used within criminal law theory in the last 25 years. As examples one could mention terms such as:

- *Feindstrafrecht* (Jakobs),[5]
- *Sicherheitsstrafrecht* (Albrecht, Hassemer),[6]
- Offensive (as opposed to defensive) criminal law (Jareborg),[7]
- Pre-active criminal law (Husabo).[8]

A common trait in this diagnosis is that the prevention of danger and harm has become the primary perspective when discussing the design of the criminal justice system. Thus, criminal law is seen not as a basic set of rules providing society with outer limits on what citizens may do, but rather as an instrument for actually achieving things, for changing society for the better. One can also say that there is a consensus among people working in the area that the interest in prevention is gaining ground in relation to such fundamental interests as legal certainty and personal integrity. The trend towards preventionism is probably most obvious in the fight against terrorism—there are, of course, good reasons to try to prevent major terrorist attacks—but it is clearly visible also in other areas of criminal law and procedure, for example in grooming (see the section entitled 'Two central examples' below).

[5] G Jakobs, 'Kriminalisierung im Vorveld einer Rechtsgutsverletzung' (1985) Zeitschrift für die gesamte Strafrechtswissenschaften 751–85. I understand this text as diagnostic or even critical. Jakobs has, however, later returned to the concept of *Feindstrafrecht* with a somewhat different approach. I do not wish to enter into the general discussion on *Feindstrafrecht* in this context.

[6] P-A Albrecht, 'Das nach-präventive Strafrecht: Abscheid vom Recht' (2006), Neue Richtervereinigung, <http://www.nrv-net.de>, and W Hassemer, 'Sicherheit durch Strafrecht' (2006) Onlinezeitschrift für Höchstrichterliche Rechtsprechung im Strafrecht, <www.hrr-strafrecht.de> 130 ff.

[7] N Jareborg, 'What Kind of Criminal Law Do We Want? On Defensive and Offensive Criminal Law Policy' in A Snare (ed), *Beware of Punishment: On the Utility and Futility of Criminal Law* (1995) 17–36.

[8] EJ Husabo, 'Pre-aktiv strafferet' (2003) Tidskrift for strafferet 97–106.

## What's new? Has not criminal law always been conceptually linked to prevention?

One initial objection to the picture just presented might be that the analysis focuses on a tendency which contains nothing new: criminal law has always been concerned with prevention.

If you look at mainstream criminal law theory it is, for example, often emphasized that the main purpose of having a criminal law system at all is to achieve some preventive effects (ie, to reduce harmful behaviour). Further, ever since the acceptance of the idea of criminalization (ie, the idea of a criminal law system built upon proscriptions which are made public in advance), it could be contended that there has been some kind of conceptual link between criminal law and prevention. The very idea of public proscriptions seems to imply a belief, or at least a hope, that the criminal law, with its proscriptions, will affect the behaviour of people. Prevention is, in other words, closely connected to the understanding of modern criminal law. Why then make a fuss about a trend towards preventionism?

The answer surely is not that the alleged connection between criminal law and prevention does not exist. It certainly does. The answer is, rather, that although prevention has a role to play within the criminal law system, this role is fairly limited: prevention is definitely one of the reasons for having a criminal law system, but this does not mean that prevention is the leading rationale when constructing and shaping the system.

If one accepts the idea that it is possible to distinguish between *the general justifying aim of the system* on the one hand, and *the distribution of punishment* on the other[9]—or if one accepts any similar division between the reasons for doing something at all and reasons for doing something in a certain way—it could be argued that (general) prevention is the most plausible answer to questions such as 'Why have a criminal law system at all?' and 'Why criminalize?', but that (general) prevention has limited relevance when it comes to the distribution of punishment.

In this regard the basic principle is rather a principle of fair retribution or, as Hart put it, 'retribution in Distribution'.[10] If one allows oneself to be a bit tautological this overarching principle runs something like the following:

> Punishment should be imposed only on those who – given the fact that we have chosen to have a criminal law system – deserve to be punished (ie, people should be punished for what they have done and not merely be treated as means to an end).

Even though one can debate what the concept of deservedness entails—it is certainly a topic on which there can be diverging views—most people would accept that the following topics must be included in some way:

[9] See, eg, J Rawls, 'Two Concepts of Rules' (1955) 64 *The Philosophical Review* 3–32; HLA Hart, *Punishment and Responsibility* (1968) 8 ff; N Jareborg, *Essays in Criminal Law* (1988) ch V; and C Roxin, *Strafrecht. Allgemeiner Teil. Band I. Grundlagen. Der Aufbau der Verbrechenslehre* (4th edn, 2006) ch §3.A.V.

[10] Hart (cited in n 9).

- Deservedness presupposes *reasonable criminalization*. It is a problem if the legislator criminalizes things which should not be criminalized at all since such criminalizations inevitably lead to undeserved punishment.
- Deservedness presupposes *that the person is actually guilty*, which is a reason for having *reasonable requirements as regards the burden of proof*—it is a problem if the system, on a regular basis, punishes people who have not committed the act that they are accused of (cf general procedural principles, especially in *dubio pro reo*).
- *Deservedness presupposes reasonable requirements as regards fair imputation*. It is a problem if the system punishes pure *casus* and does not care about whether the person can be held responsible or not (cf general principles of guilt, conformity, etc).

Thus, one can say that general prevention certainly has a role to play, but that the idea of prevention is not the primary rationale in all parts of the system. On the contrary, when it comes to the distribution of punishment prevention is of no or limited relevance and other rationales come into play.

My thesis in this chapter is that the tendency towards preventionism has led to a situation where more and more emphasis is put on prevention and that this also affects, inter alia, the distribution of punishment:

- Criminal law is, to a greater extent than before, seen as—or assumed to be—an efficient means for preventing harm and danger (though attempts to justify this assumption are seldom made),
- Crime control is, to a greater extent than before, proactive (as opposed to reactive), and
- Criminal law systems are, more than before, measured with regard to their ability to prevent harmful acts and to meet new risks, etc.

In addition, this tendency or shift in logic puts pressure on the criminal law system in the sense that it challenges traditional principles and safeguards.

Before giving a few examples of preventionist tendencies and before discussing the dangers of preventionism, I want to emphasize that I focus exclusively upon attempts to achieve preventive effects by making use of the criminal law system (in a broad sense, including measures such as coercive measures, surveillance, etc). Thus, what I say here does not in any way imply that it is problematic to strive for prevention through other types of measure (eg through situational crime prevention, providing education, trying to improve the social situation in problem areas, etc).

## Two central examples

*The first example*, (a), of how preventionist thinking affects criminal law concerns the proscriptions themselves. Here we can see a clear tendency to proscribe not only behaviour which is harmful, but also different forms of preparatory conduct. Examples are to be found in various terrorist offences—not merely the possession of weapons (with high penalties) is criminalized, but also the offence of collecting, providing, or receiving money for the purpose of or in the knowledge that it may be used in the commission of serious crimes. And in addition an attempt to commit such an act is being criminalized (ie the attempt to commit an offence which itself is inchoate).

Another example is the offence of grooming. Grooming was, until recently, not criminalized in Sweden. In 2007 the Swedish Prosecutor General presented a report which recommended that (1) to have contact with a child (2) with the purpose of committing a sexual offence against the child should be criminalized. The idea was clearly to criminalize the behaviour in order to make it possible to intervene before any harm was done. I do not say that this idea is flawed, but in this case it was taken to extremes: the only objective requirement was that the perpetrator 'had contact with a child' and all of the blameworthiness lay in the intent. One of the reasons for this quite far-reaching proposal was that anything less would be inefficient.

Later on a more restrictive offence was introduced, which required that the person set up a meeting with the child and do something to facilitate this meeting, all with the purpose of committing a sexual offence against the child.

*The second example*, (b), from Sweden concerns the use of surveillance and coercive measures for preventive reasons. Generally speaking, according to Swedish law the authority to use coercive measures and different measures of surveillance such as secret wiretapping, secret tele-surveillance, etc presupposes that there is a suspicion of an offence having been committed. However, after two terrorist attacks in Sweden in the early 1970s, a new Terrorist Act (lagen 1973:162 om särskilda åtgärder till förebyggande av vissa våldsdåd med internationell bakgrund) was introduced which allowed surveillance and coercive measures (such as searches of body and premises) in order to find out whether a foreigner (who would be deported if possible, but could not be deported for humanitarian reasons) is planning or preparing a terrorist offence. This special law was strongly criticized by legislative committees in 1989 and 1990, and was regarded as exceptional. Yet Sweden has recently enacted a new and general law allowing the use of such measures when a court has reason to believe that a person will commit a serious offence.

Thus we can see a clear shift in attitude. What was considered exceptional and basically inappropriate only twenty years ago is now apparently acceptable (at least in principle). And if one reads the preparatory materials for the legislation, one sees that the threat from international terrorism is obviously the main concern that has contributed to this shift in views. I am not suggesting that the use of surveillance measures for preventive reasons is unacceptable under any circumstances. I simply draw attention to the shift in attitude that seems to have been taking place. At the beginning of the 1990s it was said that the use of coercive measures without reference to a committed offence could be justified only under exceptional circumstances, ie when used against persons whom we would expel if only it were possible. Now we have introduced rules that, at least at the level of principle (there are differences between the Acts), are comparable and they are applicable to all citizens. This can be seen as one example of how exceptional powers are being normalized, reflecting the tendency towards preventionism.

This shift in attitudes invites us to reflect upon the development. What has changed? Is the new situation so different from the situation some twenty years ago and such that it justifies the new measures? Once again one can say that the development clearly reflects the tendency towards preventionism. Harm shall not occur, and in order to make sure that it does not, we tend to abandon our principles and find new ones.

## The logic of preventionism

### *Introduction*

Should we be worried about preventionism and, if so, why? One answer would be to refer to different consequences—or symptoms—of preventionist thinking and present each of them as 'a risk connected to preventionism'.

However, I would like to answer on a more general level with the first, overarching, most general, and most important risk connected to preventionism, and this is—as emphasized by Winfried Hassemer—*the intrinsic logic of prevention.*

Prevention is a future-oriented rationale, and the standard for measuring success is simply whether something (a terrorist offence, a robbery, a murder, etc) has been prevented or not. As Hassemer puts it, the logic of prevention is empirical in character rather than normative:

> The central problem of the paradigm of prevention is . . . its lack of limits. The boundary of the deterrent threat, the end of the rehabilitation efforts are no more than the achievement of the result, ie the realization of the preventive purpose; the limits of prevention are empirical and are not determined by normative parameters. Unlike a criminal law response thought of as retaliation—which has its own built-in limits, since a response has to be adjusted to the thing which it is an answer to—prevention has no antenna for excess. Prevention must, according to its own logic, try to improve petty habitual offenders indefinitely and use new threats and constraints, if deterrence is not served by the previously used instruments.[11]

Hassemer's concern about the preventionist paradigm can be explained and developed further by making use of a few examples where we distinguish between *preventionist punishment* (ie look at the possible consequences for criminal law in a strict sense) and *preventionist crime control* (ie look at the possible consequences for the criminal law system in a wider sense, including policing, intelligence, criminal procedure, etc).

### *Preventionist criminal law v Traditional criminal law*

Let us start by taking a look at what would happen if we were to adhere to *full-blown preventionism within criminal law* in a strict sense.

[11] W Hassemer, 'Strafrecht, Prävention, Vergeltung' (2006) Zeitschrift für Internationale Strafrechtsdogmatik 270. Rough translation by the author. Original in German.

Thus, let us assume that on the one hand we have a pure preventionist criminal law system, ie a system which not only has prevention as its general justifying aim, but also allows the interest in prevention to permeate all decisions within the system. Assume further that on the other hand we have a criminal law system which likewise has prevention as its general justifying aim, but which builds on principles of fair retribution when it comes to the construction of the system.

In the latter system we can easily find certain limitations based on some sort of principle of fair retribution. Such a system does not preclude brutality and harshness, but there is at least a normative yardstick—ie one built upon normative considerations—implying that there should be some sort of fair relation between the act and the answer to the act. Similarly, such a system would not be allowed to disregard the mental capacities of the defendant when considering whether it would be appropriate to punish him or her.

In the former system these types of limitation would be lacking. If we have chosen to adhere to a purely preventionist view of the criminal law, the question of whether a certain punishment is appropriate or not will not (any more) be answered by reference to normative, backward-looking considerations but rather by reference to empirically founded prognoses:

> What is it necessary to do in order to achieve the aim pursued (ie the result that we want to achieve)?

Thus, if we adhere to *pure preventionism* the answer to the question 'what should we do?' will be dependent upon empirical knowledge. For example: if we found out that 'three-strikes-and-you-are-out' works and is necessary for the purpose of controlling crime, then it would be fully in line with preventionist logic to punish a petty theft with imprisonment for life.

Similar examples can be provided for other normative principles such as, for example, the principle of guilt. If it turns out that it is necessary to disregard the principle of guilt to achieve a certain result it would, under a pure preventionist paradigm, be logical to do so. The yardstick is empirical (what is needed?) rather than normative (what is reasonable or just and fair?).

Thus what I suggest is that we, without proper reflection, to some extent tend to think *as if we had chosen to adhere to a purely preventionist system* (and indirectly I am also saying that such a choice would be dangerous and that it would be dangerous exactly because decision-making under a purely preventionist paradigm becomes empirical in character: everything is about consequences). Thus the tendency towards preventionism means that the criminal law system is led by expectations. This creates both:

- a pressure towards increased repression (if the things done are not enough, then we must have more of the same), and
- a pressure on the legislator to make exceptions from such basic criminal law principles (based on notions of fairness and individual autonomy) which might limit the efficiency of the system.

*Preventionist crime control v Preventionist criminal law*

The risks connected to a preventionist criminal law system are, however, rather limited if compared with the risks connected to a preventionist system of crime control.

Things are quite different if we ask ourselves what to do, *not to react to crime, but for the purpose of preventing crime*: if we do so, we will find that there are virtually no limits to our possibilities and to our thinking. This could be illustrated by a simple question:

What is necessary to ensure that another instance of 9/11 will not occur (ie to prevent a major terrorist attack involving the death of thousands of people)?

It is quite obvious that the question is almost impossible to answer: it is relatively easy to cause harm and it is even more obvious that it would be impossible—or at least would require almost unthinkable measures—to take such precautions as would rule out the possibility that major terrorist attacks could occur. This means that pure preventionist thinking puts us in a situation where there are virtually no limits.

This comparison between criminal law on the one hand and the larger system of crime control on the other could perhaps also be used as a basis for reminding us that criminal law—in all its brutality—serves not only the purpose of punishing convicted offenders, but also the purpose of securing freedom. Using criminal law is a way of making the state reactive, ie a way to take away (to some extent) the initiative from the state.

*Summary*

To summarize, preventionism is dangerous since it tends to transform the essentially normative questions about how to construct the criminal law system and how to react to crime and criminality (what should we do?) into empirical ones (what do we need to do in order to . . . ?), ie it tends to foster an approach according to which the central questions are empirical ('what needs to be done?', 'what would prevent *X* from happening?') and according to which normative questions are irrelevant or at least secondary.

When we are discussing questions of how to construct the criminal law system, different kinds of preventive or consequentialist concerns may, of course, be of importance. I am not arguing for any specific view in this regard, but rather trying to demonstrate how the trend towards preventionism may make us forget that the questions are basically normative and fall back on an unreflective 'means to an end' thinking.

## B. Criminalization of non-consummate offences

### Introduction

In this second part of the chapter I will address questions connected to the justification of nonconsummate offences. Douglas Husak suggests a definition according to which an offence:

- is nonconsummate if not all act-tokens of an act-type that is proscribed are harmful, and
- is consummate if all act-tokens of that act-type are harmful.[12]

With this definition as a point of departure it is quite obvious that there are different kinds of nonconsummate offence and that they can be divided into subcategories.[13] One possibility would be to distinguish between different kinds of nonconsummate offence depending upon *how they relate to the harm that they are supposed to prevent*. Using such a ground for categorization one could, for example, distinguish between:

(i) offences of concrete endangerment—offences which presuppose the causation of danger (of harm) in a concrete case (ie, the court must find that the conduct actually caused danger),
(ii) offences of abstract endangerment—offences which presuppose that the conduct at least typically causes such danger (ie, the court must find that the conduct has a certain 'abstract' quality of being dangerous if looked at as a type of conduct),
(iii) offences of presumed endangerment—offences which proscribe conduct which simply is presupposed (by the legislator) to cause such danger (ie, the conduct is criminalized as such and the question of danger is not relevant at the adjudicative level).

Using another standard of systematization one could distinguish between:

(i) simple nonconsummate offences (ie, offences which are criminalized as such without reference to other offences), and
(ii) complex nonconsummate offences (ie, offences which are criminalized as preparatory acts which explicitly relate to other offences, eg attempted murder, conspiracy to commit arson, etc).[14]

Typically complex nonconsummate offences build upon (1) some sort of act (eg a decision by three persons to commit an offence, an attempt to break into a house, etc) and (2) an ulterior intent requirement, ie an intent to perform the consummate offence in question.

For present purposes I will build upon the distinction between simple and complex nonconsummate offences, but adjusting the definition of complex nonconsummate offences so that it does not only cover offences which explicitly refer to another offence (doing *X* with the intent of carrying out offence *Y*), but rather covers *all nonconsummate offences which are built upon an ulterior intent* 'to do more

[12] See Husak (1995) and (2008) (cited in n 2).

[13] In addition to the ones discussed in this text, see also RA Duff, 'Criminalizing Endangerment' (2004–05) Louisiana Law Review 941–65. See also A Ashworth and L Zedner, 'Prevention and Criminalization: Justifications and Limits' (2012) New Criminal Law Review (forthcoming) for another taxonomy.

[14] Husak (1995) (cited in n 2).

than has actually been done' (doing *X* with the intent of carrying out the act *Y* whether *Y* is an offence or not). Thus:

- simple nonconsummate offences—offences which do not include an ulterior intent requirement (an intent to do more than has actually been done)—the prime example would be offences of simple possession (this category is formed by the simple nonconsummate offences according to Husak's definition *minus* such simple nonconsummate offences that include an ulterior intent requirement).
- complex nonconsummate offences—offences which do include an ulterior intent requirement, ie an intent to do more than has actually been done (this category is formed by (1) the complex nonconsummate offences according to Husak's definition *plus* (2) those simple nonconsummate offences that include an ulterior intent requirement).

In the second category I include attempts (doing an act of attempting with the intent of committing the substantive offence in question), conspiracy, and other inchoate offences, and also offences formally constructed as substantive and independent offences on the condition that they include an ulterior intent requirement. One example could be the offence of financing terrorism, which covers the provision of money on the condition that the act is done with the intent of furthering or committing a terrorist offence or any other serious crime listed in the Act (see lagen 2002:444 om straff för finansiering av särskilt allvarlig brottslighet i vissa fall).

## General problems of justification

As indicated in previous paragraphs, there are—if one accepts the idea that the general justifying aim of criminal law is to prevent harm—special justificatory problems attached to nonconsummate offences. The justificatory problems may differ depending on whether the nonconsummate offence in question is complex or simple, but I will start with three different problems arising from the fact that nonconsummate offences separate the formal consummation from the moment where the harm actually occurs.

The first problem is that the separation between formal consummation and harm-causation creates a risk of miscalculations on the part of the legislator. The legislator may simply be wrong in assuming that the criminalized conduct increases the risk of harm. With consummate offences this risk is logically excluded since each and every act-token of the act-type in question actually causes harm. But when it comes to nonconsummate offences the correlation between conduct and harm is based on a judgement made by the legislator; and as with all judgements there is room for errors. And if the risk of harm is what ultimately justifies the criminalization of the conduct it could quite reasonably be argued that the existence of such miscalculation on the part of the legislator is problematic from a justificatory perspective. This problem is perhaps less prominent for complex nonconsummate offences such as attempts,[15] but it certainly exists in the criminalization of different types of preparatory conduct.

Secondly, one could argue that the separation of formal consummation and harm-causation generally means that the relative seriousness (the penal value) of the conduct decreases correspondingly, and since the penal value of an offence arguably is correlated with the weight of the reasons for criminalizing it, this generally increases the problem of justification. One could express this by saying that increased distance between criminalized conduct and harm normally indicates decreased penal value which, in turn, means less weighty reasons for criminalization. This is a general problem, implying that, all other things being equal, the reasons for criminalizing nonconsummate offences are always less weighty than the reasons for criminalizing the corresponding consummate offence.

In this context one should note, however, that many criminal law systems comprise proscriptions which are, so to speak, at the bottom level, for example proscriptions to which only modest fines are attached. This should be taken into account in any realistic theory of (justified) criminalization. I would tentatively argue that *any reasonable theory of criminalization must be relative*, not absolute—taking into account that the act of criminalizing may mean quite different things. That is, when discussing the question of justification, one should not only focus on the conduct itself and ask whether it is worthy of criminalization, but also take into account the sanction(s) attached to the offence and perhaps also the label attached to the offence. The legislator might well be justified in proscribing behaviour of modest or minor harmfulness on the condition that only modest/minor penalties are attached to the commission of the offence. In a modern society there will be many criminal laws which are fairly neutral; and such proscriptions might very well be legitimate. Maybe one can say that the real justificatory problems start when it 'costs too much' to violate such rules. This second part of this chapter is an attempt to apply such relative thinking in a specific context.

Thirdly, one could argue that the separation between formal consummation and harm-causation creates justificatory problems as regards imputation. The distance between formal consummation and adverse (but remote) consequences that one is trying to prevent makes it questionable whether it is fair to hold a person liable for what might (under certain circumstances) happen as a (remote) consequence of his or her actions. Is it, for example, fair to hold *A*, who possesses cannabis, responsible for the harm that might occur should someone copy his or her behaviour, or responsible for the harm that might occur should someone voluntarily use the cannabis having bought it or stolen it from *A*?[16]

[15] Husak (1995) (cited in n 2) 172.

[16] See A von Hirsch, 'Extending the Harm Principle: "Remote" Harms and Fair Imputation' in AP Simester and ATH Smith (eds), *Harm and Culpability* (1996) 259 ff and von Hirsch and Wohlers (cited in n 2).

## The question of intent

### *Introduction*

From general justificatory problems I turn now to the justificatory problems that are specific to complex nonconsummate offences. The fact that complex nonconsummate offences build upon an ulterior intent (doing something with the intent of doing something additional) has several different consequences for the question of justification.

For example, it could be argued that any given complex nonconsummate offence that builds upon an ulterior intent on the part of the offender reflects a legal ideology under which citizens are not addressed as citizens with the ability to choose the good, but rather viewed as enemies or threats to the interests protected by the criminal law.

In this respect one could refer to the theory of *Feindstrafrecht* as elaborated by Günther Jakobs or to the writings of Duff who emphasizes that criminal law intervention at a stage in which harm-causation is still dependent on future acts on the part of the defendant actually implies that he or she cannot be trusted; by intervening the state shows that it is not prepared to rely on the individual's ability to make moral judgements.[17] This type of argument is, obviously, more powerful the earlier the intervention takes place. It is one thing to intervene at a stage where the individual is merely contemplating the possibility of committing an offence, and quite another to intervene when the individual is aiming at another person with a rifle.

It could also be argued that complex nonconsummate offences create special justificatory problems due to the risk that they build upon factors that are hard to prove and disprove. This is especially so if one criminalizes harmless and neutral everyday conduct on the condition that it is accompanied by an intent to commit an offence.

One does not have to build on a dualistic view of the relation between mind and body to accept the proposition that it is, at times, hard to prove that a person has thought something, believed something, or set out to do something, and it is reasonable to argue that these problems increase if one focuses on fairly neutral conduct that could be interpreted in many different ways. For example, if *A* buys a box of matches it does not follow that the only interpretation of this act is that he or she intends to commit arson. Thus, criminalizing the buying of matches with the intent to commit arson will inevitably cause severe evidentiary problems, which will have the most serious consequences for people who have already been convicted of a certain offence. This is problematic since it is unrealistic to assume that it will follow from these evidentiary problems that courts will abstain from convicting persons. The conviction rate will probably (and generally) be low, but the courts will—this is a fair assumption—reach a conviction in some cases. In these cases the decision of the court will, generally speaking, be based on a much more unreliable

[17] RA Duff, *Criminal Attempts* (1996) 37 and 387 ff. See also Duff (cited in n 13).

basis than in standard cases (ie such cases where the conduct tells us 'more' about the intent of the perpetrator).

This is problematic not only because of the risk of false convictions, but also because of the fact that the courts can be almost certain that—whether they find that the accused acted with or without intent to do *X* (eg to crack safes)—the risk that their judgment on this specific question will be defeated by new findings is minimal; this in turn makes it difficult to exercise proper control of the courts.

Against this background it could, with reference to such constitutional values that are normally summarized under the heading 'the rule of law', be argued that it is not legitimate to criminalize conduct in such a way as to cause serious evidentiary problems.

These concerns should be taken seriously, but here I focus primarily on the question of *what it actually means to include an ulterior intent requirement as a prerequisite for criminal liability* and what consequences this has for the question of justification.

## *Husak's culpability requirement*

As a point of departure I take Douglas Husak's formulation of what he calls the *culpability requirement.*

> This principle withholds liability from persons who create a risk of harm unless they have some degree of culpability for the ultimate harm risked. It is not enough that the performance of the proscribed conduct just happens to make the occurrence of the ultimate harm more likely.[18]

In earlier writings Husak was more demanding and argued that there should be a requirement that he called *the high culpability requirement.*

> It is insufficient that the performance of $a_1$ happens to make the consummate harm more likely. Selling a firearm to another ($a_1$), for example, increases the probability that a firearm offense will be committed ($a_2$), but a nonconsummate offense to proscribe such a sale cannot be justified on this basis alone. After all, many tokens of the act-type of selling a firearm might be permissible. Thus, persons who perform act-tokens of $a_1$ should not be punished unless they have a high degree of culpability with respect to $a_2$.[19]

Husak discusses this in the context of complex nonconsummate offences (according to his definition) but it seems clear that his point is to show that we seem to forget this requirement when it comes to simple nonconsummate offences. In other words he is, in this earlier text, arguing that the criminalization of nonconsummate offences is justified only on the condition that the high culpability requirement is met, ie on the condition that the offender has a high degree of culpability in relation to the consummate harm in question.

Husak's argument seems to build upon the idea that the introduction of a (high) culpability requirement in relation to the consummate harm contributes to the

[18] Husak (2008) (cited in n 2). [19] Husak (1995) (cited in n 2).

justification of the criminalization since it creates a connection between the person and the harm that ultimately justifies the criminalization. There is nothing wrong with this conclusion per se. However, I think it is too general in its assumption that an added element of culpability helps in justifying the criminalization. I will devote the last sections of the chapter to an attempt to show this.

### *Ulterior intent as a Janus-faced tool*

I now argue that there is a difference in principle between the justificatory questions that arise in relation to simple nonconsummate offences on the one hand and in relation to complex nonconsummate offences on the other. My thesis is that an ulterior intent requirement actually means:

(a) that we anticipate certain factors to the detriment of the offender (ie we indirectly charge him or her with something which he or she has not yet done), and
(b) that this creates certain quite specific 'internal' justificatory problems.

My argument is based upon the fact that *an ulterior intent-requirement not only limits the scope of the offence* (all things being equal it does, of course), *but also defines what the offender is being charged with.* This double character (being limiting and at the same time being defining) is not specific to ulterior intent requirements, but is rather something that is common to all prerequisites of an offence. For example, the requirement of a death for murder is, of course, a factor that limits responsibility: unless someone has died there can be no responsibility for murder. At the same time the fact that someone has died actually defines the charge, ie it is something for which the person is held responsible, something for which he or she is being blamed. Thus, all things being equal, a 'death requirement' limits responsibility in relation to a 'bodily harm requirement', but it also makes 'death responsibility' so much more burdensome.

This means that when we are talking about nonconsummate offences, we can say that both types of nonconsummate offence (simple and complex) proscribe conduct that is not in itself harmful, but that as regards complex nonconsummate offences there is a more direct link to the consummate harm (ie the harm that one ultimately tries to prevent). When someone is convicted of a complex nonconsummate offence, he or she is not only being held responsible for that which actually occurred (eg the act that was performed), but also being held partially and indirectly responsible for the object of his or her ulterior intention, ie the fact that he or she intended something more is substantially contributing to the seriousness of the offence. One could say that we reinterpret the act that is actually performed and add an element of seriousness which is collected from the consummate offence in question or from the connection to the consummate offence that is established by the intent of the perpetrator. In what follows I will call this an indirect truncated responsibility for the intended offence. Thus:

> In the case of a person convicted of attempted assault, not only is that person held liable for having endangered the physical well-being of the intended victim, but there is, in addition, some sort of an indirect truncated responsibility (a responsibility with a reservation or deduction) for the intended assault.
>
> In the case of a person convicted of conspiracy to murder, not only is that person held liable for the act of having decided to commit a murder together with others, but there is, in addition, some sort of an indirect truncated responsibility (a responsibility with a reservation or deduction) for the intended murder.

In more general terms one could say that the representation of an offence as an 'offence committed with the ulterior intent to *Y*' is to emphasize its close relation to *Y*. This holds true for attempts and—albeit to a lesser extent—for offences like conspiracy and other general preparatory offences. It also holds true for independent offences with an ulterior intent requirement.

When someone is held liable for a simple nonconsummate offence the extension of the charge is more limited. The offender is only charged with (actually) having done something that is connected to certain risks of harm. The connection to the harm that one ultimately tries to prevent is much less evident than it is when the offender is charged with a complex nonconsummate offence. This means that the offender is charged with less than in cases where a corresponding offence builds on an ulterior intent to do something more.

This line of argument can now be used when discussing the justification of nonconsummate offences. The typical problem when it comes to nonconsummate offences is that it is questionable whether it is justifiable to make people liable for possible remote consequences of their acts. Think, for example, of offences where the remote consequences are used as the basis for (or as the reason behind) a general criminalization of non-harmful behaviour but which have some sort of risk-relation to the harm that one is trying to prevent. In such cases the question is not (at least not in the first place) whether it is fair to hold the individual responsible for his or her own behaviour. The question is rather whether the behaviour (for which the individual is responsible) could justifiably be criminalized. For example, if a person is made liable for having bought a shotgun, the question is not whether it is fair to hold the person responsible for having bought the shotgun (of course it is), but rather whether this act of 'buying a shotgun' justifiably could be criminalized. This is illustrated in Figure 2.1, where the dotted line indicates problems of justification.

It should perhaps be added that the box with the words Act/Offence in Figure 2.1 could refer to an offence of abstract endangerment, an offence of concrete endangerment, an offence which is presumed to be dangerous, etc. That the offender could be held liable for this 'act' is established through the application of general principles and rules of criminal responsibility. The tricky question, in this example, is whether the criminalization of the act could be justified with reference to the harm that is to be prevented.

As regards complex nonconsummate offences, the justificatory problems are different and more intricate. In addition to the question of whether the criminalization could be justified by reference to the ultimate end (whether it is justified to criminalize risk-taking when one actually wants to prevent harm), one has to deal

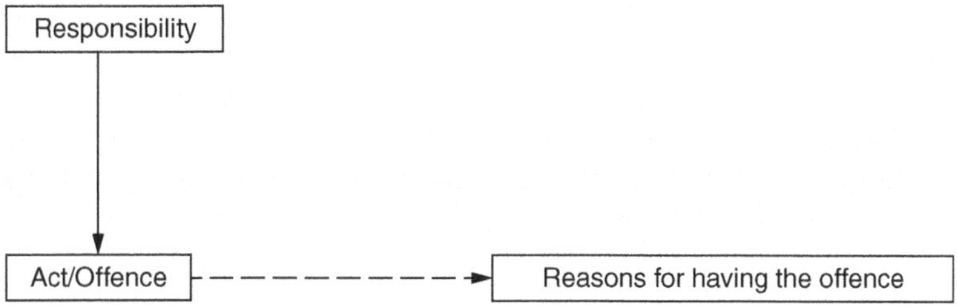


**Figure 2.1** Justification of simple nonconsummate offences

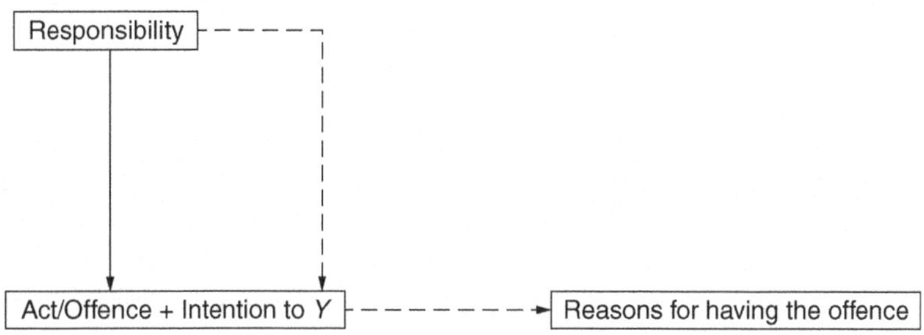


**Figure 2.2** Justification of complex nonconsummate offences

with the question of whether it is justified to hold an individual indirectly and partly responsible for what he or she has not yet done, but for merely having thought of doing it (in the sense explained in the previous discussion). This is illustrated in Figure 2.2 (where the dotted lines again indicate problems of justification).

For example, if I buy a box of matches and am charged with preparing to commit arson, the question is not only (and not primarily) whether the criminalization as such is justified by reference to the reasons for the existence of the offence, but also whether it is justified to make me partially responsible for something that I have only been contemplating, ie the actual arson. Another way of expressing this could be to say that we have to justify why we attach such weight to the connection (based on the ulterior intent of the perpetrator) to the consummate offence.[20]

To summarize, one could say that the prerequisites for liability used by the legislator are Janus-faced, thus being relevant in two respects. First, they can help in

[20] One could perhaps argue that the offender is not being held partially responsible for the consummated offence, but rather held responsible for what he or she has really done (ie performed an act combined with an ulterior intent to do more); I would argue, however, that such a view does not really solve the problem, but rather reformulates it: we still need to justify why we attach such weight to an intent which the agent has not yet transformed into more than preparatory acts.

justifying criminal responsibility (the more the offence requires as regards harm and other prerequisites, the easier it is to justify the criminalization). Secondly, they also define what the offender is charged with (the more an offence requires as regards harm, etc, the more serious it is to be convicted of the offence). From a theoretical perspective there are two different sets of questions when it comes to the justification of nonconsummate offences:

(a) as regards simple nonconsummate offences the main question is whether the offence (the criminalization) is justified having regard to the ultimate aim of the provision (given that the things done by the offender are harmless);

(b) as regards complex nonconsummate offences the main question is twofold:
  (b.i) first, it is necessary to justify the fact that we hold the offender partially responsible for something that he or she has not actually done yet (ie to hold him or her indirectly responsible for the object of his or her ulterior intent); (this question could be referred to as the *question of internal justification*, since it is a question of justification 'within' the offence);
  (b.ii) secondly, it is—in the same way as with simple nonconsummate offences; cf point (a)—necessary to consider whether the offence is justified having regard to the ultimate aim of the provision (given that the things done by the offender are harmless in themselves); (this question could be referred to as the *question of external justification*, since it is a question of justifying the offence with reference to the reasons behind the offence).

The point is thus that complex nonconsummate offences involve a partial, indirect, or truncated responsibility for things that have not happened yet and that such an intent-oriented responsibility in itself requires justification. A person convicted of a complex nonconsummate offence may justifiably ask: 'how can you base your charges on something that I have not yet done?' There are sometimes answers to this question, but not always. With this as a point of departure the crucial question is: 'under what conditions is it justified to hold a person responsible for something that he or she has not yet done, but merely intended?'

A preliminary answer might be that it is legitimate to hold a person indirectly and partly responsible for things that he or she intends to do, but has not done, *at least from the moment when he or she shows that he or she is actually prepared to accept the object of the intention as a consequence of his or her actions.*

But does that not mean that we are back to Husak? Could one not say that an intention to bring about *Y* shows that you are prepared to accept *Y* as a consequence of your actions, ie that an intention to do *Y* is what actually justifies the actor being held partially responsible for *Y*? Could one not argue that if it is ever reasonable to make a person responsible for anything, it should be to hold a person responsible for things that the person intends to bring about?

### *Two types of intent*

The answer to these questions is both yes and no, or rather *sometimes*. An ulterior intent on the part of the offender does, at times, justify holding the offender partially responsible for the object of his or her intention, but this is not always so.

The proposition that an ulterior intent on the part of the offender in itself makes it justified to hold the offender responsible for the object of the ulterior intent must be qualified. This is due to the fact that 'intent' can mean different things. In this context a distinction must be drawn between two different kinds of intent.

The first type of intent, which I will call *conduct intent*, is the normal type of intent used under criminal law and it indicates under what act descriptions a person is prepared to accept an action as his or her own. In other words, a person has conduct intent if, when presented with a description of what he or she did (such as: 'you deliberately hit him') he or she would accept that description as valid rather than, for example, replying, 'no, it was an accident, I just slipped'.

As indicated in the previous paragraphs, this type of intent is the normal type of intent used within the criminal law system and it has mainly to do with intent in relation to consequences of an act (that is being performed) or with circumstances that accompany an act (that is being performed), ie conduct intent has to do with *the actor's own understanding of an act which he or she is (present tense) performing.*

The other type of intent, which I will call *future intent*, is not primarily concerned with the act that is being performed but rather with the actor's future acts. Future intent can be pictured as a decision to perform an additional act ($act_2$) after the performance of $act_1$ (which is at present being performed with conduct intent).

The point in distinguishing between these two types of intent is that there is one important qualitative difference between them. Having *conduct intent in relation to Y* (a particular consequence of an act, a particular accompanying circumstance) indicates that the actor is prepared to accept *Y* (the consequence) as a part of his or her actions. In a way that is actually what we are 'stating' when we find that a person has committed a certain crime intentionally: you did *X* and you did it intentionally (ie at least accepted your act as an assault). However, no such inference can be made from the fact that a person acts with *future intent (in relation) to Y*. The fact that a person performs $act_1$ with the future intent of (later) performing $act_2$ (which may lead to harm) does not in itself indicate that the person, when performing $act_1$, actually is prepared to violate the interests protected by the criminal law (ie the harm that $act_2$ might lead to).

This difference is due to the fact that future intent does not presuppose a connection between the act performed ($act_1$) and the relevant harm (which is connected to $act_2$ rather than to $act_1$). On the contrary if $act_1$ is performed with future intent, there is nothing that says that the future intent (ie the intent to perform $act_2$) is going to be carried out at all. A future intent is always conditioned in different ways and it is also characterized by the fact that there is always some, and often much, distance between the time when the future intent is formed and the time when it is supposed to be carried out. One may, for example, intend to perform *act*$_2$ only if factors *A*, *B*, *C*, and *D* occur (the likelihood of which may be very low); one might when performing *act*$_1$ think that one is prepared to accept *X* as a consequence of (the future intended) *act*$_2$, but hesitate when the time comes to actually perform *act*$_2$, and so on.

Thus, when someone performs *act*$_1$ with conduct intent to cause harm by performing *act*$_1$, this implies that the actor is prepared to actually cause that harm, ie the performance of the act with conduct intent shows such preparedness. Such an inference is not possible when someone performs *act*$_1$ with future intent to cause harm, ie intends to cause harm by performing additional acts in the future.

To summarize, the distinction made between conduct intent and future intent shows that the fact that the offender intends to cause harm cannot generally justify holding the offender partly responsible for that harm at the time when he performs *act*$_1$. This can be justified when the offender has conduct intent in relation to the harm, since the existence of such an intent shows that the offender actually has been prepared to accept the harm as a consequence of his or her acts. If the offender merely has future intent in relation to the harm, this does not imply such preparedness, since the offender still keeps control over the course of events.

Before moving on it should be underlined that the fact that an ulterior intent requirement not only is a factor which contributes to the justification of an offence, but also contributes to that for which the defendant is held responsible means that it is questionable whether a (high) culpability requirement can be recommended as a criterion for judging whether a nonconsummate offence is justified or not. Since a person charged with a simple nonconsummate offence (ie an offence without an ulterior intent requirement) regularly is charged with *less* than a person who is charged with a complex nonconsummate offence, and since complex nonconsummate offences need a double justification (ie pose special justificatory problems), it could be argued that one cannot state that in principle complex nonconsummate offences (which is what we will get if we follow the high culpability requirement) are always preferable to simple nonconsummate offences.

### *When is it justified to hold a person responsible for acts that he or she has not yet performed (but merely intended)?*

In the earlier section entitled 'Ulterior intent as a Janus-faced tool', I argued that the offences with an ulterior intent requirement need a double justification. One needs not only to justify the criminalization of the offence as such, but also to justify that one is holding the person responsible for something that he or she has not yet done (but merely intended). When, then, is it justified to hold a person responsible for what he or she merely has intended (ie has not actually done)?

A preliminary answer might be that it is legitimate to hold a person indirectly and partly responsible for things that he or she intends to do, at least from the moment when he or she shows that he or she is actually prepared to accept the object of the intention as a consequence of his or her actions. Put another way, it is justified to hold a person responsible for something that he or she has intended to do, but has not yet done, *from the moment when he or she deliberately loses control of the course of events*. It is from the moment that the individual 'lets go' of control over whether harm occurs that he or she shows that he or she is actually prepared to accept its occurrence.[21]

This means (as developed in the earlier section entitled 'Two types of intent') that such a truncated responsibility for the object of the ulterior intent is justified, at least when $act_1$ is performed with conduct intent in relation to the relevant harm. For example, when a person commits an attempt by shooting at a person, the ulterior intent in relation to the death of the victim has the character of a conduct intent. The intent of the person relates to the act that he or she is (presently) performing. In such situations it seems as though the performance of $act_1$ in combination with the conduct intent in relation to the relevant harm in itself shows that the person is prepared to accept the object of his or her intention as a consequence of his or her act. Thus, it is justifiable to hold the person partially responsible for the death (that never occurred). Examples might be:

- a complete attempt, where the person has done all that is needed to complete the offence in question (eg injecting the poison into the victim with the intention of killing the victim), and
- unlawful wounding, with the intent to do grievous bodily harm (in a case where the grievous bodily harm was intended as a consequence of the wounding act already performed).

However, if a person performs an act ($act_1$) and merely has future intent in relation to the relevant harm, the intent cannot in itself justify the truncated responsibility for this harm. In these cases the ulterior intent means nothing more than an intention to perform a second act ($act_2$) and this intention does not in itself justify holding the person partially responsible for the harm connected to $act_2$. Examples might be:

- conspiracy, where two or more persons agree ($act_1$) to (later) commit an offence with the intent to commit that offence ($act_2$), or
- preparation (under Swedish law), where a person ($act_1$) buys a weapon, with the intent to use it for an offence ($act_2$) in relation to which preparation is punishable, or
- grooming (as under the Swedish proposed legislation), where a person has contact with a child ($act_1$) with the intent to (later) commit a sexual offence against the child ($act_2$).

[21] Cf the distinction between direct and indirect offences of endangerment in Duff (2004–05) (cited in n 13). In a way one can say that distinction reflects the distinction between problematic and unproblematic cases of complex nonconsummate offences.

In these cases, we must search for another justification for the truncated responsibility for the intended act. Before concluding, I offer some tentative suggestions of such other possibilities.

First, it should be noted that incomplete attempts would fall under the second category discussed in previous paragraphs, ie the category when the intent itself cannot do the justificatory work. However, it seems unreasonable to argue that criminalizing incomplete attempts would (always) be unjustified. Such a conclusion seems counter-intuitive. A first suggestion would therefore be that responsibility for intended but unrealized consequences is also justified when the perpetrator has come so close to the point of no return that it is justifiable to conclude that the person was actually prepared to fulfil his or her intentions. Then, the actor would have indirectly shown that he or she is prepared to accept the consequences of the as yet unperformed act (*act*$_2$). This line of argument needs to be developed, but the suggestion is not implausible.

A second possibility would be to argue that responsibility for intended but unrealized consequences is (also) legitimate on the condition that the offender has concerned him- or herself with objects that have an apparent criminal aim and function. If, for example, someone buys a machine gun with the intent to murder one could argue that the act in itself solves the question of internal justification, ie that the very character of the act justifies holding the person responsible for his or her ulterior intent. However, such an argument is not very convincing. The question of internal justification, ie whether it is justified to hold someone partially responsible for ulterior intentions, is simply not solved. One might argue that the conduct itself could (at times) justify the conclusion that the defendant acted with an ulterior intent to perform a murder (or some other serious offence), but from this it does not follow that it is justifiable to hold the person partially responsible for the object of his or her ulterior intentions at a time when he or she still has full control of the course of events.

Thirdly, one could argue that psychological experience shows that people's behaviour is affected by the involvement of others. For example, one could argue that it is harder to abstain from doing something once you have promised to do it, harder to abandon a plan devised with others than to abandon a plan which you have not told anyone else about, and so on. Such arguments could—and at least to some extent—legitimize making use of nonconsummate offences such as conspiracy. It could be argued that this category of conduct actually belongs to the category discussed as primary; the category of conduct which involves letting go of the control of the course of events. With a slight exaggeration one could perhaps say that the involvement of others always corresponds to a certain loss of control.

A fourth way of arguing would be to say that it is legitimate to hold a person partially responsible for his or her ulterior intentions when he or she has concerned him- or herself with objects the possession of which it would be legitimate to criminalize, even in the *absence* of ulterior intent. The line of argument would be that:

(a) it is justifiable to criminalize possession of the object irrespective of whether the offender has an ulterior intention to commit an offence;
(b) it is justifiable (and more or less inevitable) to take ulterior intentions into account when assessing the moral value of an act (ie justified to take ulterior intentions into account when assessing the seriousness of the offence);
(c) thus, it is justifiable to criminalize possession and to take the ulterior intent into account as an aggravating circumstance; and
(d) since the difference between criminalizing the possession of eg a machine gun as a simple nonconsummate offence (taking the intent to commit a murder into account merely for the purpose of sentencing) and criminalizing the same act-type as a complex nonconsummate offence (eg preparation of murder) is more or less technical, the latter type of criminalization is justified on the condition that the offence requires that the actor has concerned him- or herself with an object the possession of which it would be legitimate to criminalize.

Within this category will fall some, but not all, of the objects with an obviously criminal function, for example, a machine gun possessed with the ulterior intent to murder someone. This line of reasoning could, however, be questioned with reference to the principle of fair labelling.[22] Thus it could be argued that the very representation of an act as 'preparation for murder' or 'conspiracy to commit a murder' or suchlike emphasizes its close relation to the consummate offence and that such a representation has to be justified. And then we are back to the question that we tried to solve earlier: is it fair, at a time when the actor has not yet shown his or her preparedness to perform the intended act, to represent the act of possessing a dangerous item, with the intent to commit an offence, in such a way that the actor becomes partially responsible for the merely intended consummate offence?

## C. Epilogue

In the first part of this chapter I suggested that the interest of the legislator in nonconsummate offences is part of a larger tendency towards preventionism in criminal law, ie a tendency towards a way of thinking according to which the primary consideration is the prevention of harm. It has been argued that this '-ism' is associated with risks primarily connected to the empirical logic of prevention: risks for increased repression, risks for exceptions from traditional (normative) principles and safeguards (justified with reference to prevention), etc.

The second part of the chapter dealt with questions of justification of nonconsummate offences. It was suggested that the justification of complex nonconsummate offences is two-dimensional. It involves not only (i) the traditional justification of the

[22] Cf J Horder, 'Crimes of Ulterior Intent' in AP Simester and ATH Smith (eds), *Harm and Culpability* (1996) 161 ff.

offence as such (having regard to the ultimate aim of the offence), but also (ii) justification of the fact that we hold the actor partially responsible for something that he or she has not done yet, ie hold him or her partially responsible for the object of his or her ulterior intent. This means that it is questionable whether it is reasonable to give general priority to complex nonconsummate offences (in relation to simple noncomplex offences), ie one cannot say that complex nonconsummate offences are less problematic from a justificatory perspective due to the ulterior intent requirement, since this requirement will also add to what the defendant is being charged with. In addition I have discussed some possible standards that could be used when answering this second justificatory question. It should be evident that these findings should be read as tentative suggestions rather than as conclusions. What I am suggesting is simply that we need more discussion and analysis as regards this type of justificatory question and should not take it for granted that an ulterior intent requirement in itself provides the solution.

# 3

# Preventive Justice

## The Quest for Principle

*Markus D Dubber**

### A. Introduction

The search for principles of preventive justice is an undertaking that, at first glance, may appear too ambitious. Preventive justice has been said to encompass a wide range of legal doctrines and penal measures, substantive and procedural, legislative and executive, from reckless endangerment and dangerous driving, through possession offences in particular and inchoate liability in general, to ASBOs (anti-social behaviour orders), control orders, to a whole panoply of investigatory 'law enforcement' techniques (detecting, collecting, processing data of various sorts) and eventually to the 'preventive state' itself. Finding a set of principles that would tidy up this wide and varied lot is a daunting task.

Yet at second glance, the quest for principle may not be ambitious enough. I don't mean a limitation to substantive criminal law, though that would be somewhat surprising since preventive justice works in primarily procedural ways, or the exclusion of judicial state action from the inquiry. I mean not the scope of the search, but its depth. The search for principles of preventive justice is unlikely to succeed, or rather is misguided, if it is regarded as a process of selection, presumably among some principles of justice (or prevention?), which for some reason have not been applied, or have been applied with insufficient vigour, to a range of state actions labelled 'preventive justice' measures. In this view, preventive justice is the exception to some rule and the task is to bring the exception back in line, to rope in the new rogue penality of prevention, to re-establish the rule of law, and so on.[1]

What is at stake is not merely the principledness of preventive justice, but the principledness of penal justice as a whole, the legitimation not of the preventive state, but of the penal state. The search for principles of preventive justice is not a matter of application, or even of extension, but one of legitimatory archaeology, an

* Some of the research for this chapter was done at Humboldt-Universität zu Berlin, supported in part by a grant from the Deutsche Forschungsgemeinschaft (DFG). I am grateful to Tatjana Hörnle for making this stay not only possible but also enjoyable and productive, and to the editors of this volume for many helpful suggestions.

[1] See Dyzenhaus, this volume.

inquiry into the foundations of the modern penal state and therefore the legitimacy of state punishment in a modern liberal democracy.[2] What is needed is a critical analysis not of preventive justice, but of penal justice itself.[3]

Principled analysis would need to be pursued both horizontally and vertically, with the vertical search for principle not being content to connect one rule with another more basic one, but continuing to push deeper to unearth more fundamental layers of principle, which eventually connect to the principles of constitutional law and to the legitimacy of state power. Identifying a principle like *actus non facit reum nisi mens sit rea* or, in German law, the *Rechtsgutsprinzip* or *Schuldprinzip*, or, less clearly, the 'fundamental principle' of 'moral voluntariness' in Canadian criminal law,[4] without inquiring into its legitimatory foundation is insufficient already at the level of analysis. Simply noting that a given doctrine or practice does, or does not, comply with a principle, *mens rea*, say, or *nullum crimen sine lege*, is an instance of incomplete analysis that fails to set the stage for the move from analysis to critique, by failing to identify applicable principles and therefore also failing to note their absence. In critical analysis, the analysis is only a means to the end of critique. Exclusively horizontal analysis may help to perpetuate a penal regime that appears to be subject to principle, with occasional exceptions, yet is unrooted in the fundamental commitments of a liberal democratic state.

Wherever analysis ends, and critique starts, the objective of critical analysis of law is to test law against its inherent and distinctive claim to legitimacy. Law's claim to legitimacy is already distinctive of it as a mode of governance, in contrast to police, which lays no claim to legitimacy, and is in this sense alegitimate. Even if legitimation in general is not distinctive of the concept and project of modern law—in a state under the rule of law, the *Rechtsstaat*—the recognition of personal autonomy, or self-government, as the legitimatory *Grundnorm* is. But whatever principle emerges as the lynchpin of legitimacy, it is that principle against which the system is measured, ultimately and perhaps indirectly through various intermediary principles. This legitimacy critique is impossible with an incomplete or haphazard analysis of the positive law, as doctrine and as practice, and in context.

That contextual analysis would include an inquiry into the mode of governance reflected in the doctrine or practice in question. If one accepts that law is but one mode of governance, which can only be grasped, and was posited, in contrast to another mode of governance, call it police (or regulation, administration, management, in more recent lingo), and that modes of governance differ in, among other things, their concern for, or at least conception of, legitimacy as well as in their rationales (or logics, or even governmentalities), then the critique of a given doctrine or practice would be impossible without a contextual analysis of this sort. Arguably, the very notion of critique, and not merely critique in terms of

[2] See, eg, MD Dubber, 'Foundations of State Punishment in Modern Liberal Democracies: Toward a Genealogy of American Criminal Law' in RA Duff and S Green (eds), *Philosophical Foundations of Criminal Law* (2011) 83.

[3] On historical analysis as an instance of critical analysis of law, see MD Dubber, 'Historical Analysis of Law' (1998) 16 Law and History Review 159.

[4] See *R v Ruzic* [2001] 1 SCR 687.

legitimacy, is distinctive of the realm of law, rather than police, though of course this would depend on one's view of the distinction between these ideal types of governance.[5]

In what follows, I will sketch a critical analysis of doctrines and practices commonly identified—and identified in particular by Ashworth and Zedner—as instances of 'preventive justice'. Section B, after rehearsing briefly the distinction between law and police as alternative modes of governance best viewed in contradistinction to one another, argues that preventive justice is neither new, nor different, being instead a long familiar instance of penal police. Section C moves from analysis to critique, considering various criticisms of 'preventive justice' raised, or implied, and concluding that they miss the mark, either because they are inapposite (from the perspective of police) or unfounded (from the perspective of law).

## B. Analysis

Doctrines and practices commonly grouped under the heading 'preventive justice' are neither new nor different. They are, misleadingly labelled, instances of the exercise of the longstanding, indeed ancient, patriarchal power of police.

### Police

Briefly, the power of police (*Polizeimacht* or *-gewalt*) is the modern manifestation of householders' private unlimited arbitrary power over their household.[6] By contrast, the power of law (*Rechtsmacht or -gewalt*) is the modern manifestation of householders' public limited non-arbitrary power over each other in the Greek city-state they constitute. Police is essentially hierarchical and heteronomous, law essentially egalitarian and autonomous. Police is defined by the categorical distinction between governor (householder) and governed (household, composed of resources inanimate and animate, flora and fauna, humans, animals, plants, land, wife, children, slaves). Law is defined by the rejection of that distinction and the assertion (or discovery, if you prefer) of the radical identity of governor and governed. Police seeks, or more precisely it *is*, the welfare of the household, a state of good order and 'economy'; law seeks justice, or right. Police is the mode of governing a macro household—manifested in police ordinances and other commands, to govern the prince's subjects, and tracts (and manuals) of police science, to advise the prince in the exercise of his power. Law is the mode of governing a democracy—manifested in constitutions and published norms, binding on governor and governed alike. The state

[5] For a general discussion of this issue, see MD Dubber, *The Police Power: Patriarchy and the Foundations of American Government* (2005); for an application to penal governance, see MD Dubber, 'The New Police Science and the Police Power Model of the Criminal Process' in MD Dubber and M Valverde (eds), *The New Police Science: The Police Power in Domestic and International Governance* (2006) 107. For a critique, see L Zedner and I Loader, 'Police beyond Law' (2007) 10 New Criminal Law Review 142.

[6] For a more detailed discussion, see Dubber, *Police Power* (cited in n 5).

under police is the police state (*Polizeistaat*); the state under law is the law state (*Rechtsstaat*).

Now, to say that the ideal of the law state was specifically defined against the ideal of a police state is not to say that the law state in fact replaced the police state, and that government by law rule has replaced government by police standard. Indeed, it would be surprising if (even) the Enlightenment had managed to eliminate all traces of one of the two modes of governance that can be traced back millennia to the beginning of the Western political tradition—and its definitive texts, including Aristotle's *Politics* (which considers household government (economics) before turning to state government (politics proper)). Instead, police and law remain useful as perspectives for the analysis, and critique, of contemporary exercises of state power.

Penal police, as one aspect of police governance, then, is best thought of not as an ancient or pre-modern artefact of a mode of governance overcome by the enlightened invention of a state under the rule of law. Instead, English penality today remains firmly rooted in a policial conception of crime as the violation of the sovereign (macro or royal) householder's peace. There is thus a danger, for studies of phenomena like 'preventive justice' (or the 'preventive state' or, for that matter, 'the war on terror' or the 'security agenda against terrorism'), to present their subject as a deviation from a norm of principledness, or at least relative principledness, and perhaps even, for added emphasis, as a paradigm shift, a suggestion possibly bolstered by references to the (now already not so) new sociological phenomenon of 'the risk society' described by Ulrich Beck.[7] It is useful, however, to investigate not only the perceived impropriety of recent state actions, but also the principledness of the norm from which they are said to deviate. It may be misleading, for instance, within the context of the distinction between law and police as modes of governance, to characterize developments as the move from one ideal type to the other, from a surprisingly unexamined state of law to a state of police ('policification' (*Verpolizeilichung*)), whether that transition is portrayed as an exception to the norm or not.[8]

A focus on police, rather than on prevention (on the basic mode of governance, rather than a particular means)—and therefore on the police state, not the preventive state (or, in the German literature, the *Polizeistaat* rather than the *Präventionsstaat*[9])—supplies the inquiry into institutions of preventive justice not only with the appropriate depth, but also with the requisite, broader, scope. As a comprehensive mode of state governance, police is not limited to either substantive or procedural norms, nor to one branch—or aspect—of government rather than another.

[7] U Beck, *Risk Society: Towards a New Modernity* (1992).

[8] This shift from one mode of penal governance to another is to be distinguished from policification in the more specific sense of an expansion of the competence of the police as an institution, and of the jurisdiction of police vis-à-vis the jurisdiction of regular courts, as described for instance in the legal historiography of Nazi Germany. See, eg, A Schwegel, *Der Polizeibegriff im NS-Staat: Polizeirecht, juristische Publizistik und Judikative 1931–1944* (2005) 125.

[9] See, eg, S Huster and K Rudolph, *Vom Rechtsstaat zum Präventionsstaat* (2008).

Police manifests itself in procedural and substantive norms alike, and in fact challenges the distinction between the two, at least functionally, if not formally. Consider, for instance, the well-documented case of possession offences, which can be seen as street-sweeping tools or gateway offences that in their ubiquity and ease of detection and proof are well suited for the investigation, identification, and elimination of human dangers, and therefore as performing a function once (and still) performed by vagrancy offences since the 14th century.[10] A systematic inquiry into the phenomenon of preventive justice thus should concern itself with both substantive and procedural norms, institutions, and practices, and their interplay. At least as important, it should not limit its scope to some branches of government—the legislature, or perhaps the executive—at the exclusion of others—notably the judiciary.

All branches of government exercise the power to police. The very notion of a separation of powers, and the assignment of a given governmental power to one branch or other, is foreign to police as a mode of governance. The power to police, as we have seen, is the modern manifestation of householders' power over their household, transferred from the micro household of the traditional family (*Kleinfamilie*) to the macro household of the state, and from the personal sovereign of the householder to the abstract sovereign of the state, or the people (or the public, the *Volk*, the nation, etc).

## Peace

From the perspective of the police power, then, the various powers, or tasks, of government all spring from the same source of sovereignty; there is no need for a strict separation of powers, unless recommended by prudence, nor is there a point in then balancing these powers, should they have been separated. All state officials exercise powers delegated to them by the sovereign and all are charged with the maintenance of the household's peace. Here it is useful to recall that police, as a condition, is the modern version of the deep-rooted notion of peace, or mund, or grith. To police a territory meant to pacify it, to bring it into a well-ordered state, a state of 'good police'. Police thus was both the end and the means (including the institutional means, in the still familiar sense of police department, or police officer). The commonwealth, or commonweal, in this conception, was both the household as a group and its status, both the common and its weal(th).

This conception of the state's authority—and indeed obligation, if ultimately discretionary—to protect the peace of its constituents, is apparent in the conception of members of the executive, notably police officers but also public prosecutors (or commonwealth or district or state attorneys), as 'peace officers'.[11] It also

[10] MD Dubber, 'Policing Possession: The War on Crime and the End of Criminal Law' (2002) 91 Journal of Criminal Law & Criminology 829; A Ashworth, 'The Unfairness of Risk-Based Possession Offences' (2011) 5 Criminal Law and Philosophy 237.

[11] See, eg, *Chicago v Morales* 527 US 41, 107 (1999) (Thomas J dissenting); *People v Marrero* 69 NY 2d 382 (1987).

underlies the legislative conception, and form, of accusations of criminal conduct as offences against, or disturbances of, the king's (or the state's, or some other sovereign's) peace, both in general and in the case of particular offences.[12]

The judiciary, too, retains the power to maintain the peace, a fundamental power that becomes more clearly visible in a number of contexts. Consider, for instance, the judiciary's comprehensive and inherent power of contempt, which gives judges the discretionary and indefinable authority to take appropriate measures to keep their court's peace, directly by maintaining decorum in their presence and indirectly by disciplining those not respecting their authority—in defiance of their orders.[13] Recall also the residual power to recognize new common law misdemeanours to protect 'the public police or economy', and 'to cope with novel situations not comprehended or contemplated by the legislators'.[14]

Another significant instance of judicial police power, and one particularly relevant in the context of an inquiry into preventive justice, is the power of justices of the peace to issue bonds for keeping the peace or for good behaviour, which Blackstone discusses, with eminent pride and great emphasis, in Chapter 18 of Book IV of the *Commentaries*:

> WE are now arrived at the fifth general branch or head, under which I proposed to consider the subject of this book of our commentarie [Book the Fourth: of Public Wrongs]; viz. the means of preventing the commission of crimes and misdemesnors. And really it is an honour, and almost a singular one, of our English laws, that they furnish a title of this sort: since preventive justice is upon every principle, of reason, of humanity, and of sound policy, preferable in all respects to punishing justice; the execution of which, though necessary, and in it's consequences a species of mercy to the commonwealth, is always attended with many harsh and disagreeable circumstances.
>
> THIS preventive justice consists in obliging those persons, whom there is probable ground to suspect of future misbehaviour, to stipulate with and to give full assurance to the public, that such offence as is apprehended shall not happen; by finding pledges or securities for keeping the peace, or for their good behaviour.[15]

Blackstone evidently attaches great importance to these measures of 'preventive justice', not merely because he regards them as 'almost a singular [honour] of our English laws' (though he cites Beccaria in support of the preferability of preventive justice), but also because they occupy a central place in that part of the laws of

[12] See discussion (at n 19) of G Williams, 'Preventive Justice and the Rule of Law' (1953) 16 MLR 417 (breaches of *the* peace).

[13] For an extended discussion, and judicial defence, of the uncodified and non-statutory judicial power of contempt, see *United Nurses of Alberta v Alberta* [1992] 1 SCR 901.

[14] *Commonwealth v Keller* 35 Pennsylvania District & County Rep 2d 615 (1964). For a discussion of this fascinating opinion, which relies heavily on Blackstone's definition of 'public police and economy' as 'the due regulation and domestic order of the kingdom, whereby the individuals of the state, like members of a well governed family, are bound to conform their general behaviour to the rules of propriety, good neighbourhood and good manners, and to be decent, industrious and inoffensive in their respective stations' (*Commentaries on the Laws of England*, vol 4 (1769) 162), see MD Dubber, 'The Story of *Keller*: The Irrelevance of the Legality Principle in American Criminal Law' in R Weisberg and D Coker (eds), *Criminal Law Stories* (forthcoming 2012).

[15] Blackstone (cited in n 14) 251–2.

England which pertains to 'public wrongs'. They represent a comprehensive conception of penal justice: 'preventive justice', which is not an exception to the norm of 'punishing justice', but an alternative, and in fact a preferable one. Then, Blackstone goes even further, remarking that prevention, not expiation, or some other backward-looking consideration, is the ultimate end of 'all human punishments':

> And indeed, if we consider all human punishments in a large and extended view, we shall find them all rather calculated to prevent future crimes, than to expiate the past: since . . . all punishments inflicted by temporal laws may be classed under three heads; such as tend to the amendment of the offender himself, or to deprive him of any power to do future mischief, or to deter others by his example: all of which conduce to one and the same end, of preventing future crimes, whether that be effected by amendment, disability, or example. But the caution, which we speak of at present, is such as is intended merely for prevention, without any crime actually committed by the party, but arising only from a probable suspicion, that some crime is intended or likely to happen; and consequently it is not meant as any degree of punishment, unless perhaps for a man's imprudence in giving just ground of apprehension.[16]

In other words, not only is preventive justice preferable to punishing justice, but ultimately even punishing justice (divine punishment excluded) is preventive itself.

These passages are remarkable for several reasons. First, and most immediate, they suggest that the pursuit of 'preventive justice' is nothing new, but was familiar to Blackstone, so familiar in fact, that he traces it back at least to the 11th century (Edward the Confessor's '*fidejussores de pace et legalitate tuenda*', commonly translated as 'sureties to keep the peace and good behaviour') if not the frankpledge—originally frith-borh, or 'peace pledge' (frith, like the German *Friede*, being derived from the Old English *friðu*)—he attributes to King Alfred (9th century).

In general, the longstanding concern for preventive measures may itself reflect the centrality of the concept of peace in English governance; not prevention in general, but prevention of breaches of the peace in particular, in this light, may appear so crucially important precisely because the maintenance of the peace was not merely one concern among many, but the single most important aim of government, in fact, its *raison d'être*. In Pollock and Maitland's telling, the history of English law emerges as a history of the maintenance of peace, or rather of peaces, since, as they pointed out, 'every householder has his peace',[17] and the history of English government is also the assertion of one householder's power over another, and therefore also over his household, resulting in the gradual incorporation of micro households into the macro household of the king through a process of centralization and, literally, pacification.[18]

16 Blackstone (cited in n 14) 251–2.

17 F Pollock and FW Maitland, *The History of English Law Before the Time of Edward I*, vol 1 (2nd edn, 1898) 454.

18 See F Pollock, 'The King's Peace in the Middle Ages' (1900) 13 Harvard Law Review 177. The concept of peace also plays a crucial, if still understudied, role in American legal history. But see Laura Edwards' masterful archival study of local governance in the pre-Civil War South, LF Edwards, *The People and Their Peace: Legal Culture and the Transformation of Inequality in the Post-Revolutionary*

We will soon return to the crucial, and fascinating, question of the notion of peace and its connection to the power to police. For now, it is important to recognize that Blackstone's conception of the peace bond points not only backward, to King Alfred, but also forward, and outward, beyond the borders of English penality. Within English law, the connections between the age-old power of justices of the peace to require sureties of peace and good behaviour and more recent (and perhaps already themselves outdated) policing tools like the ASBO and various, more specific, control orders (which stand to peace bonds, and to a lesser extent ASBOs, like possession offences to vagrancy statutes) are obvious, and perhaps not particularly interesting.

## Penal Police Programmes

It might be more fruitful to see the 'preventive justice' scheme described by Blackstone in the context of other comprehensive systems of penal police. One might be tempted, looking forward from Blackstone, to think that the English conception of preventive justice has changed significantly over the past two hundred years or so. That would not appear to be the case, however. When Glanville Williams, for instance, turned his attention to the subject of preventive justice, in an article entitled 'Preventive Justice and the Rule of Law',[19] he can be seen to remain within the conception of penality recorded by Blackstone—the paradigmatic offence is an offence against the king's peace.[20] So when Williams expressed some concern about the notion of requiring sureties to keep the peace, he did not challenge this longstanding viewpoint, but invoked it: it was precisely the fact that '[e]very crime is a breach of the royal peace' which threatened to expand the scope of a peace bond beyond acceptable limits (whatever they might be). Instead, Williams declared—without argument, unless a reference to 'civil liberty' counts as an argument—that 'the notion of crimes involving a breach of *the* peace is a specific one', and further announced—also without argument—that crimes involving a breach of *the* peace were limited to crimes posing danger of violence to a person.[21] The limitation in terms of the personhood of the victim, and the nature of the violation, or at least threatened violation, may well be sensible, and may accord with a view of law rooted in the concept of the person as endowed with the capacity for autonomy; without more, however, this limitation appears as an

*South* (2009); see also CL Tomlins, 'Republican Law' in E Gray and J Kamensky (eds), *Oxford Handbook of the American Revolution* (forthcoming 2012).

[19] Williams (cited in n 12).

[20] For a close reading of Williams's article, see Andrew Ashworth, 'Preventive Orders and the Rule of Law' (on file with author).

[21] It is worth noting here that German criminal law retains two distinct offences of breach of the peace—breach of the land peace and breach of the house peace. Both offences, interestingly, are categorized under 'offences against public order'. Breach of the house peace (occasionally misleadingly, but revealingly, translated as burglary) is defined as, among other things, 'penetrating the pacified (*befriedete*) possession of another', German Criminal Code §123; see also German Criminal Code §124 (aggravated breach of the house peace).

unmotivated external ad hoc addendum fundamentally inconsistent with the conception of penality it purports to govern.

To take another example, from across the Atlantic: Roscoe Pound too had a comprehensive vision of preventive justice, though one not rooted in the protection of the royal peace, but—this being America—of its successor in the (not so) New Republic, the public peace or public welfare.[22] In a late essay, published in 1946 (and reprinted in 1964), Pound lays out a system of 'individualized justice', which includes the now familiar trio of measures of 'preventive justice': deter, rehabilitate, incapacitate. This program of peno-correctional treatment exerted enormous influence over penal policy—if not penal practice—for the better part of the 20th century and underlay not only correctional policy but even broad criminal codification efforts such as the American Model Penal Code.[23] The individualized justice Pound had in mind referred only to the offender, not to the victim, only to the punishment, not to the crime. The object of penal treatment was to protect public welfare, ie, public or social interests, not to protect the rights, or interests, of individuals as such. Note Pound's definition of justice as 'the regime of adjustment of relations and ordering of conduct through a politically organized society to the end of maintaining the inner order of that society'.[24] In other words, Pound defines justice as police. Individualized justice thus simply becomes the choice of preventive measures appropriately targeted to the specific type and degree of social dangerousness exhibited by a given individual, offender, or, preferably, potential offender. The prototype for this type of individualized justice was the juvenile court. The progressive programme calls for the expansion of the juvenile justice model (informal diagnosis and treatment of delinquency, rather than punishment based on formal ascription of criminal liability) and thus rests on the infantilization of criminal offenders (also reflected in regimes of prison management that first deprive inmates of all means of autonomy or mere self-sufficiency and then render them dependent on the distribution of 'privileges' by the prison authority).

Pound's progressive programme—despite his protestations to the contrary, and the insistence on the novelty of progressive proposals, specifically as compared to what Pound calls, in this essay, the 'methods of administering justice which we inherited from England'[25]—recalls Blackstone's view of preventive justice in several ways. As already noted, both preventive justice schemes are order-maintenance, or peace-keeping, regimes, and differ only in the sovereign whose peace is at stake, the king in one case, the amorphous public (or 'the social') in the other.

But the connection is more specific, and interesting, still: Pound's preventive means of order maintenance are Blackstone's. Recall that Blackstone, some two centuries earlier, rattled off the by then already well-known penological trifecta of

[22] Pound and his fellow progressives echoed developments on the Continent, notably work done by Franz von Liszt and his followers: eg F Liszt, 'Der Zweckgedanke im Strafrecht' (1883) 3 Zeitschrift für die gesamte Strafrechtswissenschaft 1.

[23] On the Model Penal Code treatmentist programme, see Dubber (cited in n 10).

[24] R Pound, 'The Future of Socialized Justice' (1964) 10 *Crime & Delinquency* 505 (originally published in National Probation Association 1946 Yearbook, *Society's Stake in the Offender* (1946)).

[25] Pound (cited in n 24) 506 ('Techniques').

'preventing future crimes': 'by amendment, disability, or example'.[26] What is more, this preventive trinity goes back much farther than, say, Beccaria, but can already be found in the 17th-century literature on police, most notably in the discussion, and introduction, of labour as a 'police punishment'. For instance, the alternative punishment of galley service in Germany—which regularly supplied Venice in particular with penal rowers for its fleet—was said to be reserved for offenders with rehabilitative potential. Similarly, public labour (*opus publicum*) was imposed in 17th-century Germany, as an alternative to incarceration, on corrigible vagrants, ie, the ungoverned, but not ungovernable, lordless men not under the power of a micro householder, who not surprisingly had been the paradigmatic target of household-centred order-maintenance regimes since at least the 14th century.[27] Finally, 17th-century 'houses of correction' (*Zuchthäuser*) sought, literally, to discipline the disorderly and disobedient, a group that potentially included the entire class of the governed; as a Munich *Zuchthaus* put it, simply, in the late 17th century, it was meant for 'in sum, anyone who does not do that which is appropriate' (*in Summa ein jeder der nit thut, was sich gebührt*).[28]

Secondly, Blackstone's remarks about 'preventive justice' point out that prevention is not limited to *ex ante* measures of incapacitation or deterrence, but also motivates the infliction of *ex post* punishment. This can be seen as once again pointing up the significance of the peace, and particularly the king's peace, the maintenance of which is the aim of all penal measures, *ex ante* or *ex post*. Once the peace is disturbed, the offence already has manifested itself and the king's (as any householder's) authority already has been challenged, his ability to keep the peace questioned. It is no accident, in this light, that the paradigmatic inchoate offence is high treason, an offence against the authority of the king in any form (including, for instance, counterfeiting his coin, a serious offence the prevention of which triggered one of the first, if not the first, use of possessory liability in an English criminal statute), which in its most offensive form, regicide (along with the death of the queen and the royal heir), was penalized at the stage of 'compassing' or 'imagining'.[29]

So all penal justice is preventive because the interest at stake is important, too important to await its violation. But, again, this connection is not unique to policial governance. For the same reason, as Ashworth and Zedner point out,[30] *ex ante* prevention is preferable to *ex post* punishment in a law state, grounded in the conception of the person as a being endowed with, and with nothing more than, the capacity for autonomy, or self-government. Blackstone's police state is a

[26] Blackstone (cited in n 14) 252.

[27] Statute of Labourers, 23 Edw 3, New Statute, c 1 (1349), 25 Edw 3, Stat 1, c 1 (1350), enacted shortly before the Treason Act.

[28] G Schuck, 'Arbeit als Polizeistrafe' in K Härter (ed), *Policey und frühneuzeitliche Gesellschaft* (2000) 611.

[29] Treason Act 1351, 25 Edw III St 5 c 2; on the persistence of the paradigm defined by the Treason Act, even in American penality, see MD Dubber, 'The State as Victim: Treason and the Paradox of American Criminal Law' in M Kremnitzer and K Ghanayim (eds), *Offences Against the State* (forthcoming 2012).

[30] A Ashworth and L Zedner, 'Just Prevention: Preventive Rationales and the Limits of the Criminal Law' in RA Duff and S Green (eds), *Philosophical Foundations of Criminal Law* (2011) 279.

preventive state, but that is not to say that a law state could not be a preventive state in the same sense, and for the same reason, but in pursuit of a radically, and designedly, different aim: the protection of the governed's personhood, rather than the maintenance of the governor's peace.

## Discretion

It may also be worth emphasizing the significance of discretion in all forms of policial governance centred on the maintenance of a sovereign's peace. The use of preventive justice here is associated with both the whether, and the how, of state interference. The sovereign, acting through his (or later, its) representative interprets indicia of offensiveness (or dangerousness) that, by definition, come (at least partially, even in the presence of a 'criminal record') in a form other than the official and formal ascription of criminal liability. Preventive justice, by its nature, is also a guessing game, an inexact science of attempting to predict the future (an attempt notoriously likely to fail). But, more important, even if the official has found sufficient indicia of offensiveness he nonetheless may exercise his discretion not to interfere. And even if he chooses to interfere, he will have at his disposal a wide range of possible measures, from a more or less informal warning to peace bonds to restrictions on movement, monitoring devices, institutionalization, and incarceration.

Punitive, or punishing, justice may, by contrast, be seen as constraining the sovereign's discretion on whether and how to interfere. The notion of an obligation to punish, however, would have been foreign to Blackstone; the sovereign holds the unquestionable power to pardon, or amerce, as even homicide *se defendendo* is regarded as merely excused, requiring a royal pardon, on the ground that to deprive the sovereign of any of his subjects is to give offence, which the sovereign may, in his wisdom and at his pleasure, choose to overlook.[31] There is, and can be, no imperative, categorical or not, in penal police. There is, and can be, no *Legalitätsprinzip*—literally legality principle, though usually imperfectly translated as principle of compulsory prosecution to avoid confusion with the 'legality principle', which is generally taken to be the English version of the *nullum crimen sine lege* principle.

There are imperatives, but only imperatives of obedience or execution. So the justice of the peace can be ordered to issue a peace bond 'by a mandatory writ, called a *supplicavit*, issuing out of the court of king's bench or chancery; which will compel the justice to act as a ministerial and not as a judicial officer',[32] reminding him, in other words, of his status as a minister of the king, to whom the sovereign has delegated certain, but only certain, powers. In a policial regime, the courts, as any other branch of government, merely exercise an aspect of the sovereign power, most fundamentally the power to police, ie, to maintain the peace of the household.

Finally, note Blackstone's passing, but telling, remark that preventive justice measures are 'not meant as any degree of punishment, unless perhaps for a man's imprudence in giving just ground of apprehension'. Recall that he had previously

[31] See Blackstone (cited in n 14) 182. [32] Blackstone (cited in n 14) 253.

defined the 'public police and economy' as 'the due regulation and domestic order of the kingdom, whereby the individuals of the state, like members of a well governed family, are bound to conform their general behaviour to the rules of propriety, good neighbourhood and good manners, and to be decent, industrious and inoffensive in their respective stations'.[33] Preventive justice measures, in other words, are police measures twice over: first, by preventing future offences against the king's peace, and, second, by disciplining those who already have disturbed the 'domestic[!] order of the kingdom', ie, the peace of the kingdom *qua* household, having failed by their imprudence 'to conform their behaviour to the rules of propriety, good neighbourhood and good manners', and having not been 'decent, industrious and inoffensive in their respective stations'. Blackstone's 'preventive justice' measures are police measures, not because they are preventive, but because they aim to maintain the 'public police and economy'.

## Economy

Here it is worth clarifying the meaning, and significance, of the term 'economy' in its connection with police. Economy is used, like police, in its traditional sense, of household government—from the Greek *oikos* and *nomos*. The power to police is the power to govern the state as a householder governs his household, rooted in the power of the *oikonomos* over his *oikos* and of the *paterfamilias* over his *familia*, a power that has been traced throughout English history, as 'the germ existing in every Teutonic household', from the common free man (*ceorl*) to the king.[34] This is not the place, nor am I the person, to inquire more deeply into the political (pre-)history of economics, another fascinating, though neglected, topic. Aristotle and Plato appeared to share a general approach to the question of economics—considering it a matter of prudence, rather than of justice, a realm of guidelines and manuals, rather than of principles and treatises, and generally showing little enthusiasm for the subject, at least compared to matters of (public) politics or (individual) ethics, as a subject of private concern that was perhaps most significant as setting the prerequisite for the householder's participation in the public discourse about matters of common concern. While Aristotle treats economics at the beginning of his *Politics*, he wastes little time on the subject and clearly considers the discussion preliminary to the treatment of politics, or ethics, in the sphere of public life. In fact, Aristotle takes care to draw a distinction between economics and politics, unlike Plato who in his dialogue *Politikos* insists—perhaps provocatively so—on the similarities between the two.[35]

Little has changed even when it comes to the relationship, and tension, between economics and politics, which in the wake of the Enlightenment was recast as that between police and law, without however retaining the distinction

[33] Blackstone (cited in n 14) 162.

[34] P Vinogradoff, 'Foundations of Society' (1913) 2 *Cambridge Medieval History* 630, 638.

[35] K Singer, 'Oikonomia: An Inquiry into Beginnings of Economic Thought and Language' (1958) 11 *Kyklos* 29, 30, 44.

between private and public life, and the concomitant one between economics and politics, that structured the Athenian debate. Police and law are both categories of public life, as modes of state governance, thus highlighting, and escalating, the tension between the two, by eliminating the option of confining each to a different sphere of ethical life.

The distinction between private and public life was crucial for the pre-Enlightenment interrelation between economy and politics since autonomy in one was the prerequisite for autonomy in the other. Only the householder had the capacity for autonomy in the private sphere, and therefore also in the public sphere.[36] While the household, including its human and non-human constituent resources, lacked the requisite capacity for autonomy, and therefore was marked for heteronomy, for the status of governed, the householder was the 'other' who governed the unselfgovernable and then stepped into the public sphere—the agora, the forum, the *thing*—to enter into discourse with fellow householders, his peers, to conduct the public business of the day. Whereas hierarchy and heteronomy characterized economy, equality and autonomy were the hallmarks of politics. While orders, backed by the threat of force, including physical force, moved the household, persuasion aided by rhetoric drove the government of the city. Economy was unequal other-government, politics equal self-government.

This division of spheres broke down over time with the development and expansion of macro households, and the expansion of one householder's peace at the expense of other householders' peaces which were redefined as non-originary delegated forms of sovereignty, or rather jurisdiction, the borders of which were in turn policed by the macro householder and his officials according to a new common law, ie, a royal law applicable to all, including to other householders who once held court themselves in exercise of their own inherent seigniorial jurisdiction. The erosion of the public sphere as a locus of autonomy thus went hand in hand with the expansion of the once distinctly private mode of governance into matters of state, with the king or prince assuming the power to maintain the peace of his realm.

Blackstone's association of police and economy, ie, the conception of the power to police as the power of the macro householder, reflected a conception of governance that also had long been familiar on the Continent (and even in Scotland, as Adam Smith's early Glasgow lectures on 'juris prudence' make clear[37]) and underlies, for instance, Rousseau's roughly contemporaneous definition of political economy in Diderot's *Encyclopédie* of *Economie ou oeconomie*, which 'meant originally only the wise and legitimate [sage and légitime] government of the house for the common good of the whole family', but 'was then extended to

36 O Brunner, 'Das "ganze Haus" und die alteuropäische "Ökonomik"' in *Neue Wege der Sozialgeschichte* (1956) 33, 40.

37 A Smith, 'Juris Prudence or Notes from the Lectures on Justice, Police, Revenue, and Arms delivered in the University of Glasgow by Adam Smith Professor of Moral Philosophy' in RL Meed et al (eds), *Adam Smith, Lectures on Jurisprudence* (1978) 396; see generally Dubber, *Police Power* (cited in n 5) 63–5.

the government of that great family, the State'.[38] On the Continent, a police science had developed since the 17th century, whose practitioners attempted to rationalize the prince's exercise of his police power. This science, which was particularly active and productive in France and Germany—though it also found enthusiasts elsewhere, including across the Channel, most notably Patrick Colquhoun, founder of the Thames River Police in the late 18th century—itself appears as a modern version of an advisory literature for householders, familiar at least since Xenophon's *Oikonomikos* (circa 370BC), devoted to the 'art' (and science) of householdership,[39] which also included the German *Hausväterliteratur* (which only later, in the 19th century, devolved from a familial government manual to instructions for proper housekeeping, parallel to a radical privatization and feminization of the micro family),[40] the slave manuals of the pre-Civil War American South,[41] and—as a sign of the expansion of household governance from the micro to the macro household, from a 'domestic' art to a 'royal art'[42] (or science)[43]—Machiavelli's *The Prince*.[44]

## Prevention

Here it may be appropriate briefly to comment on the connection between prevention and police, emphasized by Beccaria, Bentham, and a string of other utilitarians in their wake, including Colquhoun, the Scotsman in London who produced a steady stream of police scientific tracts of which *A Treatise on the Police of the Metropolis* (1797) is merely the best known. Since Colquhoun today is considered through the narrow, backward-looking, lens of the contemporary concept of police as an institution, rather than as a comprehensive programme of governance, it is useful to recall the scope of Colquhoun's police ambitions, as represented by his treatises on, among other things, police, poor police, education police,[45] the police of the micro household,[46] and, eventually, the macro household, a sort of *Wealth of Nations* for the British Empire.[47] At any rate, Colquhoun, through

[38] Kurt Singer's criticism of Rousseau's definition focuses on Rousseau's (apparently very common) interpretation of *nomos* as 'law': Singer (cited in n 35).

[39] Singer (cited in n 35) 47.

[40] Singer (cited in n 35) 34, 40–1; P Münch, '"Vater Staat": Staatsmänner als Vaterfiguren?' in W Faulstich and GE Grimm (eds), *Sturz der Götter? Vaterbilder im 20. Jahrhundert* (1989) 67, 72–3.

[41] See JA Bush, 'Free to Enslave: The Foundations of Colonial American Slave Law' (1993) 5 Yale Journal of Law and the Humanities 417.

[42] Singer (cited in n 35) 52.

[43] Singer (cited in n 35) 31 and 44.

[44] Blackstone's conception of police governance also bears an obvious relation to the patriarchalist tradition in English political thought, associated with Filmer and generally thought, rightly or wrongly, to have been terminated by Locke. That connection, however, is less clear than might appear at first glance, partly due to Filmer's focus on the divine, and therefore unique, origins of absolute monarchy, rather than the connection, and therefore also similarity, between the king's macro householdership and traditional household governance.

[45] *A treatise on the commerce and police of the river Thames* (1798); *A new and appropriate system of education for the labouring people . . .* (1806).

[46] *Useful suggestions favourable to the comfort of the labouring people, and of decent housekeepers . . .* (1795).

[47] *A treatise on the wealth, power, and resources of the British Empire* (1814).

this anachronistically narrow prism, today is generally regarded as the architect of 'preventive police' in England, as opposed to investigatory police institutions like the Bow Street Runners (the same slippery distinction that to this day structures the doctrine of police law, *Polizeirecht*, in Germany).[48]

Recall that Blackstone cites Beccaria for the proposition that preventive justice is preferable to punishing justice (and that England, as luck would have it, boasts the most extensive, if not the only, system of preventive justice, which he then proceeds to describe). It is no surprise that Beccaria champions (*ex ante*) prevention over (*ex post*) punishment, insofar as the former inflicts less pain for greater, or certainly no less, benefit. It is also no surprise that Bentham echoes this sentiment, along with other utilitarians like Colquhoun and John Fielding, the magistrate who ran the Bow Street Runners (and declared that '[i]t is much better to prevent even one man from being a rogue than apprehending and bringing forty to justice',[49] even though his constables were engaged in the investigation of crime, rather than its prevention). As one might expect, Bentham was not content merely to repeat Beccaria's views and recommendations, but tried to systematize them, in this case by drawing a distinction between police and justice, in terms of that between prevention and punishment:

> It is difficult to draw the line which separates these two branches of administration [police and justice]. Their functions have the same object—that of maintaining the internal peace of the state. Justice regards in particular offences already committed; her power does not display itself till after the discovery of some act hostile to the security of the citizens. Police applies itself to the prevention both of offences and calamities; its expedients are, not punishments, but precautions; it foresees evils, and provides against wants.[50]

In this view, police and justice are merely different tools (*ex ante*, and *ex post*) for the maintenance of domestic peace. Prevention, then, is associated with police only by definition, to distinguish police from (retrospective) justice. Not even in Bentham, therefore, is prevention associated with police in the broader sense invoked by, for instance, Blackstone—as a distinct mode of governance distinguished not by its means, but by its end: the maintenance of the householder's peace. In this light, Bentham's distinction between police and justice becomes irrelevant; in other words, there is only peace and therefore only police—even 'justice' is a tool of better police. (Bentham presumably would have thought a project of preventive

[48] Some decades later, an essay by Edwin Chadwick in the inaugural issue of the *London Review*, entitled 'Preventive Police', attracted the attention of prominent utilitarians, including Bentham and the Mills: E Chadwick, 'Preventive Police' (1829) 1 *London Review* 252. While the essay today is read as part of English 'police history', ie, the institutional history of police forces in England, Chadwick went on to produce an impressive and wide-ranging body of police science work of his own, notably in the area of public health, broadly construed. See the very interesting condensed version of his publications, along with an intellectual biography, published by Benjamin Richardson, with the intriguing title *The Health of Nations*: BW Richardson, *The Health of Nations: A Review of the Works of Edwin Chadwick, with a Biographical Dissertation*, 2 vols (1887).

[49] J Fielding, *An Account of the Origin and Effects of a Police Set on Foot etc.* (1758); see generally JL McMullan, 'The New Improved Monied Police: Reform, Crime Control, and the Commodification of Policing in London' (1996) 36 *British Journal of Criminology* 85 (Fielding's 'preventative machine').

[50] J Bentham, *The Theory of Legislation* (1931) 242.

justice to be oxymoronic, given that justice to him was, by definition, retrospective.)

As soon as police and justice are regarded as alternative tools for the achievement of some aim, say the maintenance of peace (in the police state, broadly conceived), and—ultimately, for the utilitarian—utility, or the greatest happiness for the greatest number, there is no reason why some other aim—say, the protection of the personhood of subject-objects in a modern liberal state—might not be substituted. Prevention, thus, once again would turn out to be distinctive of neither police, nor law.

## C. Critique

The modern conception of law as rooted in the idea of the person as capable of self-government in all spheres of life—ethics, economy, and politics—was radically inconsistent with a conception of state government as householdership, ie, as an instance of the householder's power to manage the resources of the household, where the householder is the only person capable of autonomy and therefore also of heteronomy of those fit only to be governed, not to govern (themselves or others), and where there is no categorical—and at best a prudential—distinction between the objects of government that constitute the household, including all human and non-human resources, free and unfree, animate and inanimate, as an instance of 'the power to govern men and things'[51] that encompasses the 'activities of management, or administration, applied to persons and goods belonging to an *oikos*'.[52] Heteronomy, from the autonomy-grounded perspective of law after the Enlightenment, is prima facie illegitimate. Arguably, in a modern *Rechtsstaat* the micro household cannot survive as a locus of government; instead, it becomes a locus of love and mutual support, where remnants of power are disregarded, exceptional disciplinary excesses at the margins, or ordinary instances of parental (even recognized in legal doctrine in the form of justification, or lawfulness, defences, modelled uneasily on the justification of acts of public authority[53]) discipline notwithstanding.[54]

But the Enlightenment did not challenge merely, or even primarily, traditional household governance in the micro household, the *Kleinfamilie*. The expansion of economic modes of governance from the private personal realm to the public political sphere, from the *oikos* to the *agora*, meant (among other things) the elimination of the province of autonomy under the long-standing dualism of private heteronomy and public autonomy. The police power of the macro household leaves no room for the autonomy even of micro householders, who by virtue of their householder status at one time were entitled to participate in public

[51] License Cases, 46 US (5 How.) 504, 583 (1847); see generally MD Dubber, '"The Power to Govern Men and Things": Patriarchal Origins of the Police Power in American Law' (2004) 52 Buffalo Law Review 1277.

[52] Singer (cited in n 35) 35–9.

[53] See, eg, *Canadian Foundation for Children, Youth and the Law v Canada* [2004] 1 SCR 76.

[54] Brunner (cited in n 36) 40–1.

government of equals by equals. While the political reforms and revolutions of the 19th century may thus be interpreted as an insistence by the burgeoning class of bourgeois micro householders to (re)claim their seat at the table of self-government, they were cast in the language of personhood and the capacity for and therefore the right to self-government *qua* person, not *qua* householder, thus encompassing within their critical scope all instances of heteronomy, public and private alike.

The distinction between law and police is therefore stark and fundamental. This is no surprise given the development of the modern, autonomy-based, conception of law as part of the critical enterprise of the Enlightenment, turned against, in this case, the deeply rooted taken-for-granted conception of government as the maintenance of peace. The ideal of the law state was defined against the reality of the police state. The critique that generated the ideal of the law state was radical, in the literal sense. It went at the roots of the conception of government, at the mode of governance, and at the self-conception of the state. It required a paradigm shift, a move from one ideal type to another, from prudence to justice, from discretion to duty, from arbitrariness to principledness, from guideline to norm, from competence to legitimacy, from prudence to justice, from police to law.

The Enlightenment critique did not subject the police state to a legitimacy critique; it subjected the state to a legitimacy critique, which began with radically reconceiving the state. The preventive state, however, is precisely that, a police state, or rather it is objectionable precisely *insofar as* it is just that.

This is ultimately what is at stake in the search for 'principles' of 'preventive justice'. Within the realm of police, there is no 'principle', and there is no 'justice' (unless, of course, one simply defines justice as police, with Bentham and Pound). There may be maxims, guidelines, standards, recommendations, counsel, advice, and so on. But there is no 'principle', if by principle we mean something like a norm that requires compliance because of its normative significance, ie, in politics (as opposed to in morality, or ethics), because of its legitimatory significance.

The apparent paradox between the pursuit of security, on the one hand, and the infringement of individual rights, on the other, which is said to characterize the 'preventive state' or the present regime of 'preventive justice' resolves itself once the preventive state is seen as a police state, ie, a state that pursues not the security of individual persons but of itself, or more precisely that seeks to maintain the sovereign's peace, be that sovereign a personified householder (the royal peace) or its abstract depersonified alternative (the public peace). The notion of individual rights is foreign to the police state; the victim in penal police is not the individual, the harm not to the individual's rights, nor the wrong the disrespect of one person's (or for that matter, citizen's) rights by another; nor is the offender in penal police the individual, whose rights deserve respect even in the adjudication of that individual's alleged disrespect of another's. The offence in penal police involves an individual rights bearer neither as offender, nor as victim. The offence in penal police involves a disturber of the peace and a holder of that peace.

Disturber (*Störer*), it turns out, is also the concept German police law (*Polizeirecht*) settled on, in an attempt, however half-hearted, to distinguish the police offender—subject to police sanction—from the criminal offender—subject to criminal punishment—in the early 20th century. Police law, a branch of administrative law concerned with the prevention and abatement of threats to public safety and order, wears its commitment to legalizing the police power on its sleeve, seeking to subject all instances of state action, including state action by police officials (and other administrative officials), to norms consistent with the rule of law, set out in codes of police law.[55] The project of 'police law,' or for that matter of 'administrative law' in general, thus resembles the project of 'preventive justice' by resolving the tension between police and law, prudence and justice, heteronomy and autonomy, through classificatory—and, in the case of the former two, through legislative, codificatory, or at least dogmatic—fiat, through the invention and then attachment of an oxymoronic doctrinal label, less aspirational than obfuscatory, as if the addition of the word 'law' (or 'justice') to some state action, or even an entire mode of state governance, could bring that action, or mode of governance, under the rule of law.

Interestingly, the conception of the addressee of police directives attracted very little attention in the police law literature, in sharp contrast to the prerequisites for criminal liability, which was very much on the minds of German criminal law scholars, at a time when many of the core elements for the analysis of criminal liability in German criminal law were put in place. The *Störer* was relevant as the 'cause (*Urheber*) of a state contrary to police (*polizeiwidrig*)', not for an act, nor for an intentional (or, for that matter, negligent, even civilly negligent) act, with no requirement that he recognized his behaviour as 'contrary to police'.[56] In other words, policial liability was entirely a matter of absolute, or strict, liability, an unadulterated form of result liability, the result in question being a disorderly state (contrary to police in the broad, traditional sense: a state of poor police). The question of whether a particular individual qualified as a disturber apparently was thought to be purely a question of causation, of picking the appropriate disturber out of any number of human causes of disturbance who might present themselves in a particular situation.

In other words, from a police perspective, the human, or personal, quality of the disturber was inconsequential. Police law concerned itself with the identification and abatement of causes of a state of 'poor police', preferably before they manifested themselves in an actual disturbance of the peace. Police law, after all, served—and still serves—to prevent dangers of any kind—natural, manmade, human, animal, dead, alive—and in this sense is essentially ahuman. Not only is its conception of offenderhood ahuman, so is its conception of victimhood: a general state of disorder, a breach of the peace, a disturbance. In this sense, a police offence is a pure status offence: it abates a status of disturbance or, in the language of the common law, a nuisance, an 'annoyance'. The police offender is the thing that is

[55] The history and conception of police law is a fascinating topic. For a particularly illuminating study, see P Preu, *Polizeibegriff und Staatszwecklehre: Die Entwicklung des Polizeibegriffs durch die Rechts- und Staatswissenschaften des 18. Jahrhunderts* (1983).

[56] S Naas, *Die Entstehung des Preußischen Polizeiverwaltungsgesetzes von 1931* (2003) 150, 310; see also A Schwegel, *Der Polizeibegriff im NS-Staat: Polizeirecht, juristische Publizistik und Judikative 1931–1944* (2005) 30 n 27.

abated, a nuisance, defined by Blackstone as the original police offence, ie, an offence 'against the public order and oeconomical regimen of the state'.[57] Human nuisances are abated alongside non-human ones, the prostitute along with the house of prostitution, and the possessor along with the contraband *and* the building in which it is found.[58]

From the perspective of police, there is nothing objectionable about the failure to distinguish human and non-human objects of state power. 'Principles' such as the requirement of fault, *mens rea*, *actus reus*, or personal responsibility, the *Schuldprinzip*, or for that matter the *Legalitätsprinzip*, of German criminal law, or *nullum crimen sine lege* (the 'legality principle') and its various permutations, or the various precious metallic threads of the common law (presumption of innocence, proof beyond a reasonable doubt) have no purchase in the realm of police, nor do less tangible considerations such as concerns about the 'inappropriate' or 'troubling' expansion of the scope of criminal liability (through the recognition of double inchoacy, for instance, such as liability of attempted attempts, or attempted offences that 'sound in' attempt, or attempted possession, or even possession itself, as a clear example of the imposition of criminal liability for 'pre-preparatory' conduct, despite the rule that attempt liability begins only once 'preparation' has blossomed into 'attempt'), nor references to the need to respect the autonomy, or the agency, of offenders (or victims, for that matter) or to 'the rule of law' (recall Williams's ad hoc reinterpretation of breaches of *the* peace as violent offences against the person) or, without more, to the impropriety of acts by state officials that are ultra vires, ie, beyond the authority delegated to them.[59] 'Without more', because the policing of subordinates by, for instance, monitoring their compliance with the conditions of their delegated authority, is compatible with a police regime. The same applies, as previously mentioned, to aspects of the so-called 'legality principle', which—as Fuller suggested—may be prudent also from a police perspective.

These principles can gain no traction, not only because of their substance, but also because of their form. Police governance remains unconstrained not only by principles of law, and of legitimacy, but by *principles* of any kind, insofar as principles carry normative significance and generate an expectation of compliance, and therefore the possibility of critique. From the start, norms of police governance were framed as advice, to the *oikonomikos*, the *Hausvater*, the prince. Those aspects of the legality principle that might appeal to the police governor seeking better compliance—by, for instance, telling his subordinates what he wants before disciplining them for their failure to give him what he wants—are subject to his

[57] Blackstone (cited in n 14) 167.

[58] For a recent example, see *City of New York v B250 Holding LLC, Harlems Shop Mart, Inc., Bandar A. Kalid, The Land and Building Known as 250 Bradhurst Avenue, Tax Block 2047, Tax Lot 44, County of New York, City and State of New York, the New York Liquor Authority, 'John Doe' and 'Jane Doe'* 32 Misc 3d 1202A, 2011 NY Misc LEXIS 3030 (Sup Ct NY, NY Cty 2011) (interpreting NY City Administrative Code §7–703(g), declaring a public nuisance '[a]ny building, erection or place, including one- or two-family dwellings, wherein, within the period of one year . . . , there have occurred three or more violations of any of the provisions of article 220, 221, or 225 of the penal law [including, eg, possession of drugs or drug paraphernalia]').

[59] See, eg, *MacKenzie v Martin* 1954 SCR 361, 369 (Rand dissenting).

discretion, with respect to their definition, their interpretation, and their applicability in a particular case but also with respect to their adoption or their application in fact (assuming they are found to be applicable). The police governor, for instance, may decide to discipline his subordinate for failing to comply with his wishes even in the absence of a prior, clear, executable, publicized, order, if—for instance—he decides it is prudent to encourage his subordinates in general, or this one in particular, to anticipate (and carry out) his wishes without him having to enunciate them and, perhaps, even before he had formed the wish in the first place. (The German term for this is *vorauseilender Gehorsam*, or anticipatory obedience.) At the same time, the police governor would be free *not* to discipline a subordinate despite the governor's compliance with the policial analogue to the various aspects of the legality principle.[60]

There is one other, possibly related, characteristic of police governance—besides the substantive and formal ones already mentioned—that deserves mention, if only because it can be traced through the entire history of the subject. Again and again, from Aristotle to Adam Smith, it is described as tedious and unworthy of the attention of any number of persons with presumably more exciting and more important things to think and write about. Critique of police governance, in other words, may be impossible, given its alegitimate and discretionary character; but even serious thought, or considered advice, is difficult to come by because it is concerned with such trifling matters. The lack of interest in police governance of course may reflect the pointlessness of advising someone who is free to ignore it, but it is also consistent with the insignificance of its objects. The art, or science, of police, the genre of good housekeeping advice, concerns itself with every household resource, from crops to bees to bread to honey, horses, dogs, cats, sons, slaves, soil, wind, with cleanliness, orderliness, and so on. It is unlike modern law, or ancient politics, which deal with persons, or citizens, and therefore rest on the identity of subject and object of government, and—at least in the case of citizens—are concerned with the highest-status being there is, one that matches the status of the governor. As beneath the attention of sovereigns—and those who advise them—alike, matters of police have not attracted the same sort of scrutiny, even on their own—prudential—terms, as have matters of law. In the penal realm, nuisance control—human or non-human—is itself a nuisance.

Along with its objects, police governance in general, and penal police governance in particular, thus, is suffering from neglect—malign or not.[61] Even internally, on its own terms, however vague, flexible, advisory, discretionary, suggestive rather than critical, penal police *qua* police would benefit from commentary and prudential guidance, not to mention the attention of a police science.[62]

[60] This discretion *not* to act is the focus of the German *Legalitätsprinzip*. See also KC Davis, *Administrative Law*, vol 2 (2nd edn, 1979) 216–35.

[61] Cf M Tonry, *Malign Neglect: Race, Crime, and Punishment in America* (1996).

[62] There still is a police science, which, however, as one might expect, is generally limited to the study of 'police work', ie, the activities of the police, in its narrow, institutional, sense.

The search for principles of preventive justice, however, is not concerned, it is fair to assume, with testing the effectiveness of policing measures or counselling the sovereign on how to improve the police—and the policing—of his household. This is a complicated task, one that requires establishing principles of justice, and of penal justice in particular, and then applying them to the use of preventive measures. It may appear at times as though the task instead is simply one of application, rather than of the genealogy of foundational principles of legitimacy. We already have drawn into question the underlying assumption that there is a body of principle out there that governs ordinary, or traditional, or non-preventive penality which might be extended to new, innovative, genre-busting measures of prevention, rather than of punishment.

## D. Conclusion

In closing, I want to draw attention to a particular variant of this approach: it is often said that legislatures (but presumably also officials in other branches of government) seek to evade principled (perhaps constitutional) constraints on their exercises of their penal power by classifying them as something other than punishment. The United States Supreme Court, for instance, has developed a fairly detailed taxonomy on the classification of penal measures as punishment or not-punishment (where punishment is thought to trigger certain constitutional constraints, such as the prohibition of cruel and unusual and retroactive punishments). It is of course true that protections that attach only to one category of penal measure but not another lack bite if the state is free to categorize a given measure one way or the other.[63] This question has arisen recently with respect to various purportedly non-punitive measures such as indefinite preventive detention, registration, or community notification or supervision regimes of certain (sexual, dangerous) offenders. But the evaded principles need not be constitutional, as measures such as the ASBO and, more broadly yet, possession offences illustrate, which are difficult to reconcile with traditional common law 'principles' such as fault, *mens rea*, and *actus reus*.[64]

This variant of the extension approach to the search for principles of preventive justice also assumes the existence of a body of principle that could be applied to measures of preventive justice once they are properly classified, the evasion having been exposed, and the supposed exception brought within the rule. Instead, the approach outlined here suggests regarding these measures not as not-law, or not-punishment, or *hors catégorie*, ie, as nameless deviations designed to evade the only available account of penality (namely the penal law one, or the penal punishment

[63] Cf *Kansas v Hendricks* 521 US 346 (1997) with *Engel and Others v Netherlands* (1979–80) 1 EHRR 647. Clearly it should also be troubling that a state would seek to free itself from basic constitutional constraints through categorical fiat; it would presumably be less troubling the other way around, ie, if a state categorized a given measure so as to submit itself to these constraints.

[64] For a critical analysis of possession offences along these lines, see Dubber (cited in n 10).

one, where punishment is a proxy for law), but positively as manifestations of the penal police power of the state. Rather than documenting the ways in which they violate principles of law, and proceeding to a legal critique, it may be more fruitful to begin by analysing them in light of the distinction between law and police as basic modes of governance and then to subject them to critique, or at least to discussion, in light of the applicable considerations, maxims of police in one case, principles of law in the other.[65]

Under the approach proposed here, it may turn out that what appears to be the exception is in fact the rule, that what appears to be new is in fact old, and that the task at hand is one not merely of application—and perhaps adaptation, of weaving a third, bronze thread, rather than spinning out the existing golden and silver ones—but one of fundamental reconsideration of penality in general, as a system of penal justice.

[65] On the principle of legality as a bundle of police maxims, see Dubber (cited in n 14); MD Dubber, 'The Legality Principle in American and German Criminal Law: An Essay in Comparative Legal History' in H Pihlajamäki et al (eds), *From the Judge's Arbitrium to the Legality Principle: Legislation as a Source of Law in Criminal Trials* (forthcoming 2012).

# 4

# Responsibility to Protect and Preventive Justice

*Klaus Günther**

Many modern constitutions and declarations of human rights contain rules and principles pertaining to criminal procedure and criminal law. The rights of habeas corpus are the most important and ancient ones with regard to criminal procedure: the rights which follow from the principle *nulla poena sine lege* with regard to criminal law. One could even say that the very idea of a constitution was generated out of the conflicts about criminal procedure. The experience of arbitrary imprisonment by the Crown was one of the founding moments of the general rule of habeas corpus, which was enshrined in a public and written document.

A closer look at this paradigm case reveals two general features of constitutional and human rights norms pertaining to criminal law: (1) The norms have a *negative* meaning; ie they prohibit the punishing state from doing something (like putting someone under arrest for an indeterminate time or torturing someone to get a confession). Even if they contain state duties such as bringing a detainee before a judge within a certain time, these duties are only part of a negative right: nobody shall be arrested without being brought before a judge within 24 hours. (2) The negative meaning and the function of constitutional and human rights norms pertaining to criminal law are directed against the state whose power to punish is somehow presupposed as a fact. But it seems that neither constitutions nor human rights contain any positive duty on the part of the state to punish. Some constitutions contain a norm which demands the penalization of particular kinds of behaviour, like the German Grundgesetz (or Basic Law) Art 26 which explicitly requires the punishment of offensive warfare.[1] But these constitutional duties to penalize are not as prominent and central as the negative rights. Nor do they explicitly contain a general state duty to criminalize and punish. If the European Convention of Human Rights (ECHR) Art 2.1 declares that 'Everyone's right to life shall be protected by law' this may, among other means of protection, also include criminal law, but it does not explicitly say so. With regard to the fact that

* I am grateful to all participants in the Preventive Justice Project seminar at All Souls College, Oxford, in January 2012, for their valuable and helpful comments and criticism, in particular to Andreas von Hirsch, who responded to my paper, and to the editors and Ambrose Lee for their close and critical reading, and to D Wicklein for research assistance.

[1] For further examples see G Robbers, 'Strafpflichten aus der Verfassung' in K Lüderssen (ed), *Aufgeklärte Kriminalpolitik oder Kampf gegen das Böse?*, vol 1 (1998) 147, 148.

punishment is one of the most severe violations of human integrity, it is quite surprising that many constitutions and human rights declarations primarily refer to the *modus of punishment* but not to its essential justification. Constitutions seem to presuppose the fact of the punishing state as something which is natural and obvious. The historical experience of more than two hundred years of constitutional and human rights history seems to demonstrate that citizens have to be protected against a state which exercises a punishing power it already has. The danger comes from a state which punishes too much, and not from a state which punishes too little. Part of this danger seems to be the inclination of the state to punish for preventive reasons primarily and excessively. If the prevention of crime is the main purpose of punishment in which the state is interested, any kind of measure that serves this end effectively seems to be appropriate.[2] Constitutional protections of individual rights against the state could then be considered as a counterweight to excessive prevention, which makes it possible to establish criminal law and criminal procedure law as a compromise or as a result of balancing individual rights against the public good of crime prevention.

If this explanation for the observation that constitutions contain primarily negative rights against the preventive punishing state is correct, one has to realize that it is called into question today. Many people believe that their governments are not tough enough on crime, and that the state punishes too little and not too much, that the state could do more for the prevention of crime without compromising the interests of the majority. For a long time populist movements in Western European countries as well as in the USA have argued for a 'war on crime' which is accompanied by a 'war on drugs' and a 'war on terrorism'. Although it might be true that many people suffer severely from fear of crime, governments and political parties are eager to instrumentalize fear of crime for their political purposes.[3] As David Garland has argued, the political expression of this fear has become one of the most important features of a culture of control after the end of the welfarist paradigm in criminal justice.[4] The particular situation of 'Risk Societies', facing different kinds of risks and dangers originating from new technologies and socio-economic changes, contributes to the general attitude that the state should do more to protect its citizens. Victims of crime have become the 'representative character' of middle classes in modern societies who express their emotional solidarity with them and ask the state to be more repressive against the perpetrator.[5] Fear of international terrorism is one of the latest steps in this development that makes 'security' one of the topical issues on the political agenda. Preventive justice is no longer the agenda of governments and political parties alone, it has also become the agenda of the people.

[2] P Asp, this volume.

[3] J Simon, *Governing through Crime* (2007), 75 ff; M Dubber, *Victims in the War on Crime—The Use and Abuse of Victim's Rights* (2002).

[4] D Garland, *The Culture of Control. Crime and Social Order in Contemporary Society* (2001) 144.

[5] Garland (cited in n 4); Dubber (cited in n 3).

In this chapter, I shall deal with the reasons and causes of this paradigm change and its effects on the constitutional and the human rights framework of the politics of crime prevention. What is its significance for constitutional and human rights, when their meaning changes from the negative to the positive, from constituting a negative doorlock of crime prevention to a positive door-opener for more crime prevention? Citizens claim that their rights should be protected by an efficient criminal law and by stronger law enforcement and that the relation between perpetrator and victim is out of balance because the state cares too much about the perpetrator's constitutional rights in criminal investigation and procedure and too little about the victim's rights. The protective meaning of the constitution has changed, from being a shield for the suspect and the convicted perpetrator against the state punishing for preventive purposes to being a shield for the citizen as potential or actual victim of the citizen as criminal. The state comes in as the bearer of a constitutional duty to protect the citizen-victim against the citizen-criminal. The intrinsic meaning of this request for state protection is preventive. The state shall guarantee the security of the individual, because of the individual's right to security—and security can only be guaranteed if the state intervenes as early as possible into any possibly dangerous course of events, before it becomes a concrete violation. Criminal law and criminal law enforcement are only a part of this comprehensive purpose of prevention. Prevention is only one element among others of a 'security architecture' which includes preventive police action and other administrative actions and, at the international level, intergovernmental agreements and measures like coordinated military intervention.

With the fights against international terrorism and against human rights violations by governments ('failed states') this agenda has recently developed a new dynamic. In international public law a 'responsibility to protect' (RTP) has been created by which governments are authorized to take preventive actions against severe human rights violations or even to join in a humanitarian intervention into another state.[6] The main purpose of this doctrine is a restriction and re-conceptualization of state sovereignty as it has been known and practised since the Westphalian peace treaty in 1648. State sovereignty is internally linked with the state's responsibility to protect its citizens against massive violations of the most basic human rights. A state which commits such violations or does nothing to prohibit them cannot claim sovereignty. As a consequence, the state loses its sovereignty and the RTP is transferred to the international community, which now has to take measures to stop the violations. Of course criminal law and criminal prosecution are only one little part of the RTP, which should be realized by a whole package of measures consisting of a three-stage process: the RTP is divided into a *responsibility to prevent* at the first stage,

[6] <http://www.responsibilitytoprotect.org/>; UN Resolution of the General Assembly: A/Res/60/1 (chs 138–9); E Klein (ed), *The Duty to Protect and to Ensure Human Rights* (2000); G Evans, *The Responsibility to Protect. Ending Mass Atrocity Crimes Once and For All* (2008); C Verlage, *Responsibility to Protect. Ein neuer Ansatz im Völkerrecht zur Verhinderung von Völkermord, Kriegsverbrechen und Verbrechen gegen die Menschlichkeit* (2009). For a critical view, see C Foley, *The Thin Blue Line. How Humanitarianism Went to War* (2008) 145–70; A Orford, *International Authority and the Responsibility to Protect* (2011).

which requires the international community to engage in non-military reactions to prevent human rights violations (like, eg, economic sanctions); then, at a second stage, a *responsibility to react*, which requires military intervention in a case of clear and imminent danger as well as criminal prosecution of perpetrators of human rights norms at all governmental and non-governmental levels; and, finally, at a third stage, a *responsibility to rebuild* a state after a military intervention to ensure, among other things, the efficient functioning of a criminal law system which prosecutes past violations of human rights ('transitional justice').[7] Although the RTP is still not part of the official international public law doctrine, it is very influential. It was adopted by the General Assembly of the United Nations and affirmatively mentioned by the Security Council in its resolution 1973 in 2011 which served as a justification for massive military intervention by NATO forces in the Libyan civil war.

In the following, I would like to take the RTP out of its specific international law context and take it as the paradigm of a conceptual framework by which crime prevention by governments is justified today as serving and protecting the human rights of individuals. RTP reveals or makes obvious what seems to be one of the most fundamental issues of preventive justice. According to the recent RTP paradigm, the protection of citizens against crime is considered as a human right at the international level, and as a fundamental or basic right at the national level. Its addressee at the international level is the international community, and at the national level it is the state. At both levels its essential meaning and purpose is to provide empowerment as well as to enforce a duty on the state to take protective measures against crime and against criminal citizens on its territory. Of course, there is a difference between the crime of genocide, crimes against humanity, and war crimes, which are at the core of the RTP doctrine, and the 'ordinary' crimes of everyday life in a nation state. But the preventive logic of justification is similar at all levels: the state has a duty to protect its citizens against crime—and if not it should do better and do more. Otherwise, so it is often said, our human rights are violated. 'Humanitarian intervention' is only the most extreme case of the state's (failed) responsibility to protect on a large scale which starts with 'ordinary' crime prevention. For some people the state's responsibility is already at stake in a case, eg, of abortion or a sexual relationship between two consenting adults of the same sex.[8] Therefore, when I speak of RTP I always mean this kind of justificatory reasoning which applies to national as well as international prevention of harm by criminal law enforcement. And it is the justificatory dimension in which I am primarily interested, rather than the national or international arena and the different kinds of crime.

To speak of a paradigm shift could be misleading if doing so suggests that the RTP was only recently invented and never existed before. That the state has its legitimate ground for its monopoly of violence in the duty to protect citizens against violations of their rights was never in serious doubt (with the exception of anarchism). But in the history of the modern world, cases of the abuse of the RTP

[7] See Evans (cited in n 6); Verlage (cited in n 6).

[8] Germany's constitutional law doctrine began with an explicit duty to use criminal law in the abortion cases to protect its citizens against crime (see section D).

by governments and the abuse of governments' powers for the execution of this duty for the repression of people are more present in the collective memory than cases of a violation of this duty itself. There were of course cases where a national government refrained from protecting groups of people and minorities against violations of their rights—Germany between 1933 and 1945 is one of the most infamous examples. For most of the time states and governments were not in need of an authorization of their measures by an explicit reference to an RTP for at least two reasons.

(1) The RTP was at best only an implicit part of a collective value system which was represented by the state, like 'national security' or other national interests.

(2) In most cases of criminal law legislation the state and the political system were the first to suggest a new statute which in most cases extended criminalization—and the citizens could only react by defending their rights against it.

In contrast to this one can observe today that (1) governments explicitly refer to the protection of human rights in order to take criminal law measures against rights violations, and (2) citizens themselves raise the claim to protection of their rights in the first place and governments and legislative bodies react by enacting extensive security laws, criminal law being the most important. One of the first and most prominent examples was the claim to preserve the punishment of abortion against all attempts at its repeal. In the following sections I shall:

(1) raise the question of the foundations of the RTP and its possible constitutional foundation;

(2) address the relationship between the RTP and protection by the law

(3) consider recent developments of criminal law protection; and

(4) reflect upon the human rights doctrine of protection and its use and abuse by current preventive justice policy.

## A. The foundations of the RTP: 'The end of obedience is protection'

According to the 'Declaration of Human Rights' made by the Assemblée Nationale in Paris in 1789 the purpose of a political association is the conservation of natural and inviolable human rights ('la conservation des droits naturels et imprescriptibles de l'homme'). These rights are liberty, property, security, and resistance against oppression ('Ces droits sont la liberté, la proprieté, la sureté, et la résistance à l' oppression.'). The conservation of rights is considered as the general purpose of a political association whereas the right to security is one right among others which shall be protected in particular by the political association.

These brief statements are the result of a long narrative about the justification of political power and state authority: 'the linking of state authority with the office of protection is not a new idea—indeed it is as old as the European state itself'.[9] As always this narrative of justification consists of a mix of historical experiences and interpretations as well as of reasons and arguments. There is also not only one single narrative but different narratives or at least many variations of one single narrative.

The historical narrative refers to the conflicts between particular powers which take the law into their own hands and defend themselves against violations of their rights as long as there is no centralized power available, as happened in many parts of Europe during the Middle Ages.[10] The obvious disadvantages of permanent feuds among different groups of society (noble families and their subjects) for land, for commerce, and for human flourishing in general led, so it is said, to the mutual waiver of the right to self-help or at least to a mutual abandonment of the means of violence. According to this narrative the right to self-help and the means of violence are conveyed to a centralized political power. The risk of being helpless and vulnerable against violent attacks by third parties after relinquishing one's right to self-help was compensated by the duty of the state to protect its citizens against those violations. The duty of the citizens to behave peacefully and to obey the law which is given and enforced by the state corresponds to the duty of the community and the state to protect its members and citizens.[11]

There is of course a variation of this narrative which tells the story of the neutralization of the victim of rights violations differently. According to this narrative, the relinquishment of the right to self-help and the abandonment of weapons were never satisfactorily compensated.[12] During these feudal struggles, one powerful group would win and succeed in subjugating its weaker competitors; it would secure its own power and stabilize its authority by taking the law into its own hands and by extracting taxes from its subjects.[13] Protecting the subjects against violations of their rights was simply a functional side-effect of the need to stabilize and defend the power which was won in the civil war. It was not necessary to establish an RTP because the state punished anyway, and it prosecuted and punished people not because the state wanted to protect its citizens but because the state was eager to protect itself. The primary focus was not on the actual or potential victim of a violation but on the perpetrator who demonstrated a serious lack of loyalty to the state when he committed a crime. His body and, more importantly, his soul had to be disciplined to make him become a loyal subject.[14] On the other hand, the victim also had to be disciplined by learning to keep vengeful emotions under control. The victim was individualized and neutralized because the emotions of humiliation and vengeance and the demand for satisfaction could be dangerous for the state as well, in particular when the victim was able to win the support of

[9] Orford (cited in n 6) 35.

[10] P Blickle, *Das alte Europa. Vom Hochmittelalter zur Moderne* (2008) 122–8.

[11] This is the narrative of Eberhard Schmidt and Hermann Nohl; see W Holz, *Justizgewähranspruch des Verbrechensopfers* (2007) 59–61.

[12] The subject never acquired a claim-right against the state to prosecute and punish a perpetrator.

[13] C Tilly, 'War Making and State Making as Organized Crime' in P Evans, D Rueschemeyer, and T Skocpol (eds), *Bringing the State Back In* (1985) 169–86.

[14] M Foucault, *Überwachen und Strafen* (1975).

others and to claim a right to self-help. Therefore, the prevention of crime was part of a political strategy to suppress self-help because of its dangerous effects on the state. The victim had to be disenfranchised of his right and toppled from his power to exercise self-help. As a neutralized and individualized victim he was reduced to the role of a witness in the criminal procedure, and he could only look for private satisfaction by litigating against the perpetrator in a civil court for monetary compensation.[15] A constitutionalized criminal law and criminal procedure resulted from a struggle between the citizens and a punishing state that used its monopoly of violence primarily in its own interest.

Both narratives were transformed into a justificatory argument by contractualist doctrines of natural law. According to Hobbes and Locke, the right to self-help is part of a natural law which results from two premises: in the state of nature, everybody has a natural right to liberty and a natural duty to preserve his or her own life. Each individual has a natural responsibility to protect him- and herself. As a consequence everybody has a right to do anything that he or she thinks is in his or her own interest and a right to defend him- or herself against any violation of his or her natural right. This causes a structural deficit of the state of nature. If every individual has to care for his or her own security he or she also has to determine the level and degree individually. It depends on each individual's judgement whether the level shall be higher or lower. According to one's risk-aversity or -affinity, each one chooses the degree and level of prevention and protection he or she thinks fit. From an objective point of view, the level and degree of protection and security become radically indeterminate. The claim to security is, as John Stuart Mill described it, *absolute* for each individual on the one hand, but also *indeterminate and relative* (to the anxieties of each individual) on the other.[16] Of course people in the state of nature are prudent and reasonable enough to learn that the permanent war which results from their natural rights and their duty to preserve themselves by their own individual judgement and their own means of violence can only be overcome by a mutual abandonment of a right to self-help and the mutual recognition of a contract that obliges the parties to keep the peace and to recognize the principle of equal freedom. But they are unable to live according to their own rational insight because they have to judge by themselves whether this contract was violated, and they also have to enforce it on their own. In the state of nature everybody is judge and executioner of the law of nature.[17]

Hobbes always insists that the right to preserve one's own life and body cannot be conferred to anybody.[18] 'A covenant not to defend my selfe from force, by force, is always voyd. For no man can transferre, or lay down his Right to save himselfe from Death, Wounds, and Imprisonment.'[19] The reason for this is that giving up

[15] As an example of this narrative, see K Lüderssen, 'Die Krise des öffentlichen Strafanspruchs' in K Lüderssen, *Abschaffen des Strafens?* (1995) 42.

[16] JS Mill, *Utilitarianism* (C Heydt (ed)), (2011) ch 5, 90.

[17] T Hobbes, *Leviathan* (1651) (Crawford B. Macpherson (ed)), (1985) ch 14, 199.

[18] A Ristroph, 'Respect and Resistance in Punishment Theory' (2009) 97 California Law Review 601–32.

[19] Hobbes (cited in n 17).

one's right to life and body would contradict the main purpose of the contract and the strongest motive to enter into the contract and to keep it—to get the advantage of security.[20] As a consequence the subject keeps his liberty 'in all those things, the right whereof cannot by Covenant be transferred', and the most prominent example is that a covenant not to defend a man's own body is void.[21] The right to self-defence, killing someone who assaults one, causing fear of present death, cannot be given up as long as there is no other kind of effective protection of life. 'If he wound him to death, this is no Crime; because no man is supposed at the making of the Common-wealth, to have abandoned the defence of his life, or limbes, where the Law cannot arrive time enough to his assistance.'[22] In the chapter on 'Punishments and Rewards',[23] Hobbes argues that the sovereign's right to punish cannot be transferred to him by subjects. The subject cannot give consent to his or her own punishment because this would contradict his or her natural duty of self-preservation. The subject is obliged by the covenant to assist the sovereign in the punishing of another, but this does not entail the transfer of a right to punish from the subject to the sovereign. Therefore, Hobbes concludes, the right to punish 'is not grounded on any concession, or gift of the Subjects'.[24] The subjects do not convey their right to self-help to the central political power in exchange for protection by the state. The purpose of the mutual social contract, protection of life and liberty, shall be reached in a different way. The parties to the social contract mutually agree to abandon their fundamental natural right, 'the right to every thing, and to do whatsoever he thought necessary to his own preservation'. But there is one single party that is left and is held to be exempt from the mutual agreement. This party is the one and only individual who keeps his or her natural right and continues to 'subdue, to kill, and to hurt', ie to preserve him- or herself by any means available as everybody did in the state of nature. The right to punish is a relic of the mutual abandonment of the right to everything. The sovereign does not *get* a right to punish which he or she did not have before by a transfer or by an empowerment. The sovereign keeps his or her natural right to everything and his or her means of violence become even stronger because everybody else has renounced their weapons.[25] This is, according to Hobbes, the foundation of the right to punish: 'For the subjects did not give the Soveraign that right, but oneley in laying down theirs, strengthned him to use his own, as he should think fit.'[26]

There is, however, an important difference between the natural right to everything and the right to punish. It is mentioned by Hobbes only *en passant*. The sovereign

[20] 'As first a man cannot lay down the right of resisting them, that assault him by force, to take away his life; because he cannot be understood to ayme thereby, at any Good to himselfe'(Hobbes (cited in n 17) ch 14, 192).

[21] Hobbes (cited in n 17) ch 21, 268.

[22] Hobbes (cited in n 17) ch 27, 343.

[23] Hobbes (cited in n 17) ch 28, 353–63.

[24] Hobbes (cited in n 17) ch 28, 354.

[25] According to Ristroph (cited in n 18), the sovereign is not a natural person and therefore cannot keep a natural right. The right to punish is the right of an artificial person which was created by the covenant.

[26] Hobbes (cited in n 17) ch 28, 354.

shall exercise his or her right to everything not (only) for the preservation of him- or herself but (at least concomitantly) 'for the preservation of them all'.[27] The natural right to everything turns into a right to punish when the sovereign exercises it for the preservation of his or her subjects. This is of course consistent with unequal protection—minimal protection for some and maximum protection for others, as long as the minimal protection is still such that it is better than living in the state of nature.[28] *Equal* protection comes with the positive and general law which has to be applied equally. Then subduing, killing, and hurting—the exemplary actions necessary for self-preservation in the state of nature—turn into public punishment, which is, according to Hobbes' definition, 'an Evill inflicted by publique Authority, on him that hath done, or omitted that which is Judged by the same Authority to be a Transgression of the Law; to the end that the will of men may thereby the better be disposed to obedience'.[29] As a consequence the sovereign is bound by the positive law which has to be enacted before the crime took place, and which has to be a general law that has to be applied and enforced equally.

Although Hobbes' justificatory narrative of the genesis of the right to punishment is historically more accurate it leaves unclear what exactly the normative reason is. If it is not a transfer of a right or an empowerment it can only be a permission. The driving force behind it is fear. The fear of losing one's own life in the state of nature is greater than the fear of being punished by the sovereign.

In his 'Second Treatise of Government' John Locke explicitly introduces a natural right to punish. In the state of nature human beings own two different kinds of natural rights or powers:[30] the first is similar to Hobbes' right to everything: 'to do whatsoever he thinks fit for the preservation of himself and others within the Law of Nature'.[31] The second one 'is the *power to punish the Crimes* committed against that Law'.[32] This right (and power) is not identical with a right to self-help, because it does not allow (only) self-defence against a violation of his or her own right but (also) a punishment because of a transgression of the law of nature without any reference to the individual who has been violated. In the state of nature everybody has the right and the power to punish anybody who has transgressed the law. This kind of punishment may not be a simple manifestation of emotions of humiliation and of being offended, it may not be an act of revenge in search of satisfaction for a loss. Punishment in the state of nature has to realize a general purpose that is independent of an individual intention; the purpose to enforce the law of nature by deterrence. It 'may bring such evil on any one who has transgressed that Law, as may make him repent the doing of it, and thereby deter

[27] Hobbes (cited in n 17) 354.
[28] I am grateful to Ambrose Lee for making this point clear to me.
[29] Hobbes (cited in n 17) ch 28, 353.
[30] J Locke, 'The Second Treatise of Government (1690)' in J Locke, *Two Treatises of Government* (P Laslett (ed)), (1991) 267–428. Locke speaks of a 'right' to punish in §8 (272) and of a 'power' in §§87 (323), 128 (352), and 130 (353).
[31] Locke (cited in n 30) §128 (352).
[32] Locke (cited in n 30).

him, and by his Example others from doing the like mischief'.[33] This general purpose is the normative reason for a right (and power) to punish. The only difference between the right to punish in the state of nature and in political society is that in the state of nature the right to punish can be executed by everybody and not by the political community and a judge. Everybody is the judge and the executioner of the law of nature.[34] According to Locke this is why the state of nature is insecure and dangerous. Everybody's right to judge and execute any violation of the law of nature turns into the tragedy of civil war where 'the enjoyment of the property he has in this state is very unsafe, very unsecure' so that he is willing to quit this condition which 'however free, is full of fears and continual dangers'.[35] The good intention of protecting the law of nature fails because of human nature. Biased by their interests and ignorant of the content of the law, individuals are unable to determine its meaning in order to apply it to particular cases; being partial to themselves and driven by passion and revenge with regard to their own case or being unconcerned and negligent with regard to the cases of others they are unable to judge impartially; lacking the power to support and to execute the sentence they are unable to resist the injustices of the stronger and they fear the danger of losing their life. 'The inconveniences, that they are therein exposed to, by the irregular and uncertain exercise of the Power every Man has of punishing the transgressions of others, make them take Sanctuary under the establish'd Laws of Government, and therein seek *the preservation of their Property*'.[36] Their property is insecure and unsafe not only because of everybody's right to everything (the primary cause according to Hobbes), but also (and primarily) because of everybody's right and power to be judge and executioner of the law of nature. As a consequence the state of nature can only be overcome when the people abandon both kinds of rights, the right to everything as well as the right to punish: 'the *Power* of *punishing* he wholly gives up'.[37]

Again, the question arises how the public authority of the political society gets its right to punish, how the mutual abandonment of everybody's right allows for a public right to punish. Locke argues similarly to Hobbes when he says that the first step consists of a mutual abandonment of a natural right or power. But the next step is different. The parties to the social contract give up their power to punish for the benefit of the community or the political body: 'there, and there only is Political Society, where every one of the Members hath quitted this natural Power [to punish], resign'd it up into the hands of the Community in all cases that exclude him not from appealing for Protection to the Law established by it'.[38] The natural power to punish is given up with an intention or with a purpose in the mind of everybody: 'to be exercised by such alone as shall be appointed to it amongst them; and by such Rules as the Community, or those authorised by them to that purpose, shall agree on'.[39] This could be interpreted as a (negative) abandonment of the right

[33] Locke (cited in n 30) §8 (272).

[34] Locke (cited in n 30) §§87 (324) and 125 (351).

[35] Locke (cited in n 30) §123 (350).

[36] Locke (cited in n 30) §127 (352).

[37] Locke (cited in n 30) §130 (353).

[38] Locke (cited in n 30) §87 (324).

[39] Locke (cited in n 30) §127 (352).

to punish and *uno acto* as a kind of transfer to the appointed judges. Again the general end which is pursued by everybody is protection of property (life, body, and liberty), and this aim can only be attained negatively by mutual abandonment of the power to punish and positively by establishing legislation and by appointing judges who exercise the right to punish according to a predetermined positive law. Locke's focus on the power to punish reveals a paradox: the overall end of protection of property is endangered by the natural power to punish; the first step to reach the end of protection is the abandonment (and not the strengthening) of the power to punish. Protection is protection from everybody's power to punish according to his or her interpretation of the law of nature. Protection granted by the 'Political Society' is only possible if the power to punish is concentrated into one body and disciplined by independent political legislation.

Hobbes and Locke speak only of a *right to punish* and not of a *duty* or *responsibility* to protect the subjects and citizens by enacting criminal law and by punishing perpetrators according to the pre-established and predetermined criminal law. Again it seems that the negative and disciplinary aspect of the power to punish was more important to them than the positive aspect. But one can find at least some implicit arguments which look like a duty to protect. There is, of course, the overall end of protection which is the most important reason for everybody to join the social contract. Protection is the *raison d'être* of Hobbes' *Leviathan* and of Locke's Political Society. If the state is unable to protect its subjects they exercise their right to protect themselves against any violation. But this argument does not entail a duty of the state to protect its citizens. It only describes its *raison d'être*, a constitutive rule of the state and not a regulatory rule. It also does not contain a duty to protect the subjects by punishment according to criminal law. The end of protection could be realized by different kinds of measures, not primarily by punishment which only reacts to violations of rights which have already happened (and with only a vague expectation that it would deter others from committing a similar crime in the future). An implicit argument for a duty to protect could be found in Hobbes' remark that the sovereign shall use the natural right to everything that he or she alone kept from the previous state of nature *for the preservation of all*, ie for each subject equally. And Locke's statement that everybody gives up into the hands of the appointed judges his or her power to punish could mean that the transfer of the power as well as the appointment of the judges entails also a duty (of the state) to punish any violation of the positive law which contains punishment as a sanction. One could even say that Locke's concessionary statement, that the abandonment of the power to punish and the appointment of judges were valid only 'in all cases that exclude him not from appealing for Protection to the Law established by it',[40] could allow for a claim-right of the citizen to protection of the law by punishment of the perpetrator—which has a duty of the state to punish as its correlate.[41] But there is no extensive argument about this possible correlation.

[40] Locke (cited in n 30) §87 (324).

[41] For the correlation of a claim-right and a duty, see WN Hohfeld, 'Some Fundamental Legal Conceptions as Applied in Judicial Reasoning' (1913/14) 23 Yale Law Journal 16–59.

The reason could be that a correlation of a claim-right to punishment with a duty to protect would be too strong because it would bring citizens into a position where they could mobilize the punishing state in their own interest. And this is exactly what Locke considers as the perfect state of nature. Therefore Locke is cautious, speaking of a *right to appeal* only. The right to appeal is not directed to the state, but to the pre-established and predetermined law: it is a right to litigate and to ask for the protection of the law. Punishment would be a consequence of the application of the law to a particular case by a judge. So there is only a weaker correlation between a right to appeal for protection according to the law and a duty to protect through application and enforcement of the law. It seems that this correlation is overlapped by the more general correlation between the abandonment of rights in the state of nature, be it the right to everything or the right to punish, and the general end that consists in protection: 'The end of obedience is Protection'.[42]

If one compares Hobbes' and Locke's account of the genesis of the right to punish it becomes obvious why it is not explicitly stated in a constitution. A constitution only begins where and when people abandon their responsibility to protect themselves by their individual power to punish. According to Locke, the normative as well as factual generative moment of any constitution happens when everybody is willing to give up his or her right to punish: 'there, and there only is Political Society, where every one of the Members hath quitted this natural Power'.[43] The same is true for Hobbes, when he says that the parties to the covenant lay down their right to punish. As long as everybody cares for his and her own security by his and her own means of violence according to his or her own judgement and discretion a political society and a constitution are impossible. This mutual abandonment is a *pre-constitutional moment* and a necessary prerequisite of any constitution, not a part of it. One can even say that people are only able to take part in a political society and to achieve the specific *status constituens* as equal participants in the common project of constitution-making when they have emancipated themselves from their permanent preoccupation with their individual security. The natural duty to protect oneself is just a heavy burden that constrains human flourishing, the exercise of autonomy, and finally, the natural right to liberty itself. It also prevents one from benefitting from the advantages of cooperation with others and from living one's life in a community. People are like warlords who are concerned from dawn to dusk with preventive and pre-emptive strikes to defend their security.

But this is only half the story. By abandoning their own right and power to punish, individuals at the same time recognize the sovereign's right to punish. The sovereign's right to punish is the flipside of each and every individual's abandonment of that right. Mutual abandonment means that one right and one power to punish is left over, it is a mutual abandonment for the benefit of one. One could even say that this *is* the *constitutional moment*, the performative meaning of constitution-making. This might be the meaning of Hobbes' brief statement that in

[42] Hobbes (cited in n 17) ch 21 (272).

[43] Locke (cited in n 30) §87 (324).

laying down their right to punish, the subjects strengthen the sovereign to use his or her own right. Locke is more explicit about the constitutional meaning of this moment when he says that we give up our natural power of punishing to be exercised by such alone that shall be appointed to it amongst them according to the rules of the community: 'And in this we have the original *right and rise* of both *the Legislative and Executive Power*, as well as of Governments and Societies themselves'.[44] A political society is constituted by the willingness of the people to live peacefully, to abandon their right to self-help and punishment, and to live according to those laws to which they agree and which shall be administered by institutions and persons who are authorized by us. The primary act of political autonomy is the mutual agreement on a public authority to punish. That is what the narrative of the social contract is all about. A constitution is the result of these fundamental commitments, and it is the tool with the help of which these commitments can be realized in society.

## B. Protection by the law

The conflicts which result from everybody's right to preserve him- or herself in the state of nature and of everybody's right to punish serve as a negative background to the kind of protection which shall be exercised by the political society that is born of the social contract. The state of nature is characterized by an individualized responsibility to protect—everybody has to care for his or her own security. The consequence is insecurity, because of the uncertainty and indeterminacy of the law of nature, because of ignorance and indifference, because of passions of revenge, and because of the unequal distribution of power among the individuals. The political society and the sovereign have the opposite properties: protection shall be granted according to pre-established and determinate laws which are general and equal, which shall not be applied retroactively, which shall be administered and applied by impartial and neutral judges, and which shall be enforced equally and independently from individual power-relations by the state, which has a monopoly of violence. The state is not allowed to exercise its right to punish arbitrarily but must exercise it in a disciplined manner so that the citizens get what they desired when they entered into the social contract: equal protection.

This scenario still applies to the risks and dangers which could come from a state abusing its right and power to punish which it acquired or kept by the social contract. From the subject's and citizen's point of view the focus shifts from the overall end of protection—which is realized by the social contract and the constitutional moment—to the kind of protection which they could get in a political society. When it has to become protection by and according to the law (because this marks the difference from uncertain, indeterminate, and unequal protection by self-help and by everybody's right to punish in the state of nature), the question of

[44] Locke (cited in n 30) §127 (352) (italics in original).

which kind and quality of protection a citizen receives depends on the kind and quality of the law. It does of course also depend on the willingness and power of the state to apply and enforce the law, but the primary ground of protection is the law itself. It is the law that protects in the first place, and it shall protect equally, calculably, and effectively in a threefold manner. It shall protect all those citizens who demand protection of the law against others who attempt to violate the law (and their rights as far as they are protected by the law). But it shall also protect those citizens who are uncertain whether their intentions and actions turn out to be a violation of the rights of others, or whether they are legally permissible, by offering them a determinate rule according to which they could calculate the risk of being punished. And, finally, it should protect citizens with a system in which only responsible subjects can be punished. Whether or not a right, a good, or an interest is protected depends on a law and its content. It is the general law that will solve the problem of the relative indeterminacy of protection and security according to the individual's judgement in the state of nature.

If the scope and degree of protection depends on the law, the responsibility to protect becomes the responsibility of those who make and administer the law. Who determines the content, who decides about the level, the scope, the extent, and the range of the protection that is exercised by the law? What happens when the law does not protect enough, when the scope of protection is too small, when there is a demand to the legislator to extend the scope of protection, when the citizen is excluded from appealing for the protection of the law because there is no law or a defective law, and finally, what about the situation where there is a privileged high level of protection for some and minimal protection for the many?

It seems that these questions are left unanswered by the social contract theorists because they could not imagine that basic rights and needs were not protected by the sovereign and by the political society. The protection of life, liberty, and estate, the protection of 'property' in the comprehensive Lockean sense, was obviously the one and only reason to enter into the social contract at all. If the sovereign turns out to be unable to preserve them against violations by others, the sovereign loses the reason for his or her existence and everybody returns to the state of nature where each individual cares only about his or her own security, preserves his or her rights by him- or herself, and punishes violations of his or her rights by others. But this is true only in a general sense and for clear and obvious violations of these basic rights. Whether or not a particular case of damage to body or estate is a case for protection, whether or not a certain action is the kind of damage that calls for protection by the law at all, could be controversial. And even if a judge decided that a certain action was not the kind of damage that called for protection by the law it could remain controversial whether it should be protected by a law. Here, a responsibility or duty to protect comes in.

One can of course draw some indirect conclusions about the formal characteristics of the law that are given by the social contract theorists, and that already contain some elements of protection. Life, liberty, and property shall be protected by a law which is determinate and calculable, ie which is precise enough to circumscribe the various ways of unlawful attack. This excludes any kind of all-inclusive protection against any kind of damage (with the exception of life) to liberty and property. More important are the consequences of the feature of equality. Because the law has to have the formal property of generality, it may not be applied arbitrarily. Each case and each person falling under a legal rule has to be treated equally, ie, an equal level of protection has to be bestowed on everybody according to the general rule. Although this requirement prohibits absolute arbitrariness, it is obviously compatible with some degree of relative arbitrariness. A general law which is applied equally could allow for a high, average, or minimal degree of protection, and it could allow for the privileged protection of some, as long as this follows from the general terms of the rule. Finally, the general law is compatible with arbitrary legislation by an absolutist monarch who is primarily concerned with the protection of himself and his Court, and does not care much about the protection of his subjects—as long as he puts his will in the form of a general law. To avoid these consequences, more is required than the general law itself. The general law can realize this purpose only when it is enacted by a *democratic* procedure.

The democratization of the state is, on the one hand, an attempt to tame the sovereign as a Leviathan whose monopoly of violence and whose legislative power can be abused for the interests of the monarch and the nobility. On the other hand, democratic legislation transfers the RTP to the sovereign people. In a democratic republic, every citizen has an equal right to participate in the democratic procedure of legislation; he or she enjoys the bourgeois rights of individual property and private autonomy as well as the civic rights of political participation—he or she is always an equal co-legislator. The consequences of the democratization of political power with regard to protection of rights by criminal law are manifold. Peter Ramsay has employed T H Marshall's theory on 'Citizenship and social class' to demonstrate that.[45] Ramsay focuses primarily on the correspondence between the conceptualization of the perpetrator as a responsible subject of 'free choice' and the conceptualization of crime as a violation of the equal civic status of the victim. But there are further consequences of the kind of legal protection that is enacted by democratic legislation. As a co-legislator in a democratic republic I am obliged to obey the principles of generality and reciprocity in legislation. If I, as a citizen and co-legislator, demand the protection of a certain kind of property against a certain kind of attack I have to accept equal protection for all my fellow citizens, I have to obey a law that grants to everybody else the same protection that I am asking for. Any protection I demand for my life, liberty, and property has to be a general and reciprocal one. Locke is more explicit on this point when he says that the power to punish shall be exercised only 'by such Rules as the Community, or those authorised by them to that purpose, *shall agree on*'.[46] Rousseau's conception of legislation by the general will introduces the idea of legislation the addressees of which, as

[45] TH Marshall, *Citizenship and Social Class* (1950); P Ramsay, 'The Responsible Subject as Citizen: Criminal Law, Democracy And the Welfare State' (2006) 69 MLR 45. See also P Ramsay, this volume.

[46] Locke (cited in n 30) §127 (352) (italics added).

citizens, are also the authors of the law, as co-legislators. For Rousseau—and Kant follows him in this point—the principles of generality and reciprocity, which follow from this idea, guarantee the impartiality of legislation and make privilege or discrimination by legislation impossible. Even if this requirement does not entail any criterion about whether a kind of protection by the law in certain types of cases shall be established by legislation, it offers a *procedural* criterion for the evaluation of any demand raised by a citizen for protection by a law. It has to be a protection by a law that is general and reciprocal and not a protection that privileges some and discriminates against others.

As Ramsay has already indicated, the democratization of the state also changes the meaning of protection against crime. The focus on the protection of individuals and their rights against a violation by others is extended to the protection of the equal status of civil citizenship. In a democracy, civil rights are universalized and distributed equally. Universality and equality of civil rights is a necessary condition for each citizen to become a full member of the national community. A crime also challenges this necessary condition, and because of the principle of universality also denies the equal status of the offender: 'An offender must, in addition to wronging her victim, deny to her victim the equal status of civil citizenship as such, and thereby reciprocally deny her own status.'[47] Civil rights contain not only equal rights to liberty and property, but also political rights to participate in the procedures of public will formation and legislative decision-making, eg, individual voting rights. In a democracy, the equal status of civil citizenship is also the equal status of political citizenship. As a consequence, the law is considered as an expression and manifestation of equal political citizenship, as a general will of the citizens. The responsibility to protect is theirs, and they determine the level and scope of protection—not individually, but as political citizens in a democratic legislative procedure. The protection of the individual and his or her rights is internalized by the general will of equal and reciprocal protection of all citizens by a general law. If a citizen demands a law for his or her protection he or she has to conceive him- or herself as a co-legislator of a mutual agreement or consent, as a participant in the realization of the general will. My rights can only be violated insofar as they are part of the general will; a violation of my right is always *uno acto* a violation of the general will, which recognizes my right as an equal right of each citizen. An unlawful violation of the rights of a person is a kind of unjustified domination, a violation of the right to self-determination, as is the case when a person is dominated by an unjustified political power that imposes its arbitrary will on him or her. Consequently, the citizens' justified belief in the validity of the law as a manifestation of the general will is damaged by a crime, because the perpetrator imposes his or her particular law on others by violating the general law.[48]

[47] Ramsay (2006) (cited in n 45) 45.

[48] For this kind of 'intellectual damage', see KT Welcker, *Letzte Gründe von Recht, Staat und Strafe* (1813/1964) 249–53.

## C. Protection of fundamental rights in the welfare state

Arriving at a legitimate, general, equal, and determined level of protection by means of democratic and republican legislation remains an ideal which has never been achieved. However, it has set the standard of legitimacy for all attempts to reach the constitutional moment of establishing a power of punishment. But the equal status of civil citizenship raises another problem. Civil citizenship, including political citizenship, is, as T H Marshall and Peter Ramsay have pointed out, compatible with social inequality and a society with a social class structure.[49] One consequence is the unequal distribution of wealth and of opportunities to realize the rights of civil citizenship in practical terms. The meaning of the rights of liberty becomes hypothetical for those who have to live their lives under scarce social and economic conditions, who have nothing but their labour, which they have to sell in a competitive market in order to earn less than a living. It makes an important difference whether all citizens have an equal right to life, liberty, and property and whether the social, economic, and cultural conditions which determine the scope and extent of the exercise of these rights are favourable. These practical conditions determine the value of a right for its owner. The dialectic between equal rights ownership and equal practical conditions for exercising rights changes the general constitutional framework. The protection of rights from state intervention exists alongside protection of rights through state intervention. Rights are still directed to the state, not only with the function of restraint, but also with the function of rendering a service by the state to the owner of a right. This is the paradigm of the interventionist and welfare state.

In modern societies, life, liberty, and property also become vulnerable to risks and dangers from new technologies and an increasing division of labour. Most important are dangers for life and health. These risks and dangers are often not as clear and imminent as an attack by one person on another. Evaluations of risks may differ among those who benefit from taking a risk and those who might suffer from its realization. Some risks are more abstract and some are more concrete. Whether and how a risk turns into damage depends on the degree of probability. It is therefore difficult to obtain sufficient protection against these risks. A simple preservation of life and health by a comprehensive legal prohibition of risky behaviour would prevent society from the benefits of risky technologies—automobile traffic being one of the most obvious examples. It would also prohibit citizens from exercising their right to liberty or property if a risky use of freedom and property were totally prohibited. As a consequence, all those risks which are beneficial for society are tamed by procedural norms and by standards of conduct, by rules of caution, and in some cases by a duty to take out insurance. In some cases the law prohibits behaviour before the consummate harm occurs. Some of these rules and norms can be supported by criminal law (eg German environmental law).

[49] Ramsay (cited in n 45) 48 ff.

By these means the activist and interventionist state, which intervenes in individual rights in order to protect its citizens, becomes more and more common. Public interest and public safety become the most prominent topics of protection.

The extension of civil and political citizenship to social citizenship also changes the meaning of protection by criminal law. To obtain protection from dangers requires prevention of future harms as early as possible. Criminal law becomes in large part preventive, and it becomes difficult to distinguish it from police law. Criminal law is now characterized by an internal tension between a core of protection of basic rights of civil citizenship by responsible subjects, and a penumbra of offences which violate public interest and public safety standards. In the penumbra, negligence and strict liability become the paradigm cases of legal responsibility.[50] The penumbra becomes the core when more weight is given to the public interest in protection against risks and dangers.

## D. Protection of human rights: A new beginning?

Up to this point it seems that the story has been told backwards. Instead of starting in the 17th century with the power of punishing as the rationale of the modern state and its justification by social contract theories, it seems to be more convincing to begin with human rights after 1945. The United Nations Universal Declaration of Human Rights in 1948 and the European Convention of Human Rights (ECHR) of 1950 were the starting point for further human rights conventions, and they were accompanied by an international human rights theory which led to the acknowledgement of universal human rights—although this was politically biased during the Cold War. A central element of international human rights is the responsibility of the state not only to refrain from an arbitrary and unlawful infringement of these rights, but also to actively protect them effectively against third party violations, in the most severe cases by criminal law and by prosecution.

The ECHR Art 2.1 states that 'everyone's right to life shall be protected by law'. European Court of Human Rights (ECtHR) adjudication recognizes such a duty.[51] The legal doctrine interpreting the ECHR imposes a duty on states to enact legislation prohibiting the killing of human beings and to enforce the law. Although this does not prescribe the kind of legal regulation by which this duty to protect shall be realized, it requires criminal law protection in the most severe case of a violation of the right to life, in the case of murder.[52] The requirement of criminal law protection was also recognized in cases relating to other articles of the ECHR,

[50] Ramsay (cited in n 45) 50. A further consequence of giving more importance to prevention is the circumvention of strong due process rights by resorting to police measures and to civil proceedings; see L Zedner, 'Seeking Security by Eroding Rights: The Side-stepping of Due Process' in BJ Goold and L Lazarus (eds), *Security and Human Rights* (2007) 257–75.

[51] JW Nickel, this volume.

[52] C Grabenwarter, *Europäische Menschenrechtskonvention* (2009) 139; J Meyer-Ladewig, *Europäische Menschenrechtskonvention, Handkommentar* (2nd edn, 2006) 50 (Art 2.7b and 7c).

eg, the prohibition of slavery, servitude, and forced labour in Art 4.[53] The adjudication of Art 8 (Right to respect for private life) requires the state to enact criminal law protection of mentally disabled minors against sexual assault.[54] Finally, the prohibition of torture and inhuman or degrading treatment (Art 3) requires legal prohibition, and, in severe cases like rape, criminal law protection.[55] The citizen can demand legal protection, including criminal law protection, from the state; it is considered as a claim-right which can be enforced by the ECtHR.

Independently of the development of international human rights theory and the legal doctrine of the ECHR, the Constitutional Court of Germany has established a state duty to protect the fundamental rights of the German Grundgesetz (Basic Law).[56] This doctrine started to develop in 1958 and was completed with the two abortion decisions in 1975 and 1993.[57] According to this doctrine, fundamental rights do not have only a negative meaning that is directed against unlawful and arbitrary state interventions into individual rights. They also possess an objective legal meaning ('objektiv-rechtlicher Gehalt') which constitutes a state duty to protect the owner of a fundamental right against third party violations: 'The duty of the state is comprehensive. It forbids not only—self-evidently—direct state attacks on the life developing itself but also requires the state to take a position protecting and promoting this life, that is to say it must, above all, preserve it even against illegal attacks by others.'[58] Although the Court acknowledges that the legislator has a wide margin of discretion concerning the kind and the level of legal protection, the constitution is considered to entail a minimum level of protection. The legislator may not go below this minimum level (constitutional prohibition of insufficient actions—'Untermassverbot'). In the most severe cases, for example in the case of protection of the right to life, the constitutional prohibition of insufficient actions may require the legislator to choose criminal law as the appropriate kind of legal protection.[59] Then the rights owner could have a claim-right to the legislation to enact a law which protects him or her.[60]

The human and fundamental right to protection of fundamental rights, in some cases even the right to protection by criminal law, and the corresponding state

[53] *Siliadin v France*, Application 73316/01 (26 July 2005) ECHR.

[54] *X and Y v Netherlands*, Application 8978/80 (26 May 1985) ECHR.

[55] Grabenwarter (cited in n 52) 158; F Meyer, 'Eine Geologie des Strafrechts' (2011) 123 Zeitschrift für die gesamte Strafrechtswissenschaft 1–46, 13.

[56] As Meyer (cited in n 55) 12, points out, German constitutional theory still ignores the consequences of international human rights for criminal law.

[57] Decisions of the Constitutional Court of Germany (Entscheidungen des Bundesverfassungsgerichts) vol 7, 198 (BVerfGE 7, 198; *Lüth*, 1958); vol 39, 1 (BVerfGE 39, 1; *Abortion I*, 1975); vol 88, 203 (BVerfGE 88, 203; *Abortion II*, 1993).

[58] BVerfGE 39, 149 (*Abortion I*).

[59] See as prominent examples: G Hermes, *Das Grundrecht auf Schutz von Leben und Gesundheit. Schutzpflicht und Schutzanspruch aus Art. 2 Abs. 2 Satz 1 GG* (1987); O Lagodny, *Strafrecht vor den Schranken der Grundrechte, Die Ermächtigung zum strafrechtlichen Vorwurf im Lichte der Grundrechtsdogmatik dargestellt am Beispiel der Vorfeldkriminalisierung* (1996) 254–74; I Appel, *Verfassung und Strafe. Zu den verfassungsrechtlichen Grenzen staatlichen Strafens* (1998) 62–72; K Graßhof, 'The Duty to Protect and to Ensure Human Rights Under the Basic Law of the Federal Republic of Germany' in E Klein (ed), *The Duty to Protect and to Ensure Human Rights* (2000) 33–52; Holz (cited in n 11) 52–121.

[60] Holz (cited in n 11) 94–6.

responsibility to protect, did not come out of the blue. They resulted from a historical experience, in particular the denial of these rights and the complete annihilation of the right to life and dignity of some minorities in Nazi Germany, and further atrocities committed during the Second World War. It is an experience that no social contract theorist could imagine happening (or imagine only as a regression into the state of nature), that the pre-constitutional moment of establishing a power of punishment to guarantee a minimum level of legal protection could be arbitrarily suspended for some parties to the covenant—excluding them from protection and treating them as enemies and non-humans. This experience is explicitly invoked in the preamble of the UN Universal Declaration of Human Rights, and it is also invoked by the German Constitutional Court in its first abortion decision, in 1975.[61] Together with recent atrocities committed during the civil wars in former Yugoslavia and Rwanda, these experiences also led to the treaty establishing an International Criminal Court and to the acknowledgement and adoption of an international criminal law, as well as to the doctrine of the RTP. Where there is no constitutional duty to protect, if the legislation, the judiciary, or the government of a state discriminates, suppresses, or starts to destroy the equal rights of a minority to life, health, and liberty, human rights can entail a responsibility to protect which is demanded of foreign states—that they shall intervene in order to stop human rights violations.[62] The RTP is shifted from the sovereign nation state to the international community.

Does the recognition and establishment of a human right to protection and a corresponding state responsibility to protect only make explicit the rationale of any state and of a public power of punishment? Does it only re-state the pre-constitutional moment? Is there no tension between preventive justice and the responsibility to protect? An affirmative answer to these questions would tell only half the story. The historical background of the human rights conventions and declarations makes it obvious that the responsibility to protect human rights against third party violations, through criminal law and preventive justice, relates to severe cases. One of the salient features of these cases is that the demand is for protection of a minority against a government-supported majority. These rights are 'essentially claims against the majority'.[63] Cases of severe third-party violation evoke the pre-constitutional moment, they pertain to Mill's 'groundwork of our existence', where the status of equal civil citizenship is at stake.[64] Even then the legislator has to be very cautious and has to look very closely at the facts which are presented to justify the demand for criminal law protection, whether there is an actual or potential violation of a fundamental right by a third party, and it has to apply the principle of proportionality, which requires consideration of less intrusive alternatives to

[61] Whether this is true in the case of abortion during the first three months of pregnancy depends, of course, on an affirmative answer to the question whether the foetus is already a human being.

[62] For an interpretation of human rights as norms of empowerment for humanitarian interventions, see J Raz, 'Human Rights without Foundations' in S Besson and J Tasioulas (eds), *The Philosophy of International Law* (2010) 328.

[63] A Ashworth, *Human Rights, Serious Crime and Criminal Procedure* (2002) 43.

[64] Mill (cited in n 16) 90.

criminal law, and the balancing of rights which could be infringed by criminal law protection.[65]

The other half of the story has to take into account the recent development of criminal law protection already described. Preventive justice and criminal protection have become issues of public policy which are concerned with many kinds of risks and dangers. Public interest and public values serve as a justification for a preventive policy of criminal law. It becomes even more obvious after the transition from a welfarist paradigm of criminal law policy to a culture of control.[66] Whereas the welfarist paradigm at least struggled towards integration of criminal offenders into society by means of social reform and rehabilitation programmes, the culture of control focuses primarily on a strategy of 'punitive segregation' of the majority from criminal offenders.[67] Punishment becomes more and more expressive, emotional, exclusionary, and moralizing.

The division between good and bad citizens, between a majority that, according to its own self-understanding, makes an appropriate use of its rights, and a minority that is prone to abuse its rights at other people's expense, seriously affects the responsibility to protect. The majority claims preventive justice and criminal law protection against the minority of offenders. As a consequence, public interest issues are often fused with issues of fundamental rights protection. Human rights are then used as a rhetorical device for the promotion of public interest policies. If the responsibility to protect pertains to severe cases of human rights violations where the basis of our existence is at stake and the pre-constitutional moment is evoked, it will be easy to promote preventive justice and public safety issues up to this existential level. Human rights are then 'hijacked' by governments and majorities for their own interests.[68] The anti-terrorism policy of the West and its justifications at the national as well as the international level is a telling example.

Such a majoritarian and gubernative human rights policy has at least one negative consequence. It changes the anti-majoritarian meaning and direction of human rights into a majoritarian right to protection and a corresponding responsibility to protect the majority against the minority of criminal offenders. As social contract theories have pointed out, the absoluteness and, at the same time, indeterminacy of safety as, according to Mill, 'the most indispensable of all necessaries' requires an institutionalized procedure of legislation to determine the level and degree of safety. The process of democratization of the state submitted protective legislation to the equal status of civil and political citizenship. That being so, democratic legislation has to follow the principles of generality and reciprocity. These principles require the majority to put itself in the shoes of the minority that

[65] These requirements of an application of the duty to protect were elaborated by German constitutional law theory, see BVerfGE 39 (cited in n 57) 1,46 ff; Hermes (cited in n 59); and Lagodny (cited in n 59).

[66] D Garland (cited in n 4). Garland's interpretation of this paradigm shift is not uncontroversial—see L Zedner, 'Dangers of Dystopias in Penal Theory' (2002) 22 OJLS 341–66.

[67] D Garland (cited in n 4) 70.

[68] David Dyzenhaus suggested this term during discussion of this contribution.

will be affected by criminal law protection. It is a simple thought experiment, which can be carried out by everybody. Ashworth has explained it convincingly:

> In the end . . . it will be necessary to take a view and to express a preference for the sort of society in which one wants to live. . . . those preferences may usefully be assessed by thinking of how we would wish the police and the courts to deal with members of our family or friends who find themselves suspected of crime. What safeguards would we expect, and what rights would we claim, in that situation?[69]

It is precisely this thought experiment of reciprocity that is suspended when the 'good' citizen cannot imagine what he would demand if he were on the other side of the punitive segregation, if he was suspected to be a 'bad' citizen. What then takes place is a regulatory capture of democratic criminal law legislation that suspends the procedural requirements of generality and reciprocity in such legislation.[70] The majoritarian claim to obtain protection of their fundamental rights is then balanced against the human rights of the minority of offenders. It turns out to be a zero-sum game: more legal protection of the criminal offender means less legal protection of the victim. If the responsibility to protect is applied without democratic legislation according to the principles of generality and reciprocity, it turns out to be nothing other than a tacit nullification of the social contract.[71]

[69] A Ashworth (cited in n 63) 43.

[70] K Günther, 'World Citizens between Freedom and Security' (2005) 12 *Constellations* 385; K Günther, 'From a gubernative to a deliberative human rights policy' in Council of Europe/Venice Commission (ed), *Definition and Development of Human Rights and Popular Sovereignty in Europe* (2011) 39. If one understands the constitutional order in terms of a culture of justification it becomes obvious that such an abuse of human rights violates one of its basic principles: it denies the right of the minority to be an equal inhabitant of the sphere of justifying reasons. For the 'culture of justification' see D Dyzenhaus, this volume.

[71] This is also true at the level of international relations. The lack of procedural transparency, control, and participation is one of the dangers of the international law doctrine of the responsibility to protect.

# 5

# Preventive Justice and the Rule-of-Law Project

*David Dyzenhaus**

> But the consideration of this preventing justice were worthy of the wisdom of a parliament... Blessed shall be he that lays the first stone of this building, more blessed that proceeds in it, most of all that finishes it, to... the glory of God, and the honour of our king and nation.
>
> Sir Edward Coke, epilogue to his *Third Institutes*, 243.

## A. Preventive (in)justice?

The rule-of-law project seeks to ensure that political power is always exercised within the limits of the rule of law. However, the idea of 'law' within it is ambiguous because it connotes both the positive legal regime created by a formally valid statute and the principles of legality associated with the rule of law. On the first understanding, compliance with the rule of law amounts to no more than acting in accordance with the law, whatever its content. On the second, compliance with the rule of law requires compliance with principles that need to be exhibited by a legal order; and that entails that legal actors, for example judges, are under a duty to try to ensure that such principles are observed when others, for example officials, purport to act in the name of the law.

I will argue later that these are not two rival understandings, but different aspects of the same phenomenon. For the moment it suffices to note that the 'emerging genre of preventive justice'[1] poses a serious challenge to the project at least when it is understood in the second way. For preventive justice seems to reduce the normative controls associated with the rule of law to vanishing point or worse in an area where the exercise of those controls has traditionally be seen to be most urgent: when the state deprives individuals of their liberty. Moreover, the deprivation happens not because of some proven infraction of the law but on the basis of an assessment of the

* I thank Eddie Clark for an excellent memorandum on the preventive justice measures discussed in this chapter, and for discussion, the participants in the Preventive Justice Project seminar at All Souls College, Oxford, in January 2012, especially my respondent, Murray Hunt.

[1] L Zedner, 'Pre-emptive Justice or Pre-Punishment: The Case of Control Orders' (2007) 60 Current Legal Problems 174.

risk the individual poses to some individual, group, or the community at large. However, it is difficult to make precise the wrong of the kind of preventive justice on which I will focus—preventive detention—as we find out when we explore further the intuition that preventive justice is morally suspect, perhaps even that a better label would be 'preventive injustice'.[2]

The assumption of a rule-of-law system is that a deprivation of liberty is appropriate only if the individual has been convicted of a crime serious enough to warrant such an extreme penalty. Moreover, that conviction must be the result of a fair and open trial, one characteristic of which is that the individual had the opportunity to see and challenge all the evidence on which the state relied.

There are well-recognized exceptions, and they should complicate our reaction to preventive justice since they show that our unease cannot be premised on the mere fact that a deprivation of liberty is based on an evaluation of risk. First, pre-trial detention, often for long periods, is permitted when the accused individual is considered to be a risk to others or likely to flee;[3] secondly, individuals subject to a deportation order may be detained pending deportation, again because of the risk that the person will try to disappear prior to deportation; thirdly, there is medical detention during public health emergencies when those who are a potential danger to the health of others are quarantined. In all of these situations, the decision is made on the basis of risk, precisely the evaluation that seems problematic in the preventive justice context.

There are some salient differences between these situations and the situation that creates unease. With deportation detention, detention is legitimate when and only when there is in existence a valid deportation order made after an open hearing in which the person had a full opportunity to contest the order and the detention has to be pending an actual not a notional deportation. With pre-trial detention, the detention order is again made after an open hearing when and only when an actual trial is pending. And with public health emergencies, quarantine orders are made on the basis of public information and are strictly limited by the duration of the emergency. To the extent that such detention orders are made on the basis of less exigent standards than the standard of proof required in a criminal trial, they might well be problematic. But while practice will often fall short of principle, the orders are all capable in principle of being justified by a full-blown proportionality analysis, framed by constitutionally entrenched protections of liberty, equality, and the right to an open and fair hearing.[4]

Things start to look different in the situation of deportation detention either when there is no real prospect of deportation, whatever the basis of the order, or when the basis is not that the person has been convicted of an offence that makes him or her liable to deportation, but that he or she has been determined to be a risk to national security in a procedure which does not amount to an open and fair

[2] D Husak, this volume. [3] RA Duff, this volume.

[4] See CS Steiker, this volume, for an incisive analysis of the application of proportionality analysis to the domain of preventive justice, which prescinds from the problem of normative justification of the objective.

hearing. There is no difference between his or her situation and that of someone who is detained indefinitely on national security grounds, even though governments have claimed that they would deport if only the conditions existed that made deportation possible, and courts have to their shame acquiesced in such claims.[5] Thus, a paradigm case for the wrong of preventive justice is when individuals face both of these problems at once—the deprivation of liberty either is admitted to be indefinite or is in substance so, and the basis for the detention order cannot be adequately contested.

There might, that is, not be something wrong with preventive measures as such. Rather, they go wrong substantively when they do not have a legitimate objective, just as pre-trial detention is illegitimate when it is a pretext for holding someone rather than a means necessary to ensure that the person will stand trial. And they go wrong procedurally when the person gets either no or an inadequate opportunity to contest the basis for the detention, just as a criminal trial goes wrong when the accused is not given an adequate opportunity to contest the evidence on which the state's case rests.

I have not yet made precise the wrong of preventive justice, for now we are faced with the normative problem of specifying what counts as a legitimate objective. So far there seem to be two obvious candidates for the conditions an objective has to meet in order to count as legitimate: the legal conditions and the substantive or moral conditions.

In regard to the first, I consider that it would be wrong to use pre-trial detention as a means to quarantine individuals during an epidemic, worse perhaps than quarantining them without any prior legal authorization. Medical detention becomes legitimate, that is, when it is authorized by a statute or a constitutional provision, when the conditions of detention are properly tailored to the objective, and as consistent as possible with the rights of the affected individuals. We can think of these legitimacy conditions as the specifically legal conditions of legitimacy. But they might not seem sufficient to make medical detention legitimate. There is also the fact that prior to medical detention being appropriately authorized by law, it is already considered legitimate that it be so authorized. Hence, it seems that moral considerations must supply the further condition of legitimacy.

Or does it? Consider the argument put by Alan Dershowitz for the legitimacy of torture in the wake of 9/11: torture is immoral but the security forces will use torture in a situation of perceived threat to national security; it is better that torture when it happens be legally regulated; therefore, the law should (ie it is legitimate for the law so to do) make possible the issue of torture warrants.[6] The major premise in this argument claims to recognize the immorality of torture. But since the argument also includes the claim about the necessity to resort to torture, it concludes

[5] *Re Charkaoui* (2007) 276 DLR (4th) 594; 2007 SCC 9.

[6] A Dershowitz, *Why Terrorism Works: Understanding the Threat, Responding to the Challenge* (2002). As Jeremy Waldron points out, one can 'imagine Alan Dershowitz saying that the formal regulation of torture might be as much a triumph for the Rule of Law as its prohibition': J Waldron, *Torture, Terror, and Trade-Offs: Philosophy for the White House* (2010) 250.

with the claim that legalizing torture is legitimate. And the very same argument can be made about indefinite security detention and many other preventive justice measures. The only difference between medical detention and indefinite security detention seems then to be that with the latter there is a prior moral anxiety that has to be overcome.

So the first problem I face is that it is hardly clear why we suspect preventive measures of being in substance unjust. The second problem is in part that it is also hardly clear what the rule-of-law project amounts to. But I will focus not so much on the question of injustice as on whether, even if one assumes the correctness of my own account, it is capable of responding to the challenge of preventive justice. If it cannot, a rather serious problem results since, for reasons I will elaborate, the project has no option but to try to respond. Thus, while the project might seem in the abstract to present an ideal to which legal orders should aspire, if it is doomed to failure, the aspiration might make things morally worse from the perspective of the rule-of-law ideal.

I will ultimately argue, however, that the legality conditions are more powerful than they might at first sight appear to be. They discipline the objectives within the preventive justice family that make us morally uneasy to the extent that some of these seem to be unlegalizable: they are incapable of being legalized, that is, of meeting the legality conditions of legitimacy. Or, perhaps more accurately, if this family of measures is legalized to some large extent its substantive character changes, with the result that there is substantially less to be morally anxious about; and that, I will suggest, provides a partial answer to the question of the injustice of preventive justice.

## B. Law as the public conscience

As I mentioned, the idea of 'law' within the rule-of-law project is ambiguous between positive law and principles of legality. In the 20th and 21st centuries democratic governments claim to answer to what I call the 'compulsion of legality'. They regard as a necessary condition of legitimate state action that the public officials who perform the action have a legal warrant—that there is in pre-existing law an authorization for public officials to act in this manner. Put differently, compliance with legality is seen as a necessary if not sufficient condition for legitimate state action. Indeed, such compliance often seems to be regarded as a sufficient condition for state action, since debate about the legitimacy of such action increasingly turns on the answer to the question whether the government can display a legal warrant for what it did.

Consider the controversies in the USA and the UK about the invasion of Iraq or the debate in the USA about the justification for 'extreme' interrogation techniques such as waterboarding. At times public discussion of such issues has been conducted as though it might be appropriate for governments and public officials to act outside the law in situations of extreme threats to security. However, often not only is the central question whether the decision or act is justifiable according to law, but also it is more or less assumed in such discussions that if the law justifies the action it is all-things-considered justified. On this assumption, legality begets legitimacy, a proposition that will seem counter-intuitive to many, but which I will argue later has much to commend it.

Naturally, claims for the legality of the invasion of Iraq or of extreme interrogation techniques are hotly disputed. Nevertheless, to the extent that such disputes are about what is legally justified, legality has become a kind of grammar of political morality, what Thomas Hobbes called 'the publique Conscience of the Law'.[7]

My focus here is on the public conscience of the law and a different family of examples that has come to the fore in the wake of 9/11. These are examples of preventive justice from the counterterrorism/national security context in which individuals who are considered risks to national security are removed from the community. The examples range from indefinite detention in a prison, through the 'control order' system introduced in the UK by the Prevention of Terrorism Act 2005[8] and that permitted severe forms of house arrest including confinement to a residence removed from the individual's local community with no access to mobile phones or the internet, to the supposedly less onerous forms of social control that are being substituted in the UK for the control orders: the TPIMs, so called because they have been brought into existence by the Terrorism Prevention and Investigation Measures Act 2011.

I want to highlight two features of this family. First, and evidence of the compulsion of legality, the forms of control the state exercises over the individuals who are considered risky enough to be subject to preventive justice are legal at least in the sense that they are the creatures of statute law. They are not instances of the executive relying on an idea of a prerogative, legally unbounded power to act outside of or against the law in a time of emergency. They are examples of rule *by* law.

Secondly, the forms of control are also or purport to be examples of the rule *of* law, at least in that independent judges are given by the statutes an explicit role in reviewing particular official decisions. Moreover, in playing that role, the judges are required to extend their inquiry into the legality of the acts or decisions beyond the bare terms of the statute to questions about fundamental legal values, whether these are expressed in a legal instrument such as an entrenched constitution, another statute as in the Human Rights Act 1998, an international convention as in the European Convention on Human Rights, or in the common law constitution's methods of seeking by dint of judicial interpretation to serve the individual's liberty under and equality before the law.

Legality thus begets legitimacy in two ways, corresponding with the features just identified. First, there is the democratic legitimacy that comes about because the legislature has determined that a particular legal regime is appropriate for dealing

[7] Waldron (cited in n 6) 223. For an exploration of contemporary topics in international law along similar lines, see J Brunnée and S Toope, *Legitimacy and Legality in International Law: An Interactional Account* (2010) especially chs 4 and 5. For an extensive comparative discussion of the virtues of legislative control, see K Roach, *The 9/11 Effect: Comparative Counter-Terrorism* (2011).

[8] See Zedner (cited in n 1), as well as literature cited in later notes. For a recent comprehensive account, see C Walker, *Terrorism and the Law* (2011) ch 7.

with some pressing social and political problems. I will call this 'rule-by-law' legitimacy. Secondly, there is 'rule-of-law legitimacy' that comes about when the officials who implement the regime are required to comply both with the terms of their statutory mandate and with principles of legality, and the requirements are enforced by independent judges.

However, as the next sections will help to show, these are two aspects of the legitimacy of legality rather than two different kinds. For rule-by-law legitimacy is legal legitimacy. It requires the reduction of a political programme to the explicit terms of a statute and thus converts policy into public standards, which produces a kind of legal surplus value. By this I mean that the legitimacy of official action in compliance with the statute is not simply that of compliance with a political policy that the legislature has determined to be appropriate, after debating the content of the policy. It is also the case that the conversion *adds* value because it brings into being a particular type of *public* standard. It thus permits the operation of the principles identified by Lon L Fuller as the principles of the 'inner morality of law': generality, promulgation, non-retroactivity, clarity, non-contradiction, possibility of compliance, constancy through time, and congruence between official action and declared rule.[9]

Fuller said of the last principle that it was the 'most complex', both because congruence can be destroyed or impaired in various ways and because the 'procedural devices designed to maintain it take, of necessity, a variety of forms'.[10] In the USA, he noted, it was chiefly the judiciary that is entrusted with preventing discrepancy between rules and administrative action. But he emphasized that that there would be 'serious disadvantages' in any system that looked solely to the courts 'as a bulwark against the lawless administration of the law'.[11]

Despite this important qualification, which I will come back to, Fuller's conception of the centrality of the judicial role to maintaining congruence highlights that an important component of the surplus value created by the conversion of public policy into law is that it makes possible a second process of conversion, over which judges or equivalent adjudicators preside, in which the issues submitted to them '[tend] to be *converted* into a claim of right or an accusation of guilt. This conversion is effected by the institutional framework within which both the litigant and the adjudicator function.'[12] The process of reasoned argument requires, that is, the person making the argument to present it as more than a 'naked demand'. It has to be presented as a 'claim of right', that is, as 'supported by a principle'. And that has the consequence that 'issues tried before an adjudicator tend to become claims of rights or accusations of fault'.[13] Thus Fuller regards courts as 'essential to the rule of law'. The 'object of the rule of law is to substitute for violence peaceful ways of settling disputes. Obviously, peace cannot be assured simply by treaties,

[9] These are set out in detail in LL Fuller, *The Morality of Law* (revised edn, 1969).
[10] Fuller (cited in n 9) 81.
[11] Fuller (cited in n 9) 81.
[12] LL Fuller, 'The Forms and Limits of Adjudication' in KI Winston (ed), *The Principles of Social Order: Selected Essays of Lon L. Fuller* (2001) 111(emphasis added).
[13] Fuller (cited in n 12) 111.

agreements, and legislative enactment. There must be some agency capable of determining the rights of the parties in concrete situations of controversy'.[14]

Rule-by-law legitimacy cannot be disentangled from rule-of-law legitimacy, then, since the latter amounts to little more than compliance with the same eight principles, as interpreted by judges and other officials. But it requires in addition that the principles are interpreted in such a way as to serve the individual interests in liberty under and equality before the law. As the next sections will help to show, if that requirement is not met there is also reason to doubt that rule-by-law is in place, let alone the rule-of-law.

Further, once we understand why rule by law and the rule of law cannot be disentangled, we can also appreciate why the democratic legitimacy involved in rule by law should not be conflated with a distinct kind of political legitimacy, which I will call 'expertise legitimacy'. This is the legitimacy relied upon by the legislature in delegating the authority to implement a particular legal regime to a specified group of public officials. Just how expertise legitimacy fits into legal order is an enduring problem of administrative law. It intervenes at precisely the moment when public officials have to decide how to implement their statutory mandate. It thus raises the complex problem of how to evaluate the congruence between official action and declared rule, when the officials have or are assumed to have an expertise in making policy judgements in regard to the objectives of the statute.[15]

One way to respond to this problem is by conflating expertise legitimacy with the democratic legitimacy implicated in rule by law. Such a conflation is urged by prominent academics, in particular the positivistic advocates of the idea that legal order is based ultimately in a political constitution and that law is simply the instrument of the powerful. On this view, law has no intrinsic legitimacy. It is only as legitimate as the political ends of which it is the instrument. Since these ends are determined by the government of the day, and since governments are able 'through their majority... [to] require Parliament to conform'[16] to enacting these ends, democratic legitimacy is from the perspective of the judiciary no more than what 'Ministers and others in high positions of authority' decide.[17]

This view is not confined to academics. Occasionally, judges will articulate the same view especially in cases involving national security, most notably in the post-9/11 era by Lord Hoffmann in his well-known Postscript to his speech in *Secretary of State for the Home Department v Rehman*, where he suggested that judges must defer to the executive in matters of national security because of the executive's expertise, special knowledge, and democratic credentials.[18] This instrumentalist view of law is in severe tension not only with the aspirations of the rule of law but

[14] Fuller (cited in n 12) 114.

[15] Precisely this problem led in the 1980s to a well-known debate in the USA: EL Rubin, 'Law and Legislation in the Administrative State' (1989) 89 Columbia Law Review 369 and PL Strauss, 'Legislative Theory and the Rule of Law: Some Comments on Rubin' (1989) 89 Columbia Law Review 427.

[16] JAG Griffith, 'The Common Law and the Political Constitution' (2001) 117 LQR 42, 52.

[17] JAG Griffith, 'The Political Constitution' (1979) 42 MLR 1.

[18] *Secretary of State for the Home Department v Rehman* [2002] 1 All ER 123, para 62.

also with the idea that in a regime of rule by law, law amounts to public standards that are more than the subjective views about what is best to do of the public officials who have to implement those standards. So much is recognized by judges, including by Lord Hoffmann in *Rehman*. Whilst he said that the question whether Rehman was a danger to the national security of the United Kingdom was not a 'question of law' but a 'matter of [executive] judgment and policy', he also said that the factual basis of that judgment had to be established by evidence and that a court could reject the judgment on the basis that it was *Wednesbury* unreasonable: the test established in 1948 by the Court of Appeal according to which an exercise of discretion should be reviewed only if it were so unreasonable that no reasonable authority could have ever come to it.[19]

However, in light of the Postscript and of statements in the main part of Lord Hoffmann's speech, it is clear that for him *Wednesbury* unreasonableness is not a test of whether a judgment is reasonable, but of whether it is utterly unreasonable. He based this claim explicitly on the key variable in the preventive justice context—that judgments in this context do not 'involve a yes or no answer as to whether it is more likely than not that someone has done something, but an evaluation of *risk*'.[20] His claim is thus akin to that part of Lord Greene MR's dictum in *Wednesbury* where he talked of 'something so absurd that no sensible person could ever dream that it lay within the powers of the authority',[21] or to the test prescribed for the first stage of review of control order decisions that judges should refuse permission to issue such an order only if the Home Secretary's decision is 'obviously flawed'.

If the judicial role is that implied by Lord Hoffmann's dicta, one in which judges defer submissively and supinely to the security state until the point where public officials go beyond some indeterminate and likely indeterminable pale, it is highly problematic. As I have recognized in previous work, the compulsion of legality can set in motion two very different 'cycles of legality'. In one 'virtuous cycle', the institutions of legal order cooperate in devising controls on public actors that ensure that their decisions comply with the principle of legality, understood as a substantive conception of the rule of law. In the other 'empty' cycle, the content of legality is understood in an ever more formal or vacuous manner, resulting in the mere appearance or even the pretence of legality. With this second cycle, the compulsion of legality results in the subversion of the kinds of values associated with a substantive conception of the rule of law, notably the individual interest in equality and liberty. When judges play a role in sustaining an empty cycle, they might make things worse from the perspective of the rule of law by placing what a UK judge, Sullivan J, in a control-order decision memorably described as a 'thin veneer of legality' over the 'reality' of 'executive decision-making, untrammelled by any prospect of effective judicial supervision'.[22]

[19] *Rehman* (cited in n 18) para 54, quoting from (without a specific reference to) *Associated Provincial Picture Houses Ltd v Wednesbury Corporation* [1948] 1 KB 223.

[20] *Rehman* (cited in n 18) para 57 (emphasis added).

[21] See A Tomkins, 'National Security and the Role of the Court: A Changed Landscape?' (2010) 126 LQR 543, 548.

[22] *Re MB* [2006] EWHC 1000 (Admin) [2006] H.R.L.R. 29 (2006) 150, para 103.

Thus I have also suggested in previous work, taking my cue from Lord Steyn's famous description of Guantanamo Bay as a legal 'black hole'—a space devoid of legal controls—that we should be alert to the presence of 'grey holes'. In the latter there are legal controls, but these are not substantive enough to give the affected individuals any real protection. There is just enough legality to provide government with a basis to claim that it is still governing in accordance with the rule of law, and thus to garner some legitimacy.[23] Since these holes are in substance black, their existence, I conjectured, is even more dangerous for the rule of law than black holes. A little bit of legality might, that is, be more lethal to the rule of law than none.

There is the possibility that lawyers and judges can try to turn the grey hole into something better by building more substance into the legal controls. They accept that the government and the legislature have committed themselves to ruling through the rule of law, and use that commitment as a legitimating basis for finding that the legislature must have intended real not sham controls. But it is also the case that that possibility might make such lawyers and judges complicit not only in maintaining the grey hole, but also in creating it. To the extent that judges are successful in pushing governments and legislatures in the direction of answering better to the compulsion of legality, they might achieve nothing better, to revert to Sullivan J's dictum, than a somewhat thicker veneer.

The central question in the next two sections is what the tale of the progression from indefinite detention to TPIMs tells us about these two cycles and about the predicament of the grey hole. My tentative conclusion will be that it shows that the virtuous cycle is both practicable and normatively desirable. Neither of these conclusions is obvious. In regard to practicability, that the rule of law seems to have more of a grip on the government's responses to perceived security several years after 9/11 and the London bombings might tell us only that as the threat of emergency recedes so the rule of law can enter the picture in a more substantive way.

In regard to normative desirability, the point about practicability might lead one to claim that the rule of law is a luxury, enjoyed under contingent conditions of normality, so that it is rightly pushed aside when the times prove exceptional. One might thus conclude that the rule of law is brought into disrepute when one pretends that it can operate during exceptional times, so that one should do without the thin veneer, as in Oren Gross's argument that in such times an 'extra-legal measures model' should be adopted.[24] Alternatively, one might argue that it is necessary, perhaps at the cost of some hypocrisy, to maintain the thin veneer during abnormal times in order to sustain the basis for restoring more substantive legal controls when normal times return.

Given the compulsion of legality, however, the alternatives are really between the virtuous and the empty cycles. But some of the ideas that animated Gross's argument remain of great importance, not only the general claim that the rule of

23 See D Dyzenhaus, *The Constitution of Law: Legality in a Time of Emergency* (2006).

24 O Gross, 'Chaos and Rules: Should Responses to Violent Crises Always be Constitutional?' (2003) 112 Yale Law Journal, 1011.

law will be brought into disrepute if the empty cycle prevails even if only for a limited period, but, and more important, the claim that as people become accustomed to the empty legal controls of the emergency regime, so it will be easier for such controls to seep into ordinary legal regimes, most worryingly the criminal law.

If anything, Gross underestimated the problem of seepage. It is not so much that the empty controls will seep into the ordinary legal regimes, as that once one starts to look at the realm of the 'ordinary', it becomes apparent that the barbarian is not only within the gates but has been comfortably ensconced there for some time. Perhaps one could even make the claim that governments would have been less reluctant to impose the control of legality on their preventive justice measures in response to emergencies, if only they had realized what they were already able to get away with in the ordinary regimes of preventive control.

## C. Rhetoric or reality? An Australian interlude

In an article on indefinite detention without trial during World War II in Britain, AWB Simpson sought to displace from the pantheon of great rights-protecting judgments Lord Atkin's dissent in *Liversidge v Anderson*,[25] the case about the legality of indefinite detention under the Defence (General) Regulations 1939 reg 18B. According to Simpson, Lord Atkin was 'primarily distressed' not by the faulty logic of his fellow judges in the majority nor by liberty, but by 'judicial status—the relationship of courts to the executive'. Atkin's dissent was thus more an exercise in the 'rhetoric of fiction' than in any 'practical reality' because it and similar judgments amount to no more than a hopeless rearguard stand against the trend to 'despotism'.[26]

Simpson's conclusion to his monograph on the same topic is a little different. He warns that the '[i]mposition of the rule of law upon governmental action through the courts is simply incompatible with secret administration, and in the conflict between secrecy and the rule of law secrecy wins'.[27] But he adds that a 'judiciary which does not champion the rule of law will tend to diminish the respect in which the courts are held, and there is a sense in which judges like . . . Atkin may have been right in conceiving of the conflict in terms of status: not so much their personal status, but that of the institution to which they belonged'.[28] The upshot seems to be that judges must champion the rule of law while not being able to enforce it.

Simpson's observations remain relevant today. Consider that in *South Australia v Totani*,[29] the majority of the Australian High Court found unconstitutional a state statute that introduced a scheme of control orders for alleged members of criminal gangs. The statute[30] permitted the Attorney General to declare an organization to

25 *Liversidge v Anderson* [1942] AC 206.

26 AWB Simpson, 'Rhetoric, Reality, and Regulation 18B' (1988) Denning Law Journal 130, 151.

27 AWB Simpson, *In the Highest Degree Odious: Detention Without Trial in Wartime Britain* (1992) 421.

28 Simpson (cited in n 27) 222.

29 [2010] HCA 39.

30 South Australia's Serious and Organised Crime (Control) Act 2008 (SA) s 14(1).

be one in respect of which control orders could be imposed on the individual members. The Commissioner of Police could then seek a control order from the Magistrates Court of South Australia on the basis of an individual's connection with the declared organization. The Court had to make a control order if 'satisfied that the defendant is a member of a declared organisation'. 'Member' was defined very broadly and included prospective members and persons who are treated by the organization as if they are members. A control order had a minimum content—it had to 'prohibit the defendant' from associating with other members of any declared organization. Breach of the conditions of a control order was an offence punishable by up to five years' imprisonment.

The majority's principal objection to the statute was that because there was no independent judicial inquiry into the basis of a claim that an individual was a risk, the court had been made into 'an instrument of the Executive, which undermines its independence'.[31] Because the federal Constitution guarantees the independence of state courts, the majority was able to reason that the scheme was invalid because 'it distorts that institutional integrity which is guaranteed for all State courts by Chapter III of the Constitution so that they may take their place in the integrated national judicial system of which they are part'.[32]

This decision seems a victory for the rule of law, until one tries to square it with an earlier High Court decision on control orders, this time in the national security context.[33] In *Thomas v Mowbray*,[34] the Court had to decide on the validity of a provision of the Criminal Code,[35] which allows for the imposition of interim control orders in order to prevent terrorist acts. The majority upheld the provision on a basis explained by two of the judges in the majority in *Totani* in their bid to show the consistency of their participation in the majority in both decisions. They said that in the regime created by the Criminal Code, 'the court's power to make the control order was conditioned on it being satisfied, on the balance of probabilities, that the making of the order would substantially assist in preventing a terrorist act, or that the person against whom the order was sought has provided training to, or received training from, a listed terrorist organisation'.[36]

However, in his dissent in *Thomas*, Kirby J found the scheme inconsistent with the judicial power because it denies the potential controlee procedural fairness, minimizes his or her rights, involves the withholding of evidence, and has fewer procedural protections than similar overseas systems.[37]

The combination of the majority judgments in *Thomas* and *Totani* suggests that the majority of the High Court is more concerned to preserve a formal than a

31 *Totani* (cited in n 29) para 436 (Crennan and Bell JJ).

32 *Totani* (cited in n 29) para 4.

33 For discussion see Roach (cited in n 7) 340–46. At 342, he notes that Australian officials have 'defended control orders as less intrusive than criminal prosecutions, which often involve extensive periods of pretrial detention'.

34 [2007] HCA 33.

35 Criminal Code (Cth) Division 104, Subdivision B.

36 *Thomas* (cited in n 34) para 430.

37 *Thomas* (cited in n 34) paras 364–5.

substantive constitutional role.[38] While the judges consider important the effects of any legislation or executive action on individual liberties, they regard their constitutional role not primarily as one about the protection of rights. What they care about is that they are in a position to certify that any deprivation of rights happened in accordance with the criteria set out in the legal regime. If this diagnosis is correct, it makes it hard to tell the difference between their position and that of Heydon J, who was in the majority in *Thomas* and the lone dissenter in *Totani*. For in *Totani*, Heydon reasoned that there was no basis for distinguishing that case from *Thomas*.[39]

Before his appointment to the High Court, Heydon had made public his rather conservative views on the role of judges in upholding the rule of law.[40] And at the outset of his dissent in *Totani*, he emphasized his view that the aspiration of government to the rule of law requires that governments take measures to secure the safety of the people. In this case, the executive had, he said, taken measures to forestall what it saw as very serious and socially damaging crimes. It thought that failure to implement those measures would be an abdication from duty. Like Coke, it thought that 'preventing justice excelleth punishing justice'.[41] It sought to combine established techniques to meet modern problems.[42] He was prepared to accept as a possible outcome that, if the Court were to find the provision unconstitutional, the states might be tempted 'into legislating to exert their coercive power through means other than their courts'. He continued:

> If legislation of that kind is valid, the outcomes it generates are less likely to be congenial to civil liberties than legislation employing the courts. If legislation of that kind is not valid, the capacity of the States to fulfil their obligations to protect their residents is severely impaired. Either way the rule of law is diminished.[43]

Heydon's suggestion that such legislation would be valid is the product of his view of his Court's prior jurisprudence on the constitutional protection of the judicial role in regard to involuntary detention. That is, subject to the standard exceptions, the role was confined to involuntary detention that happened only as an 'incident of judging and punishing criminal guilt'; hence, the jurisprudence, he said, has no application to 'restrictions on freedom of association falling short of detention'.[44]

This Australian interlude thus seems a complete vindication of Simpson's thesis about rhetoric and reality. Judges have no choice but to champion the rule of law if they are not to risk being shut out altogether by the legislature, but can do so only

[38] However, in his judgment in *Totani* (cited in n 29), Hayne J (who was one of the dissenters in *Thomas*) suggested a much more substantive approach than the other judges in the majority at para 236.

[39] *Totani* (cited in n 29) para 379.

[40] D Heydon, 'Judicial Activism and the Death of the Rule of Law' (2003) XLVII (1–2) Quadrant Magazine Law (January) 21. Available from <http://www.google.ca/search?client=safari&rls=en&q=heydon + judicial + activism&ie=UTF-8&oe=UTF-8&redir_esc=&ei=VEapTo6wC-bj0QGEtIC1Dg>.

[41] This appeal to Coke is misleading, as I will show (in text at n 75).

[42] *Totani* (cited in n 29) para 240, notes omitted.

[43] *Totani* (cited in n 29) para 247, notes omitted.

[44] *Totani* (cited in n 29) paras 382–83.

on condition that they do not resist the legislature's attempt to confine their role to a more or less inglorious rubber stamping of executive decisions. I will suggest, however, that the tale from detention to TPIMs may suggest a solution to the predicament, one in which judges play a central role, but which they cannot alone bring into being.

## D. The *Halliday/Liversidge* matrix[45]

Recall that in Britain during the two world wars, the indefinite detention of individuals who were perceived to be risks to national security had to follow a procedure set out in regulations. Each decision was in principle subject to an appeal to an executive committee, whose chairman had to inform detainees of the grounds of their detentions, so that they could make a case to the committee for their release. The Home Secretary could decline to follow the advice of the committee, but had to report monthly to Parliament about the orders he had made and about whether he had declined to follow advice. The committee, however, lacked rule-of-law teeth. Not only did it fail to require the real reasons for detentions from the intelligence branch, but even if it thought that someone had been wrongly detained, it also could only advise the Home Secretary of its view.

The majority of the House of Lords in the World War I decision in *Halliday*[46] and in the World War II decision in *Liversidge*[47] said that the demands of legality were satisfied by the detention regime and that such regimes were appropriate given the context—wartime emergency. While Lord Atkin's dissent has got a lot of attention, Lord Shaw's dissent in *Halliday* is hardly discussed, though it has as important a place in the rule-of-law project.[48]

The Defence of the Realm Consolidation Act 1914 did not explicitly authorize a detention regulation to be made and so Lord Shaw found invalid the precursor of Regulation 18B. He started with the assumption that Parliament must be taken to intend that its delegates act in accordance with the rule of law, which meant that it had explicitly to authorize any departures from the rule of law.[49] Judges should not ratify a 'constructive repeal of habeas corpus'[50] by the executive. He would, he said, have come to his conclusion even had the language of the statute 'been much more plain and definite than it is'.[51]

[45] I have been trying to understand the matrix created by these two decisions for over 20 years, that is, from my first book, *Hard Cases in Wicked Legal Systems: South African Law in the Perspective of Legal Philosophy* (1991), through *The Constitution of Law*, to the second edition of the first book, *Hard Cases in Wicked Legal Systems: Pathologies of Legality* (2010). The first part of this section has appeared several times before in several publications, each time though with what I hope are significant tweaks.

[46] *R v Halliday, ex parte Zadig* [1917] AC 260.

[47] *Liversidge* (cited in n 25).

[48] See Dyzenhaus (cited in n 23) 24–6, and D Foxton, '*R v Halliday, Ex Parte Zadig* in Retrospect' (2003) 19 LQR 24.

[49] *Halliday* (cited in n 46) 292–3.

[50] *Halliday* (cited in n 46) 294.

[51] *Halliday* (cited in n 46) 293.

When civil servants put together the detention regime for World War II, they took note of Shaw's dissent and so ensured that the authorizing statute explicitly permitted the establishment of a detention regime by regulation. One might view this step not as evidence of progress towards the realization of the rule of law but as adding another layer to the veneer. But, in addition to this response to a dissenting judge, the government responded to concerns raised in Parliament about the wording of the initial version of the detention regulation. It substituted 'reasonable cause to believe' when it came to the grounds for detention for the original proposal of 'if satisfied that'.

It was on the basis of that substitution that Lord Atkin held that a court was entitled to more than the government's say-so that an individual is a security risk, thus seeking to make the scheme into something better. The majority disagreed on the basis that it was inappropriate in wartime for judges to go beyond the mechanism explicitly put in place, the toothless review committee. Lord Atkin thus accused his fellow judges of being more executive-minded than the executive and of acceding to arguments that had not been put to a court since the days of the Star Chamber.[52]

In my view, *Liversidge* is best understood as the second episode in the story of a particular rule-of-law project in Britain—the project in which the writ of the rule of law progressively extends. The first episode is Lord Shaw's insistence in *Halliday* on what we would call today a 'clear statement rule', the rule that the legislature must expressly delegate authority to infringe fundamental rights, and which had the result that the explicit authorization to detain was put into the Emergency Powers (Defence) Act 1939. That subjection meant that the question of the content of the regulation as well as the question whether there should be such a regulation came up for debate in Parliament, instead of being regarded as matters of executive prerogative. And, as we have seen, debate on the former question led to the substitution in wording.

Here we see at work the process that I have claimed produces a kind of legal surplus value. When public policy is given statutory form, it is converted into a set of public standards. That conversion process adds value because it creates the potential for the operation of rule-of law principles. In addition, Lord Atkin tried to realize that potential in inferring from the substitution and from the very existence of the executive committee that the legislature did intend that some meaningful review of detention decisions was not only possible but also desirable. That is, he tried to show that the first conversion enabled the second kind of conversion to take place, one in which issues arising out of the legislative regime are 'converted into a claim of right or an accusation of guilt'.

Moreover, in the leading speech for the majority in *Liversidge*, Viscount Maugham said that if an appeal against the Home Secretary's decision 'had been thought proper, it would have been to a special tribunal with power to inquire privately into all the reasons for the Secretary's action, but without any obligation to communicate

[52] *Liversidge* (cited in n 25) 244.

them to the person detained'.[53] He too therefore thought that review is possible, even desirable, though he did not think it was possible in the absence of institutional innovation.

The combination of the insights in these two speeches is important. On the one hand, if the detention situation under Regulation 18B was such that judges who insisted on their authority to review would not be able effectively to review, one might see Atkin's dissent as not only complicit in maintaining the grey hole created by the existence of the executive committee plus the substitution of wording; for one could argue that he made things worse by adding another layer—(ineffective) judicial review—to the veneer and thus made no difference to the reality of the black hole of indefinite detention. Put differently, toothless executive committee + toothless judges ≠ teeth.

On the other hand, even if, as Maugham with quite exceptional prescience insisted, effective review required legislative intervention in order to create an institution 'with power to inquire privately into all the reasons for the Secretary's action', that would not suffice. Not only would there be an obvious problem if the inquiry had to happen, as Maugham seemed to think (again with exceptional prescience), 'without any obligation to communicate [the reasons] . . . to the person detained'. In addition, if that inquiry were shielded from judicial review, it would seem that the executive was policing itself on decisions which involved drastic deprivations of liberty. Indeed, one consequence would be that the problematic aspects of the bar on communication that Maugham thought would be necessary might not come to light. And just this constellation of issues makes up the matrix to which *Halliday* and *Liversidge* gave rise. For the kind of innovation Maugham appeared to contemplate was instituted when the UK Parliament responded to an adverse decision of the European Court of Human Rights in *Chahal*[54] on the procedure for review of deportation decisions on national security grounds.

The innovation[55] created the Special Immigration Appeals Commission (SIAC), a three-person tribunal, chaired by a High Court judge, with the other two providing expertise in immigration and security. It was created as a superior court of record, with full authority to review immigration decisions made on national security grounds. The tribunal, whose members are security cleared, has access to all the information on which the executive bases its claims and the services of a security-cleared special advocate to test the executive's case on issues where the individual and his legal representative are excluded because of the sensitive nature of the information. However, the special advocate is not permitted to communicate with the individual or his legal representative once he has seen the material considered by the Home Secretary to be 'closed', material that can be considered only in a session from which the individual and his legal representative are excluded. The special advocate can contest the decision of the Home Secretary and SIAC decides issues about disclosure when the special advocate and the Home

[53] Liversidge (cited in n 25) 220–2.
[54] *Chahal v United Kingdom* (1996) 23 EHRR 413 [*Chahal*].
[55] Special Immigration Appeals Commission Act 1997.

Secretary cannot reach agreement. However, the Home Secretary can always decide not to rely on information in order to avoid having it disclosed. Since in most, perhaps all, cases the information in the closed sessions is the effective basis for the decision by SIAC, the prohibition on communication severely hamstrings the special advocate's ability to test the evidence to the extent that several have refused to continue in the role and have publicly expressed their disillusionment with it.[56]

After 9/11, legislation was enacted that created a system of indefinite detention for aliens who were considered security risks but who could not be deported because of the risk they would be tortured or otherwise badly treated. When the House of Lords in *Belmarsh*[57] declared the system incompatible with the European Convention of Human Rights, mainly because it discriminated against aliens by reserving indefinite detention on national security grounds for them, the system of control orders was brought into being by the Prevention of Terrorism Act 2005, and applied to both citizens and aliens who were considered security risks. The Administrative Court, a division of the High Court, was thus made the primary review body.

Both the *Belmarsh* decision and the system of control orders have generated a vast body of analysis, and here I want to highlight only those features of the control order system that are most pertinent to my argument.

When the control order system was introduced, the statute distinguished between non-derogating and derogating control orders, with the latter being those that interfered with the liberty interest protected by the European Convention on Human Rights Art 5 to the extent that, in terms of Art 15, both Houses of Parliament would have to approve a derogation order. Naturally, the executive resorted only to what it alleged to be non-derogating control orders, orders whose restrictions fell short in the opinion of the Home Secretary of a deprivation of liberty. At the first stage, the order was generally made *ex parte*, without the participation or knowledge of the person suspected of involvement in terrorist activities, and the court could refuse to grant the order only if it considered that the decision was 'obviously flawed'. Within seven days, the court had to hold another hearing, in which the individual and his or her lawyer can participate and challenge the order subject to the restrictions mentioned earlier. The test for quashing the order is again whether it is 'obviously flawed'. These orders gave rise to two sets of challenges, one based on whether a non-derogation order was invalid because it breached the Art 5 protection despite the Home Secretary's claim to the contrary, the other based on whether the constraints on the hearing for non-derogating orders breached the Art 6 protection to the right to a fair trial. Both sets of

[56] For a comprehensive account of the process, see D Bonner, *Executive Measures and National Security: Have the Rules of the Game Changed?* (2007) Pt III. For the most recent public expression of disillusionment, see the Response by a group of special advocates to the 'Justice and Security Green Paper' (CM 8194), <http://adam1cor.files.wordpress.com/2012/01/js-green-paper-sas-response-16-12-11-copy.pdf>. See also the response of the Bingham Centre for the Rule of Law, <http://www.biicl.org/files/5829_bingham_centre_response_to_green_paper.pdf>.

[57] *A and Others v Secretary of State for the Home Department* [2004] UKHL 56, [2005] 2 AC 68 [*Belmarsh*].

challenges raise illuminating questions about the role of judicial review in a preventive justice system and about the connection between process and substance.

In *Secretary of State for the Home Department v JJ*,[58] drawing on jurisprudence from the Strasbourg Court, the House of Lords quashed several allegedly non-derogating control orders on the basis that they were inconsistent with the European Convention on Human Rights Art 5 because they crossed the threshold between a mere restriction on liberty and a deprivation of liberty. The control orders in question involved confinement to a small flat for 18 hours a day, forced relocation to a new location, electronic tagging, monitored telephone access, restrictions on visitors, and being subject to police searches at any time without warning.[59]

Unlike the Australian High Court majority in both *Thomas*[60] and *Totani*,[61] the majority of the House of Lords made it clear that what mattered was the impact of the restrictions on the life of the controlee, that is, on whether the restrictions amounted to a deprivation of liberty. However, Lord Hoffmann in his dissent stated that only the full deprivation of liberty (ie prison) should count as a breach of Art 5 so as to avoid placing 'too great a restriction on the powers of the state to deal with serious terrorist threats to the lives of its citizens'.[62] He therefore accepted the executive's view that seemingly unqualified rights may need to take different meanings in national security contexts and showed himself to be committed to much the same position as Heydon in *Thomas*.[63]

Moreover, while Lord Brown joined the majority, he indicated that a 16-hour curfew would have been acceptable,[64] and in subsequent decisions the House of Lords upheld curfews of 12 and 14 hours. As Helen Fenwick and Gavin Phillipson have pointed out, this kind of accommodation by the courts was interpreted by the government to show judicial support for curfews of up to 16 hours.[65]

The very same point can be and has been made in respect of the procedural challenges in terms of Art 6. In *Re MB*, the decision in which Sullivan J made the remark about the 'thin veneer' of legality, that remark was the conclusion to his observation that the procedure under the Act was 'conspicuously unfair'.[66] He then made a declaration of incompatibility under the Human Rights Act 1998 s 4.[67]

If the Court of Appeal had left Sullivan J's judgment in place it would have been a powerful political statement that the control order regime was repugnant to human rights, though unless the government chose to respond positively, there

58 [2007] UKHL 45.

59 *Secretary of State for the Home Department v JJ* (cited in n 58) para 60, Baroness Hale of Richmond.

60 *Thomas* (cited in n 34).

61 *Totani* (cited in n 29).

62 *Secretary of State for the Home Department v JJ* (cited in n 58) para 44.

63 *Thomas* (cited in n 34).

64 *Secretary of State for the Home Department v JJ* (cited in n 58) para 105.

65 H Fenwick and G Phillipson, 'Covert Derogations and Judicial Deference: Redefining Liberty and Due Process Rights in Counterterrorism Law and Beyond' (2011) 56 McGill Law Journal 863, 880–81, their emphasis, notes omitted.

66 *Re MB* (cited in n 22) para 103.

67 *Re MB* (cited in n 22) para 104.

would have been no relief for the controlee. But the Court of Appeal chose instead to rely on the interpretive obligation in the Human Rights Act 1998 s 3 that requires courts to endeavour to show that a statute complies with Convention Rights by reading into the Prevention of Terrorism Act 2005 a greater level of judicial scrutiny than Sullivan had contemplated.[68]

The choice between these remedies places the courts in a complex dilemma, most sharply illustrated by the decision of the House of Lords in *Secretary of State for the Home Department v AF (No 3)*.[69] Following the decision of the Strasbourg Court in *A v United Kingdom*,[70] the House of Lords found that Art 6 required that an irreducible minimum of disclosure be made, allowing a controlee to know the substance of the case against him, regardless of the consequences for national security. Lord Hope of Craighead said:[71]

> If the rule of law is to mean anything, it is in cases such as these that the court must stand by principle. It must insist that the person affected be told what is alleged against him.

*AF* is a powerful statement that, even when national security is at stake, some minimal standards of procedural fairness will apply. The fact that the House of Lords needed to read in additional procedural requirements showed that the control order regime under the Prevention of Terrorism Act 2005 had not previously provided such minimal standards. And yet, the government used even such a seemingly rights-affirming example of reading down to claim not only that the judges endorsed the whole control order system, but also that the endorsement showed that the system was intrinsically compliant with human rights.[72]

The particular features of the dilemma are shaped by the legal context but its nature is quite general. On the one hand, that a declaration of incompatibility based on s 4 leaves the regime unaffected should the government and Parliament decide not to respond means that those who challenged the regime get no relief. On the other hand, provision of relief by way of an interpretation of the regime based on s 3 gives the challengers what they sought to achieve and makes the regime into one that is somewhat better from the perspective of legality. The assessment of how much better is complicated because a declaration based on s 4 taints the regime with illegitimacy, whereas an interpretation based on s 3 bestows legitimacy, which, if the gain from the perspective of legality is slight, permits the government to have

[68] *Secretary of State for the Home Department v MB* [2006] EWCA Civ 1140.

[69] *Secretary of State for the Home Department v AF* [2009] UKHL 28 [*AF*]. *AF* also illustrates the difference that being deprived of information can have on a court. The same case had previously reached the House of Lords as *Secretary of State for the Home Department v MB and AF* [2007] UKHL 46 and in that decision the Court was unclear whether there ought to be an irreducible minimum of disclosure provided to controlees. Part of the reason for this failure to state an equivocal rule was an exceptionally optimistic view of how well the Special Advocate system worked. An intervention by Special Advocates in *AF* convinced several judges that the system could in fact not be relied upon so heavily. See in *AF* the speeches of Lord Hope of Craighead, paras 78–9, and Baroness Hale, paras 104–6. See also A Kavanagh 'Special Advocates, Control Orders and the Right to a Fair Trial' (2010) 73 MLR 836.

[70] [2009] ECHR 301.

[71] *AF* (cited in n 69) para 84.

[72] For a detailed and very perceptive discussion, see Fenwick and Phillipson (cited in n 65) 901–10, especially at 903, and Kavanagh (cited in n 69) 836.

nearly all of its cake, perhaps even the whole, and eat it too. And that raises questions about how much protection a human rights regime actually provides.

In addressing this dilemma, judges, as we saw Simpson suggest, have no choice but to champion the rule of law, even if it is the case that the result might be, as Heydon conjectured in *Totani*, that governments are tempted 'into legislating to exert their coercive power through means other than their courts'.[73] Recall that the dilemma, as Heydon depicted it, was between damage to the rule of law either because the statute is valid and therefore civil liberties are undermined or because the statute is not valid and therefore government cannot fulfil its obligation to protect its residents.[74]

But that depiction is mischievous. It stipulates that government cannot fulfil its obligation to protect its residents at the same time as permitting judges to play a role within a legal regime that builds in appropriate rule-of-law protections for those who are the subject of coercive measures. In addition, it countenances that one would have the rule of law, albeit a diminished rule of law, when a statute permits officials to interfere drastically with individuals' right to liberty, at the same time as barring their recourse to an independent tribunal to test the legality of the officials' decisions.

Moreover, Heydon's invocation of Coke to give common law respectability to his line of argument is misleading. Coke's remark that 'preventing justice excelleth punishing justice' was made in the context of civil liability—it occurs in a discussion of the virtues of a writ that prevents a tenant from damaging a property over an action after the damage is done.[75] Indeed, in the passage from Coke's *Institutes* from which the epigraph to my chapter is taken, he recognizes that preventive justice may work to prevent crimes, but describes the experience of its work as 'woeful'.[76]

For Coke, it seems clear, the 'safety' of the 'loyal subjects' of the king is best secured by putting in place a regime of criminal law where the particular laws meet a criterion of 'express and defined certainty', are 'equal between the king and all his subjects', and are 'rightly understood and duly executed'. It also seems clear that he thought that the domain of preventive justice should be confined to education, to ensuring the 'execution of good laws', and to confining use of the power to pardon those who have been convicted of crimes under the regime of punitive justice. It is consideration of this domain that Coke considers 'worthy of a parliament' of a sort that he considers it would be an honour to construct.[77] And it is to the theme of how a wise parliament deals with preventive justice that I now turn.

## E. The reason-demanding Parliament[78]

The failings of the special advocate system developed in the UK must trouble any argument that preventive justice measures in the context of national security can be

[73] Text to note 43. [74] Text to note 43.
[75] Coke, *Second Institutes*, 299. [76] Sir Edward Coke, epilogue to his *Third Institutes*, 243.
[77] Coke (cited in n 76) 243.
[78] I explore the idea of a reason-demanding Parliament in 'Deference, Security and Human Rights' in BJ Goold and L Lazarus, (eds), *Security and Human Rights* (2007) 125, 146–54.

made subject to rule-of-law protections. However, the adoption of a more refined version of the same kind of system in Canada with more scope for reviewing judges to order disclosure of information is instructive. This version provides a better basis for challenges by the subjects of control orders, with the result that a Canadian Federal Court judge has ordered the unconditional release of one high-profile subject of preventive justice measures because the executive withdrew evidence that the judge had ordered could be disclosed without compromising national security, and the executive was unwilling to have it disclosed.[79] In addition, the Administrative Court in the UK has found itself able in light of the enhanced procedural protections read into the Prevention of Terrorism Act 2005 on the basis of the Human Rights Act 1998 s 3 to review much more effectively the control orders that are challenged before it.[80]

To put the most optimistic gloss on the situation possible, one could say that the UK learned through *Chahal*[81] from Canada of an institutional innovation—the special advocates system.[82] Canada then relearned that lesson, but improved the innovation in light of the UK experience.[83] Hence, one could also say that courts and other institutions are now grappling with the problem of how to ensure that, both substantively and procedurally, this family of preventive justice measures is subject to the discipline of the rule of law.

This is of course the most optimistic gloss. Reasons for pessimism go beyond the customary Australian exceptionalism and the fact that in the USA the legislature never asserted proper control over the family of measures that was put in place in reaction to 9/11, a failure in large part attributable to the fact that the Supreme Court never insisted that Congress enact a statute that clearly stated that liberty had to be abridged because of a situation of national emergency and that put in place a legal regime that met Coke's criterion of 'express and defined certainty', that treated all subject to it as equal before the law, and that could be said to be 'rightly understood and duly executed'.[84]

Consider, also, that while the TPIMs will be less severe in their effect on the liberty of the individuals subject to them, and that the threshold for imposing the measures has been raised from 'reasonable suspicion' to 'reasonable belief', as the Joint Committee on Human Rights (JCHR) has noted, the standard remains lower than the civil standard of proof on the balance of probabilities, there is no full

[79] *Re Charkaoui* 2009 FC 1030 (CanLII) 353 FTR 187.

[80] See Tomkins (cited in n 21).

[81] *Chahal* (cited in n 54).

[82] In fact, the European Court of Human Rights' understanding of the Canadian situation was inaccurate.

[83] G Hughes, 'The Administration of Justice? Certificate Proceedings, *Charkaoui II*, and the Value of Disclosure' (2010) 48 Alberta Law Review 196. For constructive suggestions about how to improve things, see C Forcese and L Waldman, 'Seeking Justice in an Unfair Process: Lessons from Canada, the United Kingdom, and New Zealand on the Use of "Special Advocates" in National Security Proceedings', available at <http://ssrn.com/abstract=1623509>.

[84] D Dyzenhaus, 'The "Organic Law" of *Ex Parte Milligan*' in A Sarat (ed), *Sovereignty, Emergency, Legality* (2010) 16 and for a comprehensive account, Roach (cited in n 7) ch 4, 'The United States Responds: Executive Power and Extra-Legalism'.

merits review, and the disclosure obligation from *AF*[85] is not fully implemented.[86]

However, the JCHR's main concern is not so much with these issues as with the fact that TPIMs, like the control orders they replace, are 'essentially executive orders interfering severely with individuals' most fundamental liberties, on the basis of information not available to the individual, without any prior judicial authorisation.' They thus violate 'the well-established principle . . . that executive restrictions on liberty are such a radical departure from our common law tradition that they always require prior judicial authorisation after proper legal process'. 'It is', the JCHR continued, 'for the Government to justify this Bill's departure from that fundamental principle'.[87]

In its earlier report, the JCHR discussed with approval Lord Macdonald's review of counter-terrorism powers in which he argued that 'restrictions on the freedoms of terrorist suspects are only justifiable in constitutional and human rights terms if they are part of a continuing criminal investigation into their activities'.[88] In addition, the JCHR quoted Lord Macdonald's claim that 'where the Home Secretary is declaring to the High Court that she has reasonable grounds to believe that an individual is involved in terrorist activity, it would be utterly perverse if there were not to be a coterminous criminal investigation into that individual'.[89]

My own claim is that this perversity has become more pointed as government and Parliament have responded, however half-heartedly, to adverse judgments, public criticism, and the criticism of parliamentary bodies such as the JCHR. Indeed, as things inch closer to more substantive review of executive decisions and fuller due process, so the issue might seem less like perversity and more like absurdity that the preventive justice measures are not either made incidental to criminal proceedings or even replaced by them. Note that these developments necessarily travel together, since more due process makes substantive review possible and more substantive review seeks the kind of disclosure and testing of information that due process provides. There is then a plausible case for maintaining that a virtuous cycle of legality is not only possible but also actual when it comes to the family of preventive justice measures discussed in this chapter.[90]

Moreover, with such developments the distinction between preventive and criminal or punitive justice might start to seem a distraction from what should be the main task, which is to ensure that when the state restricts the right to liberty

[85] *AF* (cited in n 69).

[86] See Human Rights Joint Committee, *Twentieth Report Legislative Scrutiny: Terrorism Prevention and Investigation Measures Bill (Second Report)* 1.8; available at <http://www.publications.parliament.uk/pa/jt201012/jtselect/jtrights/204/20402.htm>.

[87] Human Rights Joint Committee, *Twentieth Report* (cited in n 86) 1.6, emphasis removed.

[88] *Review of Counter-Terrorism and Security Powers: A Report by Lord Macdonald of River Glaven QC* (Cm 8003, 26 January 2011); see Human Rights Joint Committee, *Sixteenth Report Legislative Scrutiny: Terrorism Prevention and Investigation Measures Bill*, at 1.16; available at <http://www.publications.parliament.uk/pa/jt201012/jtselect/jtrights/180/18002.htm>. Of course, one could easily imagine lip service being paid to this requirement, but that is true of any such requirement. The point is that one has to work on two fronts: putting the requirements in place and nurturing the culture that gives substance to them.

[89] Human Rights Joint Committee, *Sixteenth Report* (cited in n 88) 1.20.

[90] See F de Londras, *Detention in the 'War on Terror': Can Human Rights Fight Back?* (2011).

that restriction is appropriately justified. For once one comes to appreciate how legality both should and can discipline preventive justice measures, one can see that concerns about legality should be focused as well on the justifications for pre-trial and immigration detentions, which should not so easily be left to bask in the legitimacy of their objectives.

Finally, there is the vexed issue of the legitimacy of the objective. To a large extent, that question is one which cannot be settled by abstract moral argument. The ideal of the rule-of-law project is a political one, the ideal of having in place a 'culture of justification', one in which 'every exercise of power is expected to be justified; in which leadership given by government rests on the cogency of the case offered in defence of its decisions, not the fear inspired by the force at its command'.[91]

According to this ideal, the legitimacy of an objective is in large part dependent on its legality—whether it can be framed within a law of general application, and whether the means set out in the law to achieve that objective can satisfy a proportionality analysis that becomes progressively more stringent according to the impact of the legal regime on liberty and equality. This is the test I have described in other work as finding out whether an objective is 'legalizable', that is, capable of being realized within a regime of legality.[92]

I say 'in large part' because it is a mistake to suppose that the culture of justification kicks in after a statute has been enacted. A wise parliament is a reason-demanding institution, one which does not delegate entirely the task of making a legal regime human-rights- and rule-of-law-compliant to courts which perform a Human Rights Act 1998 s 3 type interpretive approach, however their legal order makes this possible. Rather, it puts in place institutions and practices that force legislators to focus on questions of legality and human rights prior to the reduction of a political programme to the explicit terms of a statute. The surplus value that is produced by the kind of public standard that this exercise creates is greatly enhanced if the legislators not only put in place institutions like the JCHR, but also make themselves and their legislation answerable to the concerns that are raised by the institution prior to the enactment of a statute.

We are now in a position to see why it is a mistake to suppose that judges are the only significant actors when it comes to review after the statute has been enacted. First, and following the last point about parliaments, for the rule-of-law project to succeed, each institution has to play its role. Grey holes are a serious problem and judges can do only so much to remedy them; but they are created in the first place by parliaments, not by judges. Secondly, just as parliaments cannot always be counted upon, so also to rely upon the judges might be to presuppose too easily a commitment by the judiciary to human rights that cannot safely be assumed.[93]

[91] E Mureinik, 'A Bridge to Where? Introducing the Interim Bill of Rights' (1994) 10 South African Journal on Human Rights 32.

[92] Dyzenhaus (cited in n 84) 45–7.

[93] See, for example, the polemic against such a commitment in the speech made by Jonathan Sumption just after his appointment to the UK Supreme Court: 'Judicial and Political Decision-Making: The Uncertain Boundary', The F A Mann Lecture, 2011; available at <http://www.legalweek.

Thirdly, and dampening the force of the second reason, because there are other significant actors, even judges who are not particularly committed to human rights find themselves operating in a culture that is not entirely of their own making and that imposes its own constraints. This is because some legal orders, and the UK is notable here, have gone some distance towards recognizing that there are certain tasks that have to be performed to maintain that commitment to which the judiciary is not best suited and so the legal orders have created institutions that are better fit for purpose.

Here we should recall that the UK's response to *Chahal*[94] put in place not only the special advocates system but also SIAC, a review body which combined in a very interesting fashion judicial, administrative, and intelligence expertise. *Rehman*[95] was a bad misstep by the House of Lords not only because of Lord Hoffmann's confusion of expertise legitimacy with democratic legitimacy. For the House of Lords also insisted that in the determination of national security the Home Secretary's view had to triumph over SIAC's; and that effectively narrowed SIAC's jurisdiction by requiring a degree of deference to the Home Secretary on the content of judgements about national security that was not dictated by the statute. Put differently, the House of Lords reduced the democratic mandate given to SIAC, a body better equipped than judges to evaluate claims by the security services, by asserting over it the expertise of the executive in a way that reinstated the kind of problem of arbitrariness to which both *Chahal* and the statute that created SIAC were a response.

It is significant that SIAC has recently reasserted its mandate in a compelling rebuke to Lord Hoffmann.[96] In my view, this reassertion is facilitated by other developments, in which the highest court in both of its incarnations, lower courts, the JCHR, and other institutions have played different but complementary roles. But the point is that there is so much human rights and rule-of-law furniture in place now that one should not overstate the importance of one particular piece.

Nevertheless, none of these developments should detract from the central role of the judiciary in the creation and maintenance of the institutional framework of a culture of justification. If judges find that they are operating within what the government may have intended to be a grey hole, they should not insult Parliament by attributing to it an intention that they should decorate decisions taken by the executive with the legitimacy that comes from judicial certification of a decision as according to law. Rather, they must take the legal regime that Parliament has provided and read into it whatever legal protections they can using the resources

com/digital_assets/3704/MANNLECTURE_final.pdf>. For a devastating response, see S Sedley, 'Judicial Politics' (2012) 34(4) *London Review of Books* 15, also at <http://www.lrb.co.uk/v34/n04/stephen-sedley/judicial-politics?utm_source=newsletter&utm_medium=email&utm_campaign=3404&hq_e=el&hq_m=1520086&hq_l=13&hq_v=1644b4ab18>.

[94] *Chahal* (cited in n 54).

[95] *Rehman* (cited in n 18).

[96] *Ektarina Zatuliveter and the Secretary of State for the Home Department*, Appeal No SC/103/2010 paras 4–8. There SIAC points out some of the tensions in the reasoning of the House of Lords in *Rehman* in order to reach a conclusion that rejects Lord Hoffmann's stance.

that will be made available to them, because they are working as judges within a legal order, and not as some other kind of official in some other kind of order; for example, the order Fuller described as managerial, in which the point of its structures is to make more efficient the transmission of commands from the top of the hierarchy to the bottom.[97]

Put differently, judges must always operate with the assumption that they are never in a legal grey hole, one that is in substance black with some trappings of the rule of law. But that requires them to assume that there is no such thing as a legal black hole. Indeed, while Lord Steyn's coinage of this term was effective as a condemnation of Guantanamo Bay, the idea that a space devoid of legal controls could be 'legal' is dangerous since legality always implies legitimacy and it is the judicial duty to champion the rule of law in the only way that can vindicate that implication.[98]

[97] Fuller (cited in n 9) 207.

[98] I am grateful to Arthur Chaskalson and Bernard Manin for setting me right on these issues.

# 6

# Pre-Trial Detention and the Presumption of Innocence

*RA Duff**

## A. Defendants, suspected terrorists, and the presumption of innocence

The Anti-terrorism, Crime and Security Act 2001 s 23 authorized the detention without trial of someone whom the Secretary of State certified (in accordance with the Act s 21) as being 'a suspected international terrorist'. That provision was controversial, and was declared by the House of Lords to be incompatible with the European Convention on Human Rights (ECHR) Arts 5 and 14—although on the narrow ground that the Act discriminated between UK nationals and others in a way that undermined the claim that derogation from the Convention was justified by the 'public emergency threatening the life of the nation' that international terrorism posed.[1] These provisions were repealed by the Prevention of Terrorism Act 2005 s 16. The 2005 Act provided instead for 'control orders' that placed often severe restrictions on those suspected of involvement in terrorist activity, breach of which would constitute a criminal offence. These provisions too proved controversial,[2] and have now been replaced by Terrorism Prevention and Investigation Measures (TPIMs), which involve fewer restrictions on liberty, but more surveillance and monitoring.[3]

Meanwhile, our prisons contain thousands of people who are detained awaiting trial: they have not been proved guilty or convicted (of the offences with which they are now charged), and thus must be presumed, as far at least as the criminal court is

* Many thanks for helpful criticisms and comments to Patrick Tomlin (my respondent at the Preventive Justice seminar at which an earlier draft of this chapter was discussed); to Andrew Ashworth and Lucia Zedner; and to the other participants in the seminar. I have also learned from Andrew Ashworth's as yet unpublished 'Preventive Detention and Criminal Procedure', and 'Negotiating the Fundamental Right to Liberty of the Person: Four Test Cases'.

[1] See *A v Secretary of State for the Home Department* [2005] 2 AC 68. The wider protests against this kind of detention were not, I think, based simply on this discriminatory dimension.

[2] See, eg, L Zedner, 'Preventive Justice or Pre-Punishment? The Case of Control Orders' (2007) 60 CLP 174; V Tadros, 'Justice and Terrorism' (2007) 10 New Criminal Law Review 658; and A J Ashworth and L Zedner, 'Preventive Orders: A Problem of Undercriminalization?' in RA Duff et al (eds), *The Boundaries of the Criminal Law* (2010) 59.

[3] Terrorism Prevention and Investigation Measures Act 2011.

concerned, to be innocent of the charges; but they are in prison because of those charges. In England and Wales 55,207 people were remanded in prison (hereafter, simply 'remanded') in 2009 to await trial; the pre-trial remand population on 31 March 2011 numbered 8,298; in 2009 the average time spent on remand was 12.3 weeks.[4] There are recurrent protests about the excessive use of pre-trial remand, and about the conditions under which those remanded are detained.[5] But the protests are not as widespread or as vociferous as those that greeted the provisions for the detention of people suspected of terrorism; there is widespread acceptance that some system of pre-trial remand is justified, even if it should be more modest in its scope, and less destructive in its conditions, than it is now. Such detention is sanctioned by the ECHR Art 5, if it is

> for the purpose of bringing [the detainee] before the competent legal authority on reasonable suspicion of having committed an offence or . . . is reasonably considered necessary to prevent his committing an offence or fleeing after having done so.

It is also sanctioned by the 'Tokyo Rules', which provide that

> Pre-trial detention shall be used as a means of last resort in criminal proceedings, with due regard for the investigation of the alleged offence and for the protection of society and the victim. . . . Pre-trial detention shall last no longer than necessary to achieve the objectives stated under rule 5.1 [ie the protection of society, crime prevention, or the promotion of respect for the law and the rights of victims], and shall be administered humanely and with respect for the inherent dignity of human beings.[6]

But this should strike us as odd: why should the detention of those suspected of involvement in something as seriously threatening as terrorism provoke so much louder protest than the far more frequent detention of those charged with, but not convicted of, far less serious crimes?[7]

There are of course significant differences between the two sorts of provision, an obvious one being that whereas the detention of someone suspected of involvement in terrorism could have been indefinite in duration, the detention of those remanded for trial lasts only until their trial, after which they will continue in detention only if convicted.[8] However, and particularly given the length of time

[4] All the figures are taken from the Prison Reform Trust, *Bromley Briefings Prison Factfile*, June 2011, p. 18. Available at <http://www.prisonreformtrust.org.uk/Portals/0/Documents/Fact%20File%20June%202011%20web.pdf>; see also R Walmsley, *World Pre-trial/Remand Imprisonment List* (2008); available at <http://www.prisonstudies.org/info/downloads/WPTRIL.pdf>; AJ Ashworth and M Redmayne, *The Criminal Process* (2010) 240–1.

[5] For some useful resources and references, see the Prison Fellowship International's *Report on Remand Prisoners*, available at <http://www.pfi.org/cjr/human-rights/vulnerable-populations/remand-prisoners>.

[6] United Nations Standard Minimum Rules for Non-custodial Measures (the Tokyo Rules), Rule 6; available at <http://www1.umn.edu/humanrts/instree/i6unsmr.htm>.

[7] Including defendants who are unlikely to face a prison sentence if convicted: the present Justice Secretary was thwarted in his ambition to rule out remand for such defendants (as reported in *The Guardian*, 29 June 2011, available at <http://www.guardian.co.uk/politics/2011/jun/29/kenneth-clarke-fresh-battle-sentencing-reforms>).

[8] I cannot discuss here the position of those remanded in custody after conviction, awaiting sentence.

that pre-trial detention can last,[9] the fact that the detention is limited in this way cannot be enough to render it morally unproblematic.

The rationale for pre-trial detention, like that for restrictions placed on those suspected of involvement in terrorism, is avowedly preventive. Under the Bail Act 1976, a defendant may be denied bail if the court is satisfied that there are substantial grounds for believing that the defendant, if released on bail (whether subject to conditions or not), would

(a) fail to surrender to custody, or
(b) commit an offence while on bail, or
(c) interfere with witnesses or otherwise obstruct the course of justice, whether in relation to himself or any other person.[10]

I will focus mainly on grounds (a) and (c), which are both aimed at ensuring that this defendant's trial can proceed properly. By contrast, ground (b) has to do with the risk that defendants will commit offences that might be independent of the alleged offence for which they face trial, and of the trial itself: I will argue later that even if pre-trial detention on grounds such as (a) and (c) can be justified, we cannot justify it on ground (b).

Amongst the considerations to which the court should attend in deciding whether to grant a defendant bail are:

(a) the nature or seriousness of the offence... (and the probable method of dealing with the defendant for it),
(b) the character, antecedents, associations, and community ties of the defendant,
(c) the defendant's record as respects the fulfilment of his obligations under previous grants of bail in criminal proceedings,
(d) ... the strength of the evidence of his having committed the offence.[11]

The 'general right to bail' that is recognized in s 4 of the Bail Act, and enshrined in the ECHR, creates a presumption in favour of bail; but that presumption can be defeated in the ways specified here.

Now the instrumental, consequentialist rationale for such provisions is obvious enough. It is important that those accused of criminal offences face trial and be available for punishment if convicted; that the trial process not be perverted or hampered; that the number of offences be reduced as far as possible. Those accused

[9] In 2002, 450 people spent more than 12 months on remand, while 900 spent between 6 and 12 months: see Ashworth and Redmayne (cited in n 4) 250.

[10] Bail Act 1976 s 4, Sch 1, Pt I, paras 2–6 (covering defendants charged with imprisonable offences; see Pt II for defendants charged with non-imprisonable offences); see Ashworth and Redmayne (cited in n 4) 236–8. For simplicity's sake I leave aside here a number of other grounds for denying bail that the Act specifies, to focus on these main reasons. See also Criminal Justice and Public Order Act 1994 s 25, which allows bail only under 'exceptional circumstances' for defendants charged with homicide, rape, or one of a list of other serious sexual offences if they have previously been convicted of such an offence.

[11] Bail Act 1976 s 4, Sch 1 Pt I para 9.

of criminal offences might be tempted to try to evade trial or to interfere with witnesses; since many of those charged with criminal offences are indeed guilty, they are also statistically more likely to commit offences whilst awaiting trial. So we have preventive reasons to subject those formally charged with criminal offences to restrictions that we do not impose on citizens generally. We must set such reasons against the defendant's interest in remaining at liberty, and against the costs and harms that pre-trial detention involves; we should therefore look for restrictions that are as mild and non-harmful as possible, and release defendants on bail, perhaps subject to any of a variety of restrictions, if we can safely do so. But if there is good reason to believe that only detention will suffice to guard against what would otherwise be the serious risk that a defendant will abscond, offend, or interfere with the trial process, the defendant's interests in liberty must be sacrificed to the interests of public safety.

Even if we take such an instrumental perspective, we must still ask why we should pick out criminal defendants for this kind of preventive treatment: should we not instead advocate a wider system of pre-emptive detention for anyone who is judged, on empirically reasonable grounds, to be likely to commit offences serious enough to warrant such costly measures? It might be argued that, given the notorious problems of finding reliable evidence on which to base predictions of future crime, it is empirically reasonable to attach significant evidential weight to the fact of being charged with a crime: if someone is facing trial, there should be 'sufficient evidence to provide a realistic prospect of conviction';[12] this surely makes it likely (more likely than is true of the population at large) that he is indeed guilty of a crime—and past offending is generally the best predictor of future offending. Since a guilty offender also has an obvious motive to abscond or to obstruct the course of justice, we might then claim to be justified in basing the predictions that remand requires on the other kinds of evidence that the Bail Act declares to be relevant—evidence that would not by itself suffice to ground such predictions.

It would be hard to establish whether this line of argument is strong enough to justify the drawing of such a sharp distinction between those who have not been charged with a crime (who may not be detained on suspicion of future crime unless they are mentally disordered), and those who have been charged, who may be detained on the basis of such suspicion. But I suspect that the general acceptance of a practice of pre-trial detention is not based on a purely consequentialist calculation of costs and benefits. Few of us are pure consequentialists: most agree that our pursuit of such consequentialist goals as crime prevention and public security must be constrained by respect for non-consequentialist demands of justice, which generally forbid the preventive detention of responsible agents who have not been convicted of a crime (I will discuss some apparent exceptions to this below). Two such constraints make pre-trial detention problematic.

[12] *Code for Crown Prosecutors,* available at <http://www.cps.gov.uk/publications/docs/code2010english.pdf> s 4.5.

The first is the requirement that we treat and respect each other, and that the state treat us, as responsible agents, who must be left free to determine their own actions until they commit a criminal wrong. It can be consistent with respect for another's responsible agency to coerce him (which might include forcibly detaining him) as an appropriate response to what he has already done, for instance by way of punishment; or in order to prevent him carrying through a wrong on which he has embarked, as when we use defensive force to intercept a criminal enterprise. If we can justify our coercive treatment as a response to what someone has done or is doing, we are not using the person 'merely as a means' to our ends; we treat her in a way that respects and responds to her own responsible agency.[13] However, pre-trial detention does not seem justifiable in either of these ways. It cannot be justified as a response to (or punishment for) what the defendant has done: he has not yet been proved to have done anything to which this could be a legitimate response. Nor is it justifiable as a defensive measure to prevent him from carrying through a wrong on which he has embarked. We could in this way justify using force to arrest a defendant who tries to abscond, and to bring him to trial: but pre-trial remand is pre-emptive rather than defensive; it coerces a defendant before he has the chance to decide whether to abscond or otherwise offend.[14] Another relevant constraint is found in the presumption of innocence (PoI). The PoI plays its most familiar, paradigmatic, role in the criminal trial: the court is not to subject a defendant to conviction and punishment unless she is proved guilty of the offence charged; and though the PoI's bare formulation is silent on the necessary standard of proof, it is natural to add that, at least when conviction and punishment are at stake, proof should be proof 'beyond reasonable doubt'. Now pre-trial detention is not (formally) punishment; it does not presuppose that the defendant is guilty of the crime for which she is to be tried (although if the defendant is convicted and sentenced to imprisonment, time spent on pre-trial remand can be counted towards that sentence as 'time served'). Furthermore, the focus of pre-trial detention is on future crimes rather than on alleged past crimes. So although the nature of the crime charged, and the strength of the prosecution's case, are factors to which the court must attend in deciding whether to grant bail, the court can still say to the defendant 'Whether you are guilty of the crime charged or not, we must detain you for these preventive reasons'. Nor indeed need the court presume that that the defendant would certainly commit the crimes that it aims to prevent: it must have 'substantial grounds' for a belief that he would do so, but that still leaves room for a recognition that he might not do so (that he might be a 'false positive'). It might therefore be argued that pre-trial detention, whatever other objections it may face, is formally consistent with the PoI.

However, it is not clear that such detention is really consistent with the PoI. First, whilst an innocent defendant might still be tempted to abscond, or to interfere with the trial process, from fear of a mistaken conviction, the risk that she

[13] For a useful discussion of the 'means principle', see V Tadros, *The Ends of Harm: The Moral Foundations of Criminal Law* (2011) ch 6.

[14] See further RA Duff, *Trials and Punishments* (1986) 139–40.

will do so is surely too small to warrant a preventive measure as coercive as detention. The 'substantial grounds for believing that the defendant, if released on bail', would abscond or obstruct the course of justice, on which the denial of bail depends,[15] must include the grounds for believing her to be guilty of the crime charged—which is on its face inconsistent with the PoI. Secondly, it is plausible to see the PoI as it operates in the criminal trial not as a separate demand of justice peculiar to the context of the criminal trial, but as an implication of a wider demand that the state should treat us (as we should treat each other in our civic lives) as both prospectively and retrospectively innocent until proved guilty. It would be very odd to insist that the state may subject us to the kind of coercion that constitutes punishment for a past offence only given proof of guilt, but to argue that the state may legitimately subject us to pre-emptive coercion that aims to prevent future crimes without proof that we would, if not thus coerced, commit such crimes; and if we are to be treated as responsible agents, proof that we will commit a crime must consist in proof that we have embarked on, or are at least preparing for, its commission. It is more plausible to say that the state should presume us to be innocent of both past and future crimes until the reverse is proved;[16] more precisely, in subjecting individuals to the kinds of punitive or preventive coercion that are taken to be warranted in relation to criminal conduct, it should presume us to be innocent of such conduct unless and until it is proved that we are not.

Any system of pre-trial detention thus faces the challenge that it seems to be inconsistent with the PoI, or with the values expressed in the PoI: inconsistent with the kind of respect, the presumption of law-abidingness, that we should expect from the state. If we then ask why this practice does not arouse more fervent opposition, or more serious questioning, one plausible answer might be that the defendant is seen as being in fact an offender, who awaits only the formal verdict of the court before receiving the punishment he deserves: that is why it is so easy (and so revealing) to slide into talking about the danger that the defendant will commit, not 'offences', but 'further offences' while on bail.[17]

Here then is the challenge. Can we show that some regime (even if not our own regime) of detention pending trial could be consistent with a plausible version of the PoI, and with the kind of respect that the state owes us as responsible citizens? If we cannot, can we then, with clear consciences, argue that we should abandon such detention as unjustified—whatever the costs of doing so might be? Or must we accept that this is a context in which the demands of justice and of respect for responsible agency must give way to the consequential demands of safety and security? This would be an uncomfortable stance to take, especially given the fact that the suspension or qualification of such demands is usually seen as justified only

15 Bail Act 1976 s 4; see text at n 10.

16 Cf J Floud and W Young, *Dangerousness and Criminal Justice* (1981) 44, on a citizen's 'right to be presumed free of harmful intentions'; see also D A Nance, 'Civility and the Burden of Proof' (1994) 17 Harvard Journal of Law and Public Policy 647, on the 'principle of civility'.

17 Thus even the Crown Prosecution Service, in its guidance on bail issues, talks twice of the risk that the defendant will commit 'further offences': available at <http://www.cps.gov.uk/legal/a_to_c/bail/#a03>.

in cases of 'national emergency'. The claim that the threat of terrorism created a 'public emergency threatening the life of the nation' was crucial to the British government's justification for the derogation from the ECHR Art 5 that detention of people suspected of involvement in terrorism involved;[18] so too, the internment of 'enemy aliens' in wartime can be justified (if at all) only on the basis of the urgent exigencies of war.[19] Both these kinds of detention are thus defended as extraordinary measures taken for a limited time in an emergency. Pre-trial detention, however, is part of the normal apparatus of criminal justice: it cannot be portrayed as an emergency measure justified by some extreme and temporary threat facing the nation.

Perhaps, however, I have overstated the challenge we face in trying to justify a system of pre-trial detention. It does involve a serious infringement of the freedom of people who have not been proved guilty of the crime of which they stand accused. However, first, we could try to reform (rather than abolish) our current practices of pre-trial detention, to make them less oppressive and more attentive to the PoI. This would involve not just seeking to minimize the length of detention, and the extent to which it disrupts the detainees' lives, and improving the conditions under which they are detained; it would also involve drawing a sharper and more public distinction between those who are remanded pending trial and convicted offenders—by, for one obvious instance, detaining them in separate facilities.

Secondly, pre-trial detention is not the only, even if it is the most onerous, burden that our systems of criminal justice lay on people who have not been convicted of a crime. Indeed, not only defendants (and suspects) are burdened. Giving evidence at a trial is burdensome, but is something that we may be required to do. Serving on a jury can be extremely burdensome, but is something that we may be required to do; indeed, juries may be sequestered (detained) during their deliberation or even during the trial.[20] I will return to jury sequestration later, but focus now on the burdens that may be laid on those who are suspected or accused of criminal offences. Those whom the police suspect of crimes may be subject to searches, questioning, even to detention. Those facing trial may have to post bail, ie guarantee a sum of money that will be forfeited if they do not appear for trial, or may be granted bail only subject to conditions that limit their freedom, including having to live in a bail hostel, having to report regularly to the police, surrendering one's passport, and staying away from specified places or people.[21] Standing trial is itself a burdensome process: the defendant is required to appear in court (on pain of arrest if she does not); even given a decent system of legal aid, this can be expensive, time-consuming, disruptive, and anxiety-inducing, even for the innocent. If pre-trial detention is inconsistent with the PoI, must we not say the same about these other kinds of burden that our criminal justice systems lay on those suspected or

[18] Under the terms of the Convention Art 15(1).

[19] Article 15(1) refers to 'time of war or other public emergency'. Even given such exigencies, of course, the detention of 'enemy aliens' was highly controversial.

[20] See, eg, M Strauss, 'Sequestration' (1996) 24 American Journal of Criminal Law 63.

[21] See J Sprack, *Emmins on Criminal Procedure* (13th edn, 2012) ch 6.

accused of committing offences? For to question or detain someone as a suspect, to require them to post bail or to accept restrictive requirements as conditions of staying free whilst awaiting trial, to require them to appear for trial, is to fail to presume them to be innocent (until proven guilty): it is not to presume them to be guilty; but it is to treat them as quite possibly guilty—as suspects.

We now have three options. First, we could hold that all these kinds of provision infringe the PoI. But to say that they are therefore unjustified in principle would be a *reductio*: the PoI cannot plausibly be taken to preclude any effective process of investigation and trial. To take this route would therefore commit us to saying that in such contexts the PoI can be justifiably infringed. In that case, however, it is not clear why pre-trial detention cannot also in principle be legitimate as a justified infringement of the PoI. Secondly, we could argue that the PoI does not apply outside the context of the criminal trial: police interrogations and detentions, bail conditions, and summoning defendants to trial do not presume innocence, but do not infringe the PoI, since they lie outside its sphere of application. In that case, however, we must say the same about pre-trial detention: whatever objections there may be to it, it does not infringe the PoI. Thirdly, we could argue that some version of the PoI does apply outside the criminal trial (to police investigations, to the process of bringing defendants to trial); but that the kinds of burden and restriction noted in previous paragraphs can be consistent with the PoI if it is properly understood as a feature of the practical attitude that a state should take towards its members. In that case, however, we cannot conclude so quickly that pre-trial detention must be inconsistent with the PoI: if these other kinds of burden and restriction can be consistent with it, why should not a (suitably reformed and limited) system of pre-trial detention also be consistent with it?

In the following section, I will pursue the third strategy. Space does not permit discussion of how the police can treat those suspected of criminal wrongdoing; but I will argue that both the process of putting someone on trial, and the imposition of certain kinds of restriction on those awaiting trial, while they implicate the PoI, can be shown to be consistent with it, once it is properly understood in the context of the idea of civic trust. Selective pre-trial detention, however, on the kinds of ground prescribed by our existing legislation, remains problematic, for reasons to be explained.

## B. Meeting the challenge?

I suggested earlier that we should ground the PoI, as it figures in the criminal trial, in the broader presumption that should guide the state's treatment of its citizens: it should presume us to be innocent of both past and future crimes until the reverse is proved; and in subjecting individuals to the kinds of coercion that may be warranted in relation to criminal conduct, it should presume us to be innocent of such conduct until it is proved that we are not. Such a presumption should also guide our conduct towards our fellow citizens.[22]

[22] I talk throughout the chapter of what citizens can demand or expect of each other, since I take it that the key moral role in a polity that aspires to be a liberal democracy is that of citizen. However, the

Apart from the general duties that we owe each other simply as human beings (duties not to attack or to unreasonably endanger each other, at least some duties of assistance), we also owe more particular duties to those with whom we live in society—to, in the political-legal context, our fellow citizens. Two dimensions of these are important here. On the one hand, we owe a certain kind of civic trust. This is not to say that we should go about our lives in a spirit of naively blinkered optimism: people might sometimes deplore the loss of those days when 'we never locked our doors', but the fact that we lock our houses and cars, and install burglar alarms and take other precautions against the possibility of being victimized, does not show that we have lost any sense of civic community—though it does speak to the extent to which fellow citizens are also very often strangers to each other.[23] But we do owe it to each other to recognize each other as fellows: not to assume in advance that others are enemies who might attack us, and against whom we need to guard ourselves. This kind of (modest) trust shows itself in our demeanour as we walk around the streets: in the fact that we do not normally cross the road to avoid others who are coming towards us (I'll comment shortly on exceptions to this), or take obvious defensive precautions against them; or in the fact that if someone approaches us we do not at once assume that their intentions are hostile. If, when I approach people to ask the way to my destination, they react by avoiding me, or taking up a defensive posture (or producing a defensive weapon), I have reason to feel insulted: not because they should realize that I, as a particular individual, am trustworthy, but because they have assumed, without a basis in anything I have done, that I am not.

On the other hand, however, we also owe certain kinds of (re)assurance to each other, to make clear to them that we can be trusted. Part of the basis for this duty lies in 'dominion' as a central value in a liberal republic: what matters is not just that others do not in fact interfere with us arbitrarily, but that we are *assured* of such freedom.[24] Trust and assurance are clearly interdependent: lack of assurance undermines trust; lack of trust generates a felt need to seek assurance. If we owe each other trust, we thus also owe the kinds of assurance that make trust possible. Such assurance may be given by our ordinary behaviour: we do not go about with a threatening or violent demeanour, we obey regulations and laws that aim to ensure safety.[25] But sometimes more than this is required. This can happen if my conduct

respect that is due to citizens is also due to residents or visitors who are not citizens, and who have the distinctive moral status of guests. See further RA Duff, 'Responsibility, Citizenship and Criminal Law' in RA Duff and SP Green (eds), *Philosophical Foundations of Criminal Law* (2011) 125.

[23] Matters become trickier when the precautions we take are directed against particular groups, rather than against the world at large; on these and other issues raised by 'situational crime prevention', see A von Hirsch, D Garland, and A Wakefield (eds), *Ethical and Social Perspectives on Situational Crime Prevention* (2000).

[24] See J Braithwaite and P Pettit, *Not Just Deserts: A Republican Theory of Criminal Justice* (1990). Lucia Zedner's work on security, and Peter Ramsay's on 'vulnerable autonomy', are relevant here: see L Zedner, 'The Concept of Security: an Agenda for Comparative Analysis' (2003) 23 LS 153 and *Security* (2009) ch. 1; P Ramsay, *The Insecurity State: Vulnerable Autonomy and the Right to Security in the Criminal Law* (2012).

[25] Thus, for instance, even if I know that I can drive as safely above the official speed limit as others can drive staying below it, I owe it to others to obey the speed limit, as a way of assuring them of my respect for the requirements of road safety: see RA Duff, *Answering for Crime* (2007) 166–72.

is such as to arouse reasonable fear. If I walk along carrying a realistic imitation gun (supposing that I have good reason for doing this), I owe it to others to find a way of assuring them that it is not real (and to explain myself if challenged); if I knock on a stranger's door late at night, I should stand back from the door to make clear that I have no intention of breaking in. Indeed, even if my behaviour is actually innocent in both fact and appearance, it might be appropriate for me to take steps to guard against the fear or suspicion that it might arouse: walking down an empty street at night, I see a woman coming towards me; realizing the anxiety that women walking alone might feel at the sight of an unknown man in this context, I cross the road or turn aside. (But care is needed here: we should not expect a black man walking down a street to cross the road because he knows that given his skin colour he might arouse anxiety in white people.)

Often the kinds of reassurance that we owe each other are given informally, without any involvement of the law. Sometimes, however, they are a matter of law. This is, for instance, part of the rationale for requiring those engaged in various kinds of risk-creating activity to have and display licences: to reassure others that the licence-holder's competence has been assessed. It is also part of the rationale for the range of airport security measures that confront travellers: as we pass through security screening, with our transparent bags of liquids, laptops removed from our briefcases, jackets, shoes, and belts taken off, part of what is going on is a matter of general mutual reassurance.

An important aspect of these kinds of measure is that they are undiscriminating: everyone engaged in the activity must have and display a licence; every traveller must pass through the same security measures. Matters are morally more problematic when such requirements are selective: we must then ask whether the criteria for selection are appropriate, which is not just a question of whether the criteria pick out those people who are empirically more likely to be dangerous. This is one of the problems in airport security, when members of particular groups are picked out for more stringent and intrusive security checks.[26]

Assurance or reassurance is also appropriate, both informally and legally, in the wake of misconduct. If I have behaved badly towards you, it is proper for me to offer, and perhaps for you to demand, assurances of my future good behaviour: I commit myself, for instance, to not missing classes in future, or to arriving on time for meetings. On some views, part of the aim of criminal punishment is also assurance: offenders owe their fellow citizens (re)assurance that they will not offend in future.[27] There are also legal provisions that can be understood as a matter of providing assurances. A person can be 'bound over' to 'keep the peace' or 'to be of good behaviour', as a civil measure, although he has not been convicted of any offence: this is intended as 'a measure of swift and effective preventative justice'.[28]

[26] On the issues raised by airport security, see (2006) 48(3) Canadian Journal of Criminology and Criminal Justice, June: a special issue on *Air Transportation and Risk Management*, J-P Brodeur (ed).

[27] See, eg, P Pettit, 'Republican Theory and Criminal Punishment' (1997) 9 *Utilitas* 59.

[28] See <http://www.cps.gov.uk/legal/a_to_c/binding_over_orders>; and Justices of the Peace Act 1968 s 1(7). Compare also the provisions for 'Acceptable Behaviour Contracts', which have no formal legal status, but are used in some areas in place of (or as preludes to) Anti-social Behaviour Orders

Provisions of this kind are normatively most plausible if two conditions are met: first, that even if they do not require a conviction, they require strong evidence of criminal conduct; secondly, that what they require from those concerned (what they are bound over to do, or what they contract to do) must not involve anything more restrictive or demanding than is anyway legally required of them. They are thus most likely to be justifiable if they are made in response to a complaint of criminal conduct supported by strong evidence (when a criminal charge is not pursued), and if all they require is that the person refrain from such criminal conduct in future: when used in this way they amount to formal warnings about the kinds of conduct that are criminal, and (when sureties are required) reinforcements of the law's demands; in agreeing to be bound over, those who are bound offer their own assurances of future good conduct.

Such provisions for binding over are obviously very like those for bail. We are, however, still a long way from making normative sense of pre-trial detention, or even of bail conditions that require anything more of defendants than to refrain from such already criminal conduct as failing to appear for trial or obstructing justice. We can see how further bail conditions can be justified by considering the difference that becoming a defendant could make to a person's normative status.

To become a defendant is to incur certain new duties or responsibilities. As a defendant, I am required to appear for trial, and am liable to be arrested and brought forcibly to court if I fail to appear. I am expected to enter a plea; depending on what the prosecution can prove, I might have to offer a response to the evidence against me if I am to avoid conviction, or offer a formal defence if it is proved that I committed the offence;[29] if convicted, I am expected to accept the judgment and sentence of the court. To summon a person to trial is not to presume that she is guilty, but it does put into public question the presumption that she is innocent of the crime charged. So if the PoI is to have any substance as a constraint on how the state can treat its members, it should protect us against being put on trial without adequate reason—reason that consists in the public provision of evidence that we have committed an offence. Now the PoI is *defeated*, in that the person may be treated as guilty, only if her guilt is proved 'beyond reasonable doubt'. We cannot set that as the standard that must be met before someone can be put on trial; but we can say that since the trial puts the PoI in question, it requires that we put someone on trial only given evidence of her guilt strong enough to constitute a case for her to answer, or strong enough to 'provide a realistic prospect of conviction'.[30]

Suppose then that I have become a defendant: I have a case to answer; there is substantial evidence that I have committed a crime. I thus acquire the responsibilities already noted, which (even given a decent system of legal aid) will be onerous.

(ASBOs): see RA Duff and SE Marshall, 'How Offensive Can You Get?' in A von Hirsch and A P Simester (eds), *Incivilities: Regulating Offensive Behaviour* (2006) 57, s III.3.

[29] On how such shifts in the burden of proof are consistent with the PoI see RA Duff, 'Presuming Innocence' in L Zedner and J Roberts (eds), *Principles and Values in Criminal Law and Criminal Justice: Essays in Honour of Andrew Ashworth* (2012).

[30] *Code for Crown Prosecutors* (cited in n 12) s 4.5.

I should, in a tolerably just polity, be willing to accept this burden and to discharge these responsibilities even if I am innocent: I should recognize the importance of responding to crime, and the value of a system that calls alleged offenders to public account; as a member of a polity living under law, I must be ready to answer to my fellow citizens if I am reasonably accused of violating our laws.

However, we also know that those accused of crimes, facing trial and possible conviction and punishment, have an incentive to abscond, or to interfere with the criminal process; other citizens may therefore reasonably fear that a defendant might try to abscond, or try to pervert the course of justice—a fear that will reasonably be greater the more serious the charge that the defendant faces. We might therefore now say that the defendant should reassure us that she will appear for trial, and not interfere with the criminal process; and (since words are cheap) that she back up her verbal reassurance with something more material—a financial bond or 'recognizance' that she will lose if she does not live up to this reassurance.[31] To require this is admittedly to say that we do not fully trust defendants: but as we have seen, the trust that citizens owe each other is a limited trust; we can in various contexts reasonably look for further assurances. Given the pressures created by facing trial, given the temptations that they can generate to abscond or to obstruct justice, given our awareness of our common human fallibility, we can see the context of a defendant awaiting trial as one such context.

This line of thought might justify a limited system of bail: defendants are required to post a bond that will be forfeited if they breach the terms of their bail; the two central terms are to appear for trial and not to interfere with the criminal process. But, first, it does not yet justify detaining defendants pending trial: it can justify detention only if this is necessary to prevent a defendant from carrying through an attempt to abscond or interfere (to be discussed below). Secondly, what is justified so far is a bail system that applies in the same way to, and imposes the same requirements on, all defendants (although it might justify varying the amount of the bond with the seriousness of the charges faced): we do not say to particular defendants that we do not trust them in the way that we trust other defendants; we say to all defendants (or all who are charged with a serious enough offence) that their distinctive normative status, which arouses reasonable anxieties in their fellow citizens, warrants requiring such reassurance from them.

Could this line of thought justify the imposition of more stringent restrictions or demands on defendants? Could it justify, for instance, requiring them to surrender their passports, so as to make it harder for them to leave the country; or to report regularly to a police station, so as to assure us that they have not absconded; or not to go near the homes of witnesses, to assure them of non-interference? We would have to ask how far such further requirements inhibit defendants' ability to lead a normal life, since we must try to minimize the extent to which facing a criminal trial disrupts a person's normal life. We would also have to ask what kind of reassurance it is reasonable to demand, and how far we must still trust people, although we

[31] Though we will need to ensure that the amount of the bond is relative to the defendant's means.

know that that trust will sometimes be broken. But we can certainly in this way render some kinds of bail condition normatively plausible, if they can be seen as ways of adding force to the reassurances that we can demand of defendants.

We can also justify a limited kind of pre-trial detention. If a defendant awaiting trial has provided the required assurances that he will not abscond or obstruct justice, but then tries to abscond or to obstruct, he can be legitimately detained, to prevent him from carrying through this attempt to frustrate the criminal process. The defendant has not yet been convicted of absconding or of attempting to obstruct justice, and if the reason for detaining him is to pre-empt any future attempts to frustrate the trial, it might be argued that we have no better reason to detain him than we have to detain those whom we suspect on other grounds of being likely to abscond or to obstruct justice (or that we have as good reason to detain them as we have to detain him).[32] However, the defendant's initial detention is not (merely) pre-emptive: it is justified not as pre-empting a predicted future crime, but as preventing the completion of a criminal enterprise on which he has already embarked;[33] and such coercion can be justified, without formal proof of guilt, if those applying it reasonably believe it to be necessary to prevent a crime that is in progress. If we ask what could justify detaining a defendant until trial, an answer might be that (provided the detention is short) this is still a matter of preventing him from continuing the criminal attempt on which he had embarked, and which he has given no sign of abandoning. Another answer might be that he, unlike other defendants, has shown by his own wrongful conduct that we cannot trust him to appear for trial and not to obstruct justice; we may therefore treat him as untrustworthy in this matter. What is of course crucial, in either case, is that if he denies that he was attempting to abscond or to obstruct justice, he must be entitled to a speedy hearing to determine that issue—and be freed if it is not proved that he was engaged in such an attempt.

If this second argument, that defendants who try to abscond or to obstruct justice have shown themselves to be untrustworthy and are therefore not entitled to be trusted in this matter, is sound, it *might* then be extended to defendants who have been proved on previous occasions to have tried to abscond, or to have tried to obstruct justice.[34] This raises issues that I cannot pursue here, about the effects that prior convictions can properly have on the extent to which we owe it to each other to restore civic trust after conviction and punishment;[35] in particular, when can we legitimately refuse to trust someone who has been convicted in the past not to commit the same kind of offence in the future? But even if we can in this way justify the pre-trial detention of those who try to abscond or to obstruct justice, *and* those

[32] Thanks to Bernard Harcourt for pressing this point.

[33] See text at nn 13–14.

[34] '[T]he defendant's record as respects the fulfilment of his obligations under previous grants of bail' is one of the factors to which courts are to attend in deciding whether to grant bail; see text at n 11.

[35] On the broader issues here about the 'collateral consequences' of punishment, see, eg, M Mauer and M Chesney-Lind (eds), *Invisible Punishment: The Collateral Consequences of Mass Imprisonment* (2002); H LaFollette, 'Collateral Consequences of Punishment: Civil Penalties Accompanying Formal Punishment' (2005) 22 *Journal of Applied Philosophy* 241–61. I have also learned from an as yet unpublished paper by Zach Hoskins, 'Are Ex-Offender Restrictions Morally Justified?'.

who have previous convictions for doing so, this still falls far short of justifying our existing system under which detention need not depend upon proved prior wrongdoing in relation to the criminal process, and requires only that there be 'substantial grounds' for suspecting future wrongdoing.

Note in particular that we cannot justify detention on the ground that the defendant might if left free commit offences other than absconding or obstructing justice.[36] We must presume the defendant to be innocent of the offence charged; since facing trial does not create an extra incentive to commit offences unconnected to the trial, we have no reason to think her more likely than other citizens to commit other offences; and even a prior record of offences, even of offences committed on bail, gives us no more reason to believe—or to act on a belief—that this defendant will commit such offences than we have to believe that other past offenders will commit new offences. Unless we are going to justify a general practice of pre-emptively detaining those whom we think likely to commit offences if left free,[37] we cannot justify this ground for denying bail; the fact that this person is facing trial cannot warrant her detention to prevent offences unrelated to her trial.

A different line of thought might now seem tempting. Someone accused of misconduct in the course of their profession might be suspended while the accusation is investigated: this is particularly likely when the alleged misconduct might lead to disqualification if it is proved. Such suspension has an obvious precautionary rationale: if the profession involves particular risks of harm from misconduct, and there are substantial grounds for thinking that this person has engaged in misconduct, we should play safe and suspend her in case the allegations are true, until we can establish whether they are true. Analogously, if a citizen is accused of committing an imprisonable offence, might we not be justified in, as it were, suspending him from participation in the normal life of the polity while the accusation is investigated? For imprisonment as a punishment amounts to a kind of suspension from normal civic life, and can be justified only by arguing that the offender's crime makes it morally impossible, for a time, to live with him in the ordinary civic realm, or to accord him the trust that is normally due to citizens;[38] if there is enough evidence to constitute a case to answer, perhaps we may play safe and suspend the person in the meantime? But as soon as we formulate the question we can see that its answer must be 'No'. Suspension from one's profession is indeed a serious restriction, from what might be an important part of one's life; but it is only part, and leaves much of normal life untouched. By contrast, pre-trial detention cannot but amount to a radical rupture from normal life. Analogies between parts and their wholes are often illegitimate and this is no exception: we cannot portray detention, as exclusion from normal life, as analogous to the suspension of one's licence to engage in a profession.

There are two other kinds of case in which people can be detained for preventive reasons without proof of wrongdoing for which such detention is a just punishment.

[36] The second factor that current law makes relevant to the question of bail or detention: see text at n 10.

[37] And this is not the place to discuss the justifiability of practices of pre-emptive incapacitation.

[38] This account of course implies that many fewer offences should be imprisonable than at present: see RA Duff, *Punishment, Communication and Community* (2001) 148–52.

Those suffering mental disorder of a type and severity that makes them a danger to others or themselves may be detained for assessment or treatment;[39] those suffering a notifiable infectious disease may be detained in hospital if 'proper precautions' against the 'serious risk of infection' to others cannot otherwise be taken.[40] However, neither of these cases is properly analogous to that of defendants awaiting trial.

The justification for detaining mentally disordered persons depends crucially not just on the risk they pose to themselves or others, but on a judgement that their disorder radically impairs their capacities for rational agency: they are legitimately detained only if their capacity to exercise rational control over their own conduct, and to deliberate rationally about their condition and its implications, is radically impaired. But if someone is rationally impaired to that degree, he is not fit to be tried:[41] the provisions for pre-trial remand apply to rationally competent defendants who must face trial, and the objection to such detention is precisely that it pre-empts the choices and actions of a responsible agent. Responsible agents ought to be left free to determine their own conduct, including their conduct in relation to the criminal law, and are properly liable to coercion only if and when they embark on a criminal enterprise. That is why the criminal law, on a traditional liberal understanding of its aims, is essentially reactive rather than proactive; that is why pre-trial detention remains normatively anomalous, since it aims to pre-empt what it is suspected the defendant might otherwise do.

The justification for quarantining someone with a dangerously infectious disease does not depend on her lack of rational competence; but it does depend on the fact that she cannot help endangering others if she goes out in the world—that 'proper precautions' cannot be taken to enable her to go about the world safely. If the risk to others is serious enough we could then justifiably require her to give up her freedom of movement for a time, by removing herself to and staying in a suitable place of quarantine. Provisions for compulsory detention could then be justified for people who refuse to obey such a requirement: for those who refuse to remove themselves to hospital, or try to leave the hospital, are by those very actions exposing others to an unjustified risk of harm; it is therefore legitimate to use coercion to prevent them from carrying through such wrongfully dangerous conduct. By contrast, a defendant awaiting trial does not expose others to risk simply by going about in the world: whether he harms others or not will depend on his own voluntary actions as he goes about the world; it is within his power, as it is not within the power of the infectious person, to go about the world without doing the kinds of harm or wrong that his detention is supposed to prevent. We therefore cannot portray his detention, as we can that of a dangerously infectious person, as preventing him from carrying through an unjustifiably dangerous course of conduct on which he has embarked.

Or could we argue that if someone is charged with a serious enough crime, and there are 'substantial grounds for believing' that he would, if left free, try to abscond or to obstruct the course of justice, he can discharge his duty to reassure his fellow

[39] See Mental Health Act 1983 Pt II.
[40] See Public Health (Control of Disease) Act 1984 ss 37–8.
[41] See Criminal Procedure (Insanity) Act 1964 ss 4A–5.

citizens only by subjecting himself to detention, because just by going about in the world he would arouse reasonable anxiety in his fellows; so that in detaining him we are merely enforcing a duty of reassurance that he already has? But this is not plausible. It is one thing to insist that a person accused of wrongdoing should offer assurances, backed by a financial bond, of her good behaviour; and perhaps that she should also accept some restrictions on her movements and activities, to make clear that she is not going to abscond or obstruct justice: such measures still allow her to lead much of her normal life with her fellows. But to require her to accept detention is to require her to accept the suspension of normal life, and removal from her fellows—as if we already know that she is rationally incompetent, or involuntarily dangerous, or criminally guilty; and that cannot be justified by the argument offered so far. We must bear in mind too that what justifies the demand for reassurances, and for restrictions that will give them material force, is not the mere fact of anxiety among others, but the reasonableness of that anxiety, and of the steps that we take in order to allay it. We might have empirically good reason to believe that a person will commit a certain type of crime, but we do not generally think it reasonable to detain him in order to prevent that commission; one aspect of a liberal democracy that treats its members as responsible agents is that those members must be willing to accept some kinds of risk, in particular the risk that others will offend against them. The fact that the person we suspect of future criminality has been charged with (but not convicted of) an offence cannot make it reasonable to detain her as if she is already guilty.

One final argument should be briefly discussed. I have already noted that juries are sometimes sequestered during their deliberations or even during the trial, if this is thought necessary to protect them (and thus protect the trial), against interference.[42] This practice surely does not violate the PoI in relation to the jurors: it does not reflect an assumption that they are corrupt; and while it is burdensome for them, it is surely a kind of burden that citizens can properly be asked to bear as part of their contribution to the common good. So can we not say the same of defendants who are detained: that this is a burden that even innocent defendants can properly be expected to bear for the sake of the integrity of the criminal process? We might add that this is not a case in which citizens have their interests set back for the sake of a good that will benefit only others: for all, including those detained (so long, at least, as the detention is as non-onerous and non-stigmatic as possible), benefit from the protection of the trial process.[43]

There is, however, a crucial difference between jury sequestration and the selective pre-trial detention that we practise. When a jury is sequestered, the whole jury is sequestered: we do not decide that this or that juror is not to be trusted, or is vulnerable, while others are not; all are sequestered together, on the basis of an assessment of the external risk of interference (and of the seriousness of the case). In sequestering a jury, we are therefore not saying, to the individual jurors, 'We do not trust *you*'. Their position is more like that of a defendant who is

[42] See text at n 20. Thanks to Carol Steiker for pressing this point.

[43] A point that could also be made about selective intensive screening at airports: see text at n 26.

required to accept restrictions placed on all defendants: we can justify the restrictions, I have argued, by pointing to the kinds of pressure or temptation to which defendants are subject as a normative category. The analogue to jury sequestration would therefore be a system under which *all* defendants (or all who face a charge of suitable seriousness) are detained. I am not sure whether this amounts to a *reductio* of the argument, or a possible way forward—towards a system of detention that we could justly impose on all defendants. What it cannot justify is a selective system under which we detain particular defendants because we will not trust them, as individuals, if that lack of trust is not based on present (or perhaps prior) attempts to commit the kinds of trial-related offence that the detention is meant to prevent.

## C. Where does that leave us?

In the previous section I explored the kinds of restriction we could reasonably impose on those awaiting trial on a criminal charge, consistent with treating them as responsible members of the polity, who are entitled, as we all are, to the presumption of innocence. We can justify a demand that they offer certain reassurances, and accept some limitations on their freedom, as ways of making clear, and of reinforcing, their commitment to appear for trial and to respect the criminal process. We can also justify detaining defendants under very limited circumstances: if they try to abscond, or to obstruct justice, we can detain them to stop them succeeding, and might be justified in detaining them until the trial; we might also be justified in detaining someone with a track record of prior breaches of bail. We *might* also be able to justify detaining *all* defendants facing charges of suitable seriousness. But we cannot justify the provisions that we now operate for selective pre-trial remands based only on the suspicion that the defendant will abscond or try to obstruct justice (and I argued earlier that we cannot justify detention to prevent defendants from committing other offences independent of their trial).

Where does that leave us? Perhaps I have missed some obvious rationale for this kind of provision, which shows that it is fully consistent with the respect and trust that citizens owe each other. Or perhaps I have exaggerated the importance or scope of that respect and trust: perhaps we should simply recognize that while in a happier world we would have no need for such measures, in our actual and imperfect world, of radically fallible human beings, respect and trust are goods that we can aspire to actualize within the limits of what is realistic, but not categorical demands that must not be violated. But if I have neither missed nor exaggerated, we face a difficult choice.

We could, on the one hand, insist that our current provisions for pre-trial detention cannot be justified, and must be abandoned: that detention is only legitimate for defendants who try, or have tried, to abscond or to interfere with the course of justice.[44] One question, to which I don't know the answer, is how

[44] Or, perhaps, for defendants who have formally admitted their guilt of an imprisonable offence for which they are likely to receive a custodial sentence, but who have not yet been formally tried or sentenced.

dangerous that would be. Another question concerns the kinds of measure we could legitimately take to monitor those who would now be released on bail. What kinds of surveillance would be consistent with respect for defendants' rights?

Alternatively, we could insist that we must, for the sake of public safety and security, and for the sake of the integrity of the criminal process, maintain at least a limited practice of pre-trial remand for defendants who have not yet tried to abscond or to obstruct justice, if there are strong grounds for believing that they would do so if left free; but that we must recognize the moral cost of doing so—the fact that we treat detained defendants unjustly. A recognition of that cost should have implications for how such defendants are treated: for the conditions under which they are detained, and the efforts that must be made to allow them to maintain as much connection with their ordinary lives as possible; and for the compensation that may be due to them. (A similar point might be made about detention in order to prevent the commission of offences other than absconding or obstructing justice. Suppose there is strong evidence not only that this defendant committed the serious offence with which he has been charged, but that he is a serial offender who is very likely to offend again if freed whilst awaiting trial—or even that he has in the past committed such offences while on bail.[45] Am I really committed to arguing that even here, the likelihood that this defendant will, if left free, commit offences other than absconding or trying to obstruct justice cannot justify detaining him pending his trial?[46] I am, I think, committed to arguing that this would be inconsistent with the PoI, and that it thus presents us with a genuine dilemma: even if we should in an extreme case detain the defendant, we must recognize the moral cost—including the cost to *his* rights—of doing so.)

I cannot explore these two possible responses in more detail here, and am still uncertain which route we should take; but I hope that I have at least done enough to show how morally problematic our practice of pre-trial detention is.

[45] Thanks to Richard Lippke for pressing this point: he imagines the case of a defendant who has several prior convictions for rape with a distinctive MO, who is now charged with a rape that (according to the police evidence) involved the same MO, and perhaps also DNA evidence linking him to the crime; and perhaps also a record of prior rapes while on bail.

[46] See text at n 36.

# 7
# Controlling Risk

*Victor Tadros**

Prevention has recently come in for greater academic scrutiny than it has ever received, especially in the context of terrorism. This is unsurprising. In the ten years since the 9/11 attacks, both the civil law and the criminal law have been extended in controversial ways.

This chapter is about preventive detention in order to prevent serious criminal wrongdoing. We can call this preventive *criminal* detention. Preventive criminal detention involves depriving a person of his or her liberty where this person is deemed to pose a risk of committing, causing, or contributing to a criminal act. This is done to reduce or eliminate the risk that this person poses. My aim is to explore one question that is important in this more general context: when is it permissible to restrict a person's liberty to reduce the risk that this person will harm others? In particular, what difference does it make that there is only a risk of harm, a risk that is difficult to quantify, that restricting the person's liberty prevents?

To provide focus for this discussion I consider one modern form of preventive detention found in UK law: control orders.[1] I will sketch the many moral considerations that are relevant to evaluating control orders. I investigate only two of those considerations in any depth. First, to what extent is it wrong to deprive a responsible person of liberty in order to prevent him or her from acting wrongfully? Does the respect that we owe to responsible agents require us to presume that they will not act wrongfully even when we can predict that they might? I will suggest that, despite its popularity, this factor is less important than it has seemed.

Secondly, can we move directly from the claim that it is permissible to restrict a person's liberty to prevent that person from harming others to the claim that it is permissible to restrict a person's liberty to eliminate a risk of a more serious harm that that person will otherwise pose? That control orders are concerned with risk

* I am grateful to the audiences at the seminar at All Souls College and at the University of Bologna at Ravenna for discussion of my paper. I am also grateful to the volume editors, especially Patrick Tomlin who suggested a number of important changes, Antony Duff, Kim Ferzan, Jackie Hodgson, and Alec Walen for thoughtful written comments.

[1] Control orders have been abolished in the UK, at least in name, and replaced by what are called Temporary Prevention and Investigation Measures (TPIMs). I will continue to refer to these as control orders for reasons I will outline.

management has been widely noted, and many consider this a troubling feature of the regime.[2] However, a systematic evaluation of the moral significance of risk is elusive. A familiar utilitarian approach to risk analysis has received criticism.[3] But no fully developed alternative model of risk evaluation has been proposed.

The utilitarian approach to risk, I will suggest, might be quite supportive of control orders. Furthermore, it is quite difficult to find non-consequentialist arguments to resist this approach. I will suggest that one approach that might have some promise focuses on the idea that utilitarian approaches to risk fail to do justice to the separateness of persons. It is quite difficult to assess the significance of this argument.[4] There is promise in an anti-utilitarian attack on control orders, then, but decisive arguments are difficult to come by.

## A. Control Orders

Since 9/11, the UK has adopted controversial measures to reduce the risk of terrorist attacks. The criminal law has been used, and part of the rationale for the expansion of terrorist offences is preventive. And some non-criminal, or perhaps better, quasi-criminal, legal techniques have been used. The Anti-Terrorism, Crime and Security Act 2001 (ACTSA) Pt IV created the power to restrict the liberty of terrorist suspects without trial, resulting in the detention of a number of people in Belmarsh prison. When the House of Lords held those provisions to violate the UK's human rights obligations, in the celebrated case of *A v Secretary of State for the Home Department*,[5] they were repealed.

ACTSA Pt IV was replaced by a new set of provisions governed by the Prevention of Terrorism Act 2005 (PTA). The PTA created a set of powers that permit the state, through an action of the responsible Secretary of State (or in the case of derogating control orders, the courts), to restrict the liberty of terrorist suspects without trial. The restriction of liberty takes the form of 'house arrest', though the Labour Government that developed these provisions resisted this phrase.[6] The orders that restrict liberty are called 'control orders'.

The Coalition Government has reviewed the scheme. At least some members of the Coalition aimed to abolish it entirely. However, the final review of the use of control orders, conducted for the Government by Lord Carlile, found that control

[2] See, for example, L Zedner, 'Preventive justice or pre-punishment? The case of control orders' (2007) 59 Current Legal Problems 174.

[3] See J Waldron, *Torture, Terror, and Trade-Offs: Philosophy for the White House* (2010) chs 2 and 5; V Tadros, 'Justice and Terrorism' (2007) 10 New Criminal Law Review 658 and 'Crimes and Security' (2008) 71 MLR 940. Some still endorse utilitarianism. See E Posner and A Vermeule, *Terror in the Balance: Security, Liberty, and the Courts* (2007).

[4] This general criticism of utilitarianism, though not the form that it takes in this chapter, stems from J Rawls, *A Theory of Justice* (revised edn, 1999) 19–24, 160–8.

[5] [2004] UKHL 56.

[6] Even the first reviewer of the provisions, Lord Carlile, who is hardly a champion of civil liberties, more or less admitted the appropriateness of this label. See *First Report of the Independent Reviewer Pursuant to Section 14(3) of the Prevention of Terrorism Act 2005* (February 2006) para 43.

orders remain necessary for a small number of cases where robust information demonstrates that the controlee poses a serious risk to the public and there is little prospect of a successful criminal prosecution.[7] The Government agreed with this assessment.[8]

It is now clear that there will be no substantial relaxation of the legal regime. The Government's review of counterterrorism policy recommended the abolition of control orders and their replacement with an alternative system called Terrorism Prevention and Investigation Measures (TPIMs). These proposals have been enacted in the Terrorism Prevention and Investigation Measures Act 2011 (TPIMA).

The differences between TPIMs and control orders are relatively marginal—there is a stricter limit on relocation of controlees and a restriction on renewing TPIMs in the absence of new evidence of terrorism-related activity.[9] Renaming control orders when claiming to abolish them is a shameful face-saving exercise by the Government. This is not the approach that citizens are entitled to expect to crucial questions of civil liberties and national security. In the light of this I will continue to refer to TPIMs as control orders.

The control orders regime is legally complex and I will make no attempt to cover all of its dimensions. The first controversial feature of the regime is the evidential threshold that must be crossed to warrant a restriction of the controlee's liberty. TPIMA ss 2 and 3 provide that the Secretary of State may impose a control order only if (a) he or she reasonably believes that the individual is, or has been, involved in terrorism-related activity, some of which is 'new'; and (b) he or she reasonably considers it necessary to impose such an order, with the particular measures contained in it, to protect members of the public from a risk of terrorism arising from the involvement in terrorism-related activity of the controlee. Involvement in terrorism-related activity is 'new' if it occurred at any time, with one exception: where a control order has already been imposed on the individual. In the exceptional case, the involvement must have occurred since the imposition of the most recent order.

The level of risk sufficient to justify the imposition of a control order is unclear. There are two dimensions to the test. One is backward-looking. It concerns the involvement of the person in terrorism-related activity. The other is forward-looking. It concerns the necessity of making the order.

The low evidential standard in the PTA, which used the phrase 'reasonably suspects' in place of 'reasonably believes', came in for a great deal of criticism. The current Government accepted this criticism and TPIMA replaces the phrase 'reasonably suspects' with 'reasonably believes'. This seems unsatisfactory—it is very unclear what the evidential standard intended is. The Government and the Joint Committee of Human Rights appear to believe that this standard is lower

[7] See *Sixth Report of the Independent Review Pursuant to Section 14(3) of the Prevention of Terrorism Act 2005* (February 2011).

[8] See *Renewal of Control Orders Legislation 2011: The Government Response to the Eighth Report from the Joint Committee on Human Rights Session 2010–11* (HMSO: CM 8096, 2011).

[9] See *Liberty's Committee Stage Briefing on the Terrorism Prevention and Investigation Measures Bill in the House of Commons* (June 2011).

than the ordinary civil standard of proof of a balance of probabilities.[10] That is unclear from the legislation. In general, if, according to one's evidence, *p* is probably not the case, it is not reasonable to believe *p*. It is only reasonable to believe that *p might* be true. But an order can be imposed only if the Secretary of State reasonably believes that the individual is, or has been, involved in terrorism-related activity, not if he or she reasonably believes that the individual might be, or might have been, involved in terrorism-related activity. Hence, the legislation implies that the evidential threshold is, contrary to the intentions of the Government, higher than a balance of probabilities.

The more puzzling aspect of the problem is that TPIMA, in common with the PTA, pays more attention to the backward-looking question than the forward-looking question. The level of risk that warrants a restriction on liberty is almost completely unspecified.[11] Whilst the backward-looking question is important, the forward-looking part of the test ought to be the main focus of attention—if control orders are to be justified, they are to be justified in virtue of their preventive effects.

One problem with the forward-looking dimension is that the word 'necessary' is ambiguous. It cannot mean that the imposition of the control order is the *only* way of preventing the threat—the threat might also be met by killing the individual, or by giving in to the demands of his or her terrorist organization. Perhaps it means that no other way of preventing the threat is permissible. But this is too demanding. Suppose that surveillance could meet the same threat, but surveillance would cost the whole of the budget for the arts. Spending that money on surveillance rather than on the arts might be permissible, at least if citizens consent to this use of resources, but that would not render the imposition of a control order wrong.

Furthermore, the level of risk that warrants the imposition of an order is unclear. There must be 'a risk of terrorism'. But, from the wording of TPIMA, even a minuscule risk appears sufficient. Consider a person who associates with terrorists, but who poses a negligible threat of completing a terrorist attack because she or he is an incompetent coward whom no one in a terrorist organization trusts. May this person's liberty be restricted even though he or she poses only a trivial risk to the public? Controlling this person may be necessary to eliminate the risk that she or he poses. But doing so is disproportionate.[12]

This discussion draws on familiar features of the morality of defensive harm. Two conditions that need independently to be satisfied to render defensive harming permissible are necessity and proportionality. It is wrong to harm a person to avert a threat where non-harmful means could avert the threat. But even if harming a person is necessary, doing so may be disproportionate if the harm imposed is much more significant than the threat averted. Using a high-powered rifle to shoot a

[10] See, eg, the government response to the Joint Committee on Human Rights report of 19 October 2011 on the TPIM Bill addressed by James Brokenshire MP to Dr Hywel Francis, Chair of the Joint Committee on Human Rights available on the Home Office website.

[11] TPIMA does add that the Secretary of State's judgement must be reasonable, and that he or she must reasonably consider it necessary to impose the specific measures in the TPIM on the individual. See s 3. This improvement, though not insignificant, is hardly sufficient to correct the problem.

[12] See Carol Steiker, this volume.

person who possesses a pea-shooter may be necessary to avert the threat that this person poses. Doing so is nevertheless disproportionate.

Whilst they are not the main focus of this chapter, it is worth mentioning two further controversies about control orders. One concerns the role of the courts. To impose a control order on an individual, the Secretary of State makes an application to the court. The role of the court at this stage is limited—to determine whether the decision of the Secretary of State is obviously flawed. If an order is imposed, the controlee is entitled to a review hearing. TPIMA does little to alter the process established in the PTA. This process has proved highly problematic and compatibility with the European Convention on Human Rights (ECHR) Art 6 has been difficult to secure.

The central problem is that the evidential basis for imposition of the order cannot typically be released to the public at large, or to the controlee, without compromising security. This has led to the use of closed proceedings to scrutinize control orders. A special advocate is assigned to the controlee to represent him or her. After the special advocate has seen the closed materials, his or her opportunities to communicate with the controlee are severely restricted. The result is that some evidential defences, alibi being the most obvious example, are effectively unavailable.[13]

A significant advance in the control orders regime was made in *Secretary of State for the Home Department v AF.*[14] In that case, the House of Lords, following (in the case of some of their Lordships, reluctantly) the European Court of Human Rights (ECtHR),[15] decided that the controlee has a core irreducible right to be told sufficient information to challenge the case against him or her by instructing the allocated special advocate. It is not completely clear how far TPIMA complies with this judgment.[16] At any rate, the use of closed proceedings remains a troubling feature of the law.

The other controversy concerns the extent of the restriction of liberty. The ambition of human rights jurisprudence in this area has been to determine when a restriction on the controlee's liberty is so severe as to amount to a deprivation of liberty contrary to the ECHR Art 5. Imprisoning a person (except where the person has been convicted of a criminal offence) clearly violates Art 5. This is why successful derogation from Art 5 was required for ACTSA Pt IV.

The current state of the law is outlined in *Secretary of State for the Home Department v JJ and others.*[17] One important aspect of the judgment in this case is that measures short of imprisonment can breach ECHR Art 5. Secondly, the test for the deprivation of liberty is counterfactual—whether Art 5 has been breached

[13] For further analysis of the difficulties caused by the special advocate system, see M Chamberlain, 'Special Advocates and Procedural Fairness in Closed Proceedings' (2009) Civil Justice Quarterly 314 and A Kavanagh, 'Special Advocates, Control Orders and the Right to a Fair Trial' (2010) 73 MLR 824.

[14] [2009] UKHL 28.

[15] In *A v United Kingdom* (Application No 3455/05, 19 February 2009).

[16] See TPIMA Sch 4 para 4(1), which does not require a summary of the relevant information to be provided to the controlee in all cases.

[17] [2007] UKHL 45.

depends on comparing the life of the controlee and the life that he or she would have been living had the order not been imposed.[18] This aspect of the judgment is not ideal. It implies that imposing a curfew on me between 8 p.m. and 10 a.m. would not amount to *any* deprivation of my liberty if I never go out between 8 p.m. and 10 a.m. This is counter-intuitive conceptually and unappealing normatively. My liberty clearly has been restricted by these conditions, and my liberty to go out at these times may be valuable to me even if I never do so. It may be valuable because having an option to do something can be valuable even if that option is not chosen,[19] and also because of the symbolic value that restricting a person's options may have.[20]

Standard measures that are deemed compatible with Art 5 include, inter alia, determining the place of residence of controlees, requiring them to wear an electronic tag, imposing curfews,[21] restricting travel, requiring monitoring and reporting, restrictions on unauthorized communication devices including limiting each controlee to possession of a single landline telephone and no computer access, restricting the person's place of worship, and restricting and scrutinizing visitors.

The TPIMA helpfully specifies what measures the Secretary of State can impose on controlees,[22] but they are extensive and are broadly in line with those imposed under the PTA. The most important new limit on the powers of the Secretary of State is that he or she cannot require controlees to relocate away from their local area. This is so despite the Government recently successfully defending a control order which relocated the controlee in *Secretary of State for the Home Department v CD*.[23] The Government has also drawn up the Enhanced Terrorism Prevention and Investigation Measures Bill and subjected it to pre-legislative scrutiny, to be enacted if this proves necessary. This Bill, if enacted, would permit the Secretary of State to relocate the controlee to a residence anywhere in the UK.

The duration of control orders was also controversial. They were imposed for 12 months, after which they could be renewed, resulting in the possibility of indefinite detention. Most controlees were subject to an order for less than two years, and by 2011 no controlee had been subject to an order for more than four years.[24] The new TPIMs regime permits restrictions on a person's liberty for a maximum of two years unless there is evidence that the person has been involved in new terrorism-related activity in that period.

In some control order cases, including *JJ* itself, the courts deemed restrictions on liberty so severe that they amounted to a breach of ECHR Art 5. In that case the controlee was under curfew for 18 hours a day and outside that curfew was required

[18] [2007] UKHL 45 at [18].

[19] See, further, V Tadros, *Criminal Responsibility* (2005) 200–7.

[20] See the related discussion in TM Scanlon, *What We Owe to Each Other* (1998) 352–3.

[21] The average length of curfews imposed by control orders is 11.9 hours. See *Sixth Report of the Independent Review* (cited in n 7) para 19.

[22] TPIMA Sch 1 Pt 1.

[23] [2011] EWHC 2087 (Admin).

[24] See *Review of Counter-Terrorism and Security Powers: Review Findings and Recommendations* (HMSO: CM 8004, 2011) 36–7.

to remain in a location where he had no family or friends.[25] This amounted to a form of social isolation. Where Art 5 was breached the court would quash the order. TPIMA has the preferable feature that it allows the court to adjust the terms of the control order to ensure Art 5 compatibility without quashing it entirely.[26]

Liberty is fundamentally important. But control orders have had severe psychological effects on controlees and their families.[27] Whilst the control orders impact on liberty less than imprisonment the effects on the controlee and his or her family may be not far short of the effects of imprisonment. This must be borne in mind when they are evaluated.

## B. The moral context

A wide range of moral and political issues is relevant to assessing preventive criminal detention, including control orders. Here are some of the most important.

*Risk prevention.* The ambition of preventive detention is risk reduction or elimination. This raises a range of questions. How precise can we be about the degree of risk, and what is the moral significance of imprecision? What is the moral significance of risk prevention when compared with harm prevention? Is the distribution of risk in a population morally significant? I will address the first, and especially the second, of these questions.[28]

*Doing/Allowing.* Restricting liberty is typically harmful. If we fail to detain the risky person we fail to prevent a risk, and if the risk is realized we fail to prevent harm. Harming may be harder to justify than failing to prevent harm.[29]

*Intentions.* Depriving a person of his or her liberty intentionally harms that person. In principle a person could be deprived of his or her liberty without being harmed. It is essential to our aim only that the person is prevented from harming others, not that he or she is harmed. This distinguishes prevention from punishment—punishment *aims* at harm (either for its impersonal value, if one is a retributivist, or to deter others, if one is not). Nevertheless preventive detention harms intentionally.[30]

[25] As the more recent case of *Secretary of State for the Home Department v AP* [2010] UKSC 24 makes clear, the extent to which some measure restricts a person's liberty depends on all of that person's circumstances, including decisions of his or her family and friends to visit if the controlee is relocated.

[26] TPIMA s 9(5)(b) and (c).

[27] See, further, Zedner (cited in n 2).

[28] For discussion of risk distribution, see J Waldron, 'Security and Liberty: the Image of Balance' in *Torture, Terror, and Trade-Offs: Philosophy for the White House* (2010) and Tadros (cited in n 3).

[29] There are some non-consequentialists who think the distinction is less important with respect to state action, but even amongst them some think that it retains importance when fundamental rights are at stake. See, eg, T Nagel, *Equality and Partiality* (1991) 99–100.

[30] For discussion of the significance of intentions, see V Tadros, *The Ends of Harm. The Moral Foundations of Criminal Law* (2011) ch 7 and references therein. Again, some think that the fact that harming is intentional is not a relevant consideration with respect to state action even if it is with respect to individual action. See, eg, D Enoch, 'Intending, Foreseeing, and the State' (2007) 13 Legal Theory 69.

*Elimination.* Although intentional, preventive detention does not harm a person as a means to an end—it eliminates a threat that the person might pose rather than using the person to avert an independent threat. It may be more difficult to justify using a person as a means (what I call *manipulative* harming) than it is to justify harming a person to eliminate a threat that he or she poses (what I call *eliminative* harming).[31]

*Responsibility.* Whether the controlee would go on to harm others were the order not imposed is typically under his or her control. This may be morally significant, though, as we will see, it is unclear whether this makes it easier or harder to justify preventive detention.

*Wrongdoing.* Control orders aim to prevent wrongdoing rather than mere harm. Some think that there are stronger reasons to prevent wrongdoing than harm.[32]

*Separation of powers.* TPIMA permits the Secretary of State to restrict liberty. Courts have only the secondary role of affirming and scrutinizing the decision.[33] This may wrongly provide the executive with direct control over the liberty of citizens, something that is particularly troubling in such a politically contentious context as terrorism.[34]

*Trials and rights.* Control orders deprive people of their liberty without the full set of protections afforded by criminal trials. This undermines public scrutiny of preventive detention, which in turn undermines confidence that the regime is being applied fairly and without wrongful discrimination. Trials may also have a more fundamental and basic significance in ensuring that citizens are treated with the respect that they are due.[35]

*Risks caused.* Control orders may inflate as well as reduce the risk of terrorism. The risk of terrorist attack might be enhanced by control orders by providing a recruiting tool for terrorist organizations.[36] This claim is difficult to evaluate empirically. It also raises normative issues. Is it always wrong to do more harm than good? Does the harm caused weigh in the moral balance as heavily as the harm prevented?

[31] The significance of the distinction between eliminative and manipulative (or what is sometimes called 'opportunistic') harming is receiving a great deal of attention in non-consequentialist ethics at the moment. See, eg, W Quinn, 'Actions, Intentions, and Consequences: The Doctrine of Double Effect' in *Morality and Action* (1993) 186; H Frowe, 'Equating Innocent Threats and Bystanders' (2008) 25 *Journal of Applied Philosophy* 277; J McMahan, *Killing in War* (2009); J Quong, 'Killing in Self-Defence' (2009) 119 *Ethics* 507; FM Kamm, *Ethics for Enemies: Terror, Torture, and War* (2011); and Tadros (cited in n 30) especially ch 11.

[32] For doubts, see J McMahan, 'Humanitarian Intervention, Consent, and Proportionality' in N Ann Davis, R Keshen, and J McMahan, *Ethics and Humanity: Themes from the Philosophy of Jonathan Glover* (2010); V Tadros (cited in n 30) chs 5 and 6.

[33] See A Ashworth and L Zedner, 'Preventive Orders: A Problem of Undercriminalization?' in *Boundaries of the Criminal Law* (2010).

[34] Political difficulties in determining the scope of terrorism are discussed in J Hodgson and V Tadros, 'The Impossibility of Defining Terrorism' (unpublished ms on file with the authors).

[35] See Ashworth and Zedner (cited in n 33). For more general analysis of the significance of trials, see A Duff, L Farmer, S Marshall, and V Tadros, *The Trial on Trial 3: Towards a Normative Theory of the Criminal Trial* (2007).

[36] See, eg, L Zedner, 'Terrorism and Counterterrorism' in L Skinns, M Scott, and T Cox, *Risk* (2011).

*Alternatives*. What alternatives are available to the state to avert the threat of terrorism, and are they better? Preventive detention might be wrong because criminal justice is better.[37] It might be wrong because immigration is better. It might be wrong because surveillance is better. It might be wrong because doing nothing is better.

*Resources*. Is it justified to spend limited resources on control orders? Any regime of control orders will be accompanied by a great deal of very expensive litigation. The use of resources is to be justified by demonstrating that the claims of others to those resources are less important than the claims of those who receive protection through preventive detention.[38]

*Creep*. Relaxing traditional restrictions on preventive detention may result in overuse of this technique to avert risks. As is familiar from the history of terrorism law, exceptional provisions soon become normalized and are extended further, often in ways that are difficult to justify, and often for illegitimate political motives. Evidence of the normalization of preventive measures is available in this context. Control orders were temporary measures which were renewed by Parliament each year. TPIMA is permanent. One central protection against overuse of state power—regular democratic scrutiny of the legal regime—has thus been removed. Even if preventive justice were to warrant the use of control orders in exceptional cases in principle, the risk of 'creep' may be too great to justify their use in practice.[39]

The philosophical groundwork for an evaluation of preventive detention is underdeveloped.[40] Some of the most significant features of detention, such as the distinction between doing and allowing, have received considerable philosophical attention. But many others have not. Risk distribution, comparative approaches to risk prevention, the significance of resources, and the significance of trials, are all underexplored. Even the significance of intentions and the eliminative/manipulative distinction have only recently received sophisticated philosophical attention. And even where philosophical work is better developed, it has not been applied very carefully in the context of preventive detention.

Furthermore, many of the philosophical questions must be related to the facts, and we don't know the facts. The level of risk that we face, the risks that preventive detention causes, the costs of preventive detention, and the costs of the alternatives are all what Donald Rumsfeld calls known unknowns.

[37] Civil libertarians often operate with the assumption that criminal justice, in this context, is preferable to protect the rights of terrorist suspects. Given the breadth, vagueness, and incoherence of terrorism offences, this view seems naive. See, further, Tadros (cited in n 3).

[38] For related discussion in the context of punishment, see Tadros (cited in n 30) ch 15.

[39] Concern about creep clearly influenced the majority decision in the recent important case of *Al Rawi v the Security Service and Others* [2011] UKSC 34. The concern with creep is familiar from philosophical work on torture. See, eg, H Shue, 'Torture in Dreamland: Disposing of the Ticking Bomb' (2006) 37 Case Western Reserve Journal of International Law 231. It is also identified in Kavanagh (cited in n 13) 857.

[40] See, eg, L Farmer, 'The Jurisprudence of Security: The Police Power and the Criminal Law' in MD Dubber and M Valverde, *The New Police Science: The Police Power in Domestic and International Governance* (2006) and Ashworth and Zedner (cited in n 33); see also D Husak, this volume.

## C. From harm to risk

One of the most important dimensions of the problem of control orders concerns risk. When a control order is imposed on a person, it is done to reduce the risk of terrorist attacks. Terrorist attacks have various bad consequences. For example, they may erode political stability, negatively affect political decisions, damage valuable buildings of cultural importance, create fear and alarm, and negatively affect the behaviour of citizens. Most seriously, they kill and maim people. I will primarily focus on the last kind of harm. Whilst philosophical writing on terrorism has focused on its other effects, especially its widespread social and psychological effects,[41] killing and maiming are the most important harms that terrorism is likely to cause.[42] This is not to downplay the other effects of terrorism, only usefully to simplify discussion of it.

The causal contribution that control orders might prevent is likely to differ from case to case. In some cases, the person would have made no contribution to acts of terrorism. In others, the person would have been a conspirator, or would have provided information, or weapons, or funds to support terrorism. Again, it will be helpful to concentrate on the simplest and most compelling case for restriction of liberty: cases where the controlee will directly perpetrate an act of terrorism. Again it must be remembered that this is a simplification.

One difficulty that I have already alluded to is that the level of risk that we face from terrorism, both in general and from particular individuals, is unknown and unquantifiable. Our grip on the significance of risk is improved if we assign precise quantities to risks that we face. For example, we might compare imposing a 50 per cent risk of some harm of degree *n* on X with imposing a 25 per cent chance of risk of harm of degree *2n* on Y. Considering risk in this way crudely models reality.

Although this approach is crude, assigning precise values to risks is unavoidable and not especially problematic. This follows from the following observation. We must sometimes make a decision whether to eliminate a precise risk or an imprecise risk. We can make such judgements, and the natural way to do so is to assign a precise figure to approximate the imprecise risk. For example, suppose that I have a choice to save one person, A, from a 50 per cent risk of harm or another person, B, from an unquantifiable risk of the same degree of harm. The right thing to do in this case is to estimate whether the risk of harm to B is higher or lower than 50 per cent. I have at least some reason to save B if the estimated risk of B being harmed is higher than 50 per cent and some reason to save A if the estimated risk of B being harmed is lower than 50 per cent. Perhaps that reason is not decisive. If the estimated risk is much higher or much lower, it will often be decisive. Rendering unquantifiable risks artificially precise is thus inevitable.

[41] See, eg, S Scheffler, 'Is Terrorism Morally Distinctive?' in *Equality and Tradition: Questions of Value in Moral and Political Theory* (2010) and J Waldron, 'Terrorism and the Uses of Terror' in *Torture, Terror, and Trade-Offs: Philosophy for the White House* (2010).

[42] See also Kamm (cited in n 31) 75–6.

I now want to outline an argument which, if it is valid, would seem powerfully to support a broad set of policies of preventive detention. I don't claim that this argument, if valid, is decisive. Some of the considerations that I have outlined may provide additional reasons to resist preventive detention. But, if it is valid, it significantly supports preventive detention. Unimaginatively, I call it *The argument for preventive detention* (*The argument* for short):

(1) It is permissible to restrict a person's liberty for a number of years if doing so is necessary to prevent him or her from certainly killing one identifiable person.

(2) It is permissible to restrict the liberty of a person to the same degree to prevent him or her from certainly killing one unidentified person in a group of 1000.

(3) When the person's liberty is restricted in the previous case, each of the 1000 is saved from a 1 in 1000 chance of being killed.

(4) It follows that it is permissible to restrict the liberty of a person to the same degree to save 1000 people from a 1 in 1000 chance of being killed.

(5) It is permissible to restrict the liberty of a person to the same degree where there is a 1 in 1000 chance that this person will otherwise kill 1000 people.

*The argument* seems to have unpalatable implications. It implies that it is permissible to restrict the liberty of a person for a number of years where that person is almost certain not to harm others.

Consider:

*Control order*: A control order is imposed on X, severely restricting his or her liberty for a number of years. Were X's liberty not restricted there is a 1 in 1000 chance that he or she would set off a bomb killing 1000.

Many people will be inclined to resist the conclusion that it is permissible to restrict X's liberty for a number of years in *Control order*. X can object that it is almost certain that he or she will harm no one. But *The argument* is not obviously unsound, and hence it is not obvious that X has a valid objection to this policy.

I am unsure whether *The argument* is sound. I will consider two challenges to it. One challenge claims the following. When we are uncertain that a person will commit a wrongful act, respect for his or her responsible agency requires us to presume that he or she will not act wrongfully. This might be thought an extension of the presumption of innocence.

If this challenge is successful, it is wrong to move from the claim that it is permissible to restrict the liberty of a person to prevent him or her from certainly killing 1 person in a group of 1000 to the claim that it is permissible to restrict the liberty of a person to the same degree to prevent a 1 in 1000 risk of him or her killing 1000. In the former case, we are certain that the person will kill a person. Respect for his or her responsible agency cannot require us to presume that he or she won't do so. In the latter case, it is extremely likely that he or she won't kill the 1000. Respect for his or her responsible agency requires that we presume that he or she won't do so.

The other challenge claims that *The argument* trades on an ambiguity about risk. In step (2) each person faces a risk of being harmed. But it is certain that one person will be harmed. The quality of the outcome is certain—a person will be killed. It is only the identity of the person killed that is uncertain. In steps (3) and (4), though, this is not specified. Where a 1 in 1000 risk is imposed on each of 1000 people the possible outcomes include no one being killed and 1000 people being killed. This difference may be morally significant.

I doubt that the first challenge, though it has some academic support, is successful. The second challenge is less well known, and is much more difficult to mount. I am uncertain whether it is successful, but I will suggest that it has more promise than the first challenge.

## D. Respect for responsible agents

Morally responsible agents ought to be treated with respect. One way to respect them, it might be argued, is to presume that they will not act wrongly unless there is very powerful evidence that they will. Presuming that morally responsible agents will not act wrongly is distinct from *predicting* that they will not act wrongly. To presume that *p* is to act as though *p* is true even in the lack of decisive evidence that *p* is true. Where I know that *p* is true I typically need not presume that *p* is true.[43]

The idea that we ought to presume that people will not act wrongly has its greatest moral significance in guiding us to act, or refrain from acting, in a way that we would otherwise act on the basis of prediction. For example, we might predict that there is a 5 per cent chance that a person will act wrongly. This might incline us to take precautions against the person so acting, precautions that might be burdensome to the person. If we ought to presume that the person will not act in this way, we ought to refrain from acting on this inclination.

In the light of this, return to *Control order*. If we ought to presume that X won't act wrongly in the absence of powerful evidence that he or she will, we ought not to restrict his or her liberty. This view holds that it is objectionable to restrict a person's liberty on a purely predictive basis. We might think of this as an extension of the ideal of the presumption of innocence.

The idea that we owe it to responsible agents to make presumptions of this kind is familiar from a range of contexts.[44] Andrew Simester and Andrew von Hirsch

[43] The idea that we should presume that people will not act wrongly even if we can predict that they might is explicitly outlined as a reason against preventive detention in A Walen, 'A Unified Theory of Detention, With Application to Preventive Detention for Suspected Terrorists' (2011) 70 Maryland Law Review 871 and 'A Punitive Precondition for Preventive Detention: Lost Status as a Foundation for a Lost Immunity' (2011) 48 San Diego Law Review 1229. It should be noted that Walen does not think that control orders are necessarily unjustifiable. See 'A Punitive Precondition' 1241–2.

[44] Even some defenders of regimes of preventive detention such as control orders think that this idea is important. See, for example, KK Ferzan, 'Beyond Crime and Commitment: Justifying Liberty Deprivations of the Dangerous and Responsible' (2011) 96 Minnesota Law Review 141. Ferzan believes that respect for autonomy would be satisfied only if control orders were to require proof that the controlee had a wrongful intention, on the grounds that we respect autonomy by treating people as though they will execute their intentions. Whilst I agree that this does respect their autonomy, I don't believe that control orders need to be restricted in this way.

have defended it in the closely related context of criminalization of remote harms. They write:

> When harmless conduct is proscribed merely because the actor, if she perpetrates it, may then be tempted to commit further acts that are harmful, she is being treated as one might a child: as someone who lacks the insight or self-control to resist the later temptation. Assuming she is a competent actor, such treatment would fail to respect her as a moral agent, capable of deliberation and self-control.[45]

It has also been used to argue against the use of previous convictions as evidence in criminal trials (including, I should say, by me).[46] Respect requires that we treat these offenders as responsive to reasons, including the reasons against criminal offending, even where we can predict that they will not respond to reasons.

These ideas now seem less powerful to me than they once seemed. Let me explain why. One very general difficulty is that it is not clear why treating a person with respect requires us not to act on purely predictive judgements. Consider Simester and von Hirsch's argument in the preceding paragraph. Suppose that it can accurately be predicted that if a person does *x* this person is more likely to be tempted to commit some wrong, *y*. Does acting on this prediction treat this person as though he or she lacks insight or self-control to resist the temptation? It does not. It treats the person as though he or she *might* lack the insight or self-control to resist the temptation.

Is it wrong to treat the person as though he or she might lack insight and self-control? Why? Given that we can accurately predict that a person who does *x* is more likely to be tempted to do *y*, treating that person in this way treats him or her as subject to ordinary human weaknesses, temptations, and bad motivations that might lead him or her to do *y*. Requiring us to presume that the person won't be tempted to do *y* seems to require that we treat the person as infallible—as incapable of being tempted to do *y*. Why would respect for others require us to treat the person in that way?

It also isn't obvious why treating a person in this way treats him or her like a child, in the morally problematic sense. Suppose that, due to their lack of insight and self-control, children are more likely than adults to be tempted to do *y* if they do *x*. If we treat an adult as though he or she is as likely as a child to do *y* if he or she does *x* we treat the adult like a child. But if we treat the adult as though he or she is as likely to do *y* as any other adult who does *x* would be, we treat this adult in the same way as we treat any other adult, and not as we would treat a child. We have good reason to treat children and adults differently because of the different predictive judgements that we make about them. What we need is an argument why we should act on our predictive judgements with respect to children but not with respect to adults.

The following argument might be offered against this view: treating a person who does *x* as more likely to do *y*, even where this is true, treats that person as though he or she lacks the *capacity* to resist doing *y*. Alec Walen argues for

[45] A Simester and A von Hirsch, *Crimes, Harms, and Wrongs: On the Principles of Criminalisation* (2011) 62.

[46] See A Duff, L Farmer, S Marshall, and V Tadros, *The Trial on Trial vol (3): Towards a Normative Theory of the Criminal Trial* (2007) 110–17. For criticism, see M Redmayne, 'The Ethics of Character Evidence' (2008) 61 CLP 371.

something like this: to subject a person to long-term preventive detention, Walen claims, 'treats autonomous and accountable persons as though they do not have the free will to choose rightly'.[47] We treat a person with disrespect when we imply that he or she is incapable of acting morally, and this is what detaining a person prior to his or her having acted wrongly does.[48]

But, in response, acting on our predictive judgements is consistent with the belief that a person possesses the capacity to choose rightly—that he or she has free will, and that he or she could exercise that will in a way that is consistent with what duty requires of him or her. To see this, suppose that a person has a capacity to resist doing *y*. This does not imply that this person will exercise his or her capacity to resist doing *y*. That depends on the judgements that he or she makes about *y*. Hence, to act on the prediction that a person might do *y* does not imply that he or she could not refrain from doing *y*.

Furthermore, even if doing *y* did demonstrate a lack of capacity to resist doing *y*, in acting on the judgement that the person might do *y* we do not imply that he or she lacks the capacity to resist doing *y*. At most we imply that he or she *might* lack such a capacity. Why is implying this disrespectful? Some people lack the capacity to resist doing *y*, and this person may be one of them. Perhaps, given that he or she has done *x*, she is more likely to be one of them. If we treat the person as though he or she *might* lack such a capacity, we treat her as we would treat any other person when we are uncertain of the capacities that they possess. If we can predict that a person who does *x* is more likely to do *y*, these judgements are hardly unwarranted.[49] If this is right, respect for autonomous agents does not provide a promising way to attack *The argument*.

This view is also supported by our intuitive judgements about cases where our predictive abilities are held constant but responsibility is not. Reflecting on these cases yields the view that we typically have *stronger* reasons to impose burdens on responsible agents when we can predict that their bad motivations will result in their performing wrongful actions when they are compared with non-responsible agents. Consider the following:

*Hostel*: It is a cold winter's night. X knocks on the door of a hostel for vulnerable people seeking shelter. Most of the people in the hostel are black. X is well known to have both racist and violent tendencies as well as a lack of self-restraint. Jane is the person who is responsible for deciding who is let into the hostel. For good reason, she believes that X may violently attack one of the vulnerable people staying in the hostel. It will be very difficult to prevent him succeeding if he does mount such an attack. If he is not admitted to the hostel, there is a good chance that X will suffer a serious illness as a result of exposure.

First let us suppose that X's racist and violent tendencies and his lack of self-restraint are a consequence of psychosis. Let us call this person X*nonres*. In deciding whether to admit X*nonres* Jane must consider the harm that he will likely suffer if he is not admitted and the potential harm that those within the hostel might suffer if

[47] Walen, 'A Unified Theory of Detention' (cited in n 43) 881.
[48] See P Ramsay, this volume.
[49] For a somewhat similar argument in the context of bad character evidence, see Redmayne (cited in n 46) 386–7.

he is admitted. There seems to be nothing wrong, in this case, with relying on predictive judgements.

Now suppose that X is fully responsible for his racist judgements, violent tendencies, and lack of self-restraint. Let's call this person X*res*. He would be fully responsible for any attack that he perpetrates on the vulnerable people in the hostel. Should this make any difference to Jane's judgement?

It is difficult to believe that respect for X*res* requires Jane to be more inclined to admit X*res* into the hostel than X*nonres*. If anything, the opposite seems true—Jane should be more inclined to admit X*nonres* into the hostel than X*res*. This is for the following powerful reason. It is much more difficult for X*nonres* than it is for X*res* to avoid posing a threat to the vulnerable people. X*res* could have done this simply by making better judgements and developing more self-restraint, something that he was, we can assume, capable of doing. X*nonres*, in contrast, is not responsible for his judgements and lack of self-restraint to the same degree.[50] This consideration seems much more significant than the idea that respect for X*res* requires Jane to refrain from acting on her predictive judgements.

Now return to control orders. As I noted in the introduction, the judgement that the Secretary of State makes in determining whether to impose a control order on a person has a backward-looking as well as a forward-looking dimension. The backward-looking dimension is that the Secretary of State believes that the controlee is, or has been, involved in new terrorism-related activity.[51] This dimension of control orders ensures that a person has at least some opportunity to avoid being subject to a control order. This person could normally do this by refraining from being involved in such activity. The circumstances of controlees are, in this way, somewhat analogous to that of X*res*. If anything, they are offered better protection against being harmed than X*res*, in that it is their actions rather than their attitudes that provide the backward-looking dimension of the decision to impose the burden on them.[52]

Of course, it will forcefully be argued that the Secretary of State cannot accurately identify whether a person has been involved in such activity. This is, of course, true. It would be foolish to suppose that all of those who are subject to control orders have been involved in terrorism-related activity given the low evidential threshold that the Secretary of State must meet.

But this factor, whilst important, is not decisive. Suppose, in *Hostel*, that Jane is not completely sure whether X has racist and violent tendencies. This does not necessarily require her to admit X to the hostel. It is a relevant factor in the evaluation of the threat to those within the hostel. This factor is equally relevant for Jane's judgement with respect to X*res* and X*nonres*.

The fact that the Secretary of State is unlikely to make perfect judgements about the actions of controlees may not provide a decisive reason to deny him or her the

50 For a more developed discussion of the relationship between avoidability and liability, see Tadros (cited in n 30) especially chs 3 and 8, drawing on Scanlon (cited in n 20) ch.6.

51 TPIMA s 3(1) and 3(2).

52 The idea that there should be an act requirement is defended in Ferzan (cited in n 44) 180–1 on the grounds that this would be an appropriate restriction on state power.

power to make those judgements. Whether it is a decisive reason depends on the degree of accuracy of those judgements, the magnitude of the threat, the harm that he or she imposes on those whose liberty is restricted, alternative ways in which the threat can be met, and so on.[53]

Furthermore, our confidence that those whose liberty is restricted have the relevant judgements can be bolstered, if again only partially, by the existence of the review procedure. Whilst this procedure is notoriously problematic and inaccurate, it is better than nothing. Again, compare *Hostel*, where Jane's ability to evaluate whether the person is a racist is quite limited and there is no review procedure.

Perhaps it might be argued that excluding X*res* in *Hostel* is importantly different from imposing a control order on a person in that excluding X*res* allows X*res* to be harmed whereas imposing a control order on a person harms that person. The distinction between the two cases, in this respect, is not sharp. Excluding X*res* might be understood as a form of harming. It prevents him from protecting himself from harm by entering the hostel. But even if this factor is important, it is independent of the question that we are considering here.

Furthermore, I doubt that the distinction between doing and allowing leads us to make different judgements about responsible and non-responsible agents. Suppose that Jane has admitted X into the hostel not knowing of X's racist and violent tendencies. She is now concerned that X will attack one of the vulnerable people in the hostel. If it was permissible for her to exclude X from the hostel, it seems also permissible for her to restrict X's liberty whilst he is in the hostel to prevent him from carrying out such an attack. Whether she is permitted to do this seems not to depend on whether X is a responsible agent, or if it does, the fact that X*res* is a responsible agent is a reason in favour of restricting his liberty.

Overall, we can conclude that the argument that control orders involve a lack of respect for responsible agents is not powerful. If anything, the fact that controlees are responsible agents points in the other direction—it militates in favour of restricting their liberty on a predictive basis rather than against it.

## E. Evaluating risks

If the idea that we must presume that responsible agents will not act wrongly cannot provide a decisive reason to reject *The Argument*, perhaps an objection can be found in the way in which it handles risk. There is something intuitively problematic about restricting a person's liberty to protect each of a large number of people from facing a very small risk that they will suffer significant harm. This seems different to restricting a person's liberty to protect one person from certain harm. The fact that the risk that each person faces is modest seems important, even

[53] As I have already noted, there is also the question of the separation of powers. The separation of powers may be justified in part on non-instrumental as well as on instrumental grounds. Consideration of this issue is beyond the scope of this chapter.

if the expected outcome of imposing this modest risk on a large population is that one or more people will be harmed. Yet the idea that we evaluate risks by considering their expected outcomes is also in its own way intuitive.[54] We need to find arguments for resisting this way of considering risks.

Let us begin by restating *The argument*:

(1) It is permissible to restrict the liberty of a person by subjecting him or her to a control order for a number of years if doing so is necessary to prevent him or her from certainly killing one identifiable person.
(2) It is permissible to restrict the liberty of a person to the same degree to prevent him or her from certainly killing one unidentified person from a group of 1000.
(3) When the person's liberty is restricted in the previous case, each of the 1000 is saved from a 1 in 1000 chance of being killed.
(4) It follows that it is permissible to restrict the liberty of a person to the same degree to save 1000 people from a 1 in 1000 chance of being killed.
(5) It is permissible to restrict the liberty of a person to the same degree where there is a 1 in 1000 chance that this person will kill 1000 people.

As I noted earlier, there is an ambiguity in the idea of risk in *The argument*. The ambiguity can be highlighted in the following way. There are some cases of risk where it is certain that someone will suffer a certain outcome. But it is uncertain who, amongst a group of people, that person will be. I call these cases 'closed risks'. There are other cases where it is not certain how many people will suffer the outcome. Each person is subject to a risk, but it is not clear whether anyone will be harmed, or it may be the case that many people are harmed. I call these cases 'open risks'.

## Closed and open risks

To see this difference more clearly, consider:

*Closed risk*. There are two people, A and B, each of whom faces a threat of harm. I can avert the threat only by flipping a coin. If I flip the coin and it comes up heads, A will automatically be rescued. If it comes up tails, B will automatically be rescued.[55]

If I flip the coin, A and B each have a 50 per cent chance of being rescued from harm and a 50 per cent chance of being harmed. But if I flip the coin it is certain that *someone* will be harmed, it is just not clear whom. Here are the two possible outcomes:

(1) Heads: B but not A is harmed (50 per cent).
(2) Tails: A but not B is harmed (50 per cent).

[54] Expected utility theory, which adopts this approach to risk, is standard fare in economics. It is also worth noting that this theory has a range of problems. For a good discussion, see L Temkin, *Rethinking the Good: Moral Ideals and the Nature of Practical Reasoning* (2012) ch 8.

[55] I have introduced the idea that the harm is automatic to avoid complications that arise when there is intervening agency.

There is no outcome where neither A nor B is harmed and no outcome where both A and B are harmed.

Compare

*Open risk.* There are two people, C and D, each of whom faces a threat of harm. If I flip a coin and it comes up heads, C will automatically be rescued. If it comes up tails, C will be harmed. If I flip another coin and it comes up heads, D will automatically be rescued. If it comes up tails, D will be harmed.

If I flip both coins C and D each have a 50 per cent chance of being harmed, just as in *Closed risk*. However, it is not certain that either C or D will be harmed. It is also possible that both C and D will be harmed. There are four possible outcomes:

(1) Heads, heads: neither C nor D is harmed (25 per cent).
(2) Heads, tails: D but not C is harmed (25 per cent).
(3) Tails, heads: C but not D is harmed (25 per cent).
(4) Tails, tails: both C and D are harmed (25 per cent).

Because the sum of the probabilities of C being harmed in (2) and (4) is 50 per cent, C has a 50 per cent chance of being harmed. Because the sum of the probabilities of D being harmed in (3) and (4) is 50 per cent, D has a 50 per cent chance of being harmed. Unlike *Closed risk*, however, in *Open risk* there is a significant chance that no one will be harmed. There is also a significant risk that both C and D will be harmed.

## Rescue, harm, and closed risks

In the light of this, let us return to *The argument*. First, let us consider step (1). There is little doubt that the proposition in step (1) is true. It is permissible to restrict a person's liberty for a number of years if that is necessary to prevent him or her from killing someone else. It is controversial whether it is permissible to harm a non-responsible threat to avert a threat of harm that is of the same magnitude or less than the harm that would be done to him or her.[56] I believe that this is permissible.[57] Even if I am wrong, it is surely permissible to harm that person to a degree that is significantly less than the harm that he or she will otherwise do to others. Restricting a person's liberty for a number of years is not a fate worse than death, or even a fate that is nearly as bad as death.

The transition from step (1) to step (2) is more controversial. It relies on the idea that when a responsible agent is deciding whether to prevent harm, it does not matter that the identity of the person rescued is uncertain. A similar idea will be familiar to criminal lawyers from the doctrine of transferred malice. If D intends to

[56] For doubts, see J McMahan, 'Self-Defense and the Problem of the Innocent Attacker' (1994) 104 *Ethics* 252 and *The Ethics of Killing: Problems at the Margins of Life* (2002) 398–421; M Otsuka, 'Killing the Innocent in Self-Defense' (1994) 23 *Philosophy and Public Affairs* 74 and D Rodin, *War and Self-Defense* (2002) 79–87.

[57] See Tadros (cited in n 30) ch 11.

kill X but actually kills Y, D is guilty of murdering Y. D need not intend to kill Y in particular to be guilty of murder. Similarly, it might be argued, there is no important difference between rescuing an identifiable person from being harmed and rescuing one of two people who face a closed risk of harm. Flipping a coin in *Closed risk* certainly saves a person. It is just not clear whom.

Perhaps it might be argued that there is some difference between saving an identified person and saving one of two people who face a closed risk. Consider:

*Storm*. Two boats, *Known* and *Unknown*, have set sail. Harry is on *Known*. Ingrid and Jane are on *Unknown*. Both boats are caught in a storm and each is sinking fast. If *Known* sinks Harry will certainly be killed. *Unknown* has a high-tech capsule on it that holds one person. Any person who enters the capsule will certainly survive. The other person will certainly die. I know that Ingrid and Jane are scrupulously fair, and will toss a coin to decide who will enter the capsule. Either Harry or one of the people on *Unknown* will certainly be killed. I can rescue one person, and I can do so at no cost to myself.[58]

It seems plausible that were I to know either that Ingrid is already in the capsule or that Jane is already in the capsule I ought to flip a coin to decide whom to rescue. Some may deny this on the grounds that the person who is not in the capsule has been given a 50 per cent chance of survival that Harry lacks. I find this difficult to believe. Perhaps this consideration is important if Ingrid, Jane, and Harry knew of the different risks that they faced when going sailing. We can control for this idea by stipulating that Ingrid and Jane did not know that the capsule was on *Unknown* when they sailed. If so, I should flip a coin to decide whether to rescue Harry or the person in the capsule.

Now consider the situation before Ingrid and Jane have flipped a coin to decide who will enter the capsule. Here is an argument in favour of rescuing Harry. Ingrid and Jane each still have a 50 per cent chance of survival even if I don't rescue the remaining person on *Unknown*. Harry, in contrast, will certainly be killed if I don't rescue him. I owe a powerful duty to Harry to prevent his death. This duty is much more powerful than the duty that I owe to either Ingrid or Jane to prevent them having a 50 per cent chance of death. Harry's objection to my failing to save him is much more powerful than Ingrid's or Jane's objection to my failing to save the person in *Unknown*. It is much more powerful because I am not certain that Ingrid is in danger or that Jane is in danger.

In response, it might be argued that both Jane and Ingrid face a 50 per cent chance of death. They can thus both object to my saving Harry. This is true. But perhaps we cannot simply add together the objections that Ingrid and Jane have in order to balance out Harry's objection. The reason for this, some might claim, is to do with the separateness of persons. Harry, Ingrid, and Jane have a right to be treated as independently important.[59]

[58] I am grateful to Patrick Tomlin for helping me to improve this example.

[59] This idea is familiar from non-consequentialist morality. See, for important examples, FM Kamm, *Morality, Mortality: vol.1: Death and Whom to Save From It* (1993) Pt II; Scanlon (cited in n 20) ch 5.

This argument lacks power in this context. Here is why. There is some fact—the person who will be selected in the coin flip—that I do not know. I know that this fact could only be either (a) Ingrid enters the capsule; or (b) Jane enters the capsule. If (a) is true I lack a reason to prefer Harry to Jane and I ought to flip a coin. If (b) is true I lack a reason to prefer Harry to Ingrid and I ought to flip a coin. Given this, it cannot be true that uncertainty whether (a) or (b) is the case can render it wrong to flip a coin. If I ought to flip a coin if (a) or if (b), I ought to flip a coin if either (a) or (b).

Perhaps some may argue that there is no fact of the matter about whether (a) or (b) is true, and that makes a difference to what I should do. This is difficult to believe. There are facts about the future. For example, suppose that I save Harry and Jane enters the capsule, resulting in Ingrid being killed. It is true, before the coin is flipped, that Ingrid would never see her family again. She did not know that this was true, but it was true nevertheless.

Even if this argument is not decisive, uncertainty about who will be harmed surely cannot make a very significant difference to the reasons that I have to rescue the person from harm. Suppose that rescuing Harry is risky whereas rescuing the person in *Unknown* is not risky. I am surely permitted to rescue the remaining person in *Unknown*. Similarly, suppose that Harry faces a risk of the loss of a limb and the person in *Unknown* faces a risk of the loss of two limbs. Again, I am surely permitted to rescue the person in *Unknown*. Even if the transition from (1) to (2) is not completely smooth, this does not count heavily against *The argument*.

## The moral difference between closed and open risks

If a person is deprived of his or her liberty by being subject to a control order, citizens are protected from an open rather than a closed risk. If a controlee had not had his or her liberty restricted, a wide range of outcomes might have occurred, ranging from nothing to the loss of very many lives. If the controlee does not have his or her liberty restricted, the risk that serious harm will occur is typically small. There is only a small chance that restricting the liberty of a person will prevent a harmful terrorist incident occurring that would not otherwise have occurred.

This is partly because some controlees lack any inclination to instigate or assist acts of terrorism. It is partly because any person with the relevant inclinations is unlikely to act on them. It is partly because any person acting on these inclinations is unlikely to be successful. It is partly because the contribution that a person makes to a terrorist attack is overdetermined—if this person does not provide the funding, or the information, or drive the car, someone else will. A result is that most controlees who have their liberty restricted are harmed without anyone being benefited.

However, if a terrorist attack occurs that would not otherwise have occurred, a great deal of harm may be caused. It is possible to cause multiple casualties through a terrorist attack. The risk of completion is small but the number of lives lost in a terrorist attack may be large.

The effect of depriving people of their liberty cannot be calculated on a purely individual basis. Restricting the liberty of one person may be completely ineffective unless the liberty of others is also restricted. This will be so if many different people could contribute effectively to the completion of an attack—a threat will be averted only if all potential causal contributors are neutralized. The contribution that control orders make to security is, in consequence, especially difficult to assess.

In this section I will explore the idea that the reasons to prevent closed risks are stronger than those to prevent open risks. To make progress, consider:

*Storm II*. Two boats, *Unknown* and *Uncertain* have set sail. Ingrid and Jane are on *Unknown* and one of them will certainly be saved in the capsule as before. *Unknown* is sinking fast into shark-infested waters. If I do nothing, whoever is not saved will certainly be killed. *Uncertain* has set sail with Kevin and Larry aboard and both have fallen into the water. They are some distance from an island but are both good swimmers. Each has a 50 per cent chance of surviving if I do nothing. I can rescue either the crew of *Unknown* or the crew of *Uncertain* but not both. I can do either thing at no cost to myself.

If I do nothing in *Storm II*, there is a 50 per cent chance that Ingrid will be killed, a 50 per cent chance that Jane will be killed, a 50 per cent chance that Kevin will be killed, and a 50 per cent chance that Larry will be killed.

If I rescue the crew of *Unknown* Ingrid and Jane both survive. In that case, the following outcomes are possible:

(1) Kevin and Larry both survive (25 per cent).
(2) Kevin survives and Larry dies (25 per cent).
(3) Kevin dies and Larry survives (25 per cent).
(4) Kevin and Larry both die (25 per cent).

If I rescue the crew of *Uncertain*, Kevin and Larry both survive. The following outcomes are possible:

(1) Jane dies and Ingrid survives (50 per cent).
(2) Ingrid dies and Jane survives (50 per cent).

Although the risk of death to each person is the same whether I rescue the crew of *Unknown* or the crew of *Uncertain*, the range of possible outcomes is not the same. If I rescue the crew of *Unknown*, there is a chance that no one will be killed. There is also a chance that two people will be killed. If I rescue the crew of *Uncertain*, in contrast, one person will certainly be killed, but there is no chance that two people will be killed.

In deciding whether to rescue the crew of *Unknown* or the crew of *Uncertain*, we need to evaluate the reasons to prevent the first set of probabilities compared with the second set of probabilities. Perhaps the reasons to prevent the first set of probabilities are significantly weaker than the reasons to prevent the second set. A first pass for an argument for this view is as follows. If I save the crew of *Unknown*, there is a 25 per cent chance that no one will be killed. There is an extremely powerful reason to preserve this possibility. The reason to preserve this possibility is much more powerful than the reason to exclude the possibility that two people will be killed.

This idea is, I think, intuitive. But we also need a more developed argument for it. One argument that might be given for this conclusion draws on the separateness of persons, an idea that I considered earlier. I am not sure whether this argument is successful, and I have space to lay it out only quite briefly.

The basic idea is this. Each person has an independent life to lead. She or he has her or his own unique and particular importance. For this reason, in deciding what to do, we do not simply maximize the good without considering who will be recipients of that good. Rather, we consider the significance of our decisions for each person considered independently. One possible implication of this idea is that the reason to save two lives is not twice as powerful as the reasons to save one life.

We can illustrate this by considering the power of the objection that a person might have to us excluding the possibility of a certain outcome. As we have already seen, the fact that it is uncertain who will be killed makes little difference where it is certain that one person will be killed. Let us suppose, then, that the person is Ingrid. Ingrid has a powerful objection to this result. Were the person on *Unknown* Jane, her objection would be equally as powerful.

The question is whether the possibility of outcome (4) is sufficiently important to outweigh Ingrid's objection. It is, of course, much worse that two people are killed rather than one. If we can save either one person from certain death or two other people from certain death, most people think that we ought to save the two.

But that may not be because we can simply add the value of independent lives and weigh them against a single life. Even if it is true that the number of people who will be killed is morally significant, it does not follow that the reason to prevent two people from being killed is twice as powerful as the reason to prevent a single person from being killed. The reason for this is that each person's life is uniquely important for him or her. The value of lives cannot simply be pooled as though we together all live one big life.

This provides some reason to think that the reason to preserve option (1) is very powerful, for in option (1) everyone is very well off. Whilst there are powerful reasons to avoid option (4), these reasons are not as powerful as the reasons to preserve option (1). We give special weight to the situation where no one is harmed.

Much more needs to be said about this argument than I have space for here. I confess to being unsure about whether it is sound. It seems to me a powerful objection to control orders that refraining from restricting a person's liberty preserves the possibility that no one is seriously harmed. There is no such possibility if a person is subject to a control order. Even though the harm averted through the use of control orders may be very great, in that many people may lose their lives, the probability that this will occur is small. The fact that terrorist attacks may have many victims, whilst it is clearly morally important, lacks the significance that it is given in *The argument*. The loss of 1000 lives does not have 1000 times the reason-giving force of the loss of one life. If this is true, we have some reason to doubt that *The argument* is sound.

## F. Conclusion

I don't claim that the argument I have presented concerning risk, even if it is valid, provides a decisive objection to control orders. I doubt that there is a single knock-down philosophical argument against control orders. I am also unsure whether the use of control orders is justified. I have my doubts, but I remain uncertain about the issue.

Evaluation of control orders requires us to consider a wide range of philosophical issues. The objection to *The argument*, if it is valid, provides a reason to think that the utilitarian risk analysis that may well underpin policies like control orders is mistaken. It is mistaken not because respect for autonomous agents requires us to presume that they will not act wrongly, it is rather because respect for the separateness of persons requires us to take more powerful measures to prevent harm and closed risks of harm than we do to prevent open risks of harm.

# 8

# Restraining Orders, Liberty, and Due Process

*James W Nickel**

This chapter discusses an important, long-established, and growing area of preventive law, namely restraining orders (ROs). This area of law in the UK and the USA includes domestic and workplace ROs, non-molestation orders, mandatory quarantines to prevent the spread of infectious diseases, gang injunctions, restraints imposed as a condition of bail while awaiting criminal trial,[1] or as a condition of release from immigration detention, sexual offences preventive orders,[2] Anti-Social Behaviour Orders (ASBOs),[3] and control orders for suspected terrorists.[4] The use of such orders in both civil and criminal contexts has greatly expanded in recent decades in both countries.[5] Growth in the types and uses of ROs is at least partly due to their attractive features. In comparison to criminal detention ROs are, generally, faster in terms of how long it takes to impose them, cheaper in their court and detention costs, and possibly less damaging than jail to the restrainee's liberty and welfare.

This chapter critically examines ROs but offers no blanket endorsement or condemnation of them. It attempts to cover a wide range of ROs and gives considerable attention to the biggest area—domestic violence restraining orders. Reflection on ROs can explore their key components, justifications, costs, impacts on liberty, compatibility with human rights standards, appropriate level(s) of procedural protections, and efficacy. The first section offers an analysis of ROs as part of

* I am indebted to Karen N. Chrisman and Alex A. Smith for excellent research assistance. I am also grateful to the editors and many others for useful criticisms and suggestions.

1 See RA Duff, this volume.

2 S Shute, 'The Sexual Offences Act 2003: Sexual Offences Prevention Orders; Foreign Travel Orders; Risk of Sexual Harm Orders' (2004) Crim LR 417–440.

3 ASBOs were introduced in the UK by the Blair administration in 1998. They are used instead of criminal prosecutions in hopes of controlling behaviour such as recreational drug use, drunkenness, fare dodging, generating high levels of noise, painting graffiti, begging, shoplifting, and vandalism. See A Ashworth and M Redmayne, *The Criminal Process* (4th edn, 2010) 405–10. In May 2012 the Home Secretary Theresa May announced that ASBOs will be replaced in England and Wales by two orders: the Criminal Behaviour Order (CBO) and a Crime Prevention Injunction (CPI). See <http://www.bbc.co.uk/news/uk-18163214>.

4 L Zedner, 'Preventive justice or pre-punishment?' (2007) 60 CLP 174–203; S Macdonald, 'ASBOs and Control Orders: Two Recurring Themes, Two Apparent Contradictions' (2007) *Parliamentary Affairs* 601–24. In the UK control orders for suspected terrorists have been replaced by Terrorism Prevention and Investigation Measures or TPIMs.

5 A Ashworth and L Zedner, 'Preventive Orders: A Problem of Undercriminalization?' in RA Duff et al (eds), *The Boundaries of the Criminal Law* (2010) 59–87.

preventive law. Quarantine orders and domestic restraining orders are discussed as examples of ROs. The next section explores the impact of ROs on personal liberty broadly conceived. The third section considers whether and how ROs can be compatible with human rights to fundamental freedoms. The fourth part of the chapter addresses the question of what sorts of procedural protections ROs should have. It argues that the grounds for due process protections in criminal law also provide reasons for substantial—but not identical—procedural protections for the initiation and review of ROs. The old idea that the procedural requirements for a case depend on whether it is 'civil' or 'criminal' should be abandoned. The chapter's final section offers a brief discussion of the efficacy of ROs.

## A. Restraining orders: analysis and examples

ROs have four key features. First, they are *official orders* or injunctions typically issued and reviewed by a judge. Secondly, ROs are directed and communicated to particular individuals and individually tailored to some degree. Like other injunctions, ROs send a customized message to the restrained party saying, 'Listen! Here are specific obligations that the legal system imposes on you personally.' Thirdly, ROs attempt to influence behaviour through the use of coercive threats. They often forbid actions that are not antecedently criminal. And finally, their main purpose is to reduce illegal, harmful, offensive, or obstructive behaviour and hence is mainly *preventive* rather than punitive (even though punitive measures are lurking in the background).

The parties to ROs include the issuing judge or official, the restrained person or persons—the *restrainee(s)*, and the protected person or persons—the *protectee(s)*. Frequently ROs are issued in response to a complaint or application. The *applicant* is often the potential protectee, but not always. Applications for ASBOs, for example, must come from police or housing officials, and applications for Workplace Violence Restraining Orders may come from employers. If the judge finds the application or complaint persuasive he or she then has the legal power to impose an RO.

Some ROs such as domestic and workplace restraining orders have as their protectees a single person or a small group such as a family or group of workers. Other ROs have neighbourhoods or even large populations as their protectees. ROs that protect larger groups include quarantine orders, ASBOs, sex offence restraining orders, and restraining orders used to limit the activities of suspected terrorists.

The lifespan of an RO can be divided into four stages. There is the *initiation stage* when the RO is imposed and is in force for some period of time; the *review stage*—which can occur at initiation or later—when the necessity and proportionality of the RO is reviewed seriously by a judge; the *sanctioning stage* that occurs when officials detect a violation of the RO and decide to impose penalties; and the *termination stage* when the RO is cancelled or expires.

## Preventive laws

Preventive measures in law use coercive threats or forceful incapacitation in hopes of preventing some future harm, crime, nuisance, or obstruction of legitimate government activities. Criminal laws are preventive in this sense since they issue coercive threats to everyone in order to prevent or minimize future crimes. ROs are also parts of preventive law but they use customized or individually-targeted coercive threats to prevent future misbehaviour.

One way to prevent a person from engaging in an unwanted action such as violent assault is to use forceful physical incapacitation. The person is made incapable of assaulting anyone by being bound, drugged, locked in a room or cell, or killed. Preventive custodial detention (that is, confining someone for preventive reasons) belongs in this category. A different way of preventing a person from engaging in a violent assault uses *coercive threats* as the primary means. A believable threat of hard treatment is used to change the restrainee's incentive structure so as to make engaging in a violent assault too costly. If the coercive threat succeeds, assaulting someone remains possible but becomes an unattractive option. Incapacitation overrides the restrainee's agency, while coercion works *through* his or her agency. To succeed, coercion requires some degree of rationality and self-control on the part of the restrainee.

Police work regularly makes use of both forms of prevention. For example, barricades are set up to prevent angry protesters from attacking an embassy (incapacitation). And protestors are threatened with arrest and penalties if they attempt to remove or climb the barricade (coercion). When coercive threats are used to control behaviour they require two sets of means (or a 'two-step process').[6] The primary means of controlling behaviour is the coercive threat itself. The secondary means come into play when violations of the order are detected and punished. Serious violations are then penalized as a way of making good on the threat. In contrast, incapacitation of persons who might engage in unwanted behaviour requires no secondary means. Incapacitation need not be backed up with threatened penalties or hard treatment—although it sometimes is, as when incarceration is backed up by laws threatening a longer sentence if the prisoner tries to escape.

## Coercive quarantine of persons with infectious diseases

Quarantine orders (QOs) are used to isolate people believed to be contagious in hopes of preventing the spread of a communicable disease. They are also a tool for dealing with biohazards and bioterrorism. Some authors distinguish *isolation* for persons known to be carriers of contagious diseases from *quarantine* for persons suspected of being or becoming contagious, but this analysis will follow ordinary usage and treat them together. QOs separate people who are or may become

[6] Ashworth and Redmayne (cited in n 3).

contagious from those who are healthy. The protectees of a QO often include a large population—anyone who lives or travels near the contagious person.

Custodial detention is a possible but heavy-handed way of putting a person in quarantine. It detains an infectious or possibly infectious person in a special room or ward. No QO is required since physical constraints are used to enclose the detainee. QOs, in contrast, use coercive threats to require contagious or potentially contagious people to stay at home or refrain from leaving the hospital. To make a QO enforceable it is often necessary to obtain a court order. QOs are typically accompanied by general laws requiring non-infected persons to stay away from people who are quarantined.

When QOs work they achieve detention without bars or guards. Since their effect is often similar to custodial preventive detention and because they require that everyone else stay away from the restrainee, QOs (along with control orders for suspected terrorists) are among the ROs with the greatest negative impact on the liberty of the people they restrain. Most ROs that limit movement do so by *excluding* the restrainee from a small geographic zone while leaving open all other zones. In contrast, a person under a QO is usually enclosed and only free to move within the walls of the enclosure. If a QO is extended in its duration it can have a very serious impact on an individual's liberty, preventing him or her from engaging in most normal activities such as visiting family and friends and going to work or religious services. Fortunately, the duration of isolation orders is usually limited to a short period (while a person is contagious and recovering from the disease). Persons with tuberculosis may, however, be restrained for long periods of time.

Great haste is often needed in dealing with serious communicable diseases. In major epidemics the number of people subjected to QOs may be so large as to make it difficult or impossible to provide access to legal process in regard to initiation, review, or termination. Further, the restrainee's appearance before a court may be dangerous since it could lead to the infection of all who are present.

QOs are likely to have better compliance rates than other ROs. Illness often makes one happy to be at home in bed. QOs typically imply no accusation or condemnation, and the restrainee will often recognize the danger he or she poses to others and thus see the need for quarantine. Further, people who are actually or possibly infected with a contagious disease come from various parts of the population and are not likely to be in any particular mental state other than anxiety about their illness. This is in contrast to the restrainees of domestic and workplace restraining orders, ASBOs, and sexual offences preventive orders—who may be, on average, less easily influenced by coercive legal threats due to anger, immaturity, sexual compulsions, or mental health problems.[7]

[7] On the frequency of criminal records among restrainees of domestic violence ROs see A Klein, 'Re-Abuse in a Population of Court-Restrained Male Batterers: Why Restraining Orders Don't Work' in E Buzawa and C Buzawa (eds), *Do Arrests and Restraining Orders Work?* (1996) 202. Klein claims that 'most male abusers do not have criminal records, but the vast majority brought to court by their victims for ROs do'.

## ROs in domestic and workplace contexts

Domestic violence continues to be a serious problem in the UK and the USA. Women are the victims in the vast majority of cases. A 2004 study in England and Wales claims that 45 per cent of women have experienced some form of domestic violence, sexual assault, or stalking.[8] And in the USA, one study suggests that one in three women have experienced rape, physical violence, and/or stalking by an intimate partner.[9] Reasonable political demands that domestic and workplace violence be controlled have led to the strengthening and greater availability of legal protections and remedies. In the USA the passage of the federal Violence Against Women Act in 1994 (and the funding it provided) played a major role in the expansion in the availability and use of domestic ROs.[10] The UK has the Domestic Violence, Crime and Victims Act 2004 and the Protection from Harassment Act 1997.

Restraining orders are widely used in the hope of preventing harassment, stalking, abuse, assaults, kidnappings, and murders. In the workplace they are used to restrain angry employees (or *ex*-employees) who may shoot up the office, store, or factory.[11] Statutory frameworks for the use of restraining orders in particular areas such as stalking, harassment, sex offences, domestic violence, and workplace violence are now common. Within the USA, Pennsylvania enacted the first of these frameworks in 1976, and currently every state has a statute authorizing judges to issue domestic ROs and specifying the procedures to be followed.[12] It is estimated that more than one million domestic ROs are issued every year in the USA. California alone issues approximately 80,000 a year.[13]

Domestic and workplace ROs are similar to QOs, in that they sometimes need to be imposed with great haste during a period of crisis and maximum danger. Protection starting a week or a month after an application is filed may be too late. For this reason, ROs are often available on an interim basis. Temporary ROs are sometimes initiated by police officers who are called to the scene of a domestic dispute or in a case of abuse. More frequently, however, ROs are initiated by fearful applicants who seek special protection for themselves, their families, or employees.

[8] S Walby and J Allen, 'Domestic violence, sexual assault and stalking: Findings from the British Crime Survey' (Home Office Research Study 276) <http://broken-rainbow.org.uk/research/Dv%20crime%20survey.pdf>.

[9] M Black, K Basile, M Breiding, S Smith, M Walters, M Merrick, J Chen, and MR Stevens, 'The National Intimate Partner and Sexual Violence Survey: 2010 Summary Report' (National Center for Injury Prevention and Control Executive Summary) <http://www.cdc.gov/ViolencePrevention/pdf/NISVS_Executive_Summary-a.pdf>.

[10] US Public Law 109–162. 119 Stat. 2960 (1994).

[11] A good description of these orders in the USA is available at: 'Workplace Violence Restraining Orders' (Know the Laws Indiana) <http://www.womenslaw.org/laws_state_type.php?id=13010&state_code=IN>. This massive website provides online access to the domestic and workplace RO statutes of every state in the USA.

[12] A Klein (cited in n 7) 192.

[13] S Sorenson and H Shen, 'Restraining Orders in California: A Look at Statewide Data' (2005) 7 *Violence Against Women* 920, 928. According to the authors' 2003 data, 72.2 per cent of ROs involved a restrained male and a protected female, 8.5 per cent were for a restrained female and a protected male, 11.4 per cent were male–male, and 7.9 per cent were female–female.

They are often initiated *ex parte* (without the potential restrainee's participation in the initiation procedure) and with minimal procedural protections. Stronger due process protections are postponed until the mandatory review stage that typically occurs days or weeks later. If the RO is sustained in that review the order becomes 'permanent' in the sense that it is in effect for an extended period of time.

Domestic and workplace ROs frequently require that a restrainee must stay away from the protectee(s) and from specified locations such as a home, workplace, or neighbourhood. And they often assign the protectee the burden of serving notice of the order on the restrainee (usually by arranging service with the local police) and of reporting any subsequent violations by telephone or filing an affidavit with the court.

## B. ROs and personal liberty

We now turn to the impact of ROs on personal liberty. The concept of personal liberty used in this section is broad; it covers valuable liberties even if they are not thought important enough to be protected by specific human rights (in the way that freedom of assembly, for example, is protected by the right to freedom of assembly). The liberties to consume alcohol, smoke tobacco, or play basketball, for example, are not parts of a 'basic liberty' or 'fundamental freedom' that is protected by human rights. The concept of liberty used here is also broad in that it does not restrict infringements to those coming from law or government. In this section liberty is treated as a value to be promoted and balanced, not as a matter of rights or duties. In the next section human rights to fundamental freedoms are discussed in more detail.

Having an ample set of liberties may be desirable because of the specific activities it allows one to engage in (or avoid) and/or the goals that it allows one to pursue (or reject).[14] Liberties may also be valuable because of the options they provide for future pursuits that are not yet known or valued, much in the way that it is valuable to have information available on the internet about every imaginable topic just in case one someday needs it. Having a wide range of options is useful to the development and exercise of autonomy.[15]

The story of the impact of ROs on liberty in this broad sense is complicated. This is partly because of the enormous variation within ROs due to their various types and levels of enforcement, and even within particular types of ROs due to differences in the burdensomeness of the individually tailored specific orders they contain. Broadly, however, ROs reduce the liberty of restrainees in hopes of increasing the liberty and security of protectees. Writing about domestic ROs, Diane L Rosenfeld says that they 'redistribute liberty back to the [protectee]'.[16] This shifting of liberties is explored in the following paragraphs.

[14] See I Carter, *A Measure of Freedom* (1999), 4 f, on the non-specific value of freedom; see also J Feinberg, *Harm to Others* (1987) 206–14.

[15] J Griffin, *On Human Rights* (2008).

[16] DL Rosenfeld, 'Why Doesn't *He* Leave?' in CA MacKinnon and RB Siegel (eds), *Directions in Sexual Harassment Law* (2004) 536.

QOs often require the restrainee to stay at home or in a hospital room; this is coercively imposed, rather than custodial house arrest with guards outside. As a type of house arrest, its impact on the restrainee's liberty is severe. All actions that require leaving one's home or room are blocked, as well as all actions that involve other persons being in close proximity to those who are contagious. On the other hand, a well-implemented system of QOs protects everyone who lives or travels near a contagious person—and hence the protectees are very numerous. They are free to move about the streets and do not need to isolate themselves in their homes or remote places in order to avoid infection. As this suggests, QOs take away liberties from the contagious and those who wish to be near them while increasing the liberties of the protectees.

A domestic RO typically limits the restrainee's liberty less than a QO. Instead of enduring coercively imposed house arrest the restrainee is usually prohibited from visiting selected locations, contacting certain persons, and/or engaging in specific types of actions. Often these prohibited actions and locations are ones that are legally permissible for most people. If the order is efficacious the protectees regain the liberty to go about their normal lives. Flight and hiding become unnecessary. When domestic ROs are effective and widely used, people similarly situated to the restrainee and to the protectee also experience impacts on their liberty. General deterrence is achieved when people who might otherwise engage in domestic abuse and violence learn of ROs and realize that judges have the power to restrict their liberties. Conversely, those enduring a significant probability of being victims of domestic abuse and violence may learn of ROs and realize that they have access to them as a form of protection. This may increase their ability to resist a controlling spouse or partner and give them the courage to lead a normal life. Overall, needed and effective domestic ROs are likely to promote liberty (in the broad sense) about as much as they restrict it.

Let's now look more closely at the impact on the liberty of the restrainee. This area of impact is the one most relevant to what sorts of procedural protections ROs should provide, and it is this impact that a judge must assess in order to decide whether the restraints are proportional to the danger posed. The impact on liberty of ROs varies significantly in accordance with the breadth and duration of the restraints imposed. A harassment restraining order may merely require the restrainee to stay a certain distance from a celebrity's home and to refrain from attempting to communicate with him or her. Here the impact is minimal. In contrast, a severe RO may block for a long period nearly everything the restrainee enjoys by forbidding many types of activities, excluding travel to most areas, and putting contact with many people off limits. This may make work, social life, and recreation difficult or impossible. From a longer-term perspective, however, an RO may help preserve a restrainee's overall liberty by offering a personalized warning that, if heeded, will allow him or her to avoid criminal prosecution and jail.

Still, the negative impact on the restrainee's liberty is often far from trivial. ROs often take away or restrict liberties to engage in actions that are generally permissible and that the restrainee was accustomed to doing and enjoying. Restrainees are often ordered to stay away from their workplaces, friends, homes, children, families, neighborhoods, and favourite hang-outs. The negative impact of ROs on liberty is generally not, however, as severe as custodial detention of equal duration.[17] Unlike detention, which *encloses* a person and makes access to anything outside the walls difficult, ROs typically *exclude* certain areas and behaviours but leave the rest of the world open and available.[18] In consequence, it is usually plausible to respond to the complaints of a person restrained by an RO by saying something like, 'Well, those restraints on your liberties are not trivial, but they're not nearly as bad for your liberty as being in jail.' The response might continue by saying that exclusion from a neighbourhood is not nearly as severe a restriction of liberty as being locked in a cell, that limited access to one's friends and children is not as bad as only seeing them when they visit you in jail, that having to detour around one's old neighbourhood in order to get to work is not as bad as losing one's job because one is in prison, and that not having access to one's gun collection is not nearly as severe a restriction on property and liberty as having access to almost none of one's belongings and having to wear a prison uniform. Further, even if an RO only excludes a small area and a few activities, liberties to be in that area and to engage in those activities may be those most valued by the addressee. Being excluded from one's workplace, home, and neighbourhood is likely to have a greater impact on one's liberty than being excluded from a local park, bar, or shopping mall.

Freedom of religion can be used by analogy to support the idea that personal attachments and commitments matter to liberty. For religious believers the most important religious liberties tend to be ones that protect their own specific religious commitments, loyalties, and practices. The liberty they care about most is not just being able to go to some place or other of religious worship, but being able to go to the services that best fit their particular religious beliefs (and perhaps the one that they have attended for a long time). The intellectually sophisticated may recognize that there is value for them and others in having much broader religious (and anti-religious) liberties, many of which they will never use. Still, the religious liberties that have the greatest value for many people are ones that protect their specific personal attachments in the area of religious belief and practice.

Once we recognize the importance of particular personal attachments we can see that a person who is subject to an RO denying him the liberty to visit his home or communicate with his children may take little solace in being told that he's not in detention and that he's only excluded from a small part of the world. He may say, 'They tell me that I'm nearly a free man, but the fact is that I'm forbidden from going to the places that are important to me and I'm blocked from seeing and communicating with my friends and loved ones'. In a similar vein, however, a woman who has to flee her home and neighbourhood in order to escape an abusive partner loses more liberty than she would if she just had to stay away from some

[17] We should recognize here that control orders are sometimes in force for longer periods than it is likely that custodial sentences for a similar sort of case would be. Further, a more likely alternative to an RO may be community-based noncustodial sanctions.

[18] There is a discussion of cases of exclusion so severe that they become inclusion or detention in Macdonald (cited in n 4) 613 f.

random house, store, or neighbourhood. Recognizing that losses of liberty are likely to be greater when they are in the area of a person's intense personal attachments complicates our thinking about liberty. Just knowing, for example, that association is restricted is insufficient; the *type* of association must be considered as well.

A recent development in the theory of liberty is Philip Pettit's view of freedom as nondomination.[19] It focuses less on the presence or absence of interference in a certain area and more on whether others have the power to interfere without much cost or risk to themselves. When others are in this position one is subject to a master or 'dominus' and one's liberty is impaired—even when the dominus does not in fact interfere. 'The ideal of freedom as nondomination would argue . . . for quite dramatic limitations on the power that one person or group of persons may have of imposing their will on another.' Fully explaining this view and applying it to ROs would make this chapter too long, but its general implications are clear.[20] It raises the worry that easily accessible ROs put angry spouses, ex-lovers, and annoyed employees into the position of master or dominus. And it raises the same worry about lower-court judges who have great power over restrainees that is not easily subject to review. But this perspective can also cut the other way by raising the worry that our social and legal institutions give the angry and aggressive too much unrestrained power over their partners, lovers, neighbours, and co-workers.

This section has shown that the impact of ROs on a restrainee's liberty is far from uniform. Some impacts on the restrainee are small (being required to stay away from the home of a celebrity that one has been stalking), while others are very large (coercively imposed house arrest), and still others are in the middle (being excluded from one's home, children, and neighbourhood). Further, the overall impact of an RO on liberty depends on whether restraining one person substantially increases the liberty of others. ROs sometimes do this and this means that they can be defended not just in terms of promoting security but also in terms of promoting liberty.

## C. ROs and human rights to fundamental freedoms

We now turn our attention to a smaller set of liberties—those covered by human rights to fundamental freedoms. There are at least nine rights in the European Convention on Human Rights (ECHR) and the International Covenant on Civil and Political Rights (ICCPR) that ROs can and sometimes do infringe. These are the freedoms of (1) movement and residence; (2) private and family life; (3) thought, conscience, and religion;[21] (4) communication or expression; (5) association; (6) peaceful assembly; (7) political participation and voting; (8) freedom to

[19] P Pettit, 'The Instability of Freedom as Noninterference: The Case of Isaiah Berlin' [2011] 121 *Ethics* 708; P Pettit, *Republicanism: A Theory of Freedom and Government* (1997).

[20] For a critical discussion of republican theory's application to criminal law, see A Ashworth and A von Hirsch, 'Not Not Just Deserts: A Response to Braithwaite and Pettit' (1992) 12 OJLS 83–98.

[21] In *Francois v Francois* 941 So. 2nd 722 (La App 2006), a Louisiana court held that a restraining order prohibiting a husband from going within 100 yards of his wife's residence did not violate the husband's constitutional right to attend his church—which was located within that excluded zone.

gain one's living through lawful work; and (9) property and possessions. An additional consideration is the impact of restraining orders on children's freedoms when they are part of the picture. For example, the Convention on the Rights of the Child Art 9.3 says that 'States Parties shall respect the right of the child who is separated from one or both parents to maintain personal relations and direct contact with both parents on a regular basis, except if it is contrary to the child's best interests'.

Human rights to fundamental freedoms do not require promoting liberty in the broad sense used earlier; they rather involve satisfying the duties owed to the rightholder(s) regarding certain limited but very important areas of liberty. It is fully possible for a human right to require governments to respect a particular liberty such as freedom of peaceful assembly, even if respecting one liberty results in an overall loss of liberty in terms of the broader conception of liberty used in the previous section. For example, the traffic jams caused by a big political demonstration may cause a net loss of liberty in the broad sense (at least in the short term). Recognition of a liberty as fundamental or basic means that we have decided that it is so important that we are willing to endure sacrifices of other liberties (and other goods as well) in order to protect it.

When a liberty is clearly covered by a human right it is sometimes impermissible to infringe it at all. Freedom of religious belief (in contrast to religious practice) is an example of this. Most rights to liberties may, however, be permissibly infringed provided that a high justificatory standard is met. To meet that standard it must be shown that the measure is proportional and that it is the least restrictive measure that will achieve a legitimate and important state interest. Suppose that a man—call him Robert—is convicted of possessing child pornography and in consequence is under an RO that forbids him from being in the company, without supervision, of juveniles under the age of 16.[22] This seems an infringement of Robert's right to freedom of association. It prohibits him from associating one-on-one with young family members such as nieces and nephews. If such an order is challenged as a violation of a human right, courts often proceed immediately to deliberations about weights and proportionality. We will return to proportionality testing, but let's first look at the question of whether the order is a prima facie violation of Robert's human rights. If it is, then his rights could be in conflict with the rights to security of the children protected. The possibilities are that Robert's unsupervised association with the children of his friends and family (1) is not covered by the scope of the right, (2) would be covered but for an exception to the right, or (3) would be covered but for Robert's having (fully or partially) forfeited the right to freedom of association. If none of these is plausible, then we return to balancing and proportionality. We might then conclude that the case does fall within the right's scope but that in Robert's case its protections are outweighed by more powerful competing considerations pertaining to the safety of children. We then have a conflict of rights that is resolved in favour of one or the other. Let's now look more closely at these four options.

[22] This example is adapted from *Helmsley v R* [2010] EWCA Crim 225.

*Outside the scope of the right.* Even if association with one's friends and family and their children is within the core of freedom of association, as I think it is, there is one clear way in which the right might fail to apply to Robert's case. If Robert's arrest for possession of child pornography led his teenage nieces to refuse to have any unsupervised visits with him, that would undermine Robert's claim under rights of association. This is because, quite generally, there is no right to associate with people who decline to associate with you. Robert has the right to freedom of association, but its application to association with any particular person is conditional on mutual consent. Enforcing Robert's exclusion from his nieces violates no right to association that he actually has.

The applicability of a number of human rights to fundamental freedoms has this sort of consent-dependence. An important consequence is that when consent is absent no right is violated if the government enforces a stay-away order. Such rights include the right to freedom of communication when that involves extended interaction; the right to freedom of co-habitation; freedoms to engage in sexual activities with other consenting persons; and the right to freedom of assembly when the assembly is not open to all.

*Exceptions.* If the scope of a right is represented by a circular pie chart, an exception is a slice of the pie that has been removed. Rights to fundamental freedoms sometimes have exceptions. For example, freedom of assembly is commonly restricted to *peaceful* assembly. A street gathering of people with guns who are discussing attacking the politicians working in the nearby parliament building is simply not covered by the freedom of assembly. Preventing such an assembly does not violate the right to freedom of assembly.

When two rights seem to conflict, we may find a clear exception within one of the rights that resolves the conflict. If the rights to life and security of the people in the parliament building are thought to conflict with the rights to assembly of the armed people gathering outside, attending to the exception restricting the latter right to *peaceful* assemblies resolves the conflict. No balancing is required.

*Forfeiture.* If Ike's right to freedom of movement allows him to create a danger to Leticia's security, we may have a conflict of rights. But if Ike has been fairly convicted of a serious crime, sent to prison, and then escapes, his freedom of movement has been, at least temporarily, forfeited—and the movements that endanger Leticia are covered by no right to free movement. Accordingly, no conflict between Ike's right to freedom of movement and Leticia's security is present.

Forfeiture is sometimes attractive as a way of explaining why someone's freedom of movement is not violated by an RO. If Kevin has been abusing Lena we may feel that he does not deserve his rights to free movement, that he lost his rights by being abusive. Caution is required here, however, since our hold on our human rights is perilously weak if it immediately breaks whenever we behave badly, and particularly when it breaks even though bad behaviour has not been proven in court. Possession of human rights is not limited to the deserving or those with perfect records. Beyond this, not all of the cases in which ROs are needed are ones in which illegal or seriously bad behaviour (that could warrant forfeiture) has already occurred.

*Balancing and overriding.* When we face a conflict of rights, balancing is another way of resolving the conflict. If we decide that one of the rights is weightier than another we say that it trumps, outweighs, or overrides the other. Human rights usually have broad formulations that contain only a few explicit exceptions. Even if an activity falls within the scope of the right and is not excluded by any specific exception or act of forfeiture, its protection under the right may still be outweighed by competing considerations. We use metaphors of weight and balancing in this type of case.

If a conflict of rights requires us to weigh the two rights against each other, this is not a matter of simply placing each undifferentiated unit on one side of a balance scale. The weight of specific areas within a right's scope often varies so the particularities of the case need to be taken into account. Within freedom of expression, for example, advertising for a political rally may have much greater weight or priority than advertising for a garage sale. Rights often have cores (areas of greatest weight), margins (areas of lesser weight), and borderline cases. For example, within the human right against torture and cruel treatment, avoiding torture has higher priority than avoiding cruel treatment—although the priority of both is very high.

Government duties to provide security against crimes are endorsed by political philosophers of almost all stripes and by contemporary human rights treaties. Political philosophers in the liberal democratic tradition have been unanimous in holding that one of the primary jobs of the state is to protect its residents against internal and external threats of crime and harm. Echoing Thomas Hobbes, John Stuart Mill said that security is the 'most indispensable of all necessaries'. As grounds for this he says that security is a good that 'no human being can possibly do without; on it we depend for all our immunity from evil, and for the whole value of all and every good, beyond the passing moment'.[23] Human rights treaties echo this view by accommodating the use of criminal punishments, short of the death penalty, provided they respect due process of law and are not cruel or degrading. Beyond this, human rights declarations and treaties require the legal protection of people's security. The ECHR Art 2.1 says that 'Everyone's right to life shall be protected by law', and Art 5.1 says that 'Everyone has the right to liberty and security of person'. The Convention on the Rights of the Child in Art 3.2 requires governments 'to ensure the child such protection and care as is necessary for his or her well-being', and Art 6.2 says that countries 'shall ensure to the maximum extent possible the survival and development of the child'.

States also have obligations under human rights treaties to protect public health. The International Covenant on Economic, Social, and Cultural Rights (ICESCR) Art 12.2(c) says that the steps to be taken by states to realize the right to health include: 'The prevention, treatment and control of epidemic, endemic, occupational and other diseases'.

Almost all of the fundamental freedoms in the ECHR and the ICCPR are accompanied by big qualification clauses. ECHR Art 8.2, which qualifies the right to respect for private and family life, is typical:

[23] JS Mill, *Utilitarianism* (1863) ch 5.

There shall be no interference by a public authority with the exercise of this right except such as is in accordance with the law and is necessary in a democratic society in the interests of national security, public safety or the economic well-being of the country, for the prevention of disorder or crime, for the protection of health or morals, or for the protection of the rights and freedoms of others.

Note, however, that restrictions must be 'necessary in a democratic society'. The European Court of Human Rights has made frequent use of this clause and has interpreted it as requiring proportionality between the liberty lost and a legitimate governmental aim of a *democratic* society such as providing protection against harmful and offensive behaviour.[24]

These qualification clauses may lead to the development of explicit exceptions to rights to fundamental freedoms or they may provide a guide to balancing by identifying considerations that can sometimes outweigh these rights. ROs have a good fit with some of these qualifications. They are designed to protect 'public safety', to prevent 'disorder or crime', and to secure 'the rights and freedoms of others'. Well-designed ROs that provide needed procedural protections and do not limit important liberties any more than necessary in a democratic society are compatible with human rights to the fundamental freedoms. Still, proportionality needs to be reviewed in every case and that will require serious thinking about how to best understand the scope and weight of rights to the fundamental freedoms.

If the arguments given in the previous section for the greater weight of liberties in areas of strong personal attachments are sound, they are relevant to how we should balance human rights to liberties against other rights. Protecting one person's right to security, say, by restricting some of another person's fundamental freedoms with an RO may be harder to justify when the relevant freedoms are in areas of strong personal attachments or are covered by privacy of home and family.

This section has illustrated some ways in which ROs can be compatible with rights to the fundamental freedoms. The compatibility of ROs with human rights also depends, however, on whether ROs are imposed with appropriate procedural requirements and display appropriate proportionality between the restraints on liberty they impose and the legitimate values actually promoted. It is to these topics that we now turn.

## D. ROs and human rights to due process

This section continues to take a human rights perspective, but now our concern is with the procedural requirements appropriate to ROs, particularly at the initiation and review stages. The strategy is to first identify some of the main grounds for due process rights in criminal proceedings and then assess their applicability to ROs.

[24] See, eg, *Lustig-Prean and Beckett v United Kingdom*, (2000) 29 ECHR 548. This case on homosexuals in the military is interesting in that it considered not only the impact on liberty of exclusion from military careers but also the impact on Art 8 privacy of the official investigation that was conducted concerning the litigants' sexual orientations.

Major international human rights treaties such as the ECHR and the ICCPR require that detention under the criminal law be accorded strong due process protections. Due process rights include a presumption of innocence and a high burden of proof for the government; being informed of the charges one faces; assistance from counsel of one's own choosing; pre-trial hearings to evaluate the grounds for detention and prosecution and to consider release pending trial; a fair trial without undue delay; to be present at one's trial; to call and examine witnesses; assistance from interpreters if needed; not to be compelled to testify against oneself or confess guilt; exclusion of hearsay evidence; no use of retroactive criminal laws; a right to appeal one's conviction and sentence; and a right against double jeopardy.[25] There is no doubt that meeting these standards has significant costs in terms of resources, personnel, slow proceedings, release of dangerous criminals for lack of sufficient evidence, and failed prosecutions of the guilty.

ROs are often imposed during criminal proceedings and in these cases their initiation is already protected in the UK and the USA by substantial due process requirements for criminal cases. Judges often order ROs as a condition of release on bail, as part of a criminal penalty (which might be a fine plus an RO), as a condition of release on parole, or even as a condition of release when the sentence has been fully served (as with sex offenders).

When ROs are imposed outside criminal proceedings it is common to provide far fewer procedural protections than are standard in criminal cases. At the initiation stage ROs are often imposed *ex parte* and with very low standards of proof. The applicant's account of an alleged danger may be sufficient, and deciding exactly which restraints to impose is often more like ticking boxes on a form than carefully designing the restraints to maximize effectiveness while minimizing losses to the restrainee's rights to liberties.[26] At the review stage when a temporary RO can be made 'permanent', both parties are expected to participate, although if the restrainee fails to appear the judge often can still decide to make the order permanent. Assistance from counsel is typically permitted at this stage. Modification of insufficient, excessive, or inappropriate restraints may be possible at this point, depending on judicial discretion. Standards of proof may be a little higher in the review stage, but a presumption that the RO is unnecessary (akin to the presumption of innocence) is rarely operative. Calling witnesses and demanding evaluation of evidence is likely to be permitted. The sanctioning phase is likely to have stronger due process protections—as indeed it should have, given that criminal penalties are possible. If judges are authorized to impose summary punishments for RO violations this promotes efficiency at the cost of procedural protections.

[25] A similar list is found in Ashworth and Zedner (cited in n 5) 82.

[26] 'Orders that conflicted were relatively common when custody of a child was involved. For example, among restrained persons who were granted sole custody, 27.9 per cent were not allowed visitation rights. In addition, orders that were difficult to implement also were relatively common. For example, when joint custody was granted, 90.0 per cent of the restrained persons were ordered not to contact the protected person': Sorenson and Shen (cited in n 13) 924.

## General grounds for due process rights

Tyrants throughout history have used the institutions, personnel, and sanctions of the criminal law as means of imposing their capricious and unjust rule. They throw their enemies and opponents into jail, have them executed, or take away their property. Historic and contemporary bills of rights recognize these dangers and accordingly give due process rights a prominent place.[27]

One rationale for due process rights is that they protect the *security* of our lives, liberties, and possessions against misuse (whether intentional, negligent, or accidental) of dangerous legal machinery such as coercive laws, powerful judges, armed police, prisons, and mental hospitals. To protect ourselves against greedy and dangerous neighbours we create government, law, and legally registered and protected property. We enact criminal laws, create courts and jails, and use these tools to convict and punish offenders. Experience soon teaches us that we need to fear not just greedy neighbours, but also the predations, corruption, and ineptitude of those controlling the laws, courts, and jails. Seeing that the criminal law system is dangerous to the law-abiding, and not just to offenders, we create due process rights to be enforced by independent courts. With success, these make it more difficult for officials to detain people without trial, improve the quality and integrity of legal deliberations, and protect our lives, liberty, and property. Like the criminal law itself, due process rights protect our security. Due process rights protect us directly when we are personally accused of crimes, but also indirectly by serving as checks on governmental power. They make less available tyrannical but perennially tempting ways of governing and thereby promote good government. Because due process rights are themselves security rights, conflicts between security rights and due process rights are not just conflicts between security and fairness. They are also conflicts between two different means of providing security.

Another rationale for due process rights is that they assist the state in vindicating its claim that it is highly probable that the accused committed the charged crime or is dangerous. By requiring careful investigations, imposing high standards of proof, and permitting appeals for reconsideration, due process rights help make it more likely that the state has adequate epistemological grounds for such stigmatizing claims. To put this more simply, they help reduce negligent and malicious errors by judges and prosecutors.

A third rationale for due process rights is that they help ensure fairness by putting the burden of proof on the state, requiring impartiality by judges and jurors, and demanding the consideration of excuses and justifications when they are offered. The centrepiece of due process rights is the right to a fair trial. Fair procedures can be seen as those that people could reasonably accept if they did not know whether they were going to be the victim, the judge, the prosecutor, the defence attorney, or the accused.

[27] This section is adapted from JW Nickel, *Making Sense of Human Rights* (2007) 106–22. This chapter is also available as 'Due Process Rights and Terrorist Emergencies' (2007) 1 European Journal of Legal Studies 1.

## Four arguments against heavy-duty due process protections for ROs

The arguments for due process rights just given do not necessarily apply to ROs except in their sanctioning stage (when criminal penalties are used to back up the coercive threats that failed to induce compliant behaviour). At the initiation and review stages ROs are commonly thought of as 'civil' remedies and, as such, are subject to much weaker procedural protections. Here I present and critically discuss four arguments for the conclusion that strong due process protections for ROs in the initiation and review stages are not necessary or appropriate.

*ROs are generally less serious matters than criminal charges.* Compared to a criminal charge, an RO is generally a less serious matter for an individual in terms of possible penalties, public condemnation, stigma or reputational loss, and loss of the right to vote.[28] This general difference helps explain why it is justifiable to have much weaker due process requirements for the initiation and review of ROs than for the imposition of criminal punishments.

Perhaps this argument's premise is broadly true, even though both the severity and duration of criminal penalties and of the restraints imposed by ROs vary widely. But the difference often is not as large as suggested, particularly if duration is held constant. The stigma of being a court-certified dangerous or violent person is severe and endangers employability. And serious criminal penalties for RO violations often lurk at the sanctioning stage.

*ROs are usually not as bad for one's liberty as custodial detention.* This argument is similar to the preceding argument but focuses specifically on the impact on a person's freedom in the broad sense. The impact on personal freedom of being jailed for a crime is usually far more severe than an RO of the same duration. This general difference also helps explain why it is justifiable to have much weaker due process requirements for the initiation and review of ROs than for the imposition of criminal punishments. We have seen, however, that ROs vary greatly in their consequences for the restrainee's liberty. Some ROs impose extended house arrest and hence have major negative impacts on liberty. And a severe RO that keeps the restrainee away from his or her children, long-time home, and jointly owned possessions also has a serious impact on liberty. Beyond this, ROs certainly have the potential to violate human rights to fundamental freedoms. Severe ROs can have more serious impacts on the restrainee's liberty than minor criminal penalties, and thus it is unwise to proceed in terms of grand categories such as civil versus criminal or restraining order versus criminal penalty.

*Adjudicating an RO is easier than a criminal prosecution.* This argument alleges that adjudicating an RO is less difficult than a criminal prosecution because the evidentiary basis may be clearer (and even 'scientific') and criminal intent (ie, *mens rea*) does not need to be shown.[29] This general difference in the difficulty of

[28] This argument is made about QOs by EP Richards, 'Dangerous People, Unsafe Conditions: The Constitutional Basis for Public Health Surveillance' (2009) 30 Journal of Legal Medicine 29.

[29] EP Richards makes this argument about QOs (but not generally about ROs): 'In public health dangerousness cases, there are usually laboratory tests or other objective evidence on infection, as well

adjudication helps explain why it is justifiable to have weaker due process requirements for the initiation and review of ROs than for the imposition of criminal punishments.

This may be generally true of QOs, but it is emphatically not true of other ROs. Estimating the dangerousness of a person is frequently *more* difficult than determining whether he or she committed a crime.[30] Estimating the probability that someone will cause serious offence or harm to others in the near future is very difficult.[31] Even the knowledge that someone was violent last week provides no sure basis for predicting that he or she will be violent today (perhaps this person has stopped consuming alcohol or has resumed taking prescribed medication). Further, judicial bias is just as possible with ROs as in criminal matters.

*ROs often need to be imposed immediately.* To prevent harm during a period of crisis ROs often need to be imposed immediately on an emergency basis. If the goal is to stop a person from spreading a serious and contagious disease, speed is vital. Similarly, if the goal is to prevent a dangerous person from harming family members or co-workers, success will be greatly handicapped by having to wait weeks for a court date. Further, if the goal is to prevent violence and there is a significant risk of its occurrence, the protectees' rights to security are in play. Security rights are very weighty and often succeed in overriding other rights. If heavy-duty due process protections were required at the initiation stage this would introduce substantial delays that would result in ROs being unavailable when most needed.[32] The need for speed helps explain why it is justifiable to have weaker due process requirements for the initiation of ROs than for the imposition of criminal punishments.

This argument works best for QOs and domestic and workplace ROs—and needs to be accommodated in cases where a judge has strong reasons to believe that an RO is urgently needed. It does not work for ROs imposed when the danger is not imminent. For example, ASBOs rightly have serious procedural requirements at the initiation stage. Further, the contrast this argument draws with criminal prosecutions is exaggerated since the incapacitation of dangerous criminals often needs to be accomplished at the very moment they are apprehended so that they will not escape and endanger others. To deal with this kind of urgency the criminal law permits immediate arrest and custodial detention, holds a short hearing within a few days of detention, permits denial of release on bail when dangerousness can be shown, and then proceeds with prosecution and trial. This is similar to what many

as specific behavior or environmental facts that point to dangerousness. The most difficult questions of criminal law—intent and mens rea—are not at issue': Richards (cited in n 28) 28–9.

30 See L Zedner, 'Neither Safe Nor Sound? The Perils and Possibilities of Risk' (2006) 48 Canadian Journal of Criminology and Criminal Justice 423–34; Zedner (cited in n 4) 190.

31 See B Harcourt, this volume.

32 As EP Richards says, 'with the exception of cases of drug-resistant tuberculosis and certain other rare communicable diseases, public health restrictions are limited either by time or intrusiveness. In all cases, the restrictions are limited to what is necessary to prevent the spread of the disease and may not be used as a punishment for being infected': Richards (cited in n 28) 28–9.

RO systems do when they impose temporary ROs on an emergency basis and then hold a review hearing within a few days or weeks.

## The case for procedural protections for the use of ROs

In spite of the four arguments just considered, the grounds offered for due process rights in criminal proceedings also apply to the initiation and review of ROs. This is true not only of very severe ROs such as control orders for suspected terrorists, but also for some of the less severe and more widely used ROs.

First, ROs have serious potential to be used maliciously or in ways that will result in the invasion or undermining of security of life, liberty, and property. Since ROs are often easy to get they are sometimes used to gain advantage in divorce and child custody disputes. Being put under an RO frequently has a negative impact on the restrainee's welfare, liberty, family relationships, property, reputation, and employability. Procedural protections for ROs help protect people's security against the state by increasing the likelihood that those who abide by the law will not be subject to an RO. Further, procedural protections help prevent an RO from wrongly stigmatizing a person as violent or dangerous by reducing errors in the initiation stage. Finally, procedural protections for ROs help ensure fairness by requiring meaningful standards of proof, impartiality, and access to review on appeal of all aspects of imposition (initiation, review, and sanctioning).

We saw earlier that in recent decades lawmakers in both the UK and the USA have created statutory schemes to guide courts in the use of domestic restraining orders. This was often good news for due process protections, since the schemes generally require a judicial review of the orders within a few weeks of initiation. Restrainees are entitled to participate in these reviews, should they choose to do so.

Nevertheless, due process protections for ROs often fall far short of those protections available in criminal prosecutions; standards of proof are low and hearsay evidence is accepted. This means that a complainant's word is often sufficient to impose a restraining order and supporting expert testimony will not generally be required. There is no presumption in favour of a potential restrainee akin to the presumption of innocence. Further, when there is a threat of harm, judges sometimes proceed on a precautionary principle holding that when irreversible damage is threatened the absence of full certainty should not be used as a reason for refusing to take action.[33] Caution of this sort serves the important goal of protecting the security rights of the complainant, but such a precautionary policy would never be permissible in a criminal proceeding and further lowers the standard of evidence required. Beyond this, ROs are often created in a very casual and standardized way—by ticking boxes on a form. Finally, and most importantly, judges have great discretion in decisions concerning ROs, including what penalties they can impose for contempt. There are no juries in RO initiation and review

[33] Zedner (cited in n 4) 188.

proceedings and judges may be biased by their knowledge of the potential restrainee's criminal record.[34]

To preserve the lower costs, timeliness, and flexibility associated with ROs, we should not overburden their initiation and review with heavy procedural protections, except when the restraints are very severe. But what counts as an excessive burden and which procedures are 'due' requires serious consideration. Table 8.1 is meant to illustrate this point. It compares procedural protections in criminal proceedings and in RO proceedings. The right-hand column offers the author's opinion of the relevance of the procedural protection in the left-hand column to the initiation and review stages of RO proceedings. In adapting the protections classified as 'fully relevant' or 'partly relevant' one needs to bear in mind considerations about timeliness and cost. Further, it may be possible to classify the severity of restraints likely to be imposed by the RO as minor, medium, and severe, for example, and to calibrate procedural protections to those levels. This approach is more discriminating than one simply based on whether the proceedings are civil or criminal.

## E. Efficacy and reliance

It is highly likely that different kinds of RO have different degrees of efficacy since the populations they restrain tend to be different.[35] Consequently, statistical studies of domestic ROs or ASBOs are not a sure guide to the efficacy of other kinds of RO. For example, most restrainees of domestic ROs have prior criminal records, which would not be the case with the restrainees of QOs. About 80 per cent of restrainees of domestic ROs are men, but this also would not ordinarily be the case with the restrainees of QOs.

There is little evidence to suggest that domestic ROs have great efficacy in reducing violence and harassment. Efficacy involves a causal claim, namely that imposing ROs and providing current levels of enforcement for them causes a reduction in the likelihood of future violence or harassment by restrainees. Causal claims in this area are hard to establish since we cannot do double-blind experiments and because statistical studies often lack control groups. Levels of enforcement provided for domestic ROs vary substantially by cities, states, and regions. We know that violation rates for domestic ROs are high but not all of these violations are serious ones. Victims of domestic abuse protected by ROs report re-abuse at high rates (around 50 per cent).[36] It is likely that domestic ROs help in some cases, but their power to influence their targets is probably modest. GPS tracking devices with victim-notification capability are now being used in some

[34] Sorenson and Shen (cited in n 13) 914.

[35] On the efficacy of control orders for suspected terrorists, see Zedner (cited in n 4) 190.

[36] For a 2010 review of studies of efficacy see C Benitez, D McNiel, and R Binder, 'Do Protection Orders Protect?' (2010) 38 *The Journal of the American Academy of Psychiatry and Law* 376–85.

**Table 8.1** Procedural protections in criminal and RO proceedings

| Criminal proceedings | RO proceedings |
| --- | --- |
| Limits to state investigative powers (limits on warrantless and severely invasive searches) | Fully relevant |
| *Miranda* warnings before interrogation | Partially relevant—restrainees need to know if their testimony in review proceedings can be used against them in criminal prosecutions |
| Right to assistance of counsel and interpreters | Fully relevant |
| Right to be informed of charges | Fully relevant—restrainees should have clear and timely official communication of the restraints imposed, their evidential basis, and procedures available for review and modification |
| Habeas corpus, right of access to courts | Fully relevant when adapted—provides the basis for review and appeals |
| Indictment hearing | N/A |
| Presumptive availability of bail | N/A |
| Right to a fair public trial without undue delay | Fully relevant when adapted; it becomes the right to a fair and prompt public proceeding at initiation or review |
| Right to impartial and competent judge | Fully relevant |
| Presumption of innocence | Partially relevant as the principle that dangerousness requires serious evidence |
| High standard of proof | Medium standard of proof at the initiation and review stages; high standard at the sanctioning stage |
| Right against retroactive criminal laws | N/A |
| Crimes defined by generally published statutes | N/A |
| Right against double jeopardy | N/A |
| Right to be present at one's trial | Fully relevant as a presumptive right to presence at initiation, review, and sanctioning hearings |
| Right to call and examine witnesses and gather evidence | Fully relevant in all proceedings |
| Right not to be forced to confess or to testify against oneself | Fully relevant in all proceedings |
| Exclusion of hearsay evidence | N/A, but there should be at least some protections against the dangers of hearsay evidence |
| Right to consideration of excuses and justifications | Fully relevant |
| Right against a cruel or grossly disproportionate sentence | Fully relevant when it becomes a proportionality requirement on restraints |
| Right to appeal conviction and sentence | Fully relevant—right of review and further appeals after initiation |
| Duty of officials to review status of incarcerated persons to ensure that they are not held beyond their sentence | Relevant to providing protection against restraints of unnecessarily extended duration |

jurisdictions in hopes of increasing efficacy; these devices send an alert to a potential victim or to the police when a restrainee enters an excluded zone.

If having domestic ROs in place does not greatly reduce the probability of violence and abuse then it is dangerously wrong to encourage people to rely on them for protection. A victim of abuse who naively believes that an RO provides significant protection may fail to take alternative steps such as fleeing to a safe refuge. Put differently, there is real risk that ROs create a false and dangerous illusion that effective protection is being provided. To reduce the use of ROs in such situations it may be necessary not just to improve enforcement but also to make greater use of criminal prosecutions. In the UK and the USA criminal law already has substantial due process requirements, so why not prevent future crimes by arresting and criminally prosecuting people who reveal their dangerousness in action?[37] If the potential restrainee has already committed a crime that can be prosecuted and proven in court, then criminal sanctions can be used instead of an RO. After a criminal conviction concern for the offender's liberties is lessened because society can then plausibly claim that he or she has forfeited his or her rights to liberties by behaviour that is morally wrong and legally a crime.

Unfortunately, this approach does not account for all of the people who could be restrained by an RO. Dangerous people can be divided into three groups: (1) those whose dangerousness is not detectable with any reasonable degree of accuracy; (2) those whose dangerousness is detectable with some reasonable degree of accuracy even though it has not been revealed through illegal actions; and (3) those whose dangerousness has been revealed through prosecutable actions. There is not much society can do about group 1, and those who fall into group 3 can be prosecuted under criminal law. The criminal law cannot help us with group 2, but preventive measures such as ROs and preventive custodial detention can (although difficult problems with detecting dangerousness are present). ROs are also helpful in dealing with group 3 by providing additional options in sentencing and upon release.

In cases where a dangerous person commits criminal acts prior to doing great harm, the criminal law can come into play. But for arrest to work preventively during a crisis period it is necessary to keep the suspect in custody. That means no release on bail. That creates human rights problems of its own. Restraining orders and electronic monitoring can also be required for release on bail, but then we're back to restraining orders.

Further, meeting criminal standards of proof and obtaining a conviction is often difficult; a lack of evidence will normally result in the charges being dropped. Even if a trial occurs a failure to convict will put the person back on the streets. Further, the case may result in a plea bargain for a lesser charge and lower punishment. Restraining orders may then be needed, but presumably can be initiated with suitable process. Still, we're then back to restraining orders.

Finally, convictions of dangerous people who have not yet done great damage are often for misdemeanours and thus only result in short sentences. In 30, 60, or 90

[37] For this suggestion see Ashworth and Zedner (cited in n 5).

days, the abuser will be back on the streets. Restraining orders may then be needed, but presumably can be initiated within the procedures of criminal law. However, this brings us full circle—back to the use of ROs.

## F. Conclusion

In hopes of improving the quality of our thinking about ROs and their use, this chapter has analysed their place within preventive law and illustrated some of the ways in which they can both restrict and promote individual liberty. The negative impact of ROs on the restrainee's liberty is sometimes substantial, and is more severe when it involves areas of strong personal commitments. Nevertheless, when ROs are efficacious they redistribute freedom from the restrainee to the protectee(s) in ways that can increase freedom overall.

One important question about ROs is their compatibility with human rights to fundamental freedoms. Although ROs can violate these rights, they often do not do so because: (1) the restrained actions are not covered by their scope, (2) they would apply were it not for a clear exception to the right that is present, (3) they would be covered but for forfeiture of the right, or (4) the protections they provide are so important to security and other values that human rights protections are outweighed.

The chapter has also addressed the question of appropriate procedural requirements for ROs and showed that the arguments supporting due process in criminal law are not without traction when applied to ROs. The great discretionary power that judges have in issuing, reviewing, and punishing violations of ROs leaves plenty of room for bias and failure to assess proportionality with sufficient care. Finally, the efficacy of ROs was briefly explored and the serious dangers that ineffective ROs can pose to persons who rely on them were emphasized. It is likely that ROs are here to stay, but continuing scrutiny of their effectiveness, impacts on liberty and human rights, and areas of use is appropriate.

# 9

# Preventive Detention as Punishment?

## Some Possible Obstacles

*Douglas Husak**

## A. Introduction

In a recent article, I expressed optimism that a narrow practice of preventive detention might be justified—and cabined within acceptable limits—if it is placed within our familiar institutions of criminal justice.[1] To this end, I proposed that (1) whatever persons have done that would lead us to detain them for preventive ends should be construed as *crimes*; and (2) the sanctions imposed on those who commit these crimes should be understood as *punishments*. If this feat can be accomplished, the normative standards to assess the practice of preventive detention could be borrowed from those that are used to assess the criminal law. Since I have argued that the normative standards that should be used to assess the criminal law are stringent,[2] it follows that the normative standards that should be used to assess preventive detention are stringent as well.

I do not insist that my proposal is the *only* possible way to defend preventive detention. Although my general thoughts on criminal justice proceed within the retributivist tradition, I concede that the deontological constraints that apply within this school of thought may be relaxed if the stakes are sufficiently high.[3] When the barbarians are at the gate, actions otherwise wrongful become permissible. In any event, alternative means to justify preventive detention must be developed in detail and evaluated on their own merits.[4] Much of the motivation of my approach is to avoid a problem that other suggestions are bound to face.

* I owe an enormous debt to Andrew Ashworth, Lucia Zedner, Patrick Tomlin, and the several attendees at the Preventive Justice Project seminar at Oxford University in September 2011.

[1] See D Husak, 'Lifting the Cloak: Preventive Detention as Punishment' (2011) 48 San Diego Law Review 1173. The thoughts in this earlier paper are extended here.

[2] The application of these standards produces a substantive criminal law I describe as *minimalist.* See D Husak, *Overcriminalization* (2008).

[3] For reservations, see L Alexander, 'Deontology at the Threshold' (2000) 37 San Diego Law Review 893.

[4] See A Walen, 'A Punitive Precondition for Preventive Detention: Lost Status as a Foundation for a Lost Immunity' (2011) 48 San Diego Law Review 1229; and KK Ferzan, 'Inchoate Crimes at the Prevention/Punishment Divide' (2011) 48 San Diego Law Review 1273.

More specifically, my proposal does not involve deception or false labelling. Most theorists who struggle to defend a system of preventive detention locate it *outside* the scope of criminal justice. They describe the preventive sanctions they try to justify as something other than *punishments* and they call what the persons have done something other than *crimes*. But changing these *names* only helps to obfuscate. On any plausible account, the persons we hope to preventively detain have *done* something that leads us to want to detain them. If so, why not enact criminal offences that proscribe the things they have done? Moreover, the state response to these persons amounts to an intentional, stigmatizing deprivation. If so, why is this sanction not a form of punishment? *My* approach, then, has the virtue of candour; it aspires to remove the 'cloak' that some commentators have contended is used to disguise schemes of preventive detention.[5] The more promising and honest strategy to justify a type of preventive detention, I think, would construe it as *punishment* for *crime*. Or so I will argue here.

I doubt that those commentators who seek to justify a scheme of preventive detention are eager to engage in subterfuge. But they are driven to describe the system of preventive detention they support as something other than penal justice for a simple reason: they believe that an acceptable form of preventive detention *cannot* be construed as I propose—that is, as punishment for crime. They contend that the obstacles to my position are both conceptual and normative. In this chapter I respond to several of these alleged conceptual and normative difficulties. Although some of these problems are worrisome, I attempt to show that they are less formidable than many commentators suppose. But first I want to clarify my proposal by discussing three potential misunderstandings.

First, I allege that preventive justice can be conceptualized and justified as penal justice *in principle*. Admittedly, a number of empirical misgivings make my proposal far more difficult to implement *in practice*. As virtually every commentator is aware, our ability to predict future dangerousness is meagre.[6] Moreover, in many of the circumstances in which we *are* able to predict proclivities to cause harm with tolerable precision, the state has a wealth of alternative devices to reduce these harms that are more easily justified and thus are preferable to preventive detention. Because these empirical points are so widely appreciated, I do not belabour them here. Unless our ability to predict future harm is relatively accurate and the risk cannot be averted by less intrusive means, the case in favour of any system of

[5] See PH Robinson, 'Punishing Dangerousness: Cloaking Preventive Detention as Criminal Justice' (2001) 114 Harvard Law Review 1429.

[6] Some social scientists are more pessimistic than others. See the serious reservations described by D Cooke and C Michie, 'Limitations of Diagnostic Precision and Predictive Utility in the Individual Case: A Challenge for Forensic Practice' (2010) 34 Law and Human Behavior 259. These authors conclude that rates of error make predictions of violence in individual cases 'practically meaningless': at 263. Others argue that none of the available instruments predicts violence significantly better than the others, see JL Skeem and J Monahan, 'Current Directions in Violence Risk Assessment' in *Current Directions in Psychological Science* (2011), available at <http://cdp.sagepub.com/content/20/1/38>. Moreover, prediction is especially problematic in cases of terrorism—the kinds of dangers on which I focus. See J Monahan (cited in n 13).

preventive detention collapses. Thus it is no *objection* to my proposal to remind me that prediction is highly fallible and that penal justice should be close to a last resort. Henceforth I simply *assume* that our predictive powers are sufficiently reliable and that the harms in question cannot be prevented by some lesser means.

Secondly, I should not be understood to attempt to justify any *existing* scheme of preventive detention—like the indefinite detention of prisoners in Guantanamo Bay. If my proposal is accepted, preventive detention as currently practised must be reformed radically. If these reforms are implemented, the scheme of preventive detention I believe will emerge will barely resemble any existing scheme with which we are familiar. I am fully aware that my proposal will make political officials far less willing to resort to preventive detention in the real world. Again, I do not construe this admission as a *difficulty* with my approach. I seek only to describe the changes that would need to be made in order for a scheme of preventive detention to be defensible as a mode of penal justice. Political officials who decline to adopt my proposal must either (a) renounce preventive detention; (b) presuppose an alternative justification for preventive detention; or (c) proceed with a system that is unjustified. In the real world that ignores the normative arguments of philosophers, I strongly suspect that most political officials will follow (c).

Thirdly, for reasons that will become clear, my proposal will permit preventive justice only to forestall the most serious harms. In particular, I allege that my approach allows preventive detention of persons who pose threats of massive destruction—such as those created by the worst kinds of terrorists. I offer no suggestions for how we might justify the preventive detention of persons we have good reason to believe pose threats of far less serious harms—such as those caused by shoplifters. I reserve judgement about which kinds of harm are sufficiently serious to qualify for preventive detention under my scheme. In particular, I offer no opinion about whether my proposal will allow the preventive detention of sexual offenders.

With these three clarifications in mind, I now turn to the supposed conceptual and normative obstacles that some commentators regard as fatal to my proposal. Some of these problems will turn out to be more formidable than others. Moreover, each of the conceptual obstacles I discuss can be reformulated as a normative obstacle with little difficulty, so the contrast between the two is far less sharp than I indicate. In any event, I discuss each kind of obstacle in turn.

## B. Conceptual obstacles

A number of legal philosophers appear to think it is relatively clear that preventive detention is *not* punishment for crime and cannot be assimilated to it. Even when they do not say so explicitly, the fact that they are driven to construct novel defences of preventive detention is ample evidence of their scepticism. I construe these philosophers to claim not only that existing systems of preventive detention are not punishment at the present time, but also that preventive detention cannot be reformed to *become* punishment for crime. Deprivations based on risks of future criminality, no matter how well grounded empirically, are widely regarded as an abuse of the criminal law.[7] I propose to challenge this claim—or, at a minimum, to show that the difficulties of defending it are greater than many legal philosophers suppose.

We cannot assess this possible obstacle unless we are able to identify what the criminal law *is*. How do we know whether a law enacted by the state qualifies as one of its *criminal* laws? I hold that the criminal law *just is* that body of law that subjects persons to state punishment. If punishment is the sanction the state is authorized to inflict for violations of a rule, it follows that that rule is part of its criminal law. Conversely, if a rule is part of the criminal law of a state, it follows that that state is authorized to punish persons who violate it. Thus the rules that allow preventive detention can be conceptualized as part of the criminal law—that is, as criminal offences—if and only if it is possible to categorize preventive detention as punishment. Is it? Despite widespread agreement that preventive detention is *not* punishment, we need to be clear *why* most penal theorists are convinced that the two institutions are conceptually distinct. In other words, we must examine why many commentators are persuaded that a preventive restriction on liberty cannot qualify as a punishment so that the rules that authorize it cannot be conceptualized as part of a state's criminal law. In order to do so, we must clarify what *punishment* is—that is, what makes a particular sanction an instance of state punishment. I contend that punishment necessarily contains (at least) two essential features: *hard treatment* (or *deprivation*) and *stigma* (or *censure*).

Almost no one denies that punishment includes the first of these components. Unless someone suffers a deprivation, we would not say he has been punished. Clearly, however, not all state inflictions of hard treatment are modes of punishment. Taxes, licence revocations, benefit terminations, and other disqualifications are not ordinarily punitive, despite the severe hardship they may cause. Thus a second condition must be satisfied before a sanction should be categorized as an instance of state punishment. I contend that a response to conduct does not qualify as punitive unless it expresses censure.[8] Clearly, each of these components is present when the state preventively detains a terrorist who threatens to cause enormous destruction. Why, then, is preventive detention almost universally regarded as something conceptually distinct from punishment? And why are the rules that authorize it generally treated as something conceptually distinct from criminal laws? In the remainder of this section, I will critically discuss four of many possible answers that might be given to this question.

I characterize the first two answers to this basic question as *formal* inasmuch as the problems they cite can easily be overcome by a few adjustments to positive law. Since I believe I have dealt adequately with these two problems elsewhere, I will only summarize my replies here.[9] The *first* possible answer invokes the principle of legality: *nulla poena sine lege*. The rule of law requires punishments to be imposed

[7] For one of many examples, see Robinson (cited in n 5) 1434.

[8] For an impressive defence of the view that punishment includes both hard treatment and censure, see A von Hirsch, *Censure and Sanctions* (1993).

[9] See Husak (cited in n 1).

only on persons who have committed (or are believed to have committed) a crime. But persons preventively detained, this first answer continues, have not committed a crime. Hence they are not punished. As one commentator expresses the point, 'criminal punishment is based solely upon a conviction for an offense and can occur only if there is such a conviction. Preventive detention is based solely upon a prediction concerning future offenses and can occur only if there is such a prediction. Therefore, preventive detention is not punishment.'[10]

But any problem created by legality is easily rectified—at least in principle. Whether or not what a person has done amounts to a criminal offence depends solely on the content of positive law. If we want to punish the persons we propose to preventively detain but need to ensure they are guilty of a criminal offence in order to do so, we need only amend existing codes and enact new statutes for these persons to breach. If predictions of future dangerousness are reasonably accurate—as I have presupposed—they must be based on traits of persons derived through actuarial generalizations.[11] Although a massive amount of empirical research has tried to identify these characteristics,[12] I make no effort to summarize or evaluate these findings here. Henceforth I simply refer to the traits that predict future dangerousness as *x*, *y*, and *z*. Again, I do not for a moment belittle the difficulties of identifying these characteristics, especially when terrorism is involved.[13] But the material elements of the new statutes to be enacted would include these traits—whatever it is that persons have done that leads us to make predictions of their future dangerousness.[14] I deliberately provide no concrete illustrations of a possible offence that the persons we want to preventively detain would commit. Examples of these statutes await developments in the social sciences that enhance the accuracy of our predictions.

Admittedly, many complaints might be lodged against any new offence the state enacts.[15] Most notably, the offence might amount to a 'status crime' in violation of the supposed 'act requirement' of the criminal law.[16] This particular complaint is important, and I will return to it in section C, 'Normative obstacles'. For now, I simply point out that the state *could* resolve whatever problems are associated with

[10] C Slobogin: 'A Jurisprudence of Dangerousness' (2003) 98(1) Northwestern University Law Review 12–13.

[11] I am aware of the supposed contrast between actuarial and clinical bases for predicting dangerousness that has been a staple of the literature since the publication by P Meehl, *Clinical Versus Statistical Prediction: A Theoretical Analysis and a Review of the Evidence* (1954). Even clinical predictions, however, must be based on generalizations derived from previous observations.

[12] See, eg, the Violence Risk Appraisal Guide (VARG) discussed in J Monahan, 'A Jurisprudence of Risk Assessment: Forecasting Harm Among Prisoners, Predators, and Patients' (2006) 92 University of Virginia Law Review 291.

[13] In particular, the traits that predict acts of terrorism may be quite unlike those that predict dangerousness generally. See J Monahan, 'The Individual Risk Assessment of Terrorism' *Psychology, Public Policy, and Law* (forthcoming 2012).

[14] Although I will not attempt to formulate any such offences, it is likely that some such traits *already* appear as elements of existing crimes. For example, the US Supreme Court has recently upheld the constitutionality of laws prohibiting the giving of material aid to designated foreign terrorist groups in *Holder v Humanitarian Law Project* 130 S.Ct. 2705 (2010).

[15] If they include political speech or religious affiliation as material elements, for example, these statutes would encounter obvious First Amendment problems under the US Constitution.

[16] See *Robinson v California* 370 US 660 (1962); and *Powell v Texas* 392 US 514 (1968).

the principle of legality by drafting statutes that would be violated by the persons we propose to detain preventively. If the absence of positive law is the problem, the enactment of positive law is the solution.

If the state were to draft new statutes that are violated by the persons we propose to detain preventively, a *second* formal attempt to show why preventive detention cannot be punishment would fail as well. Whether a sanction qualifies as punitive, it might be thought, depends partly on the *procedures* that must be observed in order to inflict it. In the USA, many of these procedures are constitutional in stature. For example, no one may be punished in the absence of a trial that includes several well-known safeguards—such as the right to confront witnesses. But few persons who are preventively detained are tried and afforded the protections that famously surround the criminal process.

Like its predecessor, however, this purported difference between punishment and preventive detention is easily remedied. We need only mandate that appropriate procedures be observed whenever persons are preventively detained. Of course, many commentators would vehemently resist or even ridicule this recommendation.[17] Officials worry that the need to charge and try individuals—or to read them their *Miranda* rights in the United States—would undermine most or all of the supposed advantages of preventive detention.[18] Much has been written both for and against this allegation; I reserve judgement about whether it is true. My point is that we *could* extend all of the procedural safeguards currently available to criminal defendants to each of those persons we preventively detain.

The more realistic concern, however, is not that the array of procedural protections presently afforded in penal justice could not possibly be extended to the persons we want to preventively detain. Instead, the more trenchant worry is that my proposal to incorporate preventive detention into the criminal law would lead to a further erosion of the procedural safeguards that currently exist in the latter domain. If indeed the procedures observed throughout the penal law undermine the objectives we hope to achieve through prevention, it would be tempting to relax those protections in the name of public safety throughout the whole of the criminal law.[19] It is hard to know how to ensure that this temptation will be resisted. Deontological and consequentialist objectives have long been thought to compete in criminal justice, and my proposal can be expected to heighten these tensions still more.

Neither of these two formal answers gets to the heart of the matter. One would not suspect that the problem of conceptualizing preventive detention as punishment could be solved so easily—by enlarging the scope of procedural protections or by enacting new statutes. The next two obstacles, however, are potentially more

[17] Some purport to find the very idea difficult to imagine. See SJ Schulhofer, 'Two Systems of Social Protection: Comments on the Civil-Criminal Distinction, with Particular Reference to Sexually Violent Predator Laws' (1995) 7 Journal of Contemporary Legal Problems 69.

[18] Some of the procedural difficulties of prosecuting terrorists in criminal court are discussed by M Waxman, 'Administrative Detention' (2009) 3 Journal of National Security Law & Policy 1.

[19] For example, see L Laudan, 'The Rules of Trial, Political Morality, and the Costs of Error: Or, Is Proof Beyond a Reasonable Doubt Doing More Harm than Good?' in L Green and B Leiter (eds), *Oxford Studies in Philosophy of Law* Vol 1 (2011) 195.

serious, and cannot be overcome by a few revisions in positive law. The third possible difficulty is as follows. Many theorists contend that preventive detention cannot be punishment, and that the rules that authorize it cannot be part of a state's criminal law, because persons *can* only be punished *for* past behaviour. According to this train of thought, punishment for future dangerousness is a logical impossibility. As Chris Slobogin bluntly contends, 'the concept of "punishment" for some future act is incoherent'.[20]

How difficult is this third problem? Notice first that it seemingly purports to resolve the ancient debate between retributivists and consequentialists by invoking a definition. If persons *can* only be punished *for* what they have done in the past, it is hard to see how punishment could possibly be justified by its tendency to attain a future benefit. Of course, retributivists (like me) reject consequentialist defences of punishment. Still, the deficiencies of consequentialist justifications of punishment must be demonstrated on normative grounds rather than through conceptual analysis. In other words, no account of what punishment allegedly *is* can refute consequentialist rationales. The 'definitional stops' on which this answer depends have a dubious legacy in the history of controversies in penal justice.[21]

Definitions take us only so far. In order to provide a substantive response to this third worry (as well as to provide a fair assessment of the debate between consequentialists and retributivists), it is crucial to recognize an ambiguity in understanding *why* a response to something is taken. In asking what punishment is imposed *for*, we may want to know either (1) in virtue of what is punishment inflicted, or (2) what is the purpose for which punishment is inflicted? These two 'why' questions are distinct, and a failure to contrast them has led to enormous confusion about punishment generally and systems of preventive detention in particular. Richard L Lippke, for example, writes, 'the more worrisome feature of preventive detention, in my view, is that it punishes individuals *for* crimes they will commit rather than for ones they have committed'.[22] If Lippke is correct, preventive detention must be conceptualized as an instance of what has come to be known as 'pre-punishment'.[23] I hope to avoid the controversy that surrounds pre-punishment, since I believe that preventive detention need not be understood as Lippke construes it.

The notorious 'for' relation must be disambiguated to appreciate why preventive detention need not be conceptualized as a form of pre-punishment. I admit that the answer to question (1) necessarily looks backwards. In this sense, any punishment under a system of preventive detention is imposed *for* or *in virtue of* possession of the traits *x*, *y*, and *z*. Even though these characteristics are incorporated into elements of offences because they predict future dangerousness, the persons to be

20 Slobogin (cited in n 10) 13.

21 See HLA Hart, *Punishment and Responsibility* (1968) especially 5.

22 RL Lippke, 'Dangerous Offenders and Preventive Detention' (2008) 27 Law and Philosophy 383 (emphasis added).

23 Recent discussion of pre-punishment has been enormous. For an important contribution, see S Smilansky, 'A Time to Punish' (2004) 54 *Analysis* 50. For an application of this perspective to preventive detention, see L Zedner, 'Preventive Justice or Pre-Punishment? The Case of Control Orders' (2007) 60 CLP 174.

punished possess them at the present time; the future is immaterial to their liability, to what they are liable *for*. It does not follow, however, that the answer to question (2) must look backwards as well. As consequentialists and nearly all retributivists recognize, it is perfectly coherent and eminently sensible to impose punishment *for* or *for the purpose of* attaining a future good.[24] The mode of preventive detention I hope to justify is an illustration; it imposes punishment in virtue of (that is, *for*) traits already possessed in order to avert (that is, *for the purpose of* averting) a subsequent harm.

Moreover, the generalizations about the criminal law on which this third problem depends are false. As several commentators have recognized, many existing offences that are relatively uncontroversial among theorists are best construed as designed to prevent future harm.[25] The state would have little need to enact *anticipatory* or *inchoate* offences, such as attempt, conspiracy, and solicitation, unless the prevention of future harm is a legitimate objective of the penal law.[26] I trust that no one would say that the statutes that proscribe attempts are something other than criminal laws or that the sanctions imposed on persons who breach these statutes are something other than punishments. And the list of crimes designed to prevent future harm is not confined to this familiar triad. Many offences that are not generally regarded as inchoate punish conduct that creates a risk of harm rather than harm itself.[27] For example, the bulk of traffic offences, such as speeding and drunk driving, share this rationale. So too do drug offences, which have placed hundreds of thousands of persons behind bars.[28] Finally, scores of possession offences—to be discussed in greater detail—must be added to the list. Thus the laws enacted under a scheme of preventive detention need not be different in kind from many existing crimes. Statutes designed to prevent future harm are neither unusual nor deviant.

How probable must the risk of future harm be in order to justify the enactment of a crime? Existing offences of risk prevention provide a clue. The culpable states of recklessness and negligence both require defendants to create a *substantial* and *unjustifiable* risk before liability may be imposed, and I believe that a similar standard should apply to all crimes committed by those we want to detain preventively.[29] Admittedly, commentators have identified no quantifiable threshold beyond which a given risk qualifies as substantial. Although no formula governs the answer, I am sure that many existing crimes of risk prevention fail to meet this

[24] I explore the basis for supposing retributivists should care about consequences such as deterrence in D Husak, 'Retributivism In Extremis', Law and Philosophy (forthcoming 2013). My general idea is that consequences provide the justification for actually giving offenders the punishments they deserve.

[25] See SJ Morse, 'Neither Desert Nor Disease' (1999) 5 Legal Theory 265. See also RJ Allen and L Laudan, 'Deadly Dilemmas III: Some Kind Words for Preventive Detention' (2010) 85 Chicago-Kent Law Review 23.

[26] G Yaffe disagrees. See his *Attempts* (2010). But see D Husak, 'Why Punish Attempts At All? Yaffe on "The Transfer Principle"', Criminal Law and Philosophy (forthcoming 2013).

[27] These offences are categorized as 'substantive offences defined in the inchoate mode' in A Ashworth and L Zedner, 'Just Prevention: Preventive Rationales and the Limits of the Criminal Law' in RA Duff and SP Green (eds), *Philosophical Foundations of Criminal Law* (2011) 279.

[28] But this rationale for drug offences may fail to satisfy the applicable normative conditions for criminalization. See D Husak, *Legalize This!* (2002).

[29] See Husak (cited in n 2) 159–77.

demanding criterion.[30] Criminal laws designed to prevent risk have been allowed to grow 'in an unprincipled manner' and violate many of the principles of criminalization that we should preserve.[31] By the same token, however, many crimes to prevent risk *do* satisfy this onerous standard.

I conclude that none of these three answers is adequate to explain why preventive detention cannot be construed as punishment. To the contrary, one might contend that the ubiquity of risk-prevention offences in the criminal law argue in favour of construing preventive detention as punishment. In any event, the fourth and most plausible reason, I submit, begins by noticing that a characterization of punishment that includes only deprivation and stigma is incomplete. In order to qualify as punishment, it must also be true that each of these two components is brought about intentionally. In other words, state sanctions do not qualify as punishments because they *happen* to impose deprivations and stigmatize their recipients. Part of the very *purpose* of a punitive state sanction is to inflict a stigmatizing deprivation on the offender.[32] To be sure, the state may have ulterior motives in punishing. A punitive response to behaviour may be the most effective way to deter future crimes, promote social cohesion, protect the rights of law-abiding citizens, vindicate the sacrifices of the law-abiding, and the like. But the existence of these ulterior motives does not undermine my claim that a sanction is not a punishment unless its purpose is to deprive and censure. No other state institution is quite comparable in this respect. Many state sanctions impose hardships and several others stigmatize. Some state practices, like involuntary confinement of the dangerous mentally ill, do both simultaneously.[33] But these sanctions differ from punishments because they lack a punitive intention. Although they *knowingly* cause a stigmatizing deprivation, that is not their point or purpose.

If I am correct about the nature of punishment, the intentions of those state actors who authorize preventive detention must be ascertained in order to decide whether the sanctions they impose should be categorized as punishments. What *is* the intention of the state in confining these individuals? Again, different systems of preventive detention are supported by different rationales; no single answer can be given in all cases. When the state preventively detains mentally abnormal sexual predators who have completed their original sentences, for example, it is plausible to suppose that it lacks an intention to punish.[34] Although it is notoriously difficult to identify the content of intentions—especially when a collective entity like the state is involved—it is not hard to imagine that state actors would prefer to adopt

[30] I argue that the large number of offences designed to prevent the risk of harm rather than harm itself is a major cause of our current predicament of overcriminalization in Husak (cited in n 2).

[31] See Ashworth and Zedner (n 27) 303.

[32] Many philosophers of punishment agree. For one prominent example, see RA Duff, *Punishment, Communication, and Community* (2001) 96–7. For arguments to the contrary, see A Kolber, 'Unintentional Punishment' Legal Theory (2012) 18 Legal Theory 1 and V Chiao, 'Punishment and Permissibility' Law and Philosophy (forthcoming, 2012).

[33] The stigmatizing effect of civil commitment is conceded in *Addington v Texas* 441 US 418 (1979).

[34] In the USA, involuntary commitment of persons who have served their sentence for a crime under the Sexually Violent Predator Act has been held not to constitute a punishment. The alleged absence of an intention to punish allows the characterization of this proceeding as civil. See *Kansas v Hendricks* 521 US 346 (1997).

some other means to protect victims of mentally abnormal violent offenders if they could do so without imposing a stigmatizing deprivation on the unfortunate individuals reluctantly confined.[35] If so, no suitable rationale for *punishing* these individuals can be developed within a retributivist framework.

But whatever may be the case with mentally abnormal violent sexual offenders, I think that terrorists who pose dangers of massive destruction are in a different situation. It is much more likely the state *has* a punitive intention in preventively detaining these individuals. I suspect that few of us would be receptive to a device to prevent these terrorists from causing enormous harm that spares them from deprivation and/or stigma. To suppose these persons should be exempted from punishment (as I construe it) seemingly entails that they have an *excuse*. What excuse could they possibly have? Of course, intuitions on many of these matters can be expected to divide sharply. Some commentators will prefer that prospective terrorists be confined reluctantly, much like the dangerous mentally ill. If they are right, the state might well lack an intention to punish such persons. But if they are mistaken, we must reject this final means to show that preventive detention cannot be punishment, and that the rules that authorize it cannot be part of the state's criminal law—at least for *some* categories of persons who are preventively detained.

How can we decide which side is correct in the dispute about whether the state has a punitive intention in detaining prospective terrorists? I see no decisive argument on either side. Some theorists might argue that the state would prefer *not* to punish prospective terrorists, but to administer them a magical pill to remove the traits *x*, *y*, and *z* that predict future harm. Perhaps so. But the same allegation might be made about *all* criminals. I suspect that such rejoinders are most likely to be voiced by those who are sceptical about whether the state should intentionally impose a stigmatizing deprivation on *any* culpable wrongdoer. Obviously, I cannot address this matter here. The possibility of a more humane response to crime in a future possible world does not show that the state lacks a punitive intention in sanctioning culpable wrongdoers here and now.

I conclude that none of these four answers demonstrates that a system of preventive detention cannot be conceptualized as punishment or that the rules that authorize it cannot be part of a state's criminal law. The pressing question is whether it can be *justified* as such. I now move from conceptual to normative obstacles to my proposal—where the problems are perhaps even more formidable than those already encountered.

## C. Normative obstacles

To this point I have neglected what may be the most crucial difference between the rules that authorize preventive detention and those that allow state punishment.

[35] One commentator maintains that 'with civil detention institutions there is no reason in principle why . . . they cannot be made pleasant and agreeable places': D Wood, 'Reductivism, Retributivism, and Civil Detention' (1997) 9 *Utilitas* 131, 137.

Retributivists (like me) agree that *desert* plays a central role in explaining why punishment is justified. It may seem unlikely, however, that desert can play a comparable role in justifying preventive detention. The reason is simple—deceptively so. Desert is thought to be necessarily backward-looking, and the rationale for preventive detention looks forward. Thus even if preventive detention *can* be punishment, it cannot be *justified* as such. Some commentators appear to believe that nothing more needs to be said to explain why our thoughts about the justification of punishment have little significance for our thoughts about the justifiability of preventive detention.[36] Don Scheid contends, 'in theory, if not always in practice, a sharp distinction is made between *punishment* for past wrongs and *detention* to prevent future wrongs. The rationales for the two are very different. Criminal *desert* arises from past wrongdoing, whereas *dangerousness* is estimated future wrongdoing.'[37]

We need to know a bit about desert in order to assess this claim. As virtually all theorists recognize, desert is a tripartite relationship between (1) *who* is deserving, (2) *what* is deserved, and (3) *why* it is deserved. In other words, all desert claims are of the form 'A deserves Ω in virtue of p'.[38] Although each of these conditions requires extensive discussion, my immediate focus is on (3). The issue to be assessed is whether the properties that warrant preventive detention (that is, characteristics *x*, *y*, and *z*) might constitute a desert base—more particularly, a basis for deserved punishment. If desert claims necessarily look backward, and the rationale for preventive detention necessarily looks forward, it would seem that no one can deserve to be punished for the reasons that lead the state to detain him preventively. Thus any justification of preventive detention cannot be grounded in desert. Since desert is central to the correct (that is, to a retributivist) defence of punishment, it follows that punishment is not justified for the reasons that warrant preventive detention.

In this section I briefly explore whether the rationale for preventive detention I have constructed thus far might have a basis in desert. To proceed with this issue, I must make several assumptions I believe to be true but that some philosophers have challenged.[39] I presuppose that persons *have* desert, that punishments are among the treatments that can be deserved, and that the culpable commission of the least controversial crimes (eg murder, rape, and the like) can provide a desert base for punishment. If the commission of these crimes can provide a basis for deserved punishments—as I believe they do—it is because they satisfy two necessary conditions. First, it is *wrongful* to commit these crimes. Secondly, persons who commit these crimes (without justification or excuse) can merit intentional inflictions of deprivation and stigma. With these assumptions in place, my case for concluding that preventive detention might be deserved draws from my retort to the first of the four conceptual challenges of construing it as punishment. As

[36] 'Dangerousness and desert are distinct criteria that commonly diverge. Desert arises from a past wrong, whereas dangerousness arises from the prediction of a future wrong': Robinson (cited in n 5) 1438.

[37] DE Scheid, 'Indefinite Detention of Mega-terrorists in the War on Terror' (2010) 29(1) *Criminal Justice Ethics* 14 (emphasis in original).

[38] See J Kleinig, *Punishment and Desert* (1973).

[39] Most recently, see V Tadros, *The Ends of Harm* (2011).

I indicated, predictions of future dangerousness have an empirical basis I represent as characteristics *x*, *y*, and *z*. Newly enacted statutes would contain these traits as material elements. In some cases, at least, I contend that the possession of these properties can ground a judgement that punishment is deserved. Suppose that it is wrongful to possess these characteristics and persons merit deprivation and stigma for having them. If so, punishment for these characteristics might be deserved.

What might be said against my claim? As far as I can see, at least two reasons might be advanced to deny that persons can be deserving of punishment in virtue of possessing the characteristics that predict future dangerousness. I alluded to one such reason in section B, 'Conceptual obstacles': the statutes that authorize preventive detention might amount to *status offences* in violation of the supposed *act requirement* of the criminal law. A status offence, as I construe it, imposes liability for what persons *are* rather than for what they *do*. Most theorists think the criminal law contains an act requirement, and thus believe that desert requires an act rather than a status.[40] If the act requirement should be accepted in penal law, and the newly minted statutes that predict future dangerousness are status crimes, persons who violate these laws would not deserve to be punished.

I offer two different replies to this challenge. First, it is doubtful that the newly enacted offences that authorize preventive detention would have to be status crimes. Of course, no one can be certain until examples of these statutes are provided—which I have conspicuously failed to do. Once again, the difficulties of predicting dangerousness cannot be exaggerated. It is noteworthy, however, that the apparent indicators of terrorism are no more likely to compose a status offence than those that predict ordinary violent crime. Social scientists have identified four (non-trivial) overlapping traits of persons that predict typical violence: criminal history, irresponsible lifestyle, psychopathy, and criminal attitudes. *None* of these four traits is a good indicator of terrorism.[41] Instead, the characteristics that best predict terrorism include ideology, affiliation, grievances, and 'moral' emotions.[42] The *affiliation* and *grievance* indicators, at least, could seemingly be used as conduct elements of a penal offence that would not be a status crime. Secondly, the act requirement is not as entrenched within criminal theory as many theorists suppose. Elsewhere, I have mounted a sustained critique of this supposed requirement.[43] I have argued that what theorists typically regard as the act requirement in criminal law is better construed as a distinct but related set of normative principles designed to ensure that persons have *control* over any state of affairs for which they are punished.[44] As I construe this requirement, a given characteristic is under the

[40] See M Moore, *Act and Crime* (1993). But see RA Duff, who proposes to replace the act requirement with an action presumption: RA Duff, *Answering for Crime* (2007) ch 5.

[41] See Monahan (cited in n 13).

[42] Monahan (cited in n 13).

[43] See my 'Does Criminal Responsibility Require an Act?' in RA Duff (ed), *Philosophy and the Criminal Law* (1998) 60; 'Rethinking the Act Requirement' (2007) 28 Cardozo Law Review 2437; and 'The Alleged Act Requirement in Criminal Law' in J Deigh and D Dolinko (eds), *Oxford Handbook of the Philosophy of Criminal Law* (2011).

[44] I defend this claim in each of the articles cited in n 43.

control of an agent as long as he or she is able to change it through an exercise of practical reasoning.[45] No one should be punished for what is beyond his or her control, and any effort to show that preventive detention may be a deserved punishment must preserve this fundamental principle. As long as the possession of the traits *x*, *y*, and *z* is under the control of persons the state preventively detains—as I would insist—punishment would be compatible with the principle I propose to substitute for the act requirement.

The control requirement would rule out including a great many characteristics in penal offences, even when they accurately predict harm. Race, gender, or age, for example, could not be among the elements of these (or any other) crimes, notwithstanding their predictive power. As long as such traits are excluded, punishment for the offences to be enacted could satisfy the control requirement and thus would not violate any of the foundational ideas theorists rightly regard as sacrosanct. They would not treat persons as though they lack free will or exhibit disrespect for their status as autonomous, rational agents, for example.[46] But I will not rehearse these controversial arguments here. In what follows, I will briefly question why theorists seem so certain that the offences we allow in our penal codes preserve the act requirement. If existing crimes that have created little controversy are no more compatible with the act requirement than the offences I propose to draft, we should not cite the act requirement as the reason to suppose that people cannot deserve to be preventively detained.

I will use possession offences to illustrate my point. State penal codes include well over one hundred possession statutes.[47] Several of these offences, of course, are enormously controversial and probably should be repealed. Still, many crimes of possession—such as that proscribing the private ownership of weapons of mass destruction—clearly are justifiable.[48] In other words, these offences are a legitimate use of the penal sanction.[49] But no one should say that the state of possessing something—like the weapons in my garage—*is* an act. Possession is better construed as a state of affairs than as an act. If criminal liability ever is imposed *for* (that is, in virtue of) the state of possession—as seems clear—it follows that criminal liability is not always imposed for an act. If the act requirement should be construed

45 See the interpretation of control defended by JM Fischer, *Deep Control* (2012).

46 Admittedly, the inclusion of status crimes in penal codes would raise many new normative issues. For example, would character evidence become more salient? See T Sampsell-Jones, 'Preventive Detention, Character Evidence, and the New Criminal Law' (2010) Utah Law Review 723.

47 See MD Dubber, 'The Possession Paradigm: The Special Part and the Police Power Model of the Criminal Process' in RA Duff and S Green (eds), *Defining Crimes: Essays on the Special Part of the Criminal Law* (2005) 91, 96–7.

48 'Theorists agree that criminal responsibility for possession should not be ruled out in principle': Duff (cited in n 40) 106.

49 Andrew Ashworth, by contrast, believes that the use of possession offences to challenge the act requirement 'looks like backwards reasoning: it more or less concedes that stretching is required': A Ashworth, 'The Unfairness of Risk-Based Possession Offences' (2011) 5 Criminal Law & Philosophy 237. Although Ashworth raises a host of objections to the justifiability of many possession offences, I do not believe that their incompatibility with the supposed act requirement is among them. In any event, he does not hold *all* possession offences to be unjustifiable.

to hold that only acts are and ought to be the objects of penal liability, it is false both descriptively and normatively.

Of course, orthodox thought in criminal law rejects my claim that possession offences are counter-examples to the act requirement. The *Model Penal Code*, for example, stipulates that 'possession is an act . . . if the possessor knowingly procured or received the thing possessed or was aware of his control thereof for a sufficient period to have been able to terminate his possession'.[50] Taken literally, however, this provision is nonsense, and seeks to preserve the act requirement by fiat. The state of affairs in which I possess a weapon is not an act, and is not magically transformed into an act simply because I am 'aware of [my] control thereof for a sufficient period'. No state of mind or passage of time can perform the alchemy needed to convert non-acts into acts. I conclude that the foregoing provision from the Model Penal Code should not be interpreted to specify the conditions under which the state of possession *is* or *becomes* an act. At best, it specifies the conditions under which persons become *blameworthy* for possession. The Code, it seems, uncharacteristically assimilates issues of *mens rea* into its treatment of *actus reus* in the context of crimes of possession. Thus I do not believe we need to be overly concerned that persons cannot deserve to be preventively detained because the statutes that authorize this sanction are status offences in violation of the act requirement. I turn now to a second and more worrisome possible reason to deny that persons can be deserving of punishment in virtue of presently possessing characteristics that predict future dangerousness. This reason derives from the principle of proportionality.[51] According to this final concern, even if those persons we propose to preventively detain are deserving of punishment, the goals of preventive detention assess the *extent* of their sentences incorrectly. Retributivists typically construe proportionality to require (*ceteris paribus*) the severity of a punishment to be a function of the desert of the offender, which in turn is a function of the seriousness of his crime.[52] But the objective of preventive detention seemingly necessitates that these individuals be confined until they no longer are dangerous. Thus the standard retributive measure of punishment severity is unhelpful when applied to preventive detention. How, then, is preventive detention compatible with a retributive theory of punishment that awards a prominent place to desert and proportionality?

I regard this second problem as the most worrisome of those entertained thus far. Notice, however, that it is not always clear *how* to preserve proportionality; its demands are notoriously difficult to identify.[53] No one should profess much confidence about the specific sentence a person deserves for committing *any* crime,

[50] American Law Institute, *Model Penal Code* §2.01(4).

[51] For further thoughts on how proportionality jeopardizes preventive detention, see C Steiker, this volume.

[52] No canonical formulation of the principle of proportionality can be found. But see A von Hirsch and A Ashworth, *Proportionate Sentencing* (2005).

[53] Many theorists believe that the difficulties of satisfying the demands of cardinal proportionality are sufficient to warrant the rejection of retributive theories. See, eg, G Roebuck and D Wood, 'Censure Without Sanction: A Retributive Argument Against Punishment' (2011) 5 Criminal Law and Philosophy 73.

let alone the newly enacted crimes containing elements *x*, *y*, and *z*. Moreover, desert is not the only factor—and perhaps not even the most important factor—that contributes to sentencing decisions by retributivists. On any sensible model, considerations of special and general deterrence play an enormous role as well.[54] But these cautionary remarks about the demands of proportionality are not very reassuring. Thus I offer two more direct responses to this obstacle, each of which concedes that a retributive justification of punishment must preserve proportionality.

First, adherence to proportionality might not require early release of persons still judged to be dangerous. Consider the seriousness of the newly enacted crimes committed by persons the state preventively detains. As I have indicated, the severity of a punishment (*ceteris paribus*) is a function of the seriousness of the crime. The seriousness of a crime, in turn, is (mostly) a function of the severity of its harm and the culpability of its perpetrator.[55] Since I have already presupposed that only risks of catastrophic harm could warrant preventive detention, it follows that the crimes these defendants commit would be extremely serious as long as offenders possess a high degree of culpability. And typically they do; no one should baulk at finding the culpability of would-be terrorists who pose risks of mass destruction to be great.[56] Thus I conclude that the newly legislated crimes these defendants commit would usually be extremely serious, making perpetrators deserving of lengthy periods of confinement. As a result, we need not worry that the objectives of preventive detention will authorize long terms of incarceration in violation of retributive principles of proportionality. Although these sentences will be lengthy, it is doubtful that violations of proportionality need occur.

The sentences allowed by proportionality and those required for preventive purposes are likely to differ only if the new crimes that are legislated are not serious. This point explains my earlier remark that the state should not be willing to detain persons to prevent minor offences such as shoplifting. Enacting new crimes to disable persons from committing less serious offences would create insuperable proportionality difficulties that are easier to avoid if the harm to be averted is massive and the culpability of the offender is great.

I hazard a second response to problems about proportionality that may apply even to less serious crimes, although my thoughts on this score are more tentative. One way to argue that the demands of proportionality can be satisfied by preventive detention construes the new crimes that trigger this sanction as *continuous* inchoate offences. Once again, consider the example of possession statutes. These crimes are continuous in the sense that they are committed over and over again as long as persons remain in possession of whatever is proscribed. The ongoing nature of these offences can extend even after a defendant is convicted. A person who is punished proportionately for illegal weapon possession, for example, would forfeit the illegal

[54] See Husak (cited in n 24).

[55] See A von Hirsch and N Jareborg 'Gauging Criminal Harm: A Living-Standard Analysis' (1991) 11 OJLS 1.

[56] I argue that crimes of risk prevention are justified only when defendants are culpable for the ultimate harm such statutes are designed to prevent. See Husak (cited in n 2) 168 ff.

weapon. He or she would be eligible for an additional punishment if he or she persists in possessing an illegal weapon—even the very same illegal weapon—after completing his or her original sentence. Jurists need not regard the additional sentence as disproportionate; its rationale would be identical to and no less justifiable than the term imposed initially.

Similarly, a defendant who continues to exhibit traits *x*, *y*, and *z*—and thus is a candidate for preventive detention—remains deserving of punishment as long as he or she possesses these properties.[57] We need not construe any part of this individual's sentence as an added punishment for the original crime that implicates the double jeopardy clause of the Fifth Amendment. Instead, we might regard him or her as perpetrating a new offence each moment he or she remains dangerous. The desert base for this person's punishment is continuous; it survives as long as he or she exhibits the characteristics that predict future harm. Of course, like the defendant who divests him- or herself of the illegal weapon, the state loses its reason to detain him or her preventively when he or she no longer exhibits the properties that predict dangerousness. Recall that the properties that comprise these statutes must conform to the control requirement and be subject to alteration by exercises of practical reasoning. Thus the defendant should be able to lose whatever properties rendered him or her liable in the first place.

## D. Conclusion

I have contended that preventive detention can be conceptualized as punishment and the statutes that authorize it can be conceptualized as crimes. Moreover, I have contended that preventive detention can be justified as such. I have discussed several obstacles to my proposal and have argued that none is fatal. Some of these obstacles are more formidable than others, and my response has been tentative at times. If I am correct, however, whatever normative standards govern the criminal law should be applied to assess the newly enacted statutes that allow preventive detention. Admittedly, the application of these standards will make political officials far less likely to resort to preventive detention in the real world, and commentators who are enthusiastic about the practice will not be grateful for my efforts. I do not regard that outcome as an objection. I have sought only to describe the changes that would need to be made in positive law if preventive detention is to become a respectable part of our system of criminal justice.

[57] Admittedly, terrorists cannot 'forfeit' their characteristics *x*, *y*, and *z*, as persons in illegal possession can forfeit their contraband.

# 10

# Proportionality as a Limit on Preventive Justice

## Promises and Pitfalls

*Carol S Steiker*[*]

Much scholarly ink has been spilled attempting to demarcate a coherent and predictable line between state punishment and (mere) prevention, because different substantive and procedural limits on state power have been assumed to prevail in the two contexts. The substantive and procedural limits on the state as criminal punisher, while always in dispute, are considerably clearer than the limits on the preventive state. This gap exists because for much of human history, the state has prevented future criminal offending largely *through* punishing, relying on the deterrent, incapacitative, rehabilitative, and expressive functions of criminal punishment. Thus, history has provided many examples of the dangers that the tool of criminal punishment can pose in the hands of a malicious or autocratic state. Only quite recently have modern states amassed the power, knowledge, and institutions to undertake large-scale preventive projects, like the monitoring, treatment, restraint, and/or removal of juvenile offenders, the mentally ill, dangerous sex offenders, and terrorist suspects. The post-9/11 world has pushed the issue of the scope of state preventive regulation more to the fore than it has ever been in the past, raising profound questions about how we should delineate the substantive and procedural limits of the state's power to prevent harmful or undesirable conduct.

Both enthusiasts and sceptics of the development of the new 'preventive state' frequently resort to the principle of proportionality—the former as a reason not to worry too much about (at least some) preventive innovations,[1] and the latter as a prescription for severely restricting the turn toward preventive policies.[2] The question this chapter addresses is how far the principle of proportionality can take us in delineating the proper constraints on prevention outside the criminal justice

* For helpful comments and suggestions, I thank Vicki Jackson, Jordan Steiker, and participants in the Preventive Justice seminar at All Souls College, Oxford, as well as participants in faculty workshops at American University Washington College of Law and at Hebrew University.

[1] C Slobogin, 'A Jurisprudence of Dangerousness' (2003) 98(1) Northwestern University Law Review (defending a regime of preventive detention of 'undeterrable' offenders if limited by proportionality).

[2] R Kitai-Sangero, 'The Limits of Preventive Detention' (2009) 40 McGeorge Law Review 903 (arguing for proportionality as one of the necessary 'strict limits' on the use of preventive detention designed to make the practice 'very difficult under normal circumstances').

system. What kinds of issues are encompassed within the proportionality rubric? Which concerns about preventive policies might be addressed by a proportionality limit? What difficulties or drawbacks does an assessment of proportionality pose? In short, what are the promises and pitfalls of proportionality as a limit on the non-punitive, preventive state?

This inquiry brackets the prior question of whether and to what extent 'purely' preventive policies are justified outside the criminal justice system (or within it, for that matter). 'Proportionality' is not a justificatory theory of prevention (any more than it is a justificatory theory of punishment). However, those who have offered various justificatory theories for non-penal prevention generally agree, despite their differences, that proportionality should be considered a key constraining feature.[3] Moreover, it is widely accepted that a proportionality constraint—unlike, for example, a constraint against *ex post facto* lawmaking or double jeopardy—is one that should limit the state outside the sphere of formal criminal regulation.[4] Thus, the contours and significance of this central constraint are worth investigating.

In considering the role of proportionality as a constraint on prevention, it is not necessary (and might even be counterproductive) to start from scratch. The concept of proportionality is already well developed, both normatively and legally, on the punitive side of the punitive/preventive line. There may be lessons to learn from this rich vein, both positive and negative. Of course, any corresponding concept of proportionality on the preventive side of the line will necessarily diverge from its punitive counterpart in light of divergences in the purposes and practices of punishment and prevention. But the two concepts cannot be hermetically sealed off from one another, because changes in the nature of the proportionality constraint on one side of the punitive/preventive divide may well have implications for the other.

On the punitive side, proportionality operates both as a moral and as a legal constraint. In moral theory, proportionality is generally associated with retributivism, which justifies (or at least authorizes) punishment that is proportional to an offender's desert, which itself is the product of the gravity of the offender's crime and the offender's degree of culpability for that crime. However, consequentialist theories of punishment posit a moral limit on punishment, too: punishment that exceeds that necessary to bring about the good consequences that justify it is nothing more than the gratuitous infliction of pain, as Bentham recognized with

[3] AM Dershowitz, *Preemption: A Knife That Cuts Both Ways* (2006) 234 (proportionality key to societal self-defence theory of prevention); KK Ferzan, 'Beyond Crime and Commitment: Justifying Liberty Deprivations of the Dangerous and Responsible' (2011) 96 Minnesota Law Review 141, 173 (proportionality key to liability-based theory of prevention); Kitai-Sangero (cited in n 2) 928–9 (proportionality key to presumption of innocence theory of prevention); Slobogin (cited in n 1) 50–3 (proportionality key to undeterrability theory of prevention).

[4] European Union, Charter of Fundamental Rights of the European Union (7 December 2000), Official Journal of the European Communities (18 December 2000) (2000/C 364/01), available at: <http://www.europarl.europa.eu/charter/pdf/text_en.pdf> (imposing the principle of proportionality in Article 52 as a general limit on governmental power, in contrast to the principle of non-retroactivity in Art 49, which is confined to the penal realm); cf *BMW of North America v Gore*, 517 US 559 (1996) (applying the Eighth Amendment's proportionality principle outside the criminal justice system to civil punitive damages), with *Kansas v Hendricks*, 521 US 346 (1997) (civil statute providing for preventive commitment of sex offenders could be not challenged on double jeopardy or *ex post facto* grounds).

his parsimony principle.[5] On the legal side, the United States Supreme Court has held that the Eighth Amendment's proscription of 'cruel and unusual punishments' imposes a (limited) proportionality constraint, but has declared the federal constitution ecumenical with regard to theories of punishment.[6] Thus, in the non-capital context, the Court asks whether a particular punishment is '*grossly* disproportionate' to the promotion of *any* legitimate penological purpose,[7] and in the capital context, it tends to ask whether a capital sentence is excessive with regard to the twin goals of retribution and deterrence (apparently excluding incapacitation).[8] The Court has also applied proportionality as a Due Process constraint on the imposition of punitive damages in civil cases, holding that such awards are unconstitutional when they are '*grossly* excessive' in relation to the state's legitimate interests in punishment (retribution) or deterrence.[9] Interestingly, the Court has been quicker to deem punitive damages awards 'grossly' out of proportion to state purposes than to deem criminal sentences disproportionate.

From either a moral or a legal perspective, the proportionality constraint on non-penal preventive policies, by definition, cannot be geared toward the retributive metric of desert, but rather toward the metric of dangerousness.[10] Thus, instead of focusing on degrees of offence severity and offender culpability, the proportionality inquiry for preventive purposes must focus on the degree of harm sought to be averted and the likelihood that the harm would occur in the absence of prevention. Such an inquiry should, like the proportionality inquiry with respect to retribution, be able to generate a spectrum of both dangerousness and permissibly proportionate responses along that spectrum. Just as it is not necessarily fatal to retributivism

[5] J Bentham, *The Rationale of Punishment* (1830) 23 ('All punishment being in itself evil, upon the principle of utility, if it ought at all to be admitted, it ought only to be admitted in as far as it promises to exclude some greater evil').

[6] *Powell v Texas*, 392 US 514, 533 (1968) (rejecting role for the Court under the Eighth Amendment as 'the ultimate arbiter of the standards of criminal responsibility, in diverse areas of the criminal law, throughout the country'); *Harmelin v Michigan*, 501 US 957, 998 (1991) (noting that 'the Eighth Amendment does not mandate adoption of any one penological theory') (Kennedy J concurring in part and concurring in judgment).

[7] *Ewing v California*, 538 US 11, 25 (2003).

[8] *Gregg v Georgia*, 428 US 153, 183 (1976) (identifying 'retribution and deterrence of capital crimes by prospective offenders' as the penological purposes served by the death penalty).

[9] *BMW of North America v Gore*, 517 US 559, 568 (1996).

[10] A number of theorists wish to constrain preventive practices either by confining them entirely within retributive punishment, see D Husak, this volume; D Husak, 'Lifting the Cloak: Preventive Detention as Punishment' (2011) 48 San Diego Law Review 1173; or by basing them on some notion of forfeiture for wrongdoing, see KK Ferzan (cited in n 3); A Walen, 'A Punitive Precondition for Preventive Detention: Lost Status as a Foundation for a Lost Immunity' (2011) 48 San Diego Law Review 1229. For these theorists, proportionality would include reference to culpability, because culpability plays a part in their attempts to justify and limit the practice of preventive detention. Because this chapter brackets the justificatory question, it starts with a notion of 'pure' prevention outside the punitive context and asks what the concept of proportionality must necessarily include. While culpability could (or even must) be encompassed within proportionality in the limited preventive regimes proposed by Husak et al, it is not necessarily encompassed within the concept of proportional prevention in the absence of acceptance of some prior constraining theory like that of Husak (or others).

that it may not be able to specify a single *exactly* proportionate response for any given offence, so one should not expect that a proportionality inquiry will generate a precisely proportionate preventive response to any determination of dangerousness: the identification of a range of permissible responses should count as a workable proportionality constraint.

The range of current preventive policies is tremendously broad, from relatively small deprivations of privacy or liberty (state monitoring, reporting requirements, restrictions on travel, etc) to long-term confinement. Although a proportionality constraint might usefully sort out the legitimate applicability of lesser deprivations, I will take as my paradigm example the most problematic form of non-penal prevention—the use of long-term confinement—and ask how a proportionality constraint can help us know in what circumstances such confinements are permissible and how long they may permissibly last. Those who are currently subject to preventive confinement in the USA present a range of diverse situations: they may be dangerous but not responsible, as in the paradigm cases of juvenile offenders and the mentally ill; they may be those deemed 'sexually violent predators' who are dangerous and have some degree of impaired responsibility; they may be those who are fully responsible but who are deemed 'enemy combatants' in the 'War on Terror'; or they may be those suspected of terrorist activities detained pursuant to specific preventive legislation,[11] or more commonly pursuant to pre-existing laws dealing with immigration violations or the detention of 'material witnesses' in criminal investigations. How, if at all, does the constraint of proportionality take account of and respond to this diverse range of circumstances?

In what follows, I will first consider the ways in which the constraint of proportionality might address some of the key issues surrounding the permissible scope of preventive policies. Section A tries to answer the question how far the preventive justice sceptic ought to be reassured by a robust proportionality limit. Section B takes up difficulties inherent in the application of a proportionality constraint and also considers some less obvious costs of such a constraint.

## A. Promises

First, let us consider how and to what extent a proportionality constraint on non-penal preventive policies might address some of the most common concerns that are raised about such policies.

*Duration.* One of the most commonly voiced reasons for uneasiness about preventive confinement is the open-ended nature of a grant of authority to confine. How can a person who is found to meet whatever initial conditions are set for

[11] The USA does not currently have a general provision for preventive detention of terrorist suspects (which is largely the reason for the controversy over the Executive's power to detain those deemed 'enemy combatants'). However, the USA PATRIOT Act does have a provision authorizing preventive detention of foreign nationals suspected of terrorist affiliations. See Uniting and Strengthening America by Providing Appropriate Tools Required to Intercept and Obstruct Terrorism (USA PATRIOT Act) Act of 2001, Pub. L. No. 107–56, 115 Stat. 272 (2001), § 412.

preventive confinement ever overcome the presumption of continued dangerousness? This concern lies in the background of justificatory accounts of certain kinds of preventive confinement—such as pre-trial detention[12] and the military detention of prisoners of war—as these accounts generally emphasize the inherently time-limited nature of the confinement at issue and the assurance that the confinement will be tailored to the temporary circumstances that necessitate it. However, confinements that are not so delimited—such as confinement of 'sexual predators' after their penal sentences are served or of 'enemy combatants' in a metaphorical, global war on terror—squarely raise the question of durational limit.

A proportionality constraint would clearly speak to the issue of duration, because length of confinement is the primary measure of the liberty deprivation at issue (using preventive detention in a locked facility as our paradigm example), just as length of sentence is the primary measure of the severity of criminal punishment (using incarceration in a prison as our paradigm example). Because dangerousness is the product of both the gravity of the harm sought to be prevented (such as the sexual assault of a child, or the commission or facilitation of terrorist acts) and the probability that such harm would occur in the absence of preventive intervention, the proportionality of a preventive intervention fluctuates with any fluctuation in harm or probability. Thus, a robust proportionality constraint would require some sort of monitoring of changes in the kind of future harm that is predicted (eg the danger posed by a committed 'sexual predator' might shift from sexual assault to illegal pornography use), as well as changes in the probability of future harm (eg therapeutic intervention might diminish the likelihood of future offending by a 'sexual predator'). Thus, preventive detention must be accompanied by periodic review to establish that the risk posed still exists at a sufficient level to justify continuing detention.

Moreover, one might conclude that the simple passage of time should presumptively diminish dangerousness, even in the absence of any positive reason (like therapeutic intervention) for a diminution. The probability of future harm depends not only on the inclinations but also on the capacities of those confined. Whether or not a confined person's inclination toward future anti-social conduct is diminished or enhanced by confinement, it seems fair to presume that some capacities will inevitably decline with the passage of time. Physical and cognitive capacities may decline with age,[13] but even more predictably, a confined person's access to information and connection with a dangerous cohort (eg in the terrorism context) will be impaired over time. In addition, people's propensity for criminal behaviour (especially of certain types) is known to diminish with age. Moreover, the very fact of confinement itself may diminish a person's likelihood of future offending. For example, publication (to authorities or to the public) of a person's record of confinement as a 'sexual predator' may reduce the opportunities for the person to offend upon release because of precautions that others might take. Similarly, the

[12] See RA Duff, this volume.

[13] Except, of course, in the context of the preventive detention of juvenile offenders—in which case, physical and cognitive capacities are presumed to *improve* with age, but in a fashion that similarly diminishes the likelihood of future anti-social conduct.

release from detention of terrorist suspects will put relevant authorities on alert and also may make the former cohorts of those released suspicious of possible cooperation with authorities. In short, confidence in a judgement of dangerousness erodes over time, leading some to argue that an appropriately robust proportionality constraint should require 'automatic release after a certain period unless new evidence of dangerousness is forthcoming.'[14]

Of course, the devil here, as in most places, is in the details. How long a maximum initial period of confinement should be authorized at various points along the spectrum of dangerousness? How much of an adjustment should be triggered by the passage of time and/or the production of new evidence of dangerousness? These questions are part of the general computational difficulties that will be addressed under the heading 'Calibration'.[15] The extent to which a proportionality constraint can adequately address the problem of duration depends on the plausibility of satisfactory resolution of such difficulties.

*Conditions of confinement.* The foregoing suggests that the fluctuating calculus of dangerousness during an individual's preventive confinement may well be affected by measures that state officials take, or fail to take, with regard to the treatment of that individual while confined. The state should not be able to bootstrap continuing confinement on the basis of dangerousness that it has helped to create or perpetuate as a result of its initial decision to confine. Thus, a robust proportionality constraint may create obligations on state actors to take affirmative steps to ameliorate dangerousness and to refrain from actions that might exacerbate it. For example, if an individual (eg a 'sexual predator') is preventively confined for a condition that is treatable by therapeutic intervention, then the state would have a duty to take reasonable measures to provide such intervention. In *Hendricks*,[16] the Kansas Supreme Court invalidated its own state's 'sexually violent predator' commitment statute partially on these grounds: the Court reasoned that the state's failure to provide therapeutic services to Hendricks revealed that it did not consider him to be mentally ill, a condition that the Court held was a prerequisite for his preventive commitment under the Due Process Clause.[17] The US Supreme Court reversed that decision, over a dissent by Breyer J that even more directly argued that that the Due Process Clause 'requires Kansas to provide treatment that it concedes is potentially available to a person whom it concedes is treatable'.[18] Breyer J's view

[14] Slobogin (cited in n 1) 52.

[15] See the beginning of section B, 'Pitfalls'.

[16] *Kansas v Hendricks*, 521 US 346 (1997).

[17] *Re Hendricks*, 259 Kan. 246, 257–8, 912 P.2d 129, 136 (1996).

[18] *Kansas v Hendricks* 521 US at 378 (Breyer J dissenting). Cf the decision of the European Court of Human Rights in *M v Germany*, App. No. 19359/04, Eur. Ct. H.R. ¶ 129(2010), available at <http://laboremiuris.kennedy.edu.ar/Documents/Tribunal%20Europeo%20Derechos%20Humanos%20%20M%20v%20Germany%20RECLUSI%C3%93N%20INDETERMINADA%20DETENCI%C3%93N%20PREVENTIVA%20(English%20Version).pdf> (holding that 'persons subject to preventive detention orders must be afforded such support and care as part of a genuine attempt to reduce the risk that they will reoffend, thus serving the purpose of crime prevention and making their release possible').

of a state's substantive Due Process obligations to those whom it preventively confines can be derived from a robust proportionality constraint.

Quite apart from the duty to provide therapeutic interventions for treatable conditions, however, the duty to refrain from treatment that might exacerbate dangerousness might well sweep even more broadly. Abusive treatment during confinement would clearly fall within this proscribed zone, but so might interference with family ties or religious counselling or other activities or associations that would help diminish a detainee's dangerousness. Indeed, preventive detention in a penal facility, such as a prison or a jail, might well presumptively violate the state's duty to refrain from imposing conditions of confinement that may exacerbate dangerousness. The scope of such a duty on the part of the state would obviously be subject to some sort of rule of reasonableness, but even if so cabined, it might still have considerable power. It would certainly be broader than the moral or legal duty that the state has to avoid conditions of confinement that would render criminal punishment excessive or 'cruel and unusual' under the Eighth Amendment,[19] because criminal punishment is, by definition, premised on the notion of hard treatment,[20] while prevention is not. The constraint of proportionality provides part of the reason why preventive confinement *cannot* partake of such treatment.

*Discrimination.* One of the concerns that has dogged incapacitation as a goal in both the non-penal preventive context and criminal sentencing (in the form of 'selective incapacitation') is its tendency to promote the use of group-based predictive measures and to have discriminatory effects along the lines of race or other protected characteristics.[21] An under-appreciated feature of the constraint of proportionality offers some potential to address this tendency. The concept of proportionality has a comparative as well as an absolute dimension, both with regard to penal sanctions and with regard to preventive confinement. The absolute or 'cardinal' dimension of proportionality is the one that is most obvious and that has been the focus of the discussion of non-penal prevention thus far—the proportionality between the restrictiveness of a preventive measure and the degree of dangerousness that it purports to address. But proportionality also has a comparative or 'ordinal' dimension, and a deprivation could be considered disproportionate if it is more restrictive than one imposed on others of equal or greater dangerousness, or even if it is *far* more restrictive than one imposed on others of only slightly lesser dangerousness.[22]

Comparative or ordinal proportionality currently plays a role, though a limited one, in the Eighth Amendment analysis of the proportionality of criminal punishment.

[19] *Farmer v Brennan*, 511 US 825, 837 (1994) (holding that 'a prison official cannot be found liable under the Eighth Amendment for denying an inmate humane conditions of confinement unless the official knows of and disregards an excessive risk to inmate health or safety').

[20] HLA Hart, 'Prolegomenon to the Principles of Punishment' in HLA Hart, *Punishment and Responsibility* (1968) 1 (the 'standard' or 'central' case of punishment 'must involve pain or other consequences normally considered unpleasant').

[21] See generally BE Harcourt, *Against Prediction: Profiling, Policing, and Punishing in an Actuarial Age* (2007) (describing and critiquing the use of predictive instruments and their racial effects).

[22] A von Hirsch, *Censure and Sanctions* (1993) 18 (comparing 'cardinal' or absolute to 'ordinal' or comparative proportionality in penal sanctions).

In non-capital cases, the Supreme Court has held that if a criminal sentence is 'grossly disproportionate' to the offence as a matter of absolute proportionality, then the court will look at inter- and intra-jurisdictional comparisons—at how similar crimes are treated in other jurisdictions, and how other crimes are treated within the sentencing jurisdiction—in order to gauge the ultimate proportionality of the sentence.[23] In capital sentencing, the treatment of similarly situated offenders across the country plays a more central role in Eighth Amendment proportionality review, as a part of an effort to divine 'evolving standards of decency'.[24] In both of these contexts, comparative proportionality is evaluated in the service of absolute proportionality; the failure of other jurisdictions to treat similarly situated offenders as severely as the jurisdiction in question is evidence of the absolute disproportionality of the challenged sentence.[25] Several state supreme courts, however, have interpreted state law to impose a more robust comparative proportionality constraint on capital sentencing than the federal Eighth Amendment requires. For example, for years before capital punishment was legislatively abolished in New Jersey in 2007, the New Jersey Supreme Court applied a form of comparative proportionality review that used statistical analysis to determine whether a particular capital sentence was out of line with the sentences imposed for similar crimes.[26] Here, the inquiry was not in the service of discerning whether an initial inference of 'gross disproportionality' was warranted, or whether 'evolving standards' forbade such a severe penalty; rather, comparative proportionality review in New Jersey started from the premise that the defendant was appropriately death eligible and asked simply whether the defendant had been accorded equal treatment—an analysis that situated equality as the central normative commitment of the enterprise.

The contrast between the federal constitutional approach and the New Jersey approach to comparative proportionality reveals the potential roles that comparative proportionality might play as a means of addressing inequality in the application of preventive confinement. On the one hand, if comparative proportionality is merely an aid in assessing absolute proportionality, then inequalities in application of preventive confinement are relevant only to the extent that they demonstrate that the preventive confinement at issue is disproportionate for anyone who presents the level of dangerousness of the targeted person or group. On the other hand, if the constraint of proportionality contains within it an equality principle, then comparative proportionality might play a more robust role in policing inequality. For example, it might offer grounds to object to preventive measures, like parts of the

23 *Ewing v California*, 538 US 11 (2003) (finding no threshold inference of gross disproportionality in a sentence of 25 years to life for a recidivist convicted of stealing four golf clubs and thus declining to consider inter- and intra-jurisdictional comparisons).

24 *Atkins v Virginia*, 536 US 304 (2003) (finding a societal consensus against the execution of offenders with mental retardation).

25 EJ Mandery, 'In Defense of Specific Proportionality Review' (2002) 65 Albany Law Review 883 (defending the role of comparative proportionality review as a guide to absolute proportionality).

26 See generally 'Symposium: Legislation, Litigation, Reflection & Repeal: The Legislative Abolition of the Death Penalty in New Jersey: Panel II: The Death Penalty on Appeal: Constitutionality, Equality, and Proportionality Review' (2008) 33 Seton Hall Legislative Journal 95.

USA PATRIOT Act, that differentiate on the basis of citizenship status.[27] Indeed, the House of Lords invalidated an analogous provision of the United Kingdom's anti-terrorism laws that allowed preventive detention of non-UK nationals, but not of UK nationals, as disproportionate under the European Convention on Human Rights.[28] Even though the available evidence suggested that the terrorist threat from UK nationals was quantitatively smaller than that from foreign nationals, it was not qualitatively different, and thus the decision to address only the threat from foreign nationals was found to be a disproportionate response to the threat. Such reasoning suggests that the constraint of proportionality generally might limit the extent to which differential burdens could be permitted to arise from inferences of dangerousness drawn from racial, ethnic, or religious group membership.

Some might object that this more robust version of comparative proportionality claims too much for itself and too little for equality, which is better conceived as an independent normative commitment that places a side constraint on the pursuit of proportionality, whether in punishment or prevention.[29] This position draws some support from the fact that only in the context of capital punishment has equality been woven so closely into the fabric of comparative proportionality as a matter of legal doctrine; outside the capital context, doctrines such as those prohibiting 'selective prosecution' under the Equal Protection Clause of the Fourteenth Amendment are the natural vehicle for individual claims regarding unequal application of the criminal law. However, as a normative matter, it remains an open question—which deserves its own analysis in a separate paper or treatise—how robust the equality component of the proportionality constraint ought to be, particularly in the sphere of regulating preventive confinement, as even sceptics would accord it some role (if only evidentiary in assessments of absolute proportionality). Thus, there remains some potential for proportionality to address concerns about inequality and discrimination in the application of preventive confinement, depending on the normative persuasiveness of such an account.

*Procedures*. The constraint of proportionality has procedural as well as substantive implications. The imposition of a preventive restraint is substantively disproportionate if it is not proportionally calibrated to the proven danger at issue. But preventive restraints can also be procedurally disproportionate if they are imposed without sufficiently reliable processes to 'prove' the underlying danger. The degree of procedural reliability that is required increases with the intrusiveness of the preventive intervention at issue, with long-term confinement requiring the greatest assurances of reliability. This sliding scale of procedural protection depending on

[27] D Cole and JX Dempsey, *Terrorism and the Constitution: Sacrificing Civil Liberties in the Name of National Security* (2006) 197 (criticizing the PATRIOT Act for 'reserving its harshest measures for immigrants, measures directed predominantly at Arab and Muslim immigrants').

[28] *A v Secretary of State for the Home Department* [2004] UKHL 56.

[29] Indeed, the House of Lords also separately addressed the differentiation between UK nationals and non-UK nationals as an issue of discrimination. See *A v Secretary of State for the Home Department* (cited in n 28). See also MS Moore, *Placing Blame: A Theory of Criminal Law* (1997) 151 (acknowledging the concern that 'attaining a certain form of justice' may pose unacceptable 'costs to other values').

the deprivation at issue is classically captured in the constitutional protection of 'due process' of law for deprivations of life, liberty, and property, in descending order of procedural protection. From this mandate has emerged the Supreme Court's conclusion that virtually all of the protections of the criminal trial (with the exception of the right to trial by jury) must attend a juvenile delinquency proceeding that may result in institutional confinement,[30] and that lesser but still demanding procedural protections must attend a civil commitment procedure of those who are mentally ill and dangerous.[31]

While the principle of procedural proportionality clearly has some bite (eg, it would not permit institutional confinement to be adjudicated under the same procedures as a much less intrusive intervention such as registration), it remains unclear and highly contested how far the principle goes in specifying the precise procedures required in any preventive context, or even their ordinal ranking. For example, the failure to require proof beyond a reasonable doubt in the civil commitment context (as compared to the juvenile delinquency context) remains controversial. This controversy stems both from normative disagreement about what 'due process of law' requires in these contexts,[32] as well as from the unexplained variation in standards of proof across different preventive contexts.[33] Moreover, given the different purposes and contexts of various preventive interventions (rehabilitation as opposed to pure incapacitation), it remains contested whether the procedures specified for criminal trials should be considered the 'gold standard' from which all other procedures descend along a linear spectrum. The Supreme Court recognized as much when it excluded the right to jury trial from the juvenile court context on the grounds that such a right was inconsistent with 'the idealistic prospect of an intimate, informal protective proceeding.'[34] Taking this critique further, one commentator has argued for a profound procedural restructuring of juvenile court, rejecting the 'adult rights or no rights' framework that has tended to govern the Due Process analysis.[35] Such continuing controversy suggests more than the inevitable indeterminacy of the Due Process sliding scale; it suggests that the procedural structure of a proceeding cannot be determined solely by the nature of the deprivation at issue. Rather, procedural form is implicated by the normative theory that justifies (if it does) the underlying practice (punishment, involuntary rehabilitation of juvenile offenders, etc).[36] Thus, the principle of proportionality can go only so far in determining the necessary procedures for preventive justice; the rest of the determination must be guided by

[30] *Re Gault*, 387 U.S. 1 (1967).

[31] *Addington v Texas*, 441 US 418 (1979) (requiring proof by 'clear and convincing' evidence in civil commitment hearings).

[32] A Tsesis, 'Due Process in Civil Commitments' (2011) 68 Washington & Lee Law Review 253 (arguing for requirement of 'proof beyond a reasonable doubt' in civil commitment hearings).

[33] In contrast to the civil commitment context, many 'sexually violent predator' statutes (including the one at issue in *Kansas v Hendricks*—see n 16) require proof beyond a reasonable doubt. See Tsesis (cited in n 32) 279–82.

[34] *McKeiver v Pennsylvania*, 403 US 528, 545 (1971).

[35] E Buss, 'The Missed Opportunity in *Gault*' (2003) 70 University of Chicago Law Review 39.

[36] Cf RA Duff et al, *The Trial on Trial, Volume Three: Towards a Normative Theory of the Criminal Trial* (2007) (developing a normative account of procedural justice in criminal punishment).

answering the question I have bracketed in this chapter—the normative justification(s) for our practice(s) of preventive detention.

Even if the principle of proportionality cannot fully answer the question of procedural form, it may still have some further procedural implications for the preventive context. First, because prevention is inherently forward looking, proportionality may require periodic review procedures to check the initial adjudication of dangerousness. Any initial adjudication will be premised on a finding of dangerousness based on calculating both the gravity of the future harm and the likelihood that the harm will occur in the absence of preventive intervention. Both of these determinations, as noted earlier, in the discussion of 'Duration',[37] are not fixed in the way that backward-looking judgments of harm and culpability are in the context of retributive justice. Rather, both the nature of the predicted harm and (especially) its likelihood of occurring are subject to fluctuation with the passage of time. Thus, even if proportionality does not impose, as some have suggested, a finite limit on preventive confinement based on a single adjudication of dangerousness,[38] it must at a minimum require some mechanism to respond to the very high probability of changed circumstances. How frequently such reviews must occur, and what the burden and standard of proof should be, are contestable, and are dependent on the grounds for assuming the durability (or changeability) of the initial determination in its particular context.

Secondly, because a determination of proportionality requires the calculation of the likelihood of future harm, the proportionality constraint requires that such a calculus be an *individual* one, rather than a conclusive presumption based on statutorily defined categories. For example, it would violate the constraint of proportionality to authorize a conclusive finding of dangerousness in the sex offender commitment context based on the fact that an offender had been convicted of a certain number of serious sex offences, without an opportunity for the offender to provide further individualized information relating to the specific likelihood of re-offending. Just as proportionality should be understood to pose constraints on the imposition of (at least some) mandatory sentences as a matter of retributive justice,[39] so, too, proportionality should pose constraints on mandatory presumptions of dangerousness.

Finally, the constraint of proportionality may have implications for the question of *who* should make determinations of dangerousness, in addition to *how* such determinations should be made. The reason that proportionality is such a widely accepted constraint on state action, in both the penal and non-penal realms, is that it constitutes one of the primary means of delimiting state power. As Alice Ristroph has helpfully explained, proportionality is best understood as 'a principle of limited

[37] See the beginning of section A, 'Promises'.

[38] Slobogin (cited in n 1) 52 (arguing that proportionality in the preventive context requires 'automatic release after a certain period unless new evidence of dangerousness is forthcoming').

[39] As a matter of constitutional law, the Supreme Court has distinguished between mandatory criminal and mandatory capital sentences, permitting the former but not the latter. Cf *Woodson v North Carolina*, 428 US 280 (1976) (declaring mandatory capital sentencing unconstitutional under the Eighth Amendment, with *Ewing v California*, 538 US 11 (2003) (upholding application of California's 'three strikes' law against Eighth Amendment challenge)).

government' that sets the outer bounds of the state's legitimate pursuit of its goals, penological or otherwise.[40] As such, Ristroph argues, the principle is crucially linked to the concept of separation of powers.[41] Ristroph argues that judicial review, in particular, is the constitutional means by which proportionality can serve as a limiting principle in both the penal and non-penal realms, in light of the reasonable presumption that governmental bodies are ill-suited to judge the proportional weight of their own ends, or to assess the adequacy of the fit between their ends and their means. If ever there was a context in which such a presumption is warranted, it is in the context of state responses to 'danger'—especially grave and/or immediate danger.[42] This need for separation of powers in the preventive context may work in tandem with the need, discussed in the preceding paragraph, for an individualized determination of dangerousness to generate the procedural requirement of a judicial hearing from the constraint of proportionality. Thus, proportionality might plausibly serve as a basis for rejecting military courts or other executive branch officials as appropriate institutional actors to make determinations of the dangerousness of suspected terrorists and the necessity for their confinement.

*Relationship to criminal prosecution.* The fact that proportionality does not necessarily demand that preventive justice provide the same procedural protections as criminal justice leaves open the possibility of a gap in the protectiveness of the procedures for punishment and prevention—a gap that we in fact see in every current preventive context. This gap creates an incentive for the state to develop and use preventive measures in order to avoid the distinctive, costly procedural protections of the criminal process. The constraint of proportionality may offer some limited means to police this potentially perverse incentive. In cases in which the state seeks preventive confinement on grounds that could also give rise to criminal charges—that is, proof of dangerousness is founded substantially on the commission of acts that are criminally proscribed—then perhaps proportionality gives rise to a right to be punished before being preventively confined. The concept of proportionality is widely understood to contain a 'tailoring' element—a requirement that government action be the least restrictive means to achieve the government's end.[43] Criminal punishment may well be viewed as a less restrictive alternative than preventive confinement, both because of the latter's indefinite duration and lesser procedural protections, and because criminal punishment

[40] A Ristroph, 'Proportionality as a Principle of Limited Government' (2005) 55 Duke Law Journal 263. See also A Barak, *Proportionality: Constitutional Rights and Their Limitations* (2012) 214–34 (exploring proportionality's relationship to democracy and the rule of law); ET Sullivan and RS Frase, *Proportionality Principles in American Law: Controlling Excessive Government Actions* (2008) (developing a theory of proportionality as an instrumental part of the rule of law and an essential check on governmental power).

[41] Ristroph (cited in n 40) 287 ('The relation between proportionality and separation of powers should be underscored.').

[42] This is the same intuition that lies behind the constitutional requirement of a judicial warrant for (some) searches and seizures under the Fourth Amendment.

[43] RS Frase, 'Excessive Prison Sentences, Punishment Goals, and the Eighth Amendment: "Proportionality" Relative to What?' (2005) 89 Minnesota Law Review 571, 618.

may obviate the need for prevention by rehabilitation or simply by the passage of time and changed circumstances.

It may seem odd to suggest that criminal punishment is a lesser evil for defendants, given its stigma (which is supposedly absent from preventive confinement), its miserable and often dangerous conditions of confinement, and its frequently draconian sentences. But surely preventive confinement, too, carries stigma, occurs in unpleasant conditions, and can last for long periods. Construing the choice to opt for punishment over prevention as a right of the defendant (rather than a duty of the government), allows defendants to assert the right when the procedural protections and sentencing limits of criminal punishment are more attractive, and to waive the right when they wish to trade off the procedural protections of a criminal trial for the potentially less stigmatizing or harsh treatment of preventive confinement. Thus, a robust proportionality constraint may give defendants the right to choose punishment over preventive confinement when they deem it to be the less restrictive alternative.

Obviously, such a right could exist only for responsible actors; for irresponsible actors, criminal prosecution is not a viable option. However, the context of responsible (or partially responsible) but dangerous offenders has proven to be the context in which the government is most likely to opt for new preventive innovations, as the regulation of 'sexually violent predators' and 'enemy combatants' in the war on terror demonstrates. To be sure, a right to opt for criminal punishment before prevention would be of little use in legislative schemes that seek to continue the detention of criminal defendants after their criminal sentences are completed, as is currently the primary focus of 'sexually violent predator' legislation. However, such a right would have teeth in forcing the initial prosecution, as opposed to military detention, of terrorist suspects.[44]

It must be recognized that the limited nature of such a right—to be criminally tried *before* (rather than *instead of*) being preventively detained—may often make its use unattractive. After all, the main reason to claim the right is to receive the distinctive procedural protections of a criminal trial. But if those procedural protections actually produced an acquittal (or only a mild sanction), nothing in the right to be tried *first* would prevent the government from then seeking preventive confinement. This is exactly what US Attorney General Eric Holder promised should key terrorist suspect Khalid Sheikh Mohammed be acquitted at his (then) planned criminal trial.[45] The only way to prevent such a 'heads I win, tails you lose' proposition is to posit a right of terrorist suspects to be tried *instead of* detained. Some argue that such a right should exist as a function of the appropriate normative limits on prevention, which should require criminal punishment rather than prevention of all responsible actors as a matter of respect for their autonomy.[46]

[44] RM Chesney, 'Terrorism, Criminal Prosecution, and the Preventive Detention Debate' (2009) 50 South Texas Law Review 669 (describing the advent of and the controversy over the military detention of terrorist suspects after 9/11).

[45] M Isikoff, '"Heads I Win, Tails You Lose": In 9/11 Case, KSM Won't Walk Free Even If Found Not Guilty' *Newsweek*, 18 November 2009.

[46] RA Duff et al (cited in n 36) 293 (arguing against preventive confinement of responsible actors because it 'den[ies] the detainee's status as a responsible agent who is capable of acting for the right reasons').

The persuasiveness of such an account is a question that I bracket in this chapter; however, what is important to see is that the conclusion that punishment must wholly displace prevention for responsible actors is not one that is derivable from the constraint of proportionality alone.[47]

## B. Pitfalls

Despite its promise to speak to some of the issues that concern sceptics of preventive policies, the constraint of proportionality also faces a number of difficulties in implementation. Even if these difficulties could be successfully overcome, preventive proportionality nonetheless poses some perhaps less obvious risks.

*Calibration*. The most obvious problem with preventive detention is the difficulty in measuring exactly the thing that calls it forth—the probability of future harm. This is the first objection that is generally raised to preventive detention in all of its guises, and it is an extremely powerful one, given the apparent fallibility of such predictions. But the problem of calibration poses a number of further, less obvious challenges as well—challenges that are conceptual rather than practical. Distinct from the question of the probability of a future harm is the prior question of the *nature* of the harm at issue. For example, in the terrorism context, the harm threatened by the release of a terrorist suspect may be the commission of a specific terrorist act or it may be the suspect's continued participation in an organization that itself is predicted to be the source of unspecified terrorist acts. The individual or organizational act or acts predicted may range from those causing the death of others, to serious bodily injury, to some lesser bodily injury, to property damage, or to more amorphous harm to national security interests. A prediction of 'dangerousness' requires an often hidden generalization about the nature of the harm at issue, which is bound up in the difficult calculation of its likelihood of occurrence.

Unpacking the distinct components of a calculation of 'dangerousness' reveals a further troubling issue for proportionality review that the growing threat of terrorism has brought to the fore: the problem of low-risk/high-harm suspects. Some terrorism suspects are clearly involved in organizations that are much to be feared, committed as they are to inflicting harms of catastrophic proportions. But those suspects may well be 'little fish'—knowingly engaged in the terrorist enterprise (and therefore posing a high probability of continued support for the enterprise if released), but not of central importance to the enterprise and therefore not likely to be critical to the success of its future operations. Emblematic of this problem is the case of Osama bin Laden's driver, Salim Ahmed Hamdan, a Yemeni national captured when the USA invaded Afghanistan in November 2001, and detained at Guantanamo Bay until his trial by military commission nearly seven years later. Hamdan worked close to the epicentre of al Qaeda in his role as

[47] If anything, the relationship goes the other way: the constraint of proportionality derives from the same respect for autonomy that drives the normative account privileging punishment over prevention.

Osama bin Laden's driver and bodyguard, but his contributions to its terrorist activities were necessarily limited, given his fourth-grade education and low status within the organization. A juror on the military commission that convicted him of 'material support' of terrorism, but acquitted him of the greater charge of conspiracy to commit terrorist acts, described Hamdan's contributions as 'toward the less significant end' of the spectrum.[48] In accord was Khalid Sheikh Mohammed himself, mastermind of the 9/11 attacks, who described Hamdan as a 'primitive' Bedouin fit only for tasks such as changing tyres and washing cars.[49] Hamdan's criminal trial, which turned on questions of *scienter*, eventually led to Hamdan's split verdict, light sentence, and return to Yemen. The appropriateness of his preventive detention, however, is harder to assess. When the harms that an organization seeks to inflict reach a certain catastrophic magnitude (such as the possibility of nuclear or biological attacks), even preventive measures that have only a small chance of thwarting them may well be deemed 'proportional'.[50]

The general policy of avoiding even small chances of great harms is sometimes described as 'the precautionary principle', which holds that if an action or policy *might* cause severe and irreversible harm to the public or the environment, the proponents of the action should bear the burden of proof of no harm, in the absence of a scientific consensus that the harm will *not* occur.[51] The implications of widespread adherence to an analogous principle in the preventive detention context are sobering: we should expect to see large numbers of low-level terrorist suspects detained, coupled with surveillance and/or detention of large numbers of people who are simply members of ethnic or religious groups or organizations from whom terrorists are commonly recruited. Such policies are, in fact, not very different from what happened in the USA in the months following the 9/11 attacks. If one finds such policies troubling, however, it is not apparent that the constraint of proportionality will preclude them, as the concept of proportionality crucially leaves undetermined the relative weights of gravity of harm and likelihood of harm in the calculus. This problem is mitigated in the criminal context by the requirement of *scienter*, which precludes liability for serious crimes of risk creation in the absence of a subjective or objective appreciation of a high likelihood of causing harm.[52]

The question of the proportionality of detaining low-risk/high-harm individuals is related to another concern that one might raise about calculations of

[48] 'Salim Hamdan's Sentence at Guantanamo: A Military Juror Speaks' blog post (10 August 2008), available at <http://www.andyworthington.co.uk/2008/08/10/salim-hamdans-sentence-at-guantanamo-a-military-juror-speaks/>.

[49] W Glaberson, 'Bin Laden's Former Driver is Convicted in Split Verdict' *New York Times*, 6 August 2008.

[50] There may be a variety of reasons for deeming an individual to present a 'low' risk of a catastrophic harm. The individual may, like Hamdan, be a peripheral player in a large organization. Or the individual might be a more central player, but one who is redundant or easily replaced. Or the individual might be the sole or central source of the harm, but very unlikely to be able to bring it about. All of these situations present the same problem of apportioning appropriate weight to the likelihood as opposed to the gravity of harm.

[51] C Sunstein, *Laws of Fear: Beyond the Precautionary Principle* (2005) (explaining various versions of and critiquing the precautionary principle).

[52] American Law Institute, *Model Penal Code* §2.02 (definitions of reckless and negligence).

proportionality in the preventive as opposed to the criminal realm. Even when preventive policies formally call for high standards of proof, it may be harder for decision-makers to adhere to them than in the criminal context. When punishment is at stake, the harm has already occurred, and thus a false negative—an incorrect acquittal—will not inevitably produce a further harm (other than the intrinsic harm of a failure of retributive justice and, in some cases, the release of a dangerous individual who may re-offend). In contrast, in the preventive context, a false negative—an incorrect failure to detain—will very likely produce the feared harm. Of course, this feature of prevention is generally the best reason to prefer preventive to punitive actions, but it poses an obstacle in the form of human cognitive bias to the implementation of high standards of proof.[53]

Finally, the question of what to do with the low-risk/high-harm suspect represents one example of a more general difficulty for the calibration of proportionality. Just as it is a challenge for retributive justice to specify a particular punishment or even a range of punishments, it is likewise difficult to say when confinement (as opposed to some lesser measure) is preventively justified, and for *how long*. Time, like money, is infinitely divisible into smaller and smaller units, so it becomes very difficult to say with certainty when a sentence or period of confinement is too long, or a punitive fine is too high. The Supreme Court's relatively robust use of constitutional proportionality to police 'grossly excessive' punitive damages awards in civil cases demonstrates the inevitably ad hoc nature of the proportionality constraint: when finally pressed to set a constitutional cap on permissible punitive damages, the Court came up with a presumptive 9 : 1 ratio, stating that 'few awards exceeding a single-digit ratio between punitive and compensatory damages . . . will satisfy due process'[54]—a standard that owes perhaps too much to the happenstance that humans have ten digits rather than eight or 12. The lack of an analogous denominator to compensatory damages in criminal cases may partially account for the Court's unwillingness to police 'grossly excessive' criminal sentences as robustly as it does punitive damages,[55] leaving criminal punishments outside the capital context essentially unregulated. The Court's arbitrary and unsatisfying forays into constitutional proportionality review in the punitive damages and sentencing contexts demonstrate well the difficulty of performing the proportionality calculus and support the rueful observation of one commentator that 'proportionality is both an inherently alluring and inevitably unsatisfactory measure of constitutionality'.[56]

[53] This bias may be exacerbated by the greater invisibility of false positives in the preventive as compared to the punitive realm. One who is incorrectly convicted of a criminal offence may later be proven innocent (and presumably compensated for the error). It is impossible to disprove a prediction of future dangerousness for one who is detained as a result, and thus false positives in the preventive detention context cannot be fixed—a problem in its own right, but also one that may further bias the initial decision to detain.

[54] *State Farm Mut. Auto. Ins. Co. v Campbell*, 538 US 408, 424 (2003).

[55] PS Karlan, '"Pricking the Lines": The Due Process Clause, Punitive Damages, and Criminal Punishment' (2004) 88 Minnesota Law Review 880, 907 ('By their very nature, then, damages cases provide a piece of information that criminal cases lack: an indication of the gravity of the offense that uses the very currency in which punishment is to be meted out').

[56] Karlan (cited in n 55) 882.

*Pretext.* Imagine, however, that despite its practical and conceptual difficulties, a robust practice of constitutional proportionality review of preventive detention practices existed. In such a world, it is possible (though not certain; discussed under 'Calibration') that courts would order the release of some 'little fish' like Hamdan on the ground that their degree of dangerousness did not justify long-term confinement. What might happen then? We do not really need to speculate here, because something close to this situation existed in the months after 9/11 in the USA. Federal law enforcement officials were scrambling to respond both to the attacks of 9/11 and to the new anthrax scare. However, they had no general statutory authority to detain dangerous citizens on American soil (and only questionable authority to detain 'enemy combatants' once the invasion of Afghanistan began). Just as in a hypothetical world of judicial enforcement of a robust proportionality constraint on preventive detention, law enforcement officials in the wake of 9/11 believed that there were dangerous people who needed to be detained, but whose detention on grounds of dangerousness was unlawful.

What happened next demonstrates the limits of even a robust practice of proportionality review of preventive confinement. In the months following 9/11, despite the absence of direct legal authorization, American government officials managed to detain large numbers of people who they believed were dangerous by pressing into service other, pre-existing detention regimes whose preconditions could easily be met—such as the massively ramped-up use of both immigration detention and the previously little-used 'material witness' statute.[57] Such detentions required no proof of dangerousness; rather, they required simply the demonstration of a violation of immigration law or a need to preserve possible testimony in connection to an on-going criminal investigation. It seems indisputable that large numbers of these detentions were pretextual: although those detained generally did meet the (non-demanding) legal preconditions for their detentions, the government would not have sought their detentions without a belief that they should be detained because of their dangerousness.

This example demonstrates the inefficacy of a proportionality constraint—*especially* a robust one—without an additional, external limit on the pretextual use of other modes of detention. However, there are some significant conceptual and practical impediments to a workable pretext doctrine. First, it is hard to know what to do with so-called 'mixed motive' cases—when government officials act in part for reasons intrinsic to the statutory scheme they invoke, but also in part for reasons of dangerousness.[58] Secondly, it is hard to find reliable evidence of government 'motive' other than the testimony of the challenged government officials, which is an invitation to undetectable and thus unpunishable perjury (or at the very least to false consciousness). These considerations no doubt informed

[57] NV Demleitner, 'Immigration Threats and Rewards: Effective Law-Enforcement Tools in the "War" on Terror?' (2002) 51 Emory Law Journal 1059 (describing and critiquing ramped-up use of immigration detention after 9/11). For the unprecedented use of the 'material witness' statute, see the litigation in *Ashcroft v al-Kidd*, 131 S.Ct. 2074 (2011).

[58] See the government's briefs in *Ashcroft v al-Kidd* (cited in n 57).

the Supreme Court's refusal to allow claims of pretext in the Fourth Amendment context.[59] The formidable challenges to preventing pretextual evasions demonstrate the limited power of even a robust and strictly enforced proportionality constraint on preventive detention.

*Perverse interactions with criminal law.* Even if a robust proportionality constraint was enforced *and* pretextual evasions were curtailed, the government's perceived need to confine dangerous individuals would find an outlet—most likely in criminal law. Already, there are many 'preventive' crimes, such as inchoate and possessory offences, which aim at preventing future harm and often result in the confinement of the convicted perpetrator. Further innovations, should non-penal preventive efforts be curtailed, are not hard to imagine. For example, in the 'sexually violent predator' context, if the current scheme of post-sentence civil commitments were substantially restricted by robust proportionality review, then legislatures might simply raise sentences for sex offences across the board, or permit predicted dangerousness to determine sentences within a broadened range, thus allowing the same degree of detention of sex offenders prospectively. In the terrorism context, the government might turn to the further creation or expanded use of crimes like 'material support' of terrorism, which authorizes lengthy sentences for those who provide any support of any kind to organizations that they know have been deemed terrorist organizations by the US government, even if they do not know that their support will aid any terrorist project, and even if their support is not in fact causally linked to any harm. The 'material support' statute thus includes within its ambit contributions to organizations (like Hamas, for example) that conduct humanitarian as well as terrorist activities, even if the contribution is specifically targeted to the organization's humanitarian projects.

These potential statutory or enforcement innovations on the criminal side pose a problem analogous to the one explored (under 'Calibration') regarding the preventive detention of low-risk/high-harm suspects—the problem of the low-culpability/high-harm offender. Consider again Salim Hamdan, Osama bin Laden's driver, *after* his conviction for 'material support' of terrorism. The terrorism that he supported was really, really bad—but his support was relatively small and his culpability relatively low (knowledge as opposed to purpose, given his acquittal on conspiracy charges). Nonetheless, the 'material support' statute authorized a possible life sentence for Hamdan. As it happened, the military commission returned what was viewed by many as a surprisingly light sentence of only five and a half years.[60] But the potential for long-term incarceration through criminal sentencing of offenders like Hamdan demonstrates the criminal law's ability to pick up the slack created by a tightly constrained system of preventive incarceration.

Thus, the only way for a proportionality constraint on preventive confinement to serve as a constraint on government power is to have some similarly robust

[59] *Whren v United States*, 517 US 806 (1996) (rejecting pretextual stop challenges under the Fourth Amendment).

[60] AC McCarthy, 'Disgraceful Hamdan Sentence Calls Military Commissions into Question' *National Review*, 8 August 2008 (calling Hamdan sentence 'astounding' in its leniency).

constraint against disproportionate *criminal* sentencing. This recognition is a corollary to the problem of pretext: given the inevitable 'slippage' that tight regulation in one area will cause, effective regulation must extend to the area of slippage, whether it is immigration regulation, 'material witness' detentions, or innovations in criminal law. But also parallel to the problem of pretext, robust criminal proportionality review does not currently exist; as we have seen, the Supreme Court's current regulation of criminal sentencing under the Eighth Amendment is highly deferential to the point of virtual extinction.[61] Moreover, the development of a robust criminal proportionality doctrine would pose many of the same conceptual and practical problems to the development of a robust proportionality constraint in the preventive context that have already been reviewed. The problem of 'slippage'—as illustrated both by the problem of pretextual detention and enhanced preventive criminal punishment—presents a daunting practical challenge for the efficacy of a proportionality constraint in the preventive context.

*Occupying the justificatory field.* A very different problem that proportionality poses as a constraint in the context of preventive justice might be termed a rhetorical one. The very widespread acceptance of proportionality as a key limit on government power makes reliance on the concept susceptible to a kind of stealthy normative hegemony. It is all too easy to slip from accepting proportionality as a *necessary* condition for preventive justice to seeing it as a *sufficient* condition—as a normative justification in itself for the practice of preventive confinement. In this way, proportionality can serve as the thin edge of the wedge for a consequentialist as opposed to a deontological frame for the question of preventive justice. It is easy to split the concept of proportionality down the middle, concluding that 'proportionality' refers to the demands of retributive justice in the criminal context (calibrating punishment to desert), and to the demands of efficacy in the preventive context (calibrating prevention to dangerousness). The fallacy here is to assume the existence of a normatively justified preventive realm and then to govern it not by its normative foundations (whatever they may be), but by the familiar constraint of proportionality. The normative foundations of the preventive realm—though bracketed in this chapter—should not be obscured by proportionality's own normative allure, which should not be mistaken for a full account of the boundaries of prevention.

## C. Conclusion

How much normative allure should proportionality rightfully have? That is the question that I have tried to address in this chapter, first sketching as generously as I could the set of issues and concerns that a robust constraint of proportionality could fairly be claimed to address in the preventive realm. In this sketch of proportionality's

[61] *Ewing v California*, discussed in text at n 7.

promise, I have also tried to be careful about where proportionality's reach was qualified or where it simply gave out and needed to be supplemented with some further normative constraint or justificatory account. I have raised some challenges, both conceptual and practical, to the power of proportionality as a constraint on preventive confinement. I hope this account is fair and balanced, but in reviewing the overall picture, I am left with a sense of scepticism about proportionality's potential as a robust normative constraint: the qualified nature of proportionality's promise combined with the daunting nature of the pitfalls it must negotiate should give pause even to proportionality's many enthusiasts.

# 11

# Democratic Limits to Preventive Criminal Law

*Peter Ramsay**

## A. Introduction

All criminal law is preventive to the extent that it deters the acts or omissions that the law prohibits. Much of the law seeks to achieve this by threatening punishment for the prohibited conduct after the event. Recent criminal legislation has, however, been marked by the prevalence of *purely* preventive criminal offences. This group includes possession offences, preparation offences, failure to report offences, and breach of preventive orders. These offences appear to be concerned with pre-empting harmful conduct before the opportunity for its commission even arises, and they have as a result been referred to as pre-inchoate offences.

This preemptive coercion encroaches significantly on individual liberty and equality. I will argue here that, although they can be thought of as illiberal, these offences nevertheless can also arise from the application of a liberal principle. Moreover, while these statutory offences appear to be the outcome of democratic politics, they can and should be understood as contrary to democratic principles. These laws proliferate not despite our commitment to individual autonomy but because of it. More specifically, they proliferate because in recent times the concept of individual autonomy to which the state offers protection has continued to develop while, at the same time, belief in, and commitment to, collective political self-determination has declined. Without the effort to achieve collective self-government, the pursuit of individual autonomy becomes self-defeating.

The emphasis here will be on the relation of criminal law to democracy rather than to liberalism. I have already made the argument in relation to liberalism elsewhere.[1] I will only briefly recapitulate it here to provide the context for raising democratic principles. While the relation of substantive law and liberalism has been exhaustively discussed in the literature, the specifically democratic principles that might limit the form and content of the criminal law are much less visited terrain.

* I am grateful for the comments and criticisms of the participants at the Preventive Justice seminar at All Souls College, Oxford, and particularly those of Patrick Tomlin and Shlomit Wallerstein.

[1] P Ramsay, *The Insecurity State* (2012).

As Nicola Lacey has pointed out, there has been very little theorization of the institutional characteristics of a criminal justice system that are specifically democratic (as opposed to liberal), and there is still less consensus as to what those characteristics might be.[2] Moreover, the focus of such detailed discussion as there has been has tended to be on the justification of punishment, and of particular penal practices, rather than on the scope of the criminal law.[3] Here I will make a tentative sketch of a democratic theory of the limits of criminal law by setting out what I take to be critical aspects of truly democratic government and suggesting why our pre-inchoate criminal offences are not consistent with them. It is tentative because I cannot hope in the space available to deal with the possible criticisms and alternatives to the principles of self-government that I propose. Nevertheless I hope to show that these principles of collective self-government impose some specific limits on the scope of the preventive law.

I begin by setting out some key legal features of the pre-inchoate offences, and indicating some of the arguments that are necessary to justify punishing people for violating them. Then I will consider the equivocal position of these laws in liberal criminal law theory before turning to democracy and the way in which these offences violate democratic principle. I will conclude by considering the potential advantages of a democratic theory of criminal law.

## B. The pre-inchoate offences

Pre-inchoate offences are comprised of conduct that may constitute the initial stage of a complete offence or of a dangerous act, but does not constitute a dangerous act in its own right.[4] Pre-inchoate offences include offences of possession, criminal preparation, failure to report, and breach of a preventive order.[5] Pre-inchoate offences are to be distinguished from inchoate offences insofar as the latter criminalize acts that are intrinsically dangerous because they require proof of some conduct in which the actor loses control of the effects of his criminal intentions (in England and Wales these offences include attempt, conspiracy, and

[2] See N Lacey, *The Prisoners' Dilemma: Political Economy and Punishment in Contemporary Democracies* (2008) 6–7.

[3] See contributions to 'Democracy and Punishment' Special Issue (2002) 5 Buffalo Criminal Law Review 321–600.

[4] The term pre-inchoate has been used in slightly different ways to this by other writers. See M Dubber, 'Legitimating Penal Law' (2007) 28(6) Cardozo Law Review 2597, 2606; MC Melia, 'The Wrongfulness of Crimes of Unlawful Association' (2008) 11(4) New Criminal Law Review 563, 564; A Ashworth, 'Criminal Law, Human Rights and Preventative Justice' in B McSherry, A Norrie, and S Bronitt (eds), *Regulating Deviance* (2009) 88–9.

[5] UK law contains numerous preventive orders. They are imposed on individuals by courts when it is thought to be necessary to prevent that individual from causing some specified harm. These orders can include prohibitions on intrinsically harmless conduct that is specific to the individual, conduct that would not be unlawful if anyone else committed it, such as restrictions on movement, associations, or possessions. For more detail see I Dennis, 'Security, Risk and Preventive Orders' in I Dennis and GR Sullivan (eds), *Seeking Security* (2012) or Ramsay (cited in n 1).

encouragement).[6] Pre-inchoate offences are purely preventive in the sense that penal liability attaches to conduct that is harmless in itself and makes manifest no wrongful danger, but is connected to some harm either by an actor's intentions or in some more remote way.[7] The substantive unity of the conduct covered by pre-inchoate offences is that it fails to reassure others about the future conduct of the defendant. The conduct that these offences prohibit is not harmful or even dangerous acts, but acts that constitute the dangerousness of the actor. This criminalization of dangerousness can be seen in the relation between the offending conduct and the harms that might justify criminalization, in the substantive content that unifies these offences, and in the effects of these offences on the privacy and equality of the law's subjects. Let's look at each in turn.

There are two ways of constructing the harm prevention of which justifies state coercion of subjects with respect to the pre-inchoate conduct. The first is that the harm that justifies liability is the eventual harm pre-empted by the pre-inchoate offence. If I make preparations or possess something intending to commit an offence, my liability to punishment could be justified because these prohibitions serve to prevent the harm that I intended to commit and might have gone on to commit had I not been pre-empted by official intervention. Even if I possess a firearm with no intention to do any harm with it, I might have gone on to use it for unlawful purposes (or have lost control of it), and so coercion of such possession would contribute to preventing any harms arising from such unlawful use. If I breach a prohibition contained in a preventive order that is necessary to prevent me from involvement in some criminal activity (for example a restriction on my movements or my association with others) then my liability to punishment is justified by the prevention of that criminal activity.

Notice that there is no requirement that the prosecution prove an increase in the risk of the eventual harm. The outcome may in fact remain under the complete control of the preparer, possessor, or breacher of the preventive order. She may desist from criminal plans or bring the possession to an end without any harm eventuating or any increased risk of harm eventuating. The connection between the prevented harm and these forms of conduct is a remote one—mediated by the intervening choices that a defendant might have gone on to make, or by the wrongful choices that others might independently have made and that became more likely as a result of the defendant's pre-inchoate conduct, choices that were not in fact made by virtue of the defendant's arrest and punishment for the pre-inchoate offence.[8] In proving the elements of these offences, the prosecution has *in substance* proved that the defendant's conduct failed to reassure the tribunal of fact that she would not go on and commit the eventual wrongful harm or, in the

[6] For more detailed discussion of the distinction, see Ramsay (cited in n 1) 142–3. This convention divides offences on a different basis from the categories 'constitutive' and 'non-constitutive' or 'consummate' and inchoate offences. See, for example, D Husak, *Overcriminalization* (2008) 160–1.

[7] The definition of attempt in the American Law Institute, *Model Penal Code* as an intentional substantial step therefore includes pre-inchoate conduct.

[8] AP Simester and A von Hirsch, *Crimes, Harms and Wrongs: On the Principles of Criminalisation* (2011) 80–1.

case of simple possession, that she would not lose control of matters so as to make it more likely that someone else would do it. In other words, the prosecution has proved that the defendant's conduct gives good grounds for suspecting that the risk of some eventual wrongful harm has been increased by virtue of this person's actions or possessions. These suspicions will be particularly strong where ulterior intent is proved.

This liability for failing to reassure by giving good grounds for suspicion can, however, be understood as giving rise to a risk of another harm. This second harm is the insecurity caused to others by the knowledge that others are making such preparations. This harm is also only remotely connected to the prohibited pre-inchoate conduct, but the nature of this remote connection is different. The simple possession of firearms may not be connected with any intention to do wrong, but by knowingly possessing them, the person is remotely connected to the harm of the insecurity caused by the knowledge that these things are possessed. This remote connection could be characterized as 'conjunctive' with all the other instances of this conduct—any one particular possession might not make a significant contribution to this harm (indeed it may be entirely secret), but the possession is morally indistinguishable from the other acts which when taken together do cause insecurity.[9] This insecurity arises from the possibility that the person in possession will in future decide on a harmful course of action or will lose possession of whatever is possessed to someone else who will have harmful intentions. A preventive order may also be breached without doing any immediate harm or having any intention to do any harm, but the defiance indicates an indifference to the law's preventive demands in the specific context in which the defendant has been burdened by a preventive order because she has been assessed to represent a particular risk of harm.[10] And, *on this construction*, this indifference causes insecurity to others. Intentional preparations and possession with ulterior intent provide possibly more significant conjunctive contributions to insecurity. Any one person making deliberate preparations to commit an offence may not cause much in the way of insecurity, but taken together such intentional preparations will contribute to insecurity.

Looked at from this point of view, the prosecution, in proving the elements of the pre-inchoate offence, is proving conduct of a sort that in substance causes the harm of insecurity. This justification of the law's coercion does not rely on the hypothetical intervening choices that might have been made but for the preventive intervention of the authorities. However, the prosecution has still only proved that people may be caused insecurity because the defendant's conduct is in some way unreassuring. On this construction too, a tribunal of fact can properly convict if it is satisfied beyond reasonable doubt that it has good grounds for suspecting that the defendant has increased the risk of the wrongful harm of insecurity.

[9] See P Ramsay, 'Preparation Offences, Security Interests and Political Freedom' in RA Duff et al (eds), *Structures of Criminal Law* (2011) adapting Simester and von Hirsch (cited in n 8) 85–6.

[10] See Ramsay (cited in n 1) 47–8.

The pre-inchoate offences involve an interference with both the equality and liberty of the law's subjects that is different from that found in other types of offence. The offence of breach of a preventive order is, on its face, unlike ordinary criminal offences in that the distribution of the liability to punishment entailed in these offences is not formally equal. The purely preventive aspects of a preventive order are prohibitions on movement or on associating with particular individuals or on possessing certain items that would be lawful for anyone not subject to the particular order. The discriminatory order is imposed in court proceedings that amount to a discretionary administrative risk assessment of the individual concerned.[11] Unlike the breach of preventive orders, the other pre-inchoate offences are apparently general rules of equal application. But they too involve an important practical aspect of administrative discretion. Pre-inchoate offences will not involve any harm being done by the commission of the offence nor any manifest threat to another's interests. These offences are unlikely to come to light except as a result of the surveillance and investigation efforts of the authorities. Arrest and conviction for these offences will in practice be dependent on official activity, on the official gaze and where it is directed.

This deeper relation between liability and executive investigative activity raises an even more important implication of these offences for individual liberty. By extending the scope of criminal liability far from the direct interference with bodily or proprietary interests, these preventive offences expand the scope of legitimate police power and executive coercion into the arena that was previously thought of as the private sphere, extending as far as the coercion of subjects' thoughts and opinions. For example, a police officer may arrest anyone who is about to commit an offence or whom she reasonably suspects is about to commit an offence.[12] But to be about to commit an offence of mere preparation is to be seriously thinking about it. The theoretical possibility of arrest on the basis of intentions, thoughts, and opinions is entailed in the pre-inchoate offences.[13] To find out if a person's externally innocuous activity conceals criminal intentions (or the dangerous possibilities that might arise from simple possession) requires surveillance and investigation of that person's communications, intentions, and opinions in advance of any externally dangerous or harmful activity.

The critical point is that insofar as the authorities have a duty to prevent crime, but that crime is limited to inchoate or constitutive offences, then the surveillance of criminal preparations and intervention against advanced preparations may be justified. But insofar as the authorities are under a duty to prevent externally innocuous preparations and possessions or breach of preventive orders because these too are offences, then surveillance of *all activity* will be required in order to identify the dangerous intentions that may be lurking there. This is the logic of

[11] See P Ramsay, 'What is Anti-Social Behaviour?' [2004] Crim LR 908, 919–20.

[12] Police and Criminal Evidence Act 1984 s 24(1).

[13] Andrew Ashworth and Lucia Zedner note that police investigating their reasonable suspicions are empowered by these offences to focus their questioning of suspects entirely on opinions, attitudes, and intentions because the conduct element is banal: A Ashworth and L Zedner, 'Just Prevention' in RA Duff and S Green (eds), *Philosophical Foundations of Criminal Law* (2011) 286.

'early intervention' and the pre-inchoate offences are an aspect of that preventive logic.[14] Such mass routine surveillance is not entailed in the existence of these powers, but the more the criminal law makes externally innocuous private activity into a penal wrong the more surveillance of that activity is legitimated.

In summary: the coercion of the law's subjects found in the pre-inchoate offences can be justified either by reference to the eventual wrongful harms that they are intended to anticipate or by reference to the insecurity caused regardless of whether or not any eventual wrongful harms are prevented; either way the substantive content of the offence is the good grounds that the defendant has given the tribunal of fact for believing that she would have gone on to commit the eventual harm; the effect of these laws is to make the distribution of criminal liability more dependent on executive discretion (formally so in respect of preventive orders), and to extend the scope of executive surveillance and coercion into the most private areas of the individual subject's existence. These latter aspects of the pre-inchoate offences may seem illiberal on the face of it, but, as we shall now see, the offences are not simply ruled out by liberal criminalization theory.

## C. Liberalism and the pre-inchoate offences

To establish whether or not criminalization of some conduct is justified, liberal criminal law theorists have tended to focus on two aspects of that conduct: does prohibiting it in some way contribute to preventing a harm to others, and is the conduct prohibited morally wrong? On both these criteria, plausible arguments can be made for the pre-inchoate offences. The harm principle and the moral wrongness criterion provide no more than preliminary filters before the real work of evaluating any criminal prohibition on criteria drawn from political theory has to be done.

The ordinary harm analysis asks the legislator to weigh the gravity and likelihood of eventual criminal harm against the social value of the conduct to be prohibited and the degree of intrusion on freedom of choice that criminalization would involve, taking particular care to observe side constraints provided by fundamental rights such as freedom of expression or privacy. The effect is that this analysis excludes criminalization of conduct that risks only trivial harms or more serious harms which are very unlikely to occur. But for any harm that is non-trivial, and where there is some realistic possibility that it may occur, everything becomes a question of evaluation: how harmful, how likely to occur, and how valuable is the conduct prohibited? Since almost all conduct risks some harm to somebody, the question becomes the essentially political evaluation of whether the harms risked by criminalization outweigh the harms avoided. The work of deciding this question

[14] On pre-inchoate offences and preventive logic, see P Asp, this volume. There are many other aspects of early intervention: one of the most far-reaching is discussed by M Hildebrandt, 'Proactive Forensic Profiling: Proactive Criminalization?' in RA Duff et al (eds), *Boundaries of Criminal Law* (2010).

cannot be done by the harm principle.[15] The side constraints could potentially offer some firm limits on the scope of criminalization, but they would do so only if they were interpreted in a very narrow way. In practice, in the UK, at least, these too involve political evaluation. Liberal legal opinion has, in recent years, had a strong commitment to the European Convention on Human Rights (ECHR). The ECHR protects the fundamental rights of free speech or privacy or freedom of religion and of association in a way that allows these rights to be limited in any way that is 'necessary in a democratic society' in the interests of such values as 'national security', 'public safety or the economic well-being of the country', 'for the prevention of disorder or crime', 'for the protection of health or morals', or 'for the protection of the rights and freedoms of others'.[16]

Consistent with these doctrines, the pre-inchoate offences can be justified on the basis of an evaluation that the harms risked by possessions, preparations, and breach of preventive orders are sufficiently grave and probable that they outweigh the minimal social value of the conduct involved in criminal preparations or (the possibly greater value) of possessing prohibited items, or of the conduct that breaches a preventive order.[17] Any interference with fundamental rights to privacy or freedom of association can be justified as necessary for the protection of the safety of others. This argument will be especially strong insofar as other citizens are thought to enjoy a 'right to security'.[18] Of course all these evaluations can be disputed, but the dispute is not addressed by the constraints imposed by the harm principle.

Noting the paucity of principled arguments about criminalization generated by the 'Standard Harm Analysis', AP Simester and Andreas von Hirsch have suggested complementing it with a remote harm analysis. The connections between the conduct prohibited by the pre-inchoate offences and the harms risked are indeed remote ones. While the remote harm analysis of these offences does produce one relevant argument of principle, it tends to confirm that, in the final analysis, the available principles of criminalization are matters of political theory.

Simester and von Hirsch's analysis rules out our first construction of the harm prevented by the pre-inchoate offences. As we saw in the previous discussion, insofar as coercion of the pre-inchoate conduct is justified by the eventual criminal harm that is anticipated by arrest and conviction for the pre-inchoate offence, the connection between pre-inchoate conduct and harm is remote by virtue of the intervening contingencies of the future but unmade choices of either the defendant or others. Without these choices being made there is no connection between the

[15] B Harcourt, 'The Collapse of the Harm Principle' (1999) 90(1) Journal of Criminal Law and Criminology 109; RA Duff, *Answering for Crime* (2007) 138.

[16] ECHR Arts 8–11.

[17] Note that the case for criminalizing intentional preparations or possession with ulterior intent will be stronger than the case for simple possession or breach of a preventive order, insofar as intention is thought to increase the risk of harm eventuating. The argument I shall develop, however, will be that neither is consistent with democratic political order. The possession of handguns or automatic weapons, items with no non-violent use, may provide a significant exception to this argument, but I have no space to explore this possibility here. See also P Asp, this volume.

[18] See Ramsay (cited in n 1) ch 6.

pre-inchoate conduct and eventual harm. As Simester and von Hirsch argue it seems unfair to impute the eventual harm to the defendant's pre-inchoate conduct on the basis that others might make criminal choices that are independent of the defendant's own actions. Alternatively, if we coerce the law's subject on the basis of her own future choices to go on and commit a constitutive offence that directly harms or wrongs another then we fail 'to respect her as a moral agent, capable of deliberation and self-control',[19] and we undermine the whole liberal project of rule by law.

The second construction of the harm prevented by criminalizing pre-inchoate conduct presents a different type of remote connection between the defendant's conduct and harm. Now the connection is mediated not by intervening hypothetical choices but by the conjunctive contribution that the defendant's conduct makes, along with all the other instances of (morally indistinguishable) pre-inchoate conduct, to the insecurity endured by other subjects who are caused to live in fear of crime. As Simester and von Hirsch point out, the fairness in principle of this type of remote connection depends on the extent to which we can impose duties of cooperation on subjects so that they are precluded from saying that the harm conjunctively imputed to them is not their business.[20] The question for our purposes becomes this: should we have duties to cooperate with each other to avoid others feeling vulnerable to the possibility of criminal victimization, and how far should these duties extend? The answer will depend on how we conceive of our political obligations to each other as citizens.[21] If we decide that our duties of cooperation should extend to awareness of what will cause others to feel insecure, we then have to undertake the standard harm analysis weighing the probable harm of insecurity against the probable harms, and the restrictions on rights, consequent on criminalization. But again we are returned to evaluations of empirical evidence that will inevitably be informed by our political commitments.

Insofar as preventing the harm of insecurity is what legitimates the pre-inchoate offences, legislators are required to make an evaluation that will be influenced by their own theories of political obligation. This is equally true of the wrongfulness criterion maintained by liberal criminalization theory. If we decide that we have good reason to impose obligations on everyone not to contribute to insecurity about crime then we can in principle justify laws that impose these obligations, and it is morally wrong to break properly enacted coercive laws where there are good instrumental reasons for the state to impose the laws.[22] Wrongfulness does not add much in the way of limiting principles once there are good reasons to justify a criminal regulation. And, in respect of the pre-inchoate offences, reasons to regulate arise in the development of liberalism's understanding of individual autonomy.

Liberal legal theory has long recognized that the individual autonomy that it seeks to uphold is more than a matter of the formal capacity to make choices. It also

[19] Simester and von Hirsch (cited in n 8) 79; see also RA Duff, *Criminal Attempts* (1996).
[20] Simester and von Hirsch (cited in n 8) 86.
[21] Simester and von Hirsch (cited in n 8) 68.
[22] Simester and von Hirsch (cited in n 8) 27–8; see also Duff (cited in n 15) 137.

requires that people enjoy the capacity to make self-determined choices that are not coerced by external circumstances beyond their control.[23] In the criminal law this protection of 'real autonomy' in part requires the protection of agency goods, often involving duties of mutual cooperation.[24] Not the least of these is the penal liability for failure to pay taxes much of which are used to fund welfare systems that serve to protect others from harm to agency goods. Insofar as the feeling of security is also regarded as an agency good, then its protection may indeed be included among our cooperative obligations to each other.[25]

This then is the problem for liberal theory. Should the liberal law's upholding of autonomy extend to cooperative obligations towards others' security or not? And, if not, on what basis should they be excluded? It is not impossible for liberal theory to make a principled case in favour of liberty over security. I have elsewhere suggested such an argument myself.[26] I will briefly restate it.

If we assume that the harms of fear and insecurity are so great that cooperative penal obligations not to contribute to a climate of insecurity are justified, we are assuming that law-abiding subjects are so sceptical of the ordinary law's effectiveness in deterring potential offenders, or of persuading them to give up their criminal intentions, that this insecurity affects their decisions sufficiently to determine their choices. We are assuming that their autonomy is vulnerable to that insecurity. It is this that justifies the state's anticipation of potential criminal wrongdoing by the prohibition of conduct only remotely connected to eventual criminal wrongdoing. But this is to assume that the subjects do not believe in the effectiveness of the sovereign's coercion, an assumption incompatible with the proposition that the sovereign's coercion is authorized by them. The pre-inchoate offences are premised on the demise of liberal political order.

My argument is that this demise of liberal order has been brought about from within: by the over-extension of the liberal principle of real autonomy to embrace fear and insecurity. The problem is that, for as long as individual liberty is the central principle of criminalization, liberal theory is vulnerable to legitimizing the pre-inchoate offences and the extensive state coercion that accompanies them. This ironic outcome can arise because our account of individual autonomy is enriched by sensitivity to the many ways in which individual decision-making can be coerced by external forces. As our account of 'real autonomy' becomes more realistic, the more agency goods we recognize as essential to its exercise. The thicker the concept of individual autonomy that is offered legal protection, the more likely it is to include security as one of those protected agency goods and so legitimate the pre-inchoate offences.

Precisely because liberal theory begins with individual autonomy, there is a tendency to understand criminal law in terms of wrongs that individuals do to

[23] See, eg, J Raz, *The Morality of Freedom* (1986) 425.

[24] See generally A Brudner, *Punishment and Freedom* (2009).

[25] Simester and von Hirsch argue that there could never be a wrong of causing fear *as such*, because doing so depends as much on the reaction of others as on the actions of a putative offender ((cited in n 8) 50). They do not explain why a liberal legal order could not impose duties of awareness.

[26] Ramsay (cited in n 1).

each other. The theorist is confronted with a field filled with moral wrongs and harms, and a plurality of rights and goods that must be balanced. This balancing involves political evaluations that are necessarily subject to the political contingencies of the moment. What liberal theory seems to lack is a clear principle for when moral wrongs or harms should become the distinctively public wrongs that are the subject matter of criminal laws.[27] There is, as a result, no clear principled limit to the scope of the criminal law,[28] so that liberal political order can in practice drift into self-contradiction.

Liberals must therefore find a way to reject fear as a protected agency good without throwing out the protection of other agency goods essential to real autonomy.[29] One strategy might be to give the side constraints true peremptory force by rejecting the balancing act of the ECHR and insisting on an interpretation of fundamental rights that only allows for much more narrowly specified limitations to those rights.[30] Another might be to insist that only the causing of feelings of insecurity that are 'justifiable' because they are 'reasonable' should be prohibited.[31] If a principled dividing line could not be found, it might still be possible to 'police the facts': to argue that the harms of insecurity are not in fact particularly grave or widespread.[32] The problem with this strategy is that it necessarily involves a controversial weighting of privacy and equality interests as against interests in subjective security that already presupposes certain political commitments.

At any rate, my claim is not that liberalism cannot possibly provide a principled argument that would recognize the protection of agency goods without the need for pre-inchoate laws. Rather, I am claiming that liberalism's tendency to undermine the authority of its own institutions, among them the civil liberties, is a real and serious one because, by setting out from individual autonomy, it is required to balance a plurality of goods and rights that are essential to freedom imagined in this way—not least individual liberty and security. It is in this context that I raise the possibility that collective self-government might provide a simpler and more robust argument from principle for the protection of formal equality and privacy from the invasion of the pre-inchoate law.

## D. Representative democracy and pre-inchoate offences

At first sight, representative democracy may not seem to offer much in the way of principled limits to preventive law. If representative democracy is thought of as no

[27] See, eg, Duff's inconclusive discussion of the content of public wrongs (cited in n 15) 140–6.

[28] See G Hegel, *Elements of the Philosophy of Right* (1991) 261.

[29] Markus Dubber's theory of police power (see Dubber, this volume) makes a powerful case for the 'alegitimacy' of the pre-inchoate offences, but this is a case that is unable to account for the legitimacy of much of the penal protection of agency goods, see Ramsay (cited in n 1) 193–202.

[30] For a theoretical critique of human rights on the grounds of their illiberality, see A Gourevitch, 'Are Human Rights Liberal?' (2009) 8(4) *Journal of Human Rights* 301.

[31] See A Cornford, 'Criminalizing Anti-Social Behaviour' (2012) 6(1) Criminal Law and Philosophy 19.

[32] See, eg, F Furedi, *Invitation to Terror* (2007) 178–80.

more than the people's right to elect their government in free and fair elections then clearly the pre-inchoate laws are consistent with that minimal vision of democracy. All of the mainstream parties in the UK have at one point or another been elected to government on programmes that included support for these laws.

But this is a thin account of representative democracy. If we set out from a slightly richer account of democracy we can see that, just as these apparently illiberal laws can be understood as the extension of a liberal principle, these same laws that enjoy the legitimacy of electoral majorities can be understood as a retreat from democratic principle. I will, therefore, take democracy to mean a state in which all the citizens collectively rule themselves by determining the laws that they will obey and the policies that they will collectively pursue. The proposition that the people may collectively achieve this by means of political representation is controversial, criticized by proponents both of minimalism,[33] and of direct democracy.[34] I will nevertheless set out a concept of political self-government that provides reasons for thinking that representation both is necessary if all the people are to rule themselves collectively and provides principled limits to the scope of state coercion.

I seek to show first that, in addition to fair elections, a necessary condition of representative government is that the citizenry is politically independent of the executive; and that this condition is undermined by the pre-inchoate offences, giving reasons of democratic principle to preclude those offences. This argument in itself, however, still leaves hanging the contested question of whether true self-government can be achieved by representation. I therefore go on to sketch a specific theory of political representation as the best means to political self-determination, understood as positive liberty. This further thickening of the concept of representative democracy is the more controversial and unfashionable part of the argument, but it gives further reasons of principle to reject the pre-inchoate offences.

## The meaning of representation

What does it mean for a government to be representative? The key, as Hannah Pitkin put it, is that: 'we show a government to be representative not by demonstrating its control over its subjects but just the reverse, by demonstrating the control that its subjects have over what it does'.[35] The people must have control of government. But for the people to have control of government it is not enough that the people's preferences are aggregated every so often and that the majority should prevail.[36] The inadequacy of this form of representation is that, in itself, all that it represents is the preferences of the people at any particular time. But to what extent can the people be said to be in control of their preferences? The vote, even if it is

[33] See, eg, A Przeworski, *Democracy and the Limits of Self Government* (2010).

[34] See, eg, B Barber, *Strong Democracy: Participatory Politics for a New Age* (1984).

[35] H Pitkin, *The Concept of Representation* (1967) 232.

[36] Majority rule is necessary nevertheless, and an effective way of making decisions that reflect the majority preference, see Przeworski (cited in n 33) 39–42.

part of a competitive election under fair procedures, tells us nothing about how preferences came to be formed. If the people do not control the environment in which their preferences are formed then the people's control may be more apparent than real.

The most important potential obstacle to popular control of the political debate is the representative institutions themselves. This will be especially true where, as a result of the aggregation of preferences expressed at an earlier time, the state has grown large and government policies have come to involve intervention and regulation of large areas of social life—education, healthcare, trade and industry, leisure, entertainment, and so on. If all these areas of social life are subject to direct government control, or at least regulation oriented towards specific ends, then the executive, with vast budgets, huge powers of patronage and a monopoly on legitimate coercion, will have an immense influence on the way the population understands social life. The official culture will exert this influence in the media, the arts, the sciences, the schools and the universities, and thereby on the preferences of individuals. This effect would be magnified if the electoral competition between political parties narrowed, so that there was an ever-larger area of agreement with controversy restricted to narrower, more technical questions. If this uncontested centre-ground of politics and its intellectual underpinnings were to become *the* major influence on the majority of individuals then who is representing whom? Is the government representing the people or the people the government?

On the other hand, there could not be a pristine people, with preferences uninfluenced by government, who turned up to elections and voted. Anything above the most minimal of representative governments is going to exercise some influence over the preferences of the population. If it did not then it would have no power. How can we ensure that representative government remains representative, that the representatives lead the people but do not end up manipulating and usurping the people?[37]

For representation of the people to mean anything, the will of the government and the will of the people must be independent entities, so that the will of the former *can* be subordinate to the will of the latter. Without that independence the one is simply identified with the other and does not *represent* it. There must be some sense in which the people retain some independence of government, while not pretending that the government has no influence on people's preferences. If we abandon the condition of independence, we will rob representative government of its meaning (because there is no independence of preference formation from government influence). If we abandon the condition of governmental influence on preferences, we rob government of its governmental power. The people cannot be completely independent of a democratic government—independent in every respect. But they must be independent *politically*, in the sense that they are able *to come to their own conclusions* about what government should do notwithstanding government's huge power and influence. What are the conditions of that independence?

[37] Pitkin (cited in n 35) 232; and B Garsten, 'Representative Government and Popular Sovereignty' in I Shapiro et al (eds), *Political Representation* (2009).

## Civil liberty and political independence

The consequence of this necessity for political independence is that the protection of civil liberty is widely recognized as a condition of democratic self-government.[38] Freedom of conscience, speech, association, and assembly are all means whereby citizens can innovate political ideas, debate and propagate them, organize around them, and so on. Without this free competition of political ideas, citizens do not know what the available political possibilities are and they are not given free range to decide which of them they prefer.[39] Without this uncoerced political process citizens will be unable to come to their own view because to come to their own view requires that citizens are able to assess their initial preferences in the light of alternative arguments, changing or retaining their preferences accordingly. The political deliberation and organization of citizens must therefore be negatively free of executive coercion (and indeed coercion by other citizens). The equal distribution of civil liberty achieved by laws of general application, laws that preclude discretionary distribution of limitations on rights, is a precondition of representative government.

If civil liberty is an essential aspect of collective self-government by representation then so too are the preconditions of that civil liberty. Two preconditions are relevant here. The first is at least some criminal law. Civil liberty presupposes at bare minimum the enforcement of homicide law, offences against the person (including sexual assaults), theft, criminal damage, and attempting to do any of these or assisting others to do them. The precise scope of these offences would need further specification but without any enforcement of these offences there can be no civil liberties. The freedom of speech will be worth little if the speaker can be attacked or killed or imprisoned with impunity. In such circumstances, would-be speakers will be forced to go mob-handed into the 'public sphere' asserting their right to free expression as a natural right or revolutionary demand. The protection of the rights of personhood by the norms established in the ordinary criminal law is a precondition of civil liberty, which is only to say that you can have a state without civil liberty, but you cannot have *civil* liberty without a state.

From the point of view of democracy, the enforcement of these offences serves to protect rights of personhood, of formal agency, rights that are the precondition of the civil liberty that is essential to democratic citizenship. Not only is the criminal law's coercion necessitated in order for the state to establish and uphold the conditions for democratic citizenship, but deliberate violation of the interests protected by offences such as homicide, assaults, and criminal damage amounts to a claim of natural right that discounts the rights of personhood that are a condition of democratic citizenship.

[38] There seems to be a consensus on this basic point among theorists of democratic representation (see, eg, R Dahl, *Democracy and Its Critics* (Yale University Press, 1989) 170). My own account draws particularly on F Neumann, 'The Concept of Political Freedom' in W Scheuerman (ed), *The Rule of Law Under Siege: Selected Essays of Franz Neumann and Otto Kirchheimer* (1996). But it overlaps with several other theories that emphasize the necessity of civil liberty to democratic political deliberation. For the differences with some of those other theories see n 54 and accompanying text.

[39] See also A Meiklejohn, *Political Freedom* (1948).

In this way the offender repudiates the rights of citizenship and renders herself liable to punishment for that reason.

It is worth noting that democracy also necessitates the provision of social rights as well as civil rights and this involves the protection of agency goods in much the same way as liberalism's real autonomy. Criminal laws can enforce duties to pay taxes, and to avoid harms to others in their working and living conditions and in the provision of goods and services in a way that protects social rights.[40] But this 'social security' is, from the democratic point of view, merely a means to the end of collective self-government, and this, as we shall see, imposes strict and unambiguous limits on the extent to which agency goods can be protected.

If the enforcement of the criminal law is one precondition of civil liberty, the protection of the accused contained in modern criminal procedure and its rules of evidence is another. Without this procedural protection the criminal law is transformed from the precondition of civil liberty into a substantial threat to it. We can see this if we consider the most important aspect of the criminal procedure: the presumption of innocence and the burden of proof lying on the prosecutor. The point of the presumption of innocence is that it provides 'a process of calling upon the executive to account for its request to have a citizen officially condemned and punished for an offence.'[41] This public accountability is achieved by the separation of powers between the executive and the courts and, as Malcolm Thorburn points out, the presumption of innocence is essential to the separation of powers. The executive will make good its request only if it can prove to a tribunal that the individual accused has violated the relevant criminal provision. The presumption of innocence is, therefore, 'fundamentally about the court's ability to ensure that we shall be condemned and punished by the state only for violations of the general rules set out by the legislature, and not merely for defying the executive branch and incurring its wrath'.[42]

Without this process of public accountability of the executive for its criminal accusations, there can be no civil liberties. If the state can accuse the citizen of criminal wrongdoing and require the citizen to disprove the allegation, then citizens are dependent on the goodwill of the state, except insofar as they are confident that they can account for their every move. But such confidence would require a self-policing, a constant concern with how everything said and done will appear in the light of an accusation. In these circumstances, accountability would flow the other way around.[43] The citizen would in effect be accountable to the executive. This amounts to coercion of the sphere of independent action apparently protected by the formal civil liberties.

[40] P Ramsay, 'The Responsible Subject as Citizen: Criminal Law Democracy and the Welfare State' (2006) 69(1) Modern Law Review 29.

[41] HL Ho, 'Liberalism and the Criminal Trial' (2010) Singapore Journal of Legal Studies 87, 90–1.

[42] M Thorburn, 'Locating the Presumption of Innocence', unpublished paper on file with the author.

[43] See also Antony Duff's discussion of the Terrorism Act 2000 s 57 in RA Duff, 'Perversions and Subversions of Criminal Law' in Duff et al (cited in n 14).

The burden of proof in making the state accountable to the citizenry for its penal coercion therefore institutionalizes a formal burden of trust among citizens. It requires that we *act as if* we trust accused fellow citizens not to do wrong until it is proved otherwise. This does not imply that prudentially citizens must trust strangers in all matters or even that we necessarily trust all others in respect of the potential violation of our fundamental rights and interests. A jury, in maintaining the presumption of innocence in its deliberations, is not required *actually to believe* the case put forward by the defendant who is on trial; it is required to satisfy itself that the prosecution has proved its accusations.[44] This *form* of trust is an essential aspect of collective self-government because this is a regime whose principle is that we are free when we obey laws that we give to ourselves. We must therefore presume that all are capable of rational legislation and of obedience to that legislation.[45] We must presume that all have moral agency and that failure to adapt to the law's norms will be exceptional. Indeed it is a *burden* of trust because democracy implies some degree of social or political division, of disagreement over fundamental values and the character of social order, so that we will have many reasons not to trust others.[46] But even though some others do not deserve our trust, democratic citizens must run that risk. Extending this form of trust is the price of independence from the state. Without it, the relations among citizens are mediated by the state's discretionary powers and the sphere of civil liberty is reduced to a formality.

The pre-inchoate offences are one institutional form through which the independence of the citizenry is eroded. The preventive orders achieve this on their face. They distribute penal liabilities, and therefore limit civil liberty, differentially through a process of discretionary administrative risk assessment overseen by the judicial branch. The penal obligations that the preventive order contains are explicitly derived from the prior administrative process. As Simester and von Hirsch have argued, this is plainly a violation of the rule of general laws and the equal distribution of civil rights.[47] It is impossible, even in theory, to say that those made subject to the prohibitions in such an order are also the authors of them.

The other pre-inchoate offences are a little more subtle. They finesse the limitation on executive power that the criminal procedure achieves by fully hybridizing the substantive law. When the executive proves beyond reasonable doubt that a defendant has committed the pre-inchoate offence it proves that the defendant is in violation of a general rule, but in so doing it has done no more than prove that its suspicions about the increased risk of future offending have some (and possibly strong) foundations. Like any criminal proceeding, the trial involves an adjudication under a general rule. But the very same adjudication is substantively not

[44] M Thorburn (cited in n 42).

[45] For a review of the literature on the practical connections between trust and the effectiveness and stability of democratic governments, see R Inglehart, 'Trust, Well Being and Democracy' in M Warren, *Democracy and Trust* (1999) 98–104.

[46] On the tensions, see M Warren 'Democratic Theory and Trust' in M Warren (cited in n 45).

[47] AP Simester and A von Hirsch, 'Regulating Offensive Conduct Through Two-Step Prohibitions' in A von Hirsch and AP Simester, *Incivilities* (2006) 180.

unlike an administrative law proceeding, in that a conviction confirms the reasonableness of executive suspicions in relation to future harms. In this hybrid process, the procedural burden of proof is formally observed but the substantive law permits executive suspicions of future activity to gain a conviction, and undermines the institution of mutual trust among citizens that the presumption of innocence serves to maintain.

The place previously occupied by the institution of mutual trust is filled by the extensive surveillance and snooping powers of the executive that, as we have seen, are legitimized by the substantive law of the pre-inchoate offences. To identify the dangerous people whose outwardly harmless and innocuous conduct conceals criminal possibilities or, worse, criminal intentions, the executive will need to trawl through our opinions and associations, our interests and our desires. These laws are a key aspect of institutionalizing mutual distrust between citizens, a distrust that is the basis upon which relations among citizens become mediated by the executive. In place of the mutual trust between citizens, citizens are required to trust the executive and its good will in knowing more and more about them. Self-government is precisely based on not doing this.[48] In this way, the independence of the citizenry from the executive is eroded, requiring that the citizenry be accountable to the state for their normal actions, rather than that the state be accountable to the citizenry.

Representative democracy as self-government requires political independence of the citizenry and, with it, the free competition of political ideas that is guaranteed by the civil liberties. This independence is undermined by the normalization of executive surveillance and suspicion that leads the relations among citizens to become dependent on the executive as citizens become accountable to the executive for their opinions and associations. The direct impact of this institutionalized distrust on individual liberty is felt in the sphere of privacy. And this attack on the private sphere—indeed its logical elimination insofar as the state institutionalizes the routine surveillance of communications among citizens as the normal order[49]—undermines another fundamental characteristic of true self-government.

## Positive liberty and privacy

Civil liberty, with its formalities of trust among the citizens and distrust of the executive, is necessary so that citizens are able to come to their own view, rather than the process of preference formation being coerced by the executive. Citizens must nevertheless still come to their own view. In a democracy, the people who rule themselves *must make decisions*.[50] Their decision may be free of governmental coercion, but citizens must still decide between competing accounts and these

[48] DJ Solove, *Nothing to Hide: The False Tradeoff Between Privacy and Security* (2011) 209.

[49] At the time of writing the UK government has published a Draft Communications Data Bill detailing its proposals to allow routine official surveillance of all Internet and email traffic in the UK. See 'Draft of Email-Snooping "Communications Data Bill" Published Online', *Wired*, 14 June 2012. Available at <http://www.wired.co.uk/news/archive/2012-06/14/communications-bill>.

[50] D Plotke, 'Representation is Democracy' (1997) 4(1) *Constellations* 27.

accounts are not going to be free of manipulation and influence from many sources including the government. Indeed, insofar as any particular group of representatives has been governing, and is seeking re-election, the available views are necessarily influenced by the actions and opinions of the executive. How are the citizens to decide?

The principle of democracy is collective self-government and, *if we take this principle seriously*, it provides us with a further basis for decision-making. If it is self-government that is the purpose of the democratic order then citizens can seek to become more self-governing by freeing themselves from the control of external necessity so that they may act only on their true interests. To know what is truly in her interests a person needs to know what that external necessity consists of, to know her 'real' situation, the objective relations that she finds herself in. Only when a person makes decisions on the basis of this knowledge of necessity can she hope to escape necessity's control, and become self-determining. Franz Neumann called this 'cognitive freedom' because only by *knowing* where she is situated with respect to external nature, human psychology, and human history is a person able to control the effects of natural forces and the human passions, and understand how the limitations of humanity's present level of development could be transcended.[51] Only insofar as people do this can they politically promote what is both truly in their interests and genuinely possible to achieve in the present.

The necessary knowledge might be carved up in different ways, but the key is that such knowledge is what allows individuals to situate themselves in the universe and determine their own interests for themselves. Only by knowing about these aspects of their lives are they able to evaluate their first-order preferences and know that these preferences are their own preferences in the sense that they serve their interests in self-determination. But how is a single individual to know these things? Even if we adopt the necessary realist philosophy, this knowledge itself is inevitably a progressive approximation and an approximation which is not knowable in its totality by any single individual. It is only knowable collectively. Moreover, there is no agreement on any of these areas of knowledge.

It is in the solution to these problems of cognitive freedom that representation wins out over direct democracy as a mechanism of self-rule. Representation achieves this to the extent that the nature of the encounter between the representative and the represented lends itself to resolving the problem of grasping the totality of knowledge and the disputes about it—at least provisionally, which is as good as anyone will ever do. As David Plotke observes, the dialogic element of representation arises in the gap between the authorization of representatives by the represented at one election and the accountability of representatives to the represented at another. In that gap representatives have to recognize the interests that compete with those of their political constituency and ask 'whether their constituents' choices are the best way to get what those constituents want'.[52]

[51] F Neumann (cited in n 38). [52] D Plotke (cited in n 50) 29.

The representative, in all but the most extremely mandatory of institutional designs, can depart from her mandate provided she is willing to face the electoral consequences. This room for manoeuvre encourages the development of a critical dialogue between the two. At the same time, the need to encompass a wide set of interests encourages would-be representatives to synthesize the apparent diversity of interests and preferences that they face into a convincing worldview, to build alliances around one of those concatenations of knowledge and interest that we call ideologies. The contest of these ideologies is the contest of competing knowledges of necessity. Citizens can, therefore, make their own approximation to necessity by engaging with the clash between these ideologies, since that clash serves to focus the human mind's ongoing dispute about the current condition and potential of humanity and the relations among its various parts.[53] In this way, the achievement of *individual* self-government through positive liberty or cognitive freedom is the *collective* endeavour of a democratic society, a collective endeavour in which the negative civil liberties are an essential moment.[54]

This positive liberty gives another reason of principle to reject the normalization of executive spying on the private sphere of mental reflection and communication of opinion that the pre-inchoate offences legitimize. The achievement of positive liberty needs a vigorous competition of ideologies that are responsive to historically changing social reality. Without these, the representative political process becomes a contest over technical competency rather than one between differing configurations of knowledge and interests through which people might achieve self-government. Ideological vigour and innovation require the uninhibited exercise of political, scientific, and artistic imagination, and, therefore, a willingness to uphold the rights of those who are officially thought to be in error.

The effect of routine and comprehensive executive surveillance of private communications will be just such an inhibition of intellectual and political creativity. The possibility of arrest and interrogation for harmless private actions, or even for questioning about the possibility of such actions, and the knowledge that these powers are exercised by the state, will inhibit subjects. It will do this in a number of ways: by creating anxiety about the possibility of executive suspicion, and particularly that the hostile or prejudiced opinions of others about them might be reported

[53] It is, of course, the historical disappearance of this clash of ideologies that is one significant source of the recent decline of representative government (see Ramsay, cited in n 1).

[54] The theory of democratic positive liberty, therefore, differs from other democratic theories that also put civil liberty at their core. In its concern with effective interest representation, this account does not equate democratic legitimacy with the reasonableness of the deliberative process or the achievement of consensual outcomes (unlike, eg, J Habermas, *Between Facts and Norms* (1996)). The theory recognizes that democracy often involves the political management of conflicting private interests in a way that will not necessarily amount to a rational discussion of the common interest (unlike Meiklejohn, cited in n 39). At the same time, in its concern for positive liberty (individual and collective), the present account does not assume that the different private interests that democratic government seeks to reconcile will always inevitably involve political conflict (unlike, eg, MH Redish and AM Mollen, 'Understanding Post's and Meiklejohn's Mistakes: The Central Role of Adversary Democracy in the Theory of Free Expression', Northwestern University School Of Law Public Law And Legal Theory Series No 08-26). The democratic pursuit of positive liberty implies that an ultimate reconciliation or elimination of those conflicts is a theoretical possibility at least.

to the state; through the resultant tendency towards conformist self-censorship and the chilling of even the private expression of non-conformist ideas, the atomization of communal life, and withdrawal from controversial public engagement.[55] The very possibility of developing the sort of personality that is able to experiment with different ideas, to take intellectual risks, or even to differentiate between the interests that are shared with others and those that are not (and so be able to judge the worth of ideological claims) may be inhibited by the complete transparency that the abolition of privacy would entail.[56] These effects will actively frustrate the spirit of free enquiry and discursive engagement that self-government's pursuit of positive liberty requires.

## E. Why democracy?

Understanding the limits on criminalization that are imposed by democratic principle has a number of potential advantages. The most obvious and most important is that the principles of collective self-government through political representation are principles worth pursuing in their own right. Readers who doubt this may be sceptical about the worth of the present analysis. That is a debate that lies beyond our present concern with criminal law theory. There is, however, a more specific aspect of democratic principles that has been my concern here. Self-determination by political representation can in principle provide a theoretical resolution to the tension between negative liberty and the protection of agency goods. This is a resolution that provides a clear limit to the preventive scope of the criminal law, a limit that serves to uphold the civil liberty of the individual subject.

I have argued here that democratic principle requires that the substantive law not be used as a means to subvert the institutions of formal trust among citizens which is a necessary condition of the executive being held to account for its accusations against citizens. It requires that the state's normal surveillance powers be limited to identifying dangerous acts rather than dangerous actors, and its coercive powers limited to punishing dangerous acts rather than dangerous actors. It does not rule out the deployment of such offences or such surveillance powers as truly exceptional emergency powers. But it does rule out their present status as ordinary criminal offences in normal statutes. Nor, it should be added, does the logic of representative democracy rule out all preventive law. It is not hostile to the coercion of private activity on the grounds of risk management as such, only to that coercion which is inconsistent with political self-determination. It is, therefore, hostile to all coercion of the private activity of *persons* that creates risks that are mediated *solely by the subjectivity* of an individual subject (the subjectivity either of the actor or of

[55] For a brief review of the literature on these points, see L Mitrou, 'The Impact of Communications Data Retention on Fundamental Rights and Democracy' in K Haggerty and M Samatas (eds), *Surveillance and Democracy* (2010) 138–41.

[56] See A Lever, *On Privacy* (2012) Kindle Locations 533–59.

another person).[57] It does not rule out the coercion of corporations for acts that are not objectively dangerous. Nor does it rule out the coercion of objectively dangerous acts by all subjects—persons and corporations alike.

Liberals might object that this account is not adding much or anything to liberal theories of the limits of state power. They might, for example, cite John Stuart Mill's celebrated defence of the liberty to be wrong and the necessity of intellectual non-conformism.[58] As I have already suggested, liberals have good reasons to defend privacy and civil liberty and could in principle insist on a similar limit on the scope of police power that I have laid out here.[59] My argument is not only that there are also democratic limits to police power, but that the democratic arguments may prove to be less compromised and stronger than the liberal ones. We have seen that the more we enrich the concept of *individual* autonomy that is protected by the state's penal laws, the more likely we are to recognize security as an agency good that should enjoy that protection. Only by making our legal protection of autonomy less sensitive to the harms that undermine it can we identify liberalism's limit to the scope of the penal law. The reverse is true of the democratic principle of *collective* self-government. It is only the minimal account of democracy—the rule of the parties with the most votes after a fair election—that offers support to the pre-inchoate offences. The more we specify the conditions in which majority rule is also the means to true collective self-government, the more intolerable are the pre-inchoate offences with their coercion of the private sphere on the grounds of preventing insecurity.

Liberalism's commitment to balancing a plurality of goods leads it to depend on neutral-sounding concepts like harm and wrong which leave all the work to the particular contents that will fill them at any particular political moment. The danger is that this leads to a focus on the satisfaction of the harm principle and the meeting of the formal requirements of criminal procedure at the expense of considering the institutionalization of distrust and the subjection of individuals to the coercive administrative discretion that is legitimized by substantively pre-inchoate offences. By contrast, if collective self-government provides the central principle, we can move away from the ethical language of individual moral wrongdoing.[60] We can instead interpret criminal wrongs as offences against political self-determination,[61] incorporating certain negative liberties as a non-negotiable

[57] Note that it is persons who cannot be coerced in this way by a democracy and not just citizens. The reason is, as we saw, that the possibility of self-government is based on the personhood of citizens. It follows that *all persons are potential citizens* and must be treated as such. A democracy that refused the same protections and liabilities under the penal law to persons who were non-citizens would deny its own democratic principle of the self-government of persons in favour of some other particularist national or ethnic identification.

[58] JS Mill, *On Liberty* (1974) 76 and 132.

[59] See, eg, Simester and von Hirsch (cited in n 8).

[60] In a different context, see N Lacey and H Pickard, 'From the Consulting Room to the Court Room? Taking the Clinical Model of Responsibility without Blame into the Legal Realm' OJLS (2013 forthcoming).

[61] See also P Ramsay, 'Voters Should not Be in Prison' *Critical Review of International Social and Political Philosophy* (forthcoming) and Ramsay (cited in n 40).

component of that core principle. A degree of insecurity and risk of harm may have to be tolerated as a necessary consequence of institutionalizing the formal mutual trust that governs relations among the citizens of a truly democratic republic. Nevertheless, a state that was the institutional form of a truly self-governing population really would enjoy the sort of awesome power that Thomas Hobbes imagined for his Leviathan.

This is an argument that makes political self-determination the central principle from which to derive the legitimacy of treating a particular wrong as a public wrong.[62] Unlike the liberal language of individual autonomy, the language of political self-determination may seem dated to some readers. This is because the recent proliferation of pre-inchoate offences has occurred at a time when the ideologies that incited the mass political engagement of the past have stagnated and their influence has declined. It is in the wake of this decline that policy has become a matter of protecting 'real autonomy' from the harm of insecurity. It may be, as I have argued here, that democratic theory can offer a more consistent principled line against the expansion of preventive offences than liberalism can. Democrats will, nevertheless, have to face the fact that, for the moment at least, the existing formally democratic political order, the one that institutionalizes mutual distrust and suspicion in its preventive criminal offences, has turned its face against substantive democratic principles.

[62] Adding to the list of proposed single principles that many theorists argue must necessarily fail, see Duff (cited in n 15) 138–9.

# 12

# On Preventive Justice

*Matt Matravers**

## A. Introduction

I take it that, as the Marxists used to say, it is 'not an accident' that academic (and other) interest in 'prevention' is on the rise. No doubt many things have prompted it, amongst which the use by the state of mandatory sentences, sexual predator laws, control orders, and situational crime control are but a few. Philosophers, criminal law theorists, criminologists, and sociologists have been vocal in declaring a new era: a 'culture of control', a 'risk society', or the rise of 'preventionism'.[1] The alarm is being sounded not only because of particular instances of the preventive use of state power that strike most civilized people as abhorrent (for example, the seemingly indefinite detention without trial of people in Guantanamo Bay), but because of the sighting of a new *trend* in which a concern for preventing future harms that in part rests on, and in part helps to generate, a split between 'us' (the safe and law abiding) and 'them' (the dangerous) threatens to ride roughshod over liberal respect for others and for their rights. Moreover, this trend is occurring despite three decades in which 'just deserts' and 'proportionality' have ruled the theoretical roost. Thus, the dominant theoretical ways of thinking about criminal justice policy are not well equipped to cope with criminal justice practice in this area (other than by denunciation on grounds of lack of proportionality).[2]

My aim in this chapter is to offer the beginnings of a normative account of preventive justice; an account that may be able to make better sense of current policies even if the sense it offers is not one that would be recognized by the authors of those policies. To do this, I want first to consider what it is that is at stake when we think about 'preventive justice'. Of course, we should not get too hung up on

* I am grateful to the participants at the Preventive Justice workshop where this chapter was first aired. I owe a particular debt to Andrew Ashworth, Ambrose Lee, and Lucia Zedner for their comments. Patrick Tomlin kindly agreed to comment on my paper at that event, and even more kindly gave me a copy of what he said; this has proved invaluable in revising it. In all cases, I am sure I have not done enough to answer all the queries.

[1] U Beck, *Risk Society: Towards a New Modernity* (1992); A Giddens, 'Risk and Responsibility' (1999) 62(1) MLR 1–10; D. Garland, *The Culture of Control: Crime and Social Order in Contemporary Society* (2001).

[2] On this, see M Tonry, *Retributivism Has A Past: Has It A Future?* (2011).

terminological matters, but if we are going to offer an account of some *x*, we do need to say something about what *x* is.

## B. Preventive justice

We might think of the term 'preventive justice' as simply a descriptive term to cover criminal justice policies concerned with preventing future crimes and, say, 'pure preventive justice' as covering those policies that are, to a large extent, concerned only with the prevention of future crimes. Or, slightly more narrowly, as describing those aspects of criminal law and policy that allow the state to 'bind', one way or another, those who have not yet committed an offence, but who are reasonably suspected of being about to do so or about to incite others to do so.[3] However, to do this is not to preclude normative enquiry. Rather, it invites questions of justification: what justifies this area of law and the policies that flow from it?

Once we engage in that kind of enquiry one question appears fairly quickly, which is whether 'preventive justice' is a phrase in which the two concepts it invokes—prevention and justice—are in tension. This seems to be the case when we consider that many standard worries about preventive justice policies seem to be grounded in the thought that such policies may conflict with the demands of justice. So, we talk of the need to *balance* security and justice as if the game is, or is close to, zero-sum such that gains in preventing serious criminal harms can only be had by equivalent losses in just treatment. The debate over Guantanamo Bay is often phrased in this form. No thoughtful person believes the treatment of detainees there is in accordance with justice, but some are prepared to allow that the price paid in justice is worth the gains made in preventing future terrorist harms. On this model, it seems that prevention is one thing, justice quite another. Of course, even on this model, when we pursue the prevention of future harms we do so given side-constraints of justice. Such a position is fairly standard: we think that, for example, surgeons may do what is best for their patients so that they do not suffer future ill-health, but we do not think that they can do so by harvesting the organs of a third party. Justice here *constrains* the pursuit of future harm prevention. On this model, 'preventive justice' might identify the sub-set of justice concerned with constraining prevention. However, this is surely not the only—or even a plausible—conception of what we mean when we invoke the idea of 'preventive justice'. Rather, what we have in mind is something more akin to a duty of justice; a duty to prevent future harms.

One obvious way to unpack this thought is to consider the functions of the state and of government. In many cases, we think that amongst these functions is the protection of citizens from future harm. Of course we can, and do, debate quite how far such protection should range, to what degree it should be paternalistic, and whether the opportunity costs of one form of protection are worth paying, but

[3] G Williams, 'Preventive Justice and the Rule of Law' (1953) 16(4) MLR 417–27.

none of that changes the conceptual claim that, at least sometimes, the state has a duty of justice to protect its citizens from future harms. Thus, for example, consider the case of a serious storm approaching an urban area. Here, we might think that the state is required by justice to warn its citizens and to take certain kinds of action to ensure that all are (insofar as possible) offered an equal chance of reducing the degree to which the storm will set back their interests.

I think this better accounts for our understanding of 'preventive justice' (at least in relation to state policies). It relates to those areas of policy in which the state has a prima facie duty to act to prevent future harms. Of course, this does not mean that the tension between justice and prevention is dissolved. Unless one is an out-and-out welfare consequentialist—in which case there cannot be a conflict between what the state ought to do to prevent net losses of welfare and the demands of justice—one confronts the problem that in pursuing much of its *raison d'être*, the state will have reason to act in ways that prevent future harms, and secure future benefits, for its citizens and the critical issue is whether, and in what way, the state's actions ought to relate to the demands of justice.

## C. Justice and aggregation

As noted in section B, saying that the state will in some instances have a duty to prevent foreseeable and preventable future harms does not tell us in what instances, or to what degree, or at what cost, and so on. Moreover, it may be that in many cases the successful pursuit of this demand of justice will be in tension with other moral demands (including other demands of justice). For some, often called 'value pluralists', such tensions may be ineliminable because values conflict and we cannot satisfy all of them simultaneously; for others the tension may only be apparent and a proper understanding of justice will show how each demand can be made compatible, but that debate need not detain us here. Whatever the truth of value pluralism, thinking through preventive justice requires first that we think through justice.

Consider first the formal definition of justice. Justice requires giving to each person that which is properly due to him or her.[4] Of course, this does not tell us very much. Like the requirement that we treat relevantly alike things that are relevantly alike, it is purely formal. What is due to people? As we have seen, for the straightforward welfare consequentialist, what is due to each person is simply whatever will maximize welfare overall for all (relevant) persons. Thus, what is due the third party in the surgeon example is to be cut up and what is due the patients is to receive the organs thus 'harvested'. The reason this is unsatisfactory is that it fails to take proper account of what John Rawls called (in a very useful phrase) 'the distinction between persons'.[5] By contrast, in offering to transport the citizens of

[4] The formal definition is often captured in the Latin tag *suum cuique tribuere*: to allocate to each his own. See B Barry and M Matravers, 'Justice' in E Craig (ed), *The Shorter Routledge Encyclopedia of Philosophy* (2005) 481–6.

[5] J Rawls, *A Theory of Justice* (1971) 27.

the urban area under threat from the storm to safety, we consider each person's claim separately.

But what is it about human beings in virtue of which we think that what is due to them is to be treated as distinct? The answer is that we regard human persons as agents who are entitled to equal respect. It is in our capacity to choose—in a special way related to reasons—and to act on those choices that our 'specialness' lies. To sacrifice one agent for the sake of saving four others is not to treat that agent with the respect that is due to him or her even if overall welfare is improved as a result. Now, it is perhaps possible to think of all state action as grounded in nothing other than respecting rights. That is, assuming we unpack treating people with respect in terms of respecting their rights, the only permissible state action will be that which honours or protects those rights. However, this is implausible; there are many actions that the state might take that will enhance its citizens' well-being, or promote their interests, that need not be grounded in honouring or protecting rights. Such actions, though, need to be subject to the constraints of respecting rights.

This raises a difficult question. Consider the following example: to reduce journey times for many people, and to reduce the risk of injury to some, the state decides to build a bypass that takes road traffic around a city-centre. Let us assume that the only available route for the bypass takes it through an area in which it is tricky, but obviously not impossible, to build. As a result it is probable that some construction workers will suffer harm (they may even be seriously injured). Why, and in what way, is this different from the surgeon case? If we are to respect the liberal notion of justice, the policy of building the bypass must respect the distinctiveness of persons. One way of capturing how it does so is offered by the philosopher Tim Scanlon. Scanlon's answer is that none of us separately, considering how our own lives might go overall, can reject a principle that allows certain inherently risky activities and social practices given that they are practised with reasonable care. Aggregating 'within' each person's life, as Scanlon puts it, explains this judgement as against aggregating 'across' lives, which is what is required—and objectionable—in the surgeon case.[6]

Moreover, contrasting cases of this kind, Scanlon argues that

> It is important in understanding our reaction to these cases [cases such as the bypass] to note that they involve failing to prevent accidental injuries rather than either intentionally inflicting harm on a few people, or withholding aid from people who need it, in order to bring small benefits to others. Our sense that it is permissible to undertake these projects also depends crucially on the assumption that precautions have been taken to make the work safe and that, in addition, workers have the choice of whether or not to undertake the risks involved. So the question in these cases is whether these precautions are adequate—whether, having taken them, it is permissible to proceed—or whether a higher level of caution is required.[7]

[6] TM Scanlon, *What We Owe to Each Other* (1998) 237.

[7] Scanlon (cited in n 6) 236.

As my intention is to apply this analysis to the system of criminal justice, it is worth saying a little more about this. Scanlon mentions 'accidental' injuries and 'small benefits', but these aspects of his thesis are specific to the examples he is considering. There is no reason to think the argument would not go through (if it does) with respect to 'mistaken' as against 'accidental' injuries and, if anything, increasing the size of the benefits involved might strengthen the case.

Scanlon himself applies his account to the system of punishment. He does this by a schematic comparison of the 'institution of punishment' with an example in which there is a justified policy of waste removal to protect the water supply; the state takes all available precautions to ensure that no one is injured, but nevertheless through negligence or recklessness some people suffer contamination. Since it seems to me that the first question in considering 'preventive justice' must concern what the conditions are such that a system of prevention can be justified at all (and since some of the specific issues mentioned will come up again later), it is worth quoting Scanlon's analysis at length:

> In each case [the case of waste removal and that of punishment] ... First, there is an important social goal: protecting the water supply in the one case, protecting ourselves and our possessions in the other. Second, there is a strategy for promoting this goal that involves the creation of another risk: the risk of contamination in the one case, the risk of punishment in the other. Third, the effect of this strategy is that there is (literally or metaphorically) a certain affected 'area' that one can no longer enter without danger. In the one case this is the area in which the excavation, transport, and disposal of the waste are being carried out; in the other case it is the metaphorical 'area' consisting of the range of activities that have been declared illegal. Fourth, even if safeguards are introduced to reduce people's exposure to the risk created, it remains overwhelmingly likely that many of those who enter the affected areas, and perhaps some others, will be harmed. Some of the safeguards that are introduced (such as requirements of due process, and careful methods of excavation and transport) serve to protect those who stay out of the affected area. Other safeguards enhance the value of choice as a protection by making it less likely that people will choose to enter this area. In the example of hazardous waste these include signs and other publicity informing people of the risk, as well as fences, guards, and the choice of an obscure disposal site where no one has reason to go. Analogous features in the case of punishment are education (including moral education), the dissemination of information about the law, and the maintenance of social and economic conditions that reduce the incentive to commit crime by offering the possibility of a satisfactory life within the law. Restrictions on entrapment by law enforcement officers also belong in this category of safeguards, as do provisions which excuse from punishment those who, because of mental illness or defect, are unable to regulate their conduct in accordance with the law.[8]

As Scanlon admits, there are differences between systems of punishment and waste disposal that make justification of the former both easier and more difficult. Amongst those that make it easier is the fact that the 'area' proscribed by the criminal law consists of activities in which it is morally wrong to engage and thus 'being deprived of the opportunity of "entering this area" without risk does not

[8] Scanlon (cited in n 6) 264.

count as a morally significant loss'. Amongst those that make it harder is the fact that it is 'no part of the waste-removal program that those who go to the excavation site should suffer contamination' whereas 'it is an essential part of the institution of punishment that those who violate the law should be punished'.[9] Nevertheless, if we are to have a system of punishment that is justified, at least in part, by its preventing future harms, then Scanlon's account makes clear where the burden of justification lies. This burden is a heavy one, on the account given so far, because of the intentional infliction of harm involved in punishment. However—again, as Scanlon realizes—the burden of justification is great not only because of the quantity (so to speak) of what is imposed on those who are punished, but also because of the quality of what is imposed. More specifically, punishment has a 'condemnatory aspect'; it expresses an authoritative judgement that the offender has, through his or her own fault, failed to behave in accordance with appropriate rules and standards. Such a judgement, of course, involves assessing the degree to which the agent is rightly blamed not just in the sense of whether 'he or she did it', but in the sense of whether in 'doing it' he or she acted in a way that makes blame appropriate (the agent chose to do it in the relevant sense, he or she did not act under duress, or as a result of an uncontrollable physical spasm, etc).[10]

It might be worth taking stock. The purpose of this discussion was to put the idea of the state's seeking to prevent future harms into some kind of theoretical structure. That is, assuming the state's preventing of future harms is sometimes a demand of justice, the question is how we should decide when, how, and at what cost. One answer—an answer I have rejected—is whenever the overall benefits outweigh the overall costs aggregated across all parties. Having rejected this answer, I then appealed to a standard liberal heuristic; a form of contract argument in which proposals are tested against 'reasonable rejectability'. Applying this to the question at hand: it is one responsibility of the state to try to ensure the future well-being of its citizens and one way in which it does this is through the criminal law. What Scanlon's analysis shows us—in common with others—is that if it is to do this it must do it in ways that could not be reasonably rejected by citizens. Policies that aggregate across persons can be so rejected, as can policies that risk criminal liability without putting into place the correct precautions so that citizens might generally avoid such liability through their choices. Rather than thinking of the pursuit of the prevention of harms as one goal—a goal that must be constrained or limited by respect for individuals—Scanlon's argument suggests a slightly different view of the matter: the prevention of harms is one instance of the state's respecting persons and

[9] Scanlon (cited in n 6) 264–5.

[10] Of course, the criminal law also contains activities that are not moral wrongs in themselves (*mala prohibita* and regulatory offences) and (in practice at least) punishments do not always have a particularly strong condemnatory nature. This makes these aspects of the criminal law both easier and more difficult to justify (but in different ways to the core offences). They are more difficult to justify precisely because they do not involve behaviour the prohibition of which does not count as a morally significant loss, but the justificatory burden is lighter insofar as the penalties are less serious.

is thus properly pursued only through policies that respect the status of persons.[11] What the comparison of the waste disposal and criminal justice policies shows us—and in particular what they have in common—is that we respect the status of persons by ensuring such policies contain the correct precautions such that citizens may avoid the risks created by the exercise of their *choices*.

Before moving to consider choice and criminal justice in more detail (which is the topic of the next section), it is worth noting that, for some people, the criminal law has nothing to do with the prevention of future harms other than as a happy side effect of the pursuit of retributive justice. Michael Moore, for example, argues that the good achieved by punishment is simply that of retributive justice: that people 'get what they deserve' and that any further benefits of the system are merely contingent: 'punishing the guilty achieves something good—namely, justice'. All other good consequences are 'simply beside the point'.[12] Thus, for Moore, the comparison of waste disposal and criminal justice is entirely otiose. I have argued elsewhere that Moore's position—theoretically impressive though it is—ought to be rejected as grounded in an untenable metaphysical moral realism.[13] Moreover, even putting to one side the metaphysical basis of Moore's argument, his overall position seems far less plausible than that of, for example, Ashworth and Zedner who argue that the 'preventive and punitive rationales are intertwined. It makes no sense to suggest that the criminal law's purpose is simply to declare the most serious wrongs and to provide for the conviction and punishment of those who commit them, as if the prevention of such wrongs is not also part of the rationale'.[14]

## D. Choice, 'entering the affected area', and liability to punishment

In this section, I want to consider two stages of criminal liability that flow from Scanlon's framework (although the distinction between these is not hard and fast). First, there is the question of what protections are necessary to ensure that the creation of criminal law with a view to preventing harms cannot be reasonably rejected. Secondly, the question of the imposition of particular penalties on those who violate that law.

With respect to those protections that are necessary if we are to have a scheme of criminal liability that cannot be reasonably rejected: as we have seen, Scanlon mentions due process; education (including moral education); the dissemination of information about the law; the maintenance of social and economic conditions

[11] Cf Ashworth and Zedner: 'In principle, as most systems of criminal law recognize, pursuit of [the rationale of preventing serious harm] should be limited by doctrines that demonstrate respect for individuals as moral agents. Thus the preventive purpose should only be pursued subject to the importance of defining the wrong clearly (so that people know what they should avoid) and of making provision for a fault element in liability and for proportionality of punishment': A Ashworth and L Zedner, 'Just Prevention: Preventive Rationales and the Limits of the Criminal Law' in A Duff and S Green (eds), *Philosophical Foundations of Criminal Law* (2011) 282.

[12] M Moore, *Placing Blame: A General Theory of the Criminal Law* (1997) 111.

[13] M Matravers, *Justice and Punishment: The Rationale of Coercion* (2000) 81–7.

[14] Ashworth and Zedner (cited in n 11) 281.

that reduce the incentive to commit crime by offering the possibility of a satisfactory life within the law; restrictions on entrapment by law enforcement officers; and provisions which excuse from punishment those who, because of mental illness or defect, are unable to regulate their conduct in accordance with the law. Criminal law theorists will be able to add—and have added—many others. My aim in the following sub-section is to establish a way of thinking about liability and preventive justice that builds on the picture of agency (and its relationship to justice) already presented. In the second sub-section, I want to offer an alternative account of preventive justice measures that puts strain on the first.

## Entering the affected area

Scanlon's list of protections necessary when creating the risk to criminal liability are not new or surprising. HLA Hart, to give just one example, in one of his discussions of the excusing conditions in the criminal law, comments that 'we can regard their function as a mechanism for... maximizing within the framework of coercive criminal law the efficacy of the individual's informed and considered choice in determining the future and also his power to predict that future',[15] and throughout Hart's work one can find a concern for the ability of individuals to determine through choice whether or not criminal sanctions will be applied to them. I find this wholly convincing, which is not to say that it is uncontroversial. Indeed, one way to think of many of the pressing issues of preventive justice—for example, the use of 'two-step prohibitions'[16]—is precisely in terms of whether they violate the need to ensure that the state's regulatory actions are enacted with sufficient protections that they cannot be reasonably rejected by citizens aggregating within their lives given the significance of the penalties attached to some violations of the state's commands. That said, the precise relationship between the protections that are necessary when formulating policy in pursuit of the good of preventing future criminal harms (that is, the protections that ensure that 'entering the area' of risk is a matter of choice) and preventive policies is a complex matter and would need to be worked out on a policy by policy basis. On the one hand, it may seem that so long as the state engages in sufficient publicity the agent cannot complain if he or she breaks the rules and suffers the consequences. On the other, it cannot be the case that the conditions of choice are met for any policy, no matter how draconian, so long as it is announced clearly in advance. What is offered here is meant as a guide to thinking about these issues rather than a catalogue of permissible versus impermissible policies, but it is worth considering a couple of examples as illustrations of how the argument might go.

Consider first sex offender registers. Clearly, the state can formulate a set of offences in the area of sexual conduct and so long as the laws meet all the standards of legality, the state can claim that 'entering' the area of risk to criminal liability is

[15] HLA Hart, *Punishment and Responsibility: Essays in the Philosophy of Law* (1968) 46.

[16] A Simester and A von Hirsch, *Crimes, Harms, and Wrongs: On the Principles of Criminalisation* (2011) 213.

(other than in cases of 'mental illness or defect') a matter of choice and thus meets that demand of justice. If it adds to the law that convicted offenders will be required to go on a sex offender register, and it publicizes this fact, is there any more to be said? The answer will depend on the nature of the register (its duration, to whom it is made available, and so on). If the agent is required to register for life, then a complaint can be brought on the basis that no future set of choices by the agent (for example, not to pose a risk of offending) can change the agent's status. If the register is made available to the agent's (future) neighbours, then the consequences of the initial offence may be that the agent cannot find housing, work, friends, and so on. Since these things are no part of the original 'area of risk', again a complaint can be brought on the basis of choice, and so on.

Consider secondly two-step prohibitions. As characterized by Simister and von Hirsch, 'these involve the issuance of (nominally) civil prohibitory orders against persons who have been found engaged in, or who are expected to engage in, undesired conduct. A breach of the order then becomes a criminal offence'.[17] Again, on the face of it, the state can announce in advance that antisocial conduct will make a person liable to the risk of receiving such a two-step order, and once done, an agent would need to choose further to violate the first step of the order in order to be liable to the second. And again, exactly how we might respond will depend on the precise nature of the legislation. However, there are a number of standard features of such orders that surely render them problematic on the choice account. First, undesired or antisocial conduct is a vague notion. Secondly, the conduct included in 'antisocial' will extend far beyond criminal conduct. Thirdly, the order that follows may include prohibitions that go beyond prohibition of that conduct (for example, a person may be ordered not to enter a shopping mall) and that were not themselves known at the time the agent chose to put him- or herself at risk of liability (by, say, behaving antisocially in a particular store within the mall). Fourthly, insofar as the initial order is imposed through civil law it avoids the due process protections of the criminal law although criminal sanctions can follow from a breach of that order.

These considerations are not decisive, and it bears repeating that the permissibility of any preventive measure will depend on the precise details of that measure, but they speak against the compatibility of two-step prohibitions and justice understood as discussed earlier. The point of the argument has been to offer a way of thinking about preventive justice as a form of justice. This way of thinking is informed by the thought that the state rightly pursues general goals (including preventive goals). In pursuing these goals, it will on occasion create risks for its citizens. Scanlon's thought experiment allows us to think about the permissibility of such risks and in particular about the protections required to ensure that citizens become liable to those risks only through their choices (although of course this will never work out perfectly). This way of thinking dovetails with Hart's, liberal, account of the criminal law 'that unless a man has the capacity and a fair

[17] Simester and von Hirsch (cited in n 16).

opportunity or chance to adjust his behaviour to the law its penalties ought not to be applied to him'.[18] It is an account that, I think, has much to commend it. However, in the next sub-section, I want to suggest a different way of thinking about preventive justice and about recent developments in this area.

### Liability to punishment

The previous sub-section is concerned with protecting agency as a requirement of justice. The picture is one of choosing, autonomous agents who have to live together in conditions of scarce resources, and whose state, in formulating policies to reduce the chances of future preventable harms, must act in ways that reflect the significance of agency. The concomitant of this, of course, is that those who choose to act in ways that make themselves liable to the risk have no complaint when it is realized. A person who knowingly climbs the ladder next to the sign saying 'Do not enter, contaminated waste' has nothing to complain about should he or she become ill (although of course it need not be anyone's plan that such persons should become ill). The offender who intentionally and without excuse violates a justifiable criminal law cannot complain when sentenced to the prescribed penalty.[19] The details are—as I hope I have indicated—immensely complicated, but the picture of agency, and of its role in justice, is relatively straightforward.

In this sub-section, I want to put this into question. In particular, I argue that we are in the midst of something of a revaluation of agency and of the relationship between agency and blame.[20] I believe that this is most clearly apparent when we have to inflict penalties on agents for their 'responsible conduct' although, of course, any revaluation of agency would affect not merely this, but also the foundations of the account of justice itself. It is one thing to think about agents entering the 'affected area' of the criminal law and rendering themselves liable to sanctions. When we do this, we call on abstract notions of agency and risk settling back into 'justificatory self-satisfaction'[21] when our theories hold together. It is another to think about a particular agent being subject to a particular penalty. My suggestion is that worries about agency manifest themselves at (but are not limited to) the second stage and that *some* preventive justice developments reflect this change in the confidence with which we think of ourselves and others as agents.

To pursue this, I want to stipulate a number of claims. First, I take it that punishment must involve hard treatment. Secondly, whilst there may be number of (seeming) desert or proportionality constraints on the use of hard treatment, the inclusion of hard treatment in punishment has a preventive rationale (that is, we might condemn an offender in a number of ways that do not involve hard treatment, but in punishing him or her we condemn *and penalize*. Attempts to

[18] Hart (cited in n 16) 11.

[19] Scanlon (cited in n 6) §3.3.

[20] N Lacey and H Pickard, 'From the Consulting Room to the Court Room? Taking the Clinical Model of Responsibility without Blame into the Legal Realm' (forthcoming, OJLS).

[21] D Ivison, 'Justifying Punishment in Intercultural Contexts' in M Matravers (ed), *Punishment and Political Theory* (1999) 107.

show that hard treatment is a non-contingent vehicle for condemnation, such as are offered by Antony Duff, in my view fail,[22] which leaves hard treatment as having (at least a significant) preventive rationale). Thirdly, I take 'agency' and (in the relevant sense) 'choice' to be both a property of persons and a social construction that needs to be interpreted. That is, I take it that there is an important sense in which being an agent—being someone able to exercise choice and who commands respect in virtue of that—is to some degree a fact about the person (for example, he or she has a certain cognitive and perhaps affective capacity). However, that is not all there is to it. Attributions of agency—the use of choice as normatively significant—are embedded in social practices. Thus, for example, the use of agency to capture the idea of (legal) responsibility is 'fundamentally relational' in that it depends on 'the character of moral, legal, and social relations among the actor, the victim, and the evaluator'.[23]

In thinking about agency in this way, it is useful to learn from the ways in which we approach ideas such as lunacy. Asking how to go about thinking about lunacy, the historian Roy Porter comments that 'the history of madness stands between histories of subjects such as plague or death and (on the other hand) histories of witchcraft. It must treat insanity... as a physical fact; but it needs to interpret it... principally as a socially constructed fact'. He goes on:

> So, is the historian to treat the lunatic as akin more to the smallpox victim or to the witch? Neither of these extremes will serve our turn. Even the doughtiest champion of the organic aetiology of insanity will concede that madness has donned and doffed radically different masks down the ages, just as those who regard 'insanity' essentially as a social label will admit that the individual suffering is none the less intense. Some integrative position is required. Insanity is both a personal disorder..., and is also articulated within a system of sociolinguistic signs and meanings.[24]

Porter's suggestion of how the historian should deal with 'lunacy' offers, in my view, a productive way of thinking for those looking to understand 'agency'.

This is not to say that there are no relevant 'facts of the matter' or that one interpretation of agency is as good as any other. Moreover, of course, one of the functions of law and legal doctrine is to *fix* the meaning of terms such as liability, responsibility, and excuse. In doing so, the law has a degree of flexibility to deviate both from the 'facts' and from popular beliefs about their meaning. Thus, the law can postulate an artificial being with agency and can resist the latest in scientific and

[22] M Matravers, 'Duff on Hard Treatment' in R Cruft, M Kramer, and M Reiff (eds), *Crime, Punishment and Responsibility* (2011).

[23] C Kutz, 'Responsibility' in J Coleman and S Shapiro (eds), *The Oxford Handbook of Jurisprudence & Philosophy of Law* (2002) 550. Cf Antony Duff, 'to *be* responsible is to be... *held* responsible by somebody within some practice': RA Duff, 'Who is Responsible, for What, to Whom?' (2005) 2(2) Ohio State Journal of Criminal Law 442. My *Responsibility and Justice* (2007) is an extended defence of this view of responsibility and its significance for distributive and retributive justice.

[24] R Porter, *Madmen: A Social History of Madhouses, Mad-Doctors, & Lunatics* (2004) 26–7. For discussion of some of the different masks 'donned and doffed' by legal responsibility, see, eg, N Lacey, 'Character, Capacity, Outcome: Toward a Framework for Assessing the Shifting Pattern of Criminal Responsibility in Modern English Law' in M Dubber and L Farmer (eds), *Modern Histories of Crime and Punishment* (2007) 14–41.

pseudo-scientific findings because responsibility in the law is responsibility in the law and not responsibility in something else. Yet, this flexibility is not boundlessly elastic. Both for reasons of maintaining public confidence and because the law is not immune to intellectual fashions and changes in the understandings of the communities it serves, the law's relation to beliefs about agency, responsibility, and so on, cannot be entirely distant.

My conjecture in this section has three parts: first, that we are undergoing something of a revaluation of the nature of agency and the relationship between agency and blame; secondly, that this revaluation is more often revealed in uncertainty about our infliction of punishment than in the design of (new) offences or defences; thirdly, that *some* of what has recently been taken to be a resurgence of a preventive rationale in the use of the criminal law reflects that uncertainty. To examine this, I want to take the second claim first and to do that I want to return briefly to Scanlon.

*Two types of responsibility.* As we saw earlier, Scanlon recognizes that there is more to punishment than the regulation of conduct. Specifically, punishment involves moral condemnation. In discussing this, Scanlon distinguishes two types of responsibility: 'responsibility as attributability' and 'substantive responsibility'.[25] Although I am not wholly convinced by the way in which Scanlon divides the two senses of responsibility,[26] the distinction is important. In brief, the former captures the idea that a given action can be attributed to an agent in 'the way that is required in order for it to be a basis for moral appraisal'. The latter expresses 'substantive claims about what people are required... to do for each other'.[27] That is, if a person is 'properly subject to praise or blame for having acted' in a certain way, that is a matter of responsibility as attributability. Whether such praise or blame should be expressed and whether as a result the person should bear the 'burdens or obligations' that result from his or her actions is a matter of substantive responsibility.[28] This is a useful distinction; we sometimes feel that it is right that someone is the proper subject of blame, but that he or she ought not to have to bear the entire burden that results from his or her actions (consider someone who stupidly goes rock climbing without checking the weather and gets into trouble. Such a person is the proper object of blame for having acted in the way that he or she did, but we may feel that he or she nevertheless deserves to be rescued). Moreover, it can be applied to—although it does not map directly on—the trial and sentencing stage of criminal law. Having satisfied ourselves of the attributability of blame to the offender, we might nevertheless feel that there is a case for mitigation in sentencing. My claim is that this can provide a safety valve for uncertainty about agency at precisely the time when that uncertainty is most likely to bite, which is when a (substantial) burden is being imposed on someone in virtue of that agency.

[25] Scanlon (cited in n 6) 248.

[26] M Matravers, 'Responsibility and Choice' in M Matravers (ed), *Scanlon and Contractualism* (2003) 77–92.

[27] Scanlon (cited in n 6) 248.

[28] Scanlon (cited in n 6) 290.

An example of this might be the English plea of diminished responsibility. This plea was introduced in the Homicide Act 1957 and allows that where a defendant accused of murder can show that his or her 'mental responsibility' was 'substantially' impaired by mental abnormality conviction can only be for manslaughter. This is a much criticized aspect of English law (and I have no wish to defend it). Although the requirements for diminished responsibility have been changed by the Coroners and Justice Act 2009 s 52, it remains true that the successful use of this plea does not 'excuse from responsibility' but, by means of a change in the offence, 'mitigates the penalty'.[29] Moreover, the change helped to stave off calls for more significant reform to the law. That is—at least arguably—a gap had opened up (and continues to exist) between one idea of agency and responsibility and the idea of agency and responsibility that underpinned the M'Naghten Rules of 1843. The autonomy of the law—its ability to dismiss, for example, 'the men of medicine' and their 'modern ideas'[30]—was under pressure and that pressure was relieved by the introduction of the plea of diminished responsibility which allowed defendants to escape the terrible choice of the label of murderer (and capital punishment) or lengthy detention as insane.

I do not want to make this distinction too stark. Debates over agency and the proper conditions under which choice can be said to be a result of agency can rage at the stage at which offences and defences are being created or discussed (as, for example, in cases of proposed defences of battered women syndrome), but even there the trigger for such discussions is often the use of the penalty appropriate to agency as determined by law. What these and other discussions show, I think, is confusion and uncertainty about the nature of agency, which is the first part of my conjecture to which I now turn.

*Agency*. The first part of my conjecture is that there is a general sense of confusion and uncertainty about agency. The second part, already discussed, is that some of that uncertainty emerges when agency matters (when we are about to impose large costs on people because of judgements of responsibility). To some extent the second part, if true, would be evidence for the first. However, I think there is more to be said. The claim I would like to make is of the following form: there is in our thinking about agency and responsibility a story analogous to the one told by David Garland in *The Culture of Control*,[31] but with a further chapter.

The equivalent of the post-war welfarist consensus in Garland is what Hart analysed as 'a new scepticism' beginning in 1957:

> a scepticism of the whole institution of criminal punishment so far as it contains elements which differentiate it from a system of purely forward looking social hygiene in which our only concern when we have an offender to deal with, is with the future and the rational aims of the prevention of further crime, the protection of society and the care and if possible the cure of the offender.[32]

[29] HLA Hart, *The Morality of the Criminal Law. Two lectures* (1965) 11.
[30] SJF Stephen, *A History of the Criminal Law of England* (1883) ch XIX.
[31] Garland (cited in n 1). [32] Hart (cited in n 29) 13.

This scepticism—according to Hart who associated it with Barbara Wootton[33]—in its most extreme form stemmed from a belief in the impossibility of drawing lines between normal and abnormal offenders.[34]

Following Garland's chronology, Hart's worries about this scepticism of course proved unfounded. Instead, what emerged in the 1970s was a resilient individualism in politics and the law and a resurgence of something associated with retributivism. As I have argued elsewhere, this retributive turn was not grounded in desert or on any solid, pre-justicial foundations.[35] That lack of foundations makes it vulnerable to changes in the ordinary conception of agency and responsibility (changes that may well be prompted by something of a backlash against the individualism initiated under US President Ronald Reagan and British Prime Minister Margaret Thatcher). The extension of the argument then is that what we are seeing is a combination of political, cultural, and legal pressures on the idea of agency as it is currently enshrined in law. The public realm is awash with papers and projects on law and neuroscience and even popular magazines and newspapers are reporting that changes in the way we understand the brain will fundamentally change the way we view criminal responsibility.[36] At the same time, the promised revised version of the American Psychiatric Association's *Diagnostic and Statistical Manual of Mental Disorders* (DSM-5) proposes to move away from categorical to dimensional diagnoses of personality disorders.[37] Of course, this is not to say that brain scans will make the law redundant or that the psychiatric profession is suddenly committed to the view that we are all mad (or that there is no difference between the sane and the mad), but these—together with things like the rise of therapeutic justice—are perhaps harbingers of change.

This story, broken into three parts as it is, oversimplifies. Social, political, and cultural life does not break neatly into sections. Even one of criminal law's most treasured stories of this kind—of the rise of consequentialist theories of punishment and their displacement by 'just deserts' in the 1970s—obscures many of the ways in which retributivist strands were present prior to the 1970s and consequentialist ones afterwards.[38] Nevertheless, it would be a mistake, I think, to reject the story

33 Wootton held that the purpose of the criminal law was to prevent antisocial behaviour and the purpose of criminal punishment was to achieve this by treating offenders so as to modify their future behaviour. For Wootton, *mens rea* considerations were relevant 'after a breach of the law has been proved' because of 'the light which they throw on the likelihood of his offending again, and upon the most hopeful way of dealing with him': B Wootton, *Crime and Penal Policy: Reflections on Fifty Years' Experience* (1978) 224.

34 As Wootton (cited in n 33 at 227) puts it, 'if mental health and ill-health cannot be defined in objective scientific terms that are free of subjective moral judgements, it follows that we have no reliable criterion by which to distinguish the sick from the healthy mind'.

35 M Matravers, 'Is Twenty-First Century Punishment Post-Desert?' in Tonry (cited in n 2).

36 The most famous and arguably most serious being the Law and Neuroscience Project <http://www.lawneuro.org/index.php>. For examples of the popular reception of these ideas, see, eg, D Eagleman, 'The Brain on Trial' in *The Atlantic* <http://www.theatlantic.com/magazine/archive/2011/07/the-brain-on-trial/8520/4/>.

37 For a discussion of this, and of some of the controversies surrounding the change, see the papers included in the special edition of *Personality and Mental Health* (2011) 5(2).

38 M Tonry, 'Crime and Public Policy' in M Tonry (ed), *The Oxford Handbook of Crime and Public Policy* (2009) 3–21.

outright because it is not the whole story. There was a rise of retributivist thinking and practice in the 1970s and it had real-world consequences, many of which were unwelcome to its most fervent supporters. I do not think that there is a rise of straightforward consequentialist thinking in any analogous way—although I think that some of the confusion that is on the rise is fuelled by a feeling that current practices of blame and punishment neither reflect our beliefs about justice nor do much to reduce future offending. Rather, there is a growing unease about whether the lines of criminal responsibility can be drawn with such confidence.

*Prevention and uncertainty*. The third part of my conjecture is that all of this discussion has something to do with the ostensible topic of this chapter, which is preventive justice. To substantiate this, I want to try to capture the arguments of the other parts of the conjecture in a slightly different way. In a short piece on responsibility, Galen Strawson declares the problem of free will to be 'like a carousel'. His argument is that we seek the kind of responsibility (call it 'ultimate' moral responsibility) that can underwrite—make comfortable *for us*—our practices of blaming and punishing. Faced with the impossibility of any such responsibility, the compatibilist offers us a different sense of responsibility (one that is compatible with our beliefs about causality, science, and so on). However, the kind of responsibility that the compatibilist can rescue is too thin to reassure us in our practices of blame and punishment (and so we return to the stronger notion that is incompatible with causality and round we go again).[39] The two parts of my conjecture map onto these stages of the carousel. It is when we are punishing that we worry most about agency and our worries about agency are being compounded by science and culture. For example, we have a far greater awareness of the social determinants of actions now than we did, but we do not know quite what to do with this information. This dilemma manifests itself in many ways, for example in the schizophrenic reaction of some in the population and press to sex offenders and, in particular, paedophiles: 'they must be punished', but 'they cannot help themselves', so 'they must also be watched (or worse)'.

Of course, there is no conceptual connection between these kinds of incompatibilist worries and preventive measures. In other words, a crisis in our understanding of agency need not necessarily lead to more preventive criminal justice; it might just as easily lead to less criminal justice all round. However, I think there is a way of understanding recent developments in preventive justice—including the increase in preventive policies—that might be thought a plausible development from a revaluation of agency and might offer a distinctive and interesting way of thinking about those policies. If we think of ourselves not as 'ultimately' responsible (in the Strawson sense), but equally not as mere handmaidens of chance, we might come to a view of responsible agency as fragile. That is, for all sorts of reasons, we hang on to a picture of ourselves that is as Scanlon or Hart have it, but we are also conscious of the degree to which our fates are not fully our own or determined by our choices.

[39] G Strawson, 'Luck Swallows Everything' (1998) *Times Literary Supplement*. A similar worry, albeit in support of a very different conclusion can be found in G Watson, 'Two Faces of Responsibility' (1996) 24(2) *Philosophical Topics* 227–48.

Combine that with the appalling consequences of criminal conviction both for ourselves and for those around us and we come to a vision of preventive justice policies as helping fragile agents avoid the often catastrophic consequences of their own criminal behaviour. On such a picture, the two-step prohibition order or the CCTV camera might be thought of as responding to the agent as someone who struggles with her or his behaviour and as needing help to ensure that she or he does not become liable to the criminal penalties that we otherwise need for social stability.

This is not, of course, how those who introduce such preventive measures think of those measures. Rather, they offer such policies as protecting the law-abiding 'us' from the feral 'them'. On my account, these measures when properly instituted are best thought of as protecting all of us from ourselves in the particular circumstances of the criminal law where making a mistake has such terrible consequences. This is not to negate the Scanlon/Hart position on the importance of choice, and it does not render redundant the mechanisms for evaluating preventive measures already suggested. For the moment, choice and agency matter, but the issue is over how much they matter in particular social practices. My conjecture is that we are uncomfortable with the degree to which they matter when the stakes are high—as of course they are in criminal justice—but we have not yet found a suitable response. If so, recent developments in preventive justice might be thought of in the light of this and, in my view, rendered less threatening.

## E. Conclusion

My claim—in its least controversial form—is that criminal justice has always had a concern for prevention as well as for punishment and we should not be too surprised when the balance between these rationales shifts in particular domains. In addition, it seems to me that Scanlon's accounts of aggregating within lives and of how to capture the value of choice when thinking about the pursuit of public policy, offer a useful way of theorizing about these issues. My grander claim is that the shift in this balance is indicative of a wider confusion about agency and a growing scepticism about the traditional conception of agency grounded in choice. This confusion manifests itself in punishment as it is there that the issues seem most urgent. Moreover, tinkering with the outcomes of our judgements of responsibility is less threatening to our understanding of ourselves than is rethinking those judgements from scratch (to mitigate a sentence to reflect unease about the agency of a particular offender is one thing, to give up on *mens rea* in the construction of offences is quite another). In short, allowing that our idea of agency may be more fragile than we think, and that we worry about this most when the stakes are high, allows a different way of thinking about preventive justice.

What I have not done is say anything about whether the changes and confusion that I have conjectured exist are unwelcome or welcome developments, or something in between. For what it is worth, I think the direction of travel is welcome but in need of theorizing.[40] That is, I think it is a serious mistake simply to reject these developments out of hand as 'disproportional', 'a return to the treatment model', or whatever. I also think it is a mistake to assume that they can only be made acceptable if transformed into something familiar and retributive. Proportionality and punishment are not free of conceptions of agency, and it is agency that is in question. It might be, in the end, that our current understandings of justice, agency, and blame are vindicated, but, if nothing else, our understanding of them will be improved for considering how best they meet the challenge.

[40] I try to take seriously the Strawsonian challenge with respect to our current practices of distributive and retributive justice in Matravers (cited in n 23). As will be clear from this discussion, I am not yet sure about how to theorize an alternative to those practices. That is the wider project of which this chapter is a part.

# 13

# Punitive Preventive Justice

## A Critique

*Bernard E Harcourt**

In 1966, New York City's newly elected mayor, John Lindsay, took office promising to reform city government with more efficient cost-benefit budgeting—what was known at the time as Planning-Programming-Budgeting System analysis (PPBS)—and invited the RAND Corporation to develop new strategies to prevent crime in New York. PPBS had been pioneered by Secretary of Defense Robert S McNamara at the Pentagon starting in 1961, and Lindsay brought the new technique to New York City 'to improve budgeting and operations'.[1] Within a few years, Mayor Lindsay had helped establish the New York City RAND Institute as a joint project of New York City and the California-based RAND Corporation.[2] The primary focus of RAND's New York City satellite would be the New York City Police Department.

At a news conference on 8 January 1969, with great fanfare, Mayor Lindsay and Henry Rowen, the president of RAND and, previously, deputy assistant secretary of defense under McNamara, unveiled the new project: an initial contract with New York City worth over $600,000, a Madison Avenue office 'staffed by 40 economists, sociologists, engineers, cost analysts and other researchers', and four focus areas, the most important of which was the New York City Police Department (NYPD) (the other three were the New York City Fire Department, Housing Administration, and Health Services).[3] Expecting a tight collaboration with New York City, the *New York Times* predicted that 'The city's relationship with RAND would be similar to the one RAND has had with the Air Force since World War II'.[4]

* Special thanks for comments on a prior draft to Andrew Ashworth, Markus Dubber, Antony Duff, Cecile Fabre, Doug Husak, Nicola Lacey, Ian Loader, Laurence Lustgarten, Pat O'Malley, Adam Samaha, Carol Steiker, Victor Tadros, Patrick Tomlin, and Lucia Zedner. Special thanks to Christopher Berk, Alan Chen, Maxwell Kampfner, and Patricio Martínez for excellent research and useful comments on an earlier draft.

[1] JS Light, *From Warfare to Welfare: Defense Intellectuals and Urban Problems in Cold War America* (2003) 67.

[2] Light (cited in n 1) 68–72.

[3] R Reeves, 'City Hires Rand Corp. to Study Four Agencies' *New York Times* (9 January 1968) 31; Light, *From Warfare to Welfare* (cited in n 1) 68–70.

[4] Reeves (cited in n 3) 31.

Within a few years, the New York City RAND Institute issued a number of statistical analyses aimed at crime prevention, and both the NYC RAND Institute and the starship RAND Corporation proposed a number of preventive justice measures. The first series of reports were extremely technical, narrow operations-research reports,[5] with titles such as 'A Hypercube Queueing Model for Facility Location and Redistricting in Urban Emergency Services' (Richard C Larson, R-1238-HUD, 1973), 'Response of Emergency Units: The Effects of Barriers, Discrete Streets, and One-Way Streets' (Richard C Larson, R-675-HUD, 1971), 'Allocation of Emergency Units Response Areas' (Jan M Chaiken, P-4745, 1971), 'Analysis of the Night and Weekend Arraignment Parts in the Bronx and Queens Criminal Courts' (John B Jennings, R-1236-NYS, 1973), 'Using Simulation To Develop and Validate Analytical Emergency Service Deployment Models' (Edward Ignall, Peter Kolesar, and Warren Walker, P-5463, 1975), and 'Determining the Travel Characteristics of Emergency Service Vehicles' (J Hausner, R-1687-HUD, 1975). These studies applied complex mathematical models to examine minute dispatching and routing efficiencies. They resembled the classic early applications of operations research outside the military—applications that had included determining, for instance, 'how Post Office pick-up trucks should be routed to collect mail from deposit boxes, or whether computers should be rented or purchased, or what type of all-weather landing system should be installed in new commercial aircraft'.[6]

Gradually, and interspersed in these operations-research reports, there emerged a number of studies using a 'systems analysis' approach that extended operations research beyond its original narrow confines.[7] The systems analysis approach was a 'method of analyzing a problem by listing the desired objectives and available resources and then detailing alternative methods of using the resources to accomplish the objectives'.[8] The NYC RAND Institute's systems analysis studies did

[5] Operations research was developed during World War II as a way to 'provide quantitative aids to defense decision makers' with the goal of 'optimizing the operational employment of existing weapons (or other military) systems' (BLR Smith, *The Rand Corporation: Case Study of a Nonprofit Advisory Corporation* (1966) 6). Famous early applications of operations research were studies of the placement and use of aircraft-detection radar devices and of anti-submarine tactics involving depth-charge explosions in the early phases of World War II (Smith, 6–7). In a very strict sense, operations research applied a mathematical algorithm or 'model' to a management problem, such as, for instance, transportation routes or stock control (ES Quade, *Systems analysis techniques for planning-programming-budgeting* (1966) 3); the only question was how to optimize efficiency where the measure of efficiency was clearly defined, or, as Edward Quade explained (at 3), how 'to increase the efficiency of a man-machine system in a situation where it is clear what "more efficient" means'.

[6] Quade (cited in n 5) 18.

[7] Systems analysis extended the operations research approach to a broader set of problems—for instance, from the narrow issue of a weapon system to the broader question of a military defence policy. Systems analysis is often confused with operations research, from which it evolved. However, operations research tends to have more elaborate mathematical models and solves lower-level problems (Smith, *The Rand Corporation* (cited in n 5) 8); in systems analysis, by contrast, the pure mathematical computation generally applies to sub-parts of the overall problem. Systems analysis is 'less quantitative in method and more oriented toward the analysis of broad strategic and policy questions, and particularly in seeking to clarify choice under conditions of great uncertainty' (Smith, *The Rand Corporation* (cited in n 5) 8).

[8] Reeves (cited in n 3) 31.

indeed focus on a narrow objective—preventing crime—and began to compare a wide range of different alternative policies to try to determine the most efficient. One such report, by Michael I Liechenstein, is illustrative.[9]

The Liechenstein study, which was sponsored by Mayor Lindsay's Criminal Justice Coordinating Council, analysed techniques for improving crime prevention and security in New York City Housing Authority buildings. It took a 'broad operational view of a security system',[10] analysing 15 alternative policies, including tenant training and education, tenant patrols, qualifications to live in the projects, extended recreational opportunities for teenagers, rent rebates, elaborate building-entry restrictions, locked lobbies, intrusion detectors, weapon detectors, surveillance, and increased police or guard manpower. In order to compare the alternatives, the study developed 'effectiveness criteria' and then coupled those to 'compatibility and cost criteria' in order to 'derive estimates of an overall figure of merit (e.g., the ratio of effectiveness-to-cost with a constraint on either minimum effectiveness or maximum cost)'.[11] In addition to the security effectiveness and compatibility criteria, the report also listed cost-benefit criteria: 'Research and development cost (equipment, maintenance, administration before production); Capital cost (equipment, maintenance, and administrative costs during production); Operating cost (equipment, maintenance, administration costs during use); Scrap value (residual value at end of use); Expected total benefit.'[12] The report then generated a graph of the cost-effectiveness of all 15 alternatives. This is reproduced here as Figure 13.1.

The 15 different measures ranged across the political spectrum—from education for low-income tenants on issues of criminal offending, preventive measures, and self-defence, to providing recreational facilities for poor urban teenagers, to offering subsidies and other positive financial incentives to poor tenants, to raising admissibility and tenure standards for housing assistance, to increasing the police presence. They included everything from education to recreation, to target-hardening, to policing. But in the end, the most cost-effective preventive measure, it turned out, consisted of increased police presence and more guards. The most efficient technique, according to RAND, had a decidedly coercive edge. RAND's systems analysis method, it seemed, tilted toward a style of prevention indexed on policing and punishing, what might be called 'punitive preventive measures' because of their reliance on surveillance and the threat of penal sanction. The approach foreshadowed a turn—or return—to 'punitive prevention'.[13]

[9] MI Liechenstein, *Reducing Crime in Apartment Dwellings: A Methodology for Comparing Security Alternatives* (June 1971) P-4656, available at <http://www.rand.org/pubs/papers/2008/P4656.pdf>.

[10] Liechenstein (cited in n 9) 4.

[11] Liechenstein (cited in n 9) 5.

[12] Liechenstein (cited in n 9) 6.

[13] The term 'punitive prevention' is intended to distinguish preventive measures that rely on policing and the threat or use of legal punishment (the criminal sanction), from preventive measures that are based on educational, welfare, recreational, or other non-penal interventions. This is not to suggest, naturally, that these other non-penal interventions are necessarily non-coercive. There has been much important scholarship that has demonstrated the coercive or 'social control function' of welfare. See, eg, FF Piven and RA Cloward, *Regulating the Poor: The Functions of Public Welfare.* Updated Edition (1993 [1971]). But there is a boundary to be drawn around measures that explicitly utilize law enforcement and the threat and/or use of the criminal or quasi-criminal sanctions, and it is these measures that I refer to here as 'punitive preventive measures'.

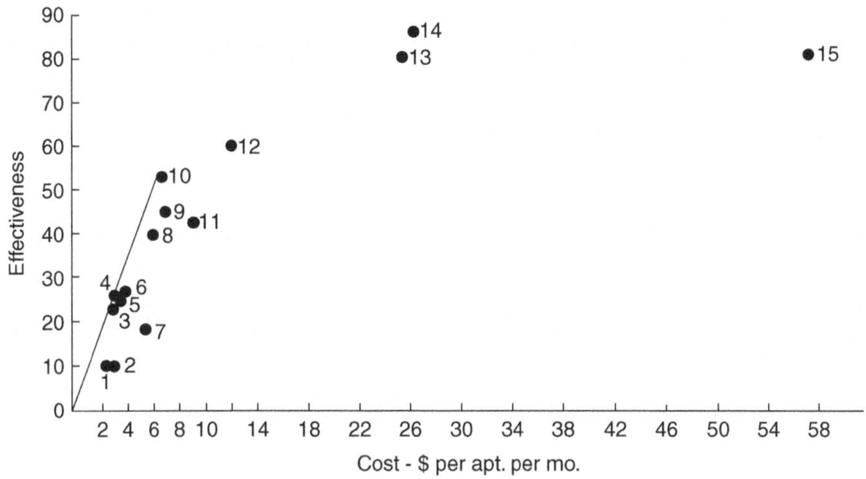


**Figure 13.1** Average effectiveness/cost ratios of security options

*Source*: Reproduced from M I Liechenstein, Reducing Crime in Apartment Dwellings: A Methodology for Comparing Security Alternatives (New York City–Rand Institute, 1971) 23.

Today, we are surrounded by preventive measures. Not all of them are punitive, naturally. We are inundated with preventive measures that take a number of forms: public service announcements in subways and buses, educational safety and awareness campaigns about 'crime in our community', campus-wide public safety e-mails announcing the latest armed robbery, mandatory car-ignition-locks for habitual drinkers, 'if you see something, say something' campaigns at the airport, covert anti-terrorism surveillance, traffic control measures,[14] even ordinary pre-trial detention (the denial of bail).[15] We are surrounded by so much prevention, in fact, that we tend to take it for granted.

As in the past, the preventive state is Janus-faced and offers both rewards and punishments. Many of the entitlements that the state provides are extended at least in part, and often justified in whole, as preventive measures. The University of Chicago economist and Nobel-laureate, James Heckman, has had the Obama administration's ear promoting early childhood education—what we call 'Head Start' in the United States—as a way to *prevent* juvenile delinquency and crime.[16] Under President Bill Clinton, the federal government began encouraging and funding local programmes intended to offer enticing entertainment alternatives, like basketball games for inner-city youths—referred to as 'Midnight Basketball'—again as a way to *prevent* crime.

[14] P O'Malley, this volume.

[15] RA Duff, this volume.

[16] J Heckman and D Masterov, 'The Productivity Argument for Investing in Young Children', Working Paper No. 5, *Invest in Kids Working Group*, October 2004, available at <http://ideas.repec.org/p/iza/izadps/dp2725.html>.

At the other end of the spectrum are the more punitive techniques. These include the preventative detention of 'violent sexual predators' in the USA after they have served their adjudicated sentence, a form of detention that the US Supreme Court condoned in its 1997 decision in *Kansas v Hendricks* upholding the indefinite commitment of those convicted of a sex offence who are deemed to pose a continuing threat;[17] the passage of similar measures called '*rétention de sureté*' in France in 2008, also affirmed by the Conseil constitutionnel that same year; and the advent of control orders with the passage of the Prevention of Terrorism Act 2005 and Terrorism Prevention and Investigation Measures (TPIMs) in the UK.[18] Though less extreme, punitive prevention also includes the use of order-maintenance techniques, such as broken-windows policing in New York City, zero-tolerance approaches in France, and Anti-Social Behaviour Orders (ASBOs) and other disorder management in England;[19] the use of profiling measures, including racial profiling, on the highways and borders, to interdict drug trafficking and illegal immigration; and, as seen in New York City, the stop-and-frisks of ordinary citizens on the street—a practice that, remarkably, exceeded 600,000 persons stopped and searched in 2010, and more than 685,000 in 2011.

It is these latter measures, what could be called 'punitive preventive measures' or 'punitive preventive justice', that have garnered increased attention, and concern, in Western democracies in the last three decades. The uncomfortable overlap of prevention and punishment has raised both legal and political questions that have yet to be resolved. From the more classical or formalist legal tradition, the finding of guilt for a criminal act conventionally served to justify punishment and assuage our moral and political conscience; and in the absence of a criminal act as predicate, it has generally been scientific expertise (such as a psychiatric diagnosis of mental illness in the case of the involuntary commitment of the mentally ill) or procedural protections ensured by a neutral magistrate that have satisfied our sense of justice. But where the predicate criminal act is absent and the claim of expertise becomes more attenuated, our concerns are heightened about the dangers of punitive prevention.

These concerns, naturally, are not new—nor are the phenomena themselves. Practically all of these contemporary punitive preventive practices have parallels in history, sometimes even more egregious. Eugenics and forced sterilization in the early 20th century were undoubtedly preventive measures; and many 'dangerous' persons have been preventively detained in mental hospitals since the birth of the asylum in the early 19th century. In fact, many persons have been executed over the centuries because, we feared, they were not safe to be kept alive.

[17] *Kansas v Hendricks*, 521 US 346 (US Supreme Court, 1997).

[18] See generally L Zedner, 'Preventive Justice or Pre-Punishment? The Case of Control Orders' (2007) 60(1) CLP 174. Terrorism Prevention and Investigation Measures (TPIMs), introduced by the Terrorism Prevention and Investigation Measures Act 2011, replaced control orders at the end of 2011, though critics suggest TPIMs are simply control orders rebranded (V Tadros, this volume).

[19] See generally A Ashworth, 'Social control and antisocial behaviour: the subversion of human rights?' (2004) 120 LQR 263–291.

As Andrew Ashworth, Lucia Zedner, and Patrick Tomlin discuss, the notion of prevention goes back centuries. Blackstone believed that 'preventive justice' was preferable to 'punishing justice', but also more dangerous;[20] of course, the combination would prove to be even more dangerous. The notion of the preventive state traces its genealogy to 17th- and 18th-century cameralism and the police sciences;[21] and there is a long history of the police state as a 'preventive' agent. But the fact that these practices—and our concerns about these practices—are not new should not stop us from investigating punitive preventive measures more closely.

As an empirical matter, the purported need for punitive preventive measures is, on balance, factually overstated and generally unproven. Once all of the facts are on the table, it often appears that the stated need and consequentialist arguments in support of these measures serve as a cover for the political redistribution of societal resources. But these empirical concerns foreground a deeper theoretical problem, namely that the modern approach displaces political debate and contestation. The central problem with the modern approach to punitive prevention is its reliance, predominantly, on economic, cost-benefit analytic studies that serve to marginalize political decision-making. Like earlier punitive preventive interventions—whether eugenics, phrenology, or the larger 'psy-' disciplines—the modern punitive preventive approach is grounded on technical, scientific knowledge; but in the more contemporary context, that technical knowledge privileges efficiency over most other political values and, in the process, displaces politics. The modern approach claims to be objective, apolitical, and neutral. It claims to be merely pursuing the most efficient policy option given an agreed-upon narrow objective. But it ultimately reintroduces political values and choices into the analyses, paradoxically, by bracketing explicit discussion of politics. The approach also obfuscates criticism by making it harder for the layman to identify the political values embedded in the technical models. For the uninitiated, and even for those with experience in the technical domain, it is an opaque method that makes it exceedingly difficult to know how or what to resist. In the end, it insidiously degrades our public sphere and masks the redistribution of political goods in society.

Section A explores why these types of punitive preventive justice have generally been regarded as more dangerous than ordinary punishments. Section B rehearses some of the empirical evidence—or lack thereof—regarding three significant and popular punitive preventive measures: broken-windows policing and ASBOs, profiling and stop-and-frisks, and selective incapacitation and mass incarceration. Section C offers a theoretical critique of the modern punitive preventive approach—specifically, that it displaces politics and corrodes our public sphere.

20 A Ashworth, L Zedner, and P Tomlin, 'Introduction', this volume.

21 M Dubber, 'Preventive Justice: The Search for Principles', this volume; see also M Dubber, *The Police Power: Patriarchy and the Foundations of American Government* (2005); M Dubber and M Valverde (eds), *The New Police Science: The Police Power in Domestic and International Governance* (2006).

## A. Why punitive preventive measures are viewed as different

Historically, in Anglo-American justificatory discourse, punishment and prevention have been neatly delineated and distinguished—but also carefully defended—based on the existence of a predicate act, namely the criminal act. The adjudication of a crime traditionally served the important function of demarcating the terrain for legal punishment, but it also justified preventive measures: punishment was inextricably linked to the criminal act, but prevention was always connected to *avoiding* the possibility of a crime. In both cases, the criminal act did practically all the work. Though it did not, naturally, differentiate the two realms completely, it played a key function in the justificatory discourse of punishment theory—whether retributivist or consequentialist.

For the consequentialists—for whom prevention was the central purpose of punishment—the criminal act served as *the* safeguard against excess (especially against the retributivist trope that a consequentialist would be willing to convict an innocent person if it overwhelmingly benefitted others in society). For the consequentialists, punishment was forward looking: there was no way to undo the crime, so punishment had to serve either as a deterrent to future crime, as a mode of correcting the convict, or as a way of incapacitating the convict so as to prevent any future offending.[22] In this sense, prevention was always already embedded as a part of punishment; and the criminal act was both a necessary gateway for entering the criminal justice system (only criminals are punished) and the basis of the future-oriented preventive focus (it is crime that we hope to avoid). At the same time, for the consequentialists, punishment was a central part of prevention: it was, for instance, fully justified to lengthen a sentence (to punish more) for a recidivist because the recidivist carried a higher likelihood of reoffending. The likelihood of future dangerousness was a cost that was to be factored into the punitive calculus and fully justified a longer sentence—even death under certain circumstances. In other words, prevention was a part of punishment, and punishment a part of prevention, but both were justified by wrongdoing.

Retributivists were the ones who traditionally had the greatest difficulty with punitive preventive measures. For them, or at least for most of them, punishment was intended to be backward looking, justifiable only in terms of desert for a past crime.[23] As Antony Duff writes, retributivism 'justifies punishment in terms not of its contingently beneficial effects but of its *intrinsic* justice as a response to crime; the justificatory relationship holds between present punishment and past crime, not between present punishment and future effects'.[24] By contrast, preventive measures were entirely forward looking, and therefore required some other justification. But generally the kind of justification that was sought *assumed* that prevention had a

[22] See generally C Beccaria, *On Crimes and Punishments* (1995) 31.

[23] There are, of course, exceptions, most notably Andrew von Hirsch, a leading retributivist, who took the view that desert and deterrence are both essential features of punishment.

[24] RA Duff, *Punishment, Communication, and Community* (2001) 19–20.

punitive dimension and therefore required the type of justification that would serve to legitimate punishment. It is in this sense, for instance, that Doug Husak argues in this volume that preventive justice is really no different from punishment and requires the same kind of justification—and in the end, that there can be limited uses of preventive justice.[25] That justification often turns on future crime. The spectre of the crime reappears as a central justificatory mechanism. Here too, then, punishment can be a part of prevention, but when deployed, it must receive the kind of due process protections afforded the criminally accused.[26]

Overall, then, prevention can be, and often is, part of punishment—especially for those who espouse punishment theories of deterrence, correction, or incapacitation. At the same time, punishment can be, and often is, part of prevention—that is certainly the case with indefinite preventive detention in administrative facilities that are no different from prisons.[27] And on both sides of the theory divide, punishment theorists privilege wrongdoing. To dispense with the adjudicated crime destabilizes. It is what makes 'punitive preventive measures' seem so dangerous. This perilous slippage—away from the adjudicated criminal act—can be visualized in Table 13.1, which catalogues, incrementally, more and more problematic forms of punitive preventive detention.

As we move down Table 13.1—eventually eliminating the criminal act predicate, but also watering down the additional element and related scientific expertise—our concerns about punitive preventive detention grow. Both the vertical movement down the table and the diagonal movement across the table, from predicate to additional elements, increase our apprehension about the corresponding forms of detention. The least problematic case, naturally, is when there exists the predicate of an adjudicated criminal conviction; the most problematic is when there is nothing more than that 'additional' element of future dangerousness. In between, the predicate diminishes as we go down the table, as does the reliability of the expertise associated with the additional element—and this, correspondingly, increases our apprehension.

Punitive preventive measures tend to raise difficult questions. Often, they are justified on empirical grounds. But those empirical grounds, more often than not, prove elusive.

[25] See D Husak, this volume.

[26] So in the context of preventive detention of sexual offenders, for instance, Carol Steiker has argued that the *Hendricks* measures *are* punitive, not just administrative as the US Supreme Court had held, and therefore that the due process protections afforded the criminally accused should extend to this domain. See C Steiker, 'Foreword: The Limits of the Preventive State' (1998) 88(3) Journal of Criminal Law and Criminology (Spring) 771–808.

[27] This is certainly the argument many made against the decisions by the US Supreme Court and the Conseil Constitutionnel that these measures are administrative in nature, not punitive. See *Kansas v Hendricks*, 521 US 346 (US Supreme Court, 1997); Conseil constitutionnel, 'Décision n 2008–562 DC du 21 février 2008. Loi relative à la rétention de sûreté et à la déclaration d'irresponsabilité pénale pour cause de trouble mental'.

**Table 13.1** Forms of Punitive Preventive Detention

| Category of detention | Predicate | Additional element |
|---|---|---|
| Imprisonment for a crime | Adjudicated criminal conviction | |
| Involuntary commitment to mental hospital or asylum | Diagnosed mental illness | Diagnosed and adjudicated future danger to self or other |
| Pre-trial detention | Probable cause accusation of crime | Adjudicated risk of flight or danger to witnesses |
| Sex offender preventive detention (USA) | Prior conviction for sexual offence | Adjudicated future danger to others |
| Guantanamo Bay detention | Captured in the battlefield | Suspected of terrorist allegiances and suspected danger to others |
| Control orders (UK) under Prevention of Terrorism Act 2005 | Suspicion of involvement in terrorist activity | Suspicion of danger to others |
| Pure preventive detention | | Risk of future dangerousness to others |

## B. A review of the empirical evidence

As I will demonstrate, the empirical arguments for the use of punitive preventive measures tend to be overstated and often mask other political forces that are, in reality, far more salient. The empirical arguments for punitive prevention tend to serve as a pretext for redistribution of societal resources and as a way to shift relations of power. Let me turn, then, to the three most significant and popular categories of punitive preventive measures.

### Order-maintenance practices: the broken-windows theory and zero tolerance

With regard, first, to order maintenance practices, there have been a large number of empirical studies testing both aspects of the famous broken-windows theory[28]—both the causal theory of crime (namely, that minor disorder, left unattended, causes serious crime) and the remedial theory of policing (namely, that order-maintenance policing reduces serious crime). In 2000, John Eck and Edward Maguire reviewed the empirical evidence and studies on broken-windows policing in their contribution to Alfred Blumstein's *The Crime Drop in America*, and found that there was little evidence to support the claim that broken-windows policing

[28] In 1982, James Q Wilson and George L Kelling suggested in an influential article in the *Atlantic Monthly* that targeting minor disorder—loitering, panhandling, prostitution, graffiti—could help reduce more serious crime. See JQ Wilson and GL Kelling, 'Broken Windows: The Police and Neighborhood Safety' (1982) *Atlantic Monthly* (March) 29, 38.

contributed to the sharp decrease in crime during the 1990s.[29] More recently, Adam Samaha conducted an extensive review of the empirical literature—what amounted in effect to a Campbell collaborative evaluation—and concluded that, 'On the available evidence, a sensible conclusion is that the probability of generating a beneficial self-fulfilling prophecy with broken windows policing is uncertain, low, or confined in important ways.'[30]

Regarding the causal theory of crime, many proponents of the broken-windows hypothesis originally pointed to the research of Wesley Skogan, especially his 1990 monograph *Disorder and Decline: Crime and the Spiral of Decay in American Neighborhoods*, arguing that it empirically verified the broken-windows theory.[31] Subsequent research, however, cast doubt on the conclusions that could properly be drawn from Skogan's analysis.[32] Following that, Robert Sampson and Stephen Raudenbush conducted one of the most comprehensive and thorough examinations of the causal theory, in their 1999 study, 'Systematic Social Observation of Public Spaces'.[33] With regard to the disorder-crime nexus, Sampson and Raudenbush found that disorder and predatory crime were only moderately correlated, but that, when antecedent neighbourhood characteristics were taken into account, the connection between disorder and crime 'vanished in 4 out of 5 tests—including homicide, arguably our best measure of violence'.[34] As an alternative to the broken-

[29] JE Eck and ER Maguire, 'Have Changes in Policing Reduced Violent Crime? An Assessment of the Evidence' in A Blumstein and J Wallman (eds), *The Crime Drop in America* (2000) 207, 228 ('Overall, the evidence is mixed on the efficacy of generic zero-tolerance strategies in driving down rates of violent crime, though serious questions have been raised about their effects on police–community relations'). See also BE Harcourt, *Illusion of Order* (2001) 88 (concluding, on the basis of existing social-scientific data, that neighbourhood disorder is not significantly related to more serious crimes when poverty, stability, and race are held constant); BE Harcourt, 'Reflecting on the Subject: A Critique of the Social Influence Conception of Deterrence, the Broken Windows Theory, and Order-Maintenance Policing New York Style' (1998) 97 Michigan Law Review 291, 389 (challenging broken-windows policing by arguing that the alleged correlation between disorder and serious crime fails to take into account other factors that may contribute to the deterioration of a neighbourhood).

[30] A Samaha, 'Regulation for the Sake of Appearance' (2012) 125 Harvard Law Review 1563, 1629.

[31] WG Skogan, *Disorder and Decline: crime and the spiral of decay in American neighborhoods* (1990) 120–4; GL Kelling and CM Coles, *Fixing Broken Windows: Restoring Order and Reducing Crime in Our Communities* (1996) 23–7; DM Kahan, 'Social Influence, Social Meaning, and Deterrence' (1997) 83 Virginia Law Review 349, 369; see also DM Kahan, 'Between Economics and Sociology' (1997) 95 Michigan Law Review 2477, 2488 n 62 ('According to criminologists, the primary cue that crime is tolerated or expected is visible public disorder').

[32] Harcourt, *Illusion of Order* (cited in n 29) 78 (concluding that 'there are *no* statistically significant relationships between disorder and purse-snatching, physical assault, burglary, or rape when other explanatory variables are held constant.... [Thus] the data do not support the broken windows hypothesis'); RB Taylor, *Breaking Away from Broken Windows: Baltimore Neighborhoods and the Nationwide Fight against Crime, Guns, Fear, and Decline* (2001) 22 (finding that, although certain types of incivilities were associated with crime or urban decay, others were not, and concluding that a more integrated perspective, which combines the current results regarding incivilities and contemporary knowledge regarding the multiplicity of factors affecting neighbourhoods over time, should be developed).

[33] RJ Sampson and SW Raudenbush, 'Systematic Social Observation of Public Spaces: A New Look at Disorder in Urban Neighborhoods' (1999) 105 *American Journal of Sociology* 603, 637.

[34] Sampson and Raudenbush, 'Systematic Social Observation' (cited in n 33) 637 (offering results contradicting a strong version of the broken-windows thesis but concluding that the role of disorder

windows theory, Sampson and Raudenbush suggested that disorder is of the same aetiology as crime—being, so often, a form of minor crime—and that both crime and disorder have the same antecedent conditions. 'Rather than conceive of disorder as a direct cause of crime, we view many elements of disorder as part and parcel of crime itself.'[35] Thus, 'a reasonable hypothesis is that public disorder and predatory crimes are manifestations of the same explanatory process, albeit at different ends of a "seriousness" continuum.'[36]

In subsequent research, Jens Ludwig and I tested the causal theory of crime using data from a unique randomized experiment conducted by the US Department of Housing and Urban Development (HUD) known as Moving to Opportunity (MTO).[37] MTO had been in operation since 1994 in five cities, including the three largest cities in the country that had adopted aspects of broken-windows policing (New York, Chicago, and Los Angeles), as well as Baltimore and Boston. Under MTO, a total of around 4,600 low-income families living in public housing communities characterized by high rates of crime and social disorder were randomly assigned housing vouchers to move to less disadvantaged and disorderly communities.[38] Our results from MTO suggested that moving people to communities with less social or physical disorder—the key intervening factor in the original Wilson and Kelling broken-windows hypothesis—on balance did *not* lead to a reduction in their criminal behaviour.

Regarding the remedial theory of policing, James Q Wilson here too sparked the debate, primarily with his 1968 book *Varieties of Police Behavior*, and his research with Barbara Boland on the effects of police arrests on crime.[39] Wilson and Boland hypothesized that aggressive police patrols, involving increased stops and arrests, have a deterrent effect on crime. A number of contributions ensued, both supporting and criticizing these findings, but, as Robert Sampson and Jacqueline Cohen suggested in 1988, the results were 'mixed'.[40] There have been strong contributions to the literature, such as the 1999 study led by Anthony Braga, entitled *Problem-Oriented Policing in Violent Crime Places*,[41] and Jeffrey Fagan and Garth Davies's

remained theoretically relevant for other purposes; disorder may have indirect, neighbourhood effects on crime by influencing 'migration patterns, investment by businesses, and overall neighbourhood viability').

[35] Sampson and Raudenbush (cited in n 33) 608.

[36] Sampson and Raudenbush (cited in n 33) 608.

[37] See generally BE Harcourt and J Ludwig, 'Broken Windows: New Evidence from New York City and a Five-City Social Experiment' (2006) 73 University of Chicago Law Review 271.

[38] See L Orr et al, 'Moving to Opportunity: Interim Impacts Evaluation' ii–iv (HUD Office of Policy Development 2003) ii-iv (describing the MTO programme) available online at <http://www.huduser.org/Publications/pdf/MTOFullReport.pdf>.

[39] See JQ Wilson, *Varieties of Police Behavior: The Management of Law and Order in Eight Communities* (1968) 281–2; see also JQ Wilson and B Boland, 'The Effects of the Police on Crime: A Response to Jacob and Rich' (1981) 16 Law and Society Review 163, 168–9; JQ Wilson and B Boland, 'The Effect of the Police on Crime' (1978) 12 Law and Society Review 367, 380.

[40] RJ Sampson and J Cohen, 'Deterrent Effect of the Police on Crime: A Replication and Theoretical Extension' (1988) 22 Law and Society Review 163, 166.

[41] AA Braga et al, 'Problem-Oriented Policing in Violent Crime Places: A Randomized Controlled Experiment' (1999) 37 *Criminology* 541, 571. See also AA Braga, *Problem-Oriented Policing and Crime Prevention* (2002) 123.

2003 research entitled *Policing Guns: Order Maintenance and Crime Control in New York*.[42] But the research is unable generally to distinguish between the broken-windows hypothesis and more traditional explanations of incapacitation and deterrence associated with increased police arrests, presence, contact, and surveillance.[43]

In 2001, George Kelling and William Sousa published a study asking, and answering in the affirmative, the question *Do Police Matter?*[44] Their study triggered another flurry of research, including a quantitative study by Jens Ludwig and myself which showed that, contrary to their findings, when mean reversion is included in the model,[45] increased misdemeanour arrests actually—and paradoxically—correlate with increased violent crime.[46] Mean reversion is the best explanation for the drops in crime in New York City. As we explain there, '[P]recincts that received the most intensive broken-windows policing during the 1990s are the ones that experienced the largest increases in crime during the city's crack epidemic of the mid-to-late 1980s'.[47]

Another important contribution to the literature was Steve Levitt's 2004 review essay in *Journal of Economic Perspectives*, in which he argued that policing practices probably do not explain much of the crime drop in the 1990s because crime went down everywhere, even in places where police departments did not implement new policing strategies.[48] Instead, Levitt attributed the massive period effects on crime throughout the USA during the 1990s to some combination of increased imprisonment, increases in the number of police, the ebbing of the crack epidemic that started in many big cities in the mid-1980s, and the legalization of abortion during

[42] J Fagan and G Davies, 'Policing Guns: Order Maintenance and Crime Control in New York' in BE Harcourt (ed), *Guns, Crime, and Punishment in America* (2003) 191, 205.

[43] The problem is somewhat endemic to the design of these studies. As Sampson and Cohen conclude with regard to their own work, 'It is true . . . that our analysis was not able to choose definitely between the two alternative scenarios': Sampson and Cohen, 'Deterrent Effect of the Police on Crime' (cited in n 40) 185.

[44] GL Kelling and WH Sousa, Jr, 'Do Police Matter? An Analysis of the Impact of New York City's Police Reforms' *Manhattan Institute Center for Civic Innovation* (Civic Report No 22, 2001) 18 ('[D]espite the root-cause theories that have dominated criminological, criminal justice, and much popular thinking about crime control, police can have a significant effect on crime levels in neighborhoods and communities. One singularly important way of doing this is by restoring and maintaining order, through "broken windows" policing').

[45] Reversion to the mean, in this context, means an eventual return to average crime levels in each precinct. Ludwig and I were able to include earlier crime levels for each precinct as a way to control for mean reversion.

[46] See Harcourt and Ludwig (cited in n 37) 296 and 297, Table 3; and 'Errata' (2007) 74 University of Chicago Law Review 407 (Table 3, Row 1 should display positive coefficients for misdemeanour arrest changes in Models 2–5).

[47] Harcourt and Ludwig (cited in n 37) 276. Another study by H Corman and N Mocan, 'Carrots, Sticks and Broken Windows' (2005) 48 Journal of Law and Economics 235, 262, found a positive effect of misdemeanour arrests on crime ('A 10 per cent increase in misdemeanour arrests decreases motor vehicle thefts by 1.6 to 2.1 per cent, [and] robberies by 2.5 to 3.2 per cent. . . . We do not find strong evidence to support the contention that a broken-windows policing strategy affects the other crimes'). However, Jens Ludwig and I demonstrate the fallacy of their simplistic assumption of single-jurisdiction data in Harcourt and Ludwig (cited in n 37).

[48] SD Levitt, 'Understanding Why Crime Fell in the 1990s: Four Factors that Explain the Decline and Six that Do Not' (2004) 18 *Journal of Economic Perspectives* 163, 177, 184.

the early 1970s.[49] In the end, as Sampson and Raudenbush remarked, the evidence suggests that '[a]ttacking public disorder through tough police tactics may thus be a politically popular but perhaps analytically weak strategy to reduce crime'.[50]

Several recent studies confirm this conclusion.[51] One such study, by Richard Rosenfeld and his colleagues, finds that order-maintenance policing had a discernible effect on homicide and robbery trends over the 1990s, but that the discernible effect was at best small, accounting for between 1 and 5 per cent of the total annual drop in robbery rates and between 6 and 12 per cent of the total annual reduction in homicide rates. A second study, by Steven Messner and his colleagues, uses a different statistical model and finds, interestingly, that both order-maintenance policing and changes in patterns of cocaine use had a statistical effect on gun-related homicides but *not* on non-firearm homicides.[52] (There is nothing in the broken-windows theory that would explain different results for gun and non-gun homicides.) In contrast, crack cocaine markets were closely connected to illegal gun use. This suggests—in line with the research of Jeffrey Fagan and Franklin Zimring[53]—that order-maintenance policing, if it affected crime, did so predominantly via guns. The pathway was probably not order maintenance, but instead the gun seizures attendant to an aggressive policy of stops, frisks, arrests, and searches.

These conclusions make intuitive sense given that the crime drop in the 1990s and 2000s was a national phenomenon that affected most large cities, including those cities that resisted Giuliani-style broken-windows policing. As Richard Rosenfeld concludes, 'substantial crime reductions likely would have occurred even without the growth in [order-maintenance policing]'.[54] Taken together, the wealth of research provides no support for a simple disorder–crime relationship as hypothesized by Wilson and Kelling in their broken-windows theory, nor for the proposition that broken-windows policing is the optimal use of scarce law enforcement resources.

My conclusion is that the broken-windows theory is really window dressing, and what it masks or hides are more profound processes of real estate development and wealth redistribution. I came to this conclusion in my ethnographic work in Los Angeles, where it became clear that the broken-windows policing by the Los Angeles Police Department and by private security firms was part of a gentrification effort led by several real estate developers.[55] There is a dearth of research in this

[49] Levitt (cited in n 48) 184.

[50] Sampson and Raudenbush (cited in n 33) 638.

[51] See R Rosenfeld, R Fornango, and AF Rengifo, 'The Impact of Order-Maintenance Policing on New York City Homicide and Robbery Rates: 1988–2001' (2007) 45 *Criminology* 355, 369, 377; SF Messner et al, 'Policing, Drugs, and the Homicide Decline in New York City in the 1990s' (2007) 45 *Criminology* 385, 401, 405; M Cerdá et al, 'Misdemeanor Policing, Physical Disorder, and Gun-Related Homicide: A Spatial Analytic Test of Broken-Windows Theory' (2009) 20 *Epidemiology* 533, 533.

[52] Messner et al (cited in n 51).

[53] J Fagan, FE Zimring, and J Kim, 'Declining Homicide in New York City: A Tale of Two Trends' (1998) 88 Journal of Criminal Law and Criminology 1277, 1322.

[54] Rosenfeld et al (cited in n 51) 377.

[55] BE Harcourt, 'Policing L.A.'s Skid Row: Crime and Real Estate Development in Downtown Los Angeles [An Experiment in Real Time]', (2005) University of Chicago Legal Forum 325–404.

area, sadly. To be sure, there are studies demonstrating a link between crime rates and real estate *values*.[56] In one such study in New York City, for instance, researchers found that falling crime rates were 'responsible for about a third of the post-1994 boom in property values'.[57] But the direction of influence is more complicated. The simple narrative—namely, that lower crime causes increased real estate values—'ignores the revitalization of New York City's poorer communities'.[58] The focus on real estate values does not do justice to the processual dynamics of how a neighbourhood is redeveloped, gentrified, or commercialized. It does not begin to scratch at the dynamic relationship between real estate *redevelopment* and crime. There are crucial intervening steps: significant investments by commercial and residential real estate developers, political initiatives by city planners, and competing efforts by not-for-profit homeless agencies to secure housing for their clients. Crime and crime reduction may well be a cover, under which there is a tumultuous battle over real property and the economic restructuring of these disorderly neighbourhoods. In this more complete story, the most important players are high-end commercial and residential real estate developers, city urban planners, and non-profit housing advocates for the homeless. The police and their policing are ancillary.

Times Square, the Bowery, the near-west side of Chicago—these disorderly neighbourhoods of major urban centres were the subject of heated debate and much political initiative at the turn of the 21st century. Some, like Chicago's near-west side, vanished—bulldozed down and redeveloped—the beneficiaries of massive urban renewal projects. In Chicago, the single-room occupancy hotels (SROs) and flophouses were gutted, the missions and saloons were closed, and in their place rose high-end, residential apartments—such as the Presidential Towers, four 49-storey modern high-security towers with over 2,300 apartments and over 900 spaces of sheltered parking.[59] Other neighbourhoods, like Times Square, had radical surgery—massive, planned, precision redevelopment. While some of the landmark buildings and theatres were refurbished, office towers and corporate, commercial, and media headquarters rose in their midst. Times Square morphed from red lights to large-scale LED displays and signage, and became a vibrant and luxurious commercial, hotel, media, business, and entertainment centre.[60] Still

[56] A Schwartz, S Susin, and I Voicu, 'Has Falling Crime Driven New York City's Real Estate Boom?' (2003) 14 *Journal of Housing Research* 101, 102, available online at <http://www.fanniemae-foundation.org/programs/jhr/pdf/jhr_1401_schwartz.pdf>.

[57] Schwartz et al (cited in n 56) 102.

[58] Schwartz et al (cited in n 56) 102.

[59] For fascinating discussions of the elimination of Chicago's near-west side skid row, see R Miller, *Here's The Deal: The Buying and Selling of a Great American City* (1996) 3–93; A Ijomah, 'The Role of Major Institutions in the Redevelopment of Chicago's Near West Side, 1940–1990' (PhD dissertation) (1991); and R Miller, *The Demolition of Skid Row* (1982) 8–25. For a description of Presidential Towers, see P Gapp, 'Presidential Towers No Beauty, But It Works Like A Charm' *Chicago Tribune* (22 December 1985) Art 6.

[60] For a general discussion, see J Traub, *The Devil's Playground: A Century of Pleasure and Profit in Times Square* (2004); J Traub, 'Common Of Earthly Delights' *New York Times* (14 March 2004) B48.

others, like Los Angeles' Downtown, are only being gentrified now, in the early 21st century. I firmly believe that this is what has really driven urban renewal: real estate development and profit, not broken-windows policing.

## Profiling and preventive searches: highway patrol, street stop-and-frisks, and anti-terrorism

A number of economists in the USA and the UK have justified preventive profiling techniques, including racial profiling, as a form of 'statistical discrimination' as opposed to racial bigotry: the former uses group traits to promote more efficient policing and extends only to the point where law enforcement has maximized the efficiency of their interventions—as evidenced, for instance, in the parity of the success rate of police searches as between members of different racial groups.[61] At that point, these economists suggest, law enforcement has achieved the best allocation of resources in a non-discriminatory manner. It is only when law enforcement uses group traits *beyond the point of equality* (*efficiency*) that their use of race or ethnicity becomes invidious. The economist Vani Borooah has suggested, for instance, that 'statistical discrimination, untainted by bigotry, is optimal from a policing perspective because it maximizes the number of arrests consequent upon a given number of persons stopped'.[62]

In a lengthy and technical treatment,[63] I demonstrate that, contrary to the claims of the economists, statistical discrimination is likely to be counterproductive to the law enforcement objective of reducing crime, and therefore misguided as a preventive measure. Two problems in particular undermine statistical discrimination in the criminal justice context. First, if we assume a rational choice framework—in other words, if we assume deterrence and the general framework of economic, consequentialist models of criminal behaviour—statistical discrimination is likely to be counterproductive to the ultimate objective of law enforcement by causing *more* crime. Under the conservative assumption that the targeted population (the population with higher offending) is less responsive (less elastic) to policing than the non-targeted population, statistical discrimination will ultimately increase overall societal offending levels as the non-profiled population (more elastic) responds more sharply to the shift in policing. This will have counterproductive effects on the law enforcement objective of reducing crime. Secondly, if we do not assume a rational action approach and believe that people are inelastic to policing, statistical discrimination is going to lead to a ratchet effect on members of the profiled

[61] For a detailed treatment of this, see BE Harcourt, 'Rethinking Racial Profiling: A Critique of the Economics, Civil Liberties, and Constitutional Literature, and of Criminal Profiling More Generally' (2004) 71 University of Chicago Law Review 1275–1381.

[62] VK Borooah, 'Racial Bias in Police Stops and Searches: An Economic Analysis' (2001) 17 *European Journal of Political Economy* 19. In the USA, the leading works in the area include J Knowles, N Persico, and P Todd, 'Racial Bias in Motor Vehicle Searches: Theory and Evidence' (2001) 109 *Journal of Political Economy* 203–29; R Hernández-Murillo and J Knowles, 'Racial Profiling or Racist Policing? Bounds Tests in Aggregated Data' (2004) 45(3) *International Economic Review* 959–89.

[63] BE Harcourt, *Against Prediction: Policing, Profiling, and Punishing in an Actuarial Age* (2007).

population with highly detrimental consequences on their employment, educational, familial, and social outcomes. This, in turn, is likely to result, again, in counterproductive effects on crime.[64]

Ultimately, criminal profiling is likely to be counterproductive to the crime-fighting goal.[65] We need to know more about comparative elasticities and offending rates as between different groups in society before engaging in actuarial policing—and we know nothing about comparative elasticities today. What is even more troubling is that there are good reasons to suspect that the elasticity of the targeted may be *less* than that of the non-targeted. Elasticity is going to depend in large part on the existence of legitimate work alternatives, and, as the work of William Julius Wilson demonstrates, there is a deep and complex relationship between work opportunities, race, and the inner city.[66] As a result, there is no good reason to assume that the higher-offending group is as responsive to policing as the lower-offending group. The two groups do, we presume, have different offending rates—otherwise the police would be profiling on a spurious trait. Whether the different offending rates are due to different socio-economic backgrounds, to different histories, cultures, or education, we know not—but if their offending rates are different, there is every reason to believe that their elasticity will be as well. If they are, for instance, offending more because they are socio-economically more disadvantaged, then it would follow logically that they may also have less elasticity of offending to policing because they have fewer alternative opportunities. There is, therefore, every reason to believe that non-spurious racial profiling would actually increase crime in society.

It is worth adding—given that so much of the preventive state is now aimed at international and domestic terrorism—that the same logic applies in the terrorism context. Surprisingly, although international terrorism is by no means a new phenomenon, there is little reliable empirical research on the effectiveness of preventive (also called 'defensive') counterterrorist measures, and there is no reliable empirical research on the use of profiling in this context. The little evidence there is on counterterrorism measures more generally suggests that such preventive policing techniques may backfire, largely due to a phenomenon called 'substitution'. 'Substitution' encompasses several possible responses to profiling by terrorist organizations, for example: (1) the recruitment of more individuals from non-profiled groups, which expands the overall pool of potential terrorists; and (2) the substitution

[64] I am taking at face value the law enforcement objectives only. Naturally, community relationships, self-respect among profiled groups, and other values should be taken into account. Most citizens do not *only* want to live in a crime-free world, but rather in a world in which people feel respected and valued as members of the community. But for the purposes of the argument in this text, it is an internal critique that takes at face value the law enforcement objectives.

[65] In a more recent working paper, John Knowles and his co-author, Jeff Dominitz, recognize that maximizing the search success rates may lead to maximizing crime, see their 'Crime Minimization and Racial Bias: What Can We Learn From Police Search Data?' (18 February 2005) PIER Working Paper 05–019 available at <http://ssrn.com/abstract=719981>. Charles Manski also recognizes the conflict between crime minimization and hit-rate maximization in his draft, 'Search Profiling with Partial Knowledge of Deterrence' (unpublished paper, 2005).

[66] WJ Wilson, *The Truly Disadvantaged: The Inner City, the Underclass, and Public Policy* (1987); WJ Wilson, *When Work Disappears: The World of the New Urban Poor* (1996).

of different types of terrorist attack that are more immune to profiling and yet more devastating in terms of deaths and injuries. These potential responses raise a host of technical empirical questions that are at present entirely unresolved, but suggest that we should be wary, here too, of unsubstantiated claims of effectiveness.[67]

## From selective incapacitation to mass incarceration

In the early 1980s, the RAND Corporation established the Habitual Offender Project with the aim of studying preventive measures aimed at recidivists. The idea originated in response to studies of California prisons that revealed, surprisingly, small differences in prison sentences as between low- and high-rate offenders. The idea behind the RAND proposal, ultimately, was to efficiently reshuffle inmate sentencing: by locking up high-rate offenders for longer periods, a state could both reduce its crime rate and simultaneously decrease its prison population. The policy promised budgetary savings *and* reduced crime. The approach would eventually become known under the rubric of 'selective incapacitation' and be considered the single most cost-effective measure to reduce crime—a mixed technique that packed a powerful preventive punch in a punitive glove.

Peter Greenwood, with Allan Abrahamse, issued a RAND report in 1982 that set forth the most fully articulated plan for implementing the strategy of selective incapacitation—a strategy that had, at its heart, 'the notion of preventive detention'.[68] Entitled 'Selective Incapacitation,' it studied the feasibility of predicting future dangerousness as a vehicle to lengthier sentencing. The study then tried to estimate the cost-effectiveness of selecting on dangerousness.

The researchers based their prediction research on self-report surveys from 2100 male prison and jail inmates from California, Michigan, and Texas in 1977.[69] They focused on robbery and burglary offences, excluding more serious crimes such as murder or rape (given that low-base-rate crimes are so much more difficult to predict) and developed a seven-factor test to identify high-rate offenders (focusing primarily on prior criminal record, history of drug abuse, and employment history). They assigned each offender a score from zero to seven: a positive response on any one of these seven factors resulted in one point on the offender's score. The resulting score was used to distinguish between low-, medium-, or high-rate offenders. When the researchers tested their predictions, they found that their test identified low- and medium-rate offenders with greater reliability than high-rate offenders: 91 to 92 per cent of those scoring 0 or 1—the lowest possible scores—turned out to be low- or medium-rate offenders; by contrast, only 50 per cent of those scoring 5, 6, or 7 turned out to be high-rate burglars or robbers.[70]

[67] See BE Harcourt, 'Muslim Profiles Post-9/11: Is Racial Profiling an Effective Counterterrorist Measure and Does it Violate the Right to be Free from Discrimination?' in B Goold and L Lazarus, *Security and Human Rights* (2007).

[68] PW Greenwood and AF Abrahamse, *Selective Incapacitation* (1982) xx and 92 (RAND Report R-2815-NIJ).

[69] Greenwood and Abrahamse (cited in n 68) xii.

[70] Greenwood and Abrahamse (cited in n 68) 53.

Despite the poor results, Greenwood concluded the study on an upbeat note: 'Increasing the accuracy with which we can identify high-rate offenders or increasing the selectivity of sentencing policies can lead to a decrease in crime, a decrease in the prison population, or both. Selective incapacitation is a way of increasing the amount of crime prevented by a given level of incarceration.'[71] Even though Greenwood found that predicting future dangerousness was inexact—and five years later would revise the report and issue it with a slightly different title: 'Selective incapacitation revisited: why the high-rate offenders are hard to predict'[72]—Greenwood nevertheless painted a rosy picture from what were not very cost-efficient conclusions.[73]

A close reading of their findings revealed that the crime-reduction benefits required—in three out of four cases—*increased prison populations*. In effect, the idea of *selective* incapacitation had really just morphed into a theory of simple incapacitation. Nevertheless, the Greenwood report had high impact and contributed importantly to the rise and theoretical prominence of incapacitation theory and eventually to the massive increase in prison populations in the USA.[74]

Incapacitation is inevitably going to produce negative effects on the rate of crime (outside the prison).[75] The problem is that the incapacitation theory in and of itself does not set a limit on the balance between imprisonment and crime—we have to go outside that analysis to find principled limits on punishment. It will never tell us how much incarceration is appropriate. The result, in the USA, is mass incarceration, which is supported not so much because of its effect on crime (crime has been falling continuously), but for its other political economy consequences. In the USA at least, counties with prisons, feeling the economic pinch of the Great Recession of 2008, have begun vocally to oppose the closing of prisons merely because of the contributions prisons have made to the local economies. All in all, it is fair to conclude that this third category of punitive preventive justice—whether we call it 'selective' or 'massive' incarceration—is anything but efficient. Here too, the purported need for these preventive measures is, as an empirical matter, factually overstated and unproven.

## C. A further critique of punitive preventive measures

These empirical problems, however, pale in comparison to a more fundamental issue with the modern punitive preventive approach. The economic cost-benefit

[71] Greenwood and Abrahamse (cited in n 68) xiii.

[72] PW Greenwood, S Turner, and National Institute of Justice (US), 'Selective Incapacitation Revisited: Why the High-Rate Offenders are Hard to Predict' (1987).

[73] Greenwood and Abrahamse (cited in n 68) xix.

[74] See generally BE Harcourt, *Against Prediction: Profiling, Policing, and Punishing in an Actuarial Age* (2007) 88–92.

[75] BE Harcourt, 'An Institutionalization Effect: The Impact of Mental Hospitalization and Imprisonment on Homicide in the United States, 1934–2001' (2011) 40 Journal of Legal Studies (January) 439–83.

approach that typically underlies these measures inverts the relationship between politics and policy-making by transforming political values into mere instrumentalities of public policy decision-making. Instead of public policy serving as a means to ensure the efficient implementation of political visions, these modern approaches to punitive prevention influence, shape, and distort political ideals—'distort' in the sense that they affect political values without openly engaging, debating, confronting, or negotiating the very balance of political values at the heart of our *polis.*

The root of the problem can be seen in the very discourse of the RAND policy analysts of the 1960s. As Edward Quade cautioned, alternative policies are not always 'obvious substitutes for one another', nor do they always 'perform the same specific function'.[76] Nevertheless, as Quade admitted, 'education, antipoverty measures, police protection, and slum clearance may all be alternatives in combating juvenile delinquency'.[77] In other words, cost-benefit analyses may well give us the tools to decide whether, as Quade wrote, 'additional money might be better spent on space exploration or economic opportunity programs';[78] or whether to 'reduce unemployment to less than 2 per cent in two years or add a certain number of miles to the interstate highway system'.[79] But those decisions obviously have important political dimensions that are not fully reflected or contested in the cost-benefit analyses themselves.

Edward Quade's pregnant remark reveals the nub of the problem with systems analysis: 'education, antipoverty measures, police protection, and slum clearance may all be alternatives in combating juvenile delinquency'. This simple statement exposes a radical inversion of politics: notice how the narrow objective—here, combating juvenile delinquency—takes priority over fundamental political values such as an educated citizenry and a robust public sphere ('education'), political and economic equality or equality of opportunity ('antipoverty measures'), political freedom, security, and civil liberties ('police protection'), as well as urban politics and planning ('slum clearance'). An innocent and narrow objective has turned these political ideals into mere instrumental goods, it has displaced political contestation, wrangling, horse-trading, and debate, and it has imposed, under the veil of neutral, objective, positivistic science, a *political outcome.*

Contemporary cost-benefit analyses—which are at the core of today's punitive preventive public-policy approach—are ingenious methods for *displacing* politics. They seduce by offering the hope of avoiding the quagmire of partisan politics and by focusing our attention on narrow objectives that no one could possibly object to—reducing crime or juvenile delinquency, for instance. They ingeniously propose a 'common sense' approach: rather than get caught up in endless political debates, purportedly we simply agree on more basic, measurable objectives (note that this privileges factors that can be subject to quantification), evaluate the different alternative ways of achieving those narrow objectives, and then choose

[76] Quade (cited in n 5) 7.
[77] Quade (cited in n 5) 7.
[78] Quade (cited in n 5) 18.
[79] Quade (cited in n 5) 4–5.

the most efficient alternative. The methodology is unimpeachable: only someone who would be willing to *waste* social resources—an irrational person—would object.

The trouble is that the set of alternative policies cuts across multiple political dimensions and, as a result, the conclusions, if they are implemented, will necessarily *affect, shape*, and *distort* our political ideals and value systems. By selecting on the basis of easily quantifiable sub-categories—here, for instance, juvenile delinquency rates—rather than on the larger political ideals of, for instance, youth welfare, or the even larger categories of equality or political freedom, the public policy approach converts political values—an educated citizenry (education), equality (anti-poverty measures), and liberty (police protection)—into mere levers, and imposes (under a veil of neutrality) political values. It shapes the political environment, and it does so by means of recurring mechanisms that have important political effects on society and directly affect the balance of political values such as liberty, equality, wealth distribution, civil rights, etc. The public policy analysis, it turns out, *changes our political environment—it shapes our politics*. In sum, by choosing a narrow objective and then simply costing alternative policies, we have *shaped* our political value system without ever having explicitly engaged *politics*.

## D. Conclusion

In January 1968, Mayor John Lindsay hailed the new arrangement with the RAND Corporation to tackle crime in New York City. He declared:

> This agreement will greatly assist our introduction into city agencies of the kind of streamlined, modern management thinking that Robert McNamara applied in the Pentagon with such success during the past seven years.... I regard this as the most important development in the search for effectiveness in city government in many, many years.[80]

History was not kind to Lindsay's mayoralty, especially not to its cost-effectiveness. The NYC RAND Institute folded in 1975 amidst significant—I might add, ironic—controversy over Lindsay's profligate spending on consultants.[81] History was also not kind to Secretary McNamara—though whether it was McNamara or President Johnson who was primarily responsible for engulfing the country in the Vietnam War remains hotly contested today.

The RAND housing security study discussed at the beginning of this chapter was symptomatic. Ultimately, the study found that even the most effective security measures—extensive surveillance, increased police, and posting of armed guards at each building—were too expensive.[82] As a result, the report did not recommend any of the security measures analysed, and instead urged a different solution: more research money for RAND!

80 Reeves (cited in n 3) 31.
81 Light (cited in n 1) 74.
82 Liechenstein (cited in n 9) 24.

> [T]he heuristic methodology that we have presented here is further testimony to the paucity of formalized design procedures for translating security goals into detailed system requirements. The present crime situation has created an undeniable demand for quantitative models which can account for behavioural and sociological phenomena which can adequately predict the impact of security measures on society, and which can clarify our presently fuzzy notions of what security really means.[83]

But sometimes history gets things right—at least partially. I would argue that it was, ultimately, a good thing for the NYC RAND Institute to close its doors so rapidly. The punitive preventive approach that it promoted—relying so extensively on economic cost-benefit analysis—was plagued with difficulties. And it remains so today. The approach is seductively simple and appealing, but it is an approach that maximizes the wrong objective and, in the process, dangerously displaces politics.

[83] Liechenstein (cited in n 9) 25.

# 14

# The Politics of Mass Preventive Justice

*Pat O'Malley*

## A. Introduction

'Preventive justice' may be distinguished by a focus on risk and perhaps more precisely, on the risk of harm.[1] While it is arguable that preventive justice is not a novel development, not least because deterrence has long been a key aim of law, that issue is perhaps less important than issues created by preventive justice's accelerating momentum and its proliferation and diversification during the 20th century. 'Actuarial justice' has been perhaps the most discussed such development, in which a jurisprudence of risk emerges that justifies the long-term incapacitation or risk-neutralization of offenders.[2] Alongside this, increasing numbers of preventive offences have been created for which risk calculations are embedded in the law itself. The governance of drink-driving is almost a paradigm of preventive justice of this sort. This is an offence *defined* by risk. It is not required that the offenders be driving in an erratic fashion. To the naked eye their driving may be perfect. Rather, at issue is that they are in a risk-creating condition. In turn, as this risky condition may only be detectable by scientific instruments, the offence itself comes to be defined in terms of this technology—driving with a certain blood alcohol content (BAC) as measured by one or other kinds of legally defined and approved device.[3]

On the other hand, the sanction also is risk based. While deterrence clearly is a preventive rationale associated with such laws, equally characteristic is that the sanction—licence disqualification—specifically incapacitates the offender as risk creator. And hovering around this development, indeed arguably a key element of its success is the fact that a 'risk jurisprudence' has emerged. This is a set of legal debates and justifications for legal governance characterized by the fact that it embodies a scientific (or purportedly scientific) discourse on risk. Its intention is

[1] A Ashworth and L Zedner, 'Defending the criminal law: reflections on the changing character of crime, procedure and sanctions' (2007) 2 Crime Law and Philosophy 21–51; A Ashworth and L Zedner, 'Just prevention: Preventive justice and the limits of the criminal law' in S Green and RA Duff (eds), *The Philosophical Foundations of the Criminal Law* (2009).

[2] M Feeley and J Simon, 'Actuarial Justice: the Emerging New Criminal Law' in D Nelken (ed), *The Futures of Criminology* (1994) 173–201.

[3] For an analysis of the political and technical process involved in this transformation of drunk driving, see R Light, *Criminalizing the Drink-Driver* (1994).

to demonstrate 'objectively' the scientific reality of risky conditions that have to be acted upon—frequently criminalized—in order to prevent harm. So effective has this jurisprudence proven, that nowadays it is very rare to find public opposition to the offence of having a blood alcohol level above a permissible maximum—an offence that did not exist in the same fashion half a century ago, when the test for drink-driving was the demonstration of behavioural incapacity.

While this chapter will not focus on drink-driving, I regard it as archetypical of preventive justice not just because it is embedded in a risk jurisprudence, has risk-based offences, and has risk-based sanctions, but also because it is embedded in the governance of traffic. While mundane in many respects, in terms of volumes of criminal and quasi-criminal prosecutions and civil procedures, traffic regulation represents the bulk of all criminal justice. Even by the early 1990s, Fox indicated that for every summary charge coming before the magistrates' courts in Australia, more than seven criminal matters were dealt with by on-the-spot fines—of which over 90 per cent were related to traffic matters.[4] Conversely, as discussed in the following sections of this chapter, traffic regulation has been a domain heavily marked by preventive justice, and is one in which preventive justice has made rapid and far-reaching advances. Yet in many respects, driving under the influence and related offences are a relatively small, if very salient, part of such preventive justice. By far the bulk of this domain—if we discount the marginal infractions associated with parking—is made up of offences related to speed. These offences and their characteristic form of justice are the focus of this chapter.

## B. Speed and the emergence of 'mass preventive justice'

As with drink-driving, 'speeding' underwent something of a transformation in the last half of the 20th century. From the beginning of the 20th century, speeding appeared as a criminal offence, but was highly contested. Alongside 'simple' speeding offences were those more serious wrongs such as 'dangerous driving' and 'furious driving'. In some more or less taken-for-granted fashion, the element of dangerousness in these latter offences was judged directly from the performance of the driver. Speed might be considered a factor, and frequently it was, but it need not be—and even when this was the case, speed itself was always relative to context. Dangerous driving is a complex and in some degree unique combination of circumstances to be considered case by case by the court. It was still open to argument that speed alone did not constitute dangerous driving. As late as the 1960s, the racing driver Stirling Moss was able successfully to argue against a dangerous driving charge in Australia on the grounds that he was a safer driver at high speed than most motorists were at very moderate speeds. Speeding was like drink-driving in the days before BAC. Drink-driving then was judged by a

[4] R Fox, *Criminal Justice on the Spot: Infringement penalties in Victoria* (1996) 89–94. See also P O'Malley, *The Currency of Justice* (2009); P O'Malley, 'Simulated Justice. Risk, Money and Telemetric Policing' (2010) 50 *British Journal of Criminology* 795–807.

behaviour rather than the quantity of alcohol consumed. It was measurable by tests such as walking the white line, and was thus subject to individual differences in the capacity to 'hold one's drink'. Both dangerous driving and drunk-driving were individual behaviours rather than risks.

But there was a key difference between dangerous driving and speeding: Stirling Moss would not escape a speeding charge. Speeding constituted an offence regardless of subjective or judicial judgements of dangerousness. This was to become the basis for a politics still highly relevant to preventive justice in the 21st century. In the early part of the 1900s, motoring associations in both Britain and the USA had argued that given the existence of dangerous driving laws, there was no justification for speeding to be an offence.[5] In Britain speeding was referred to as 'a tax on progress'. In opposition to this, enforcement of speeding charges was justified on many grounds ranging from public safety (for example, frightening horses), to complaints that speeding damaged (dirt) roads and caused a public nuisance because of the dust raised.[6] This latter, in turn, created a second aspect of the politics of speed that also is central to the current politics of prevention, for the fines raised were frequently deployed to repair roads (or at least that was the claim) so that opponents argued that speeding fines were merely a tax to feed the coffers of government, enforced by criminal law. One last matter in these early politics, to which we will also have need to return, concerned the fact that the subjects of speeding law were not the traditional targets of criminal justice. Wealthy defendants and motoring associations often were able to argue successfully that the law targeted respectable people, and so speeding was only a 'technical' offence rather than properly part of criminal law. Not only did this mean that fines were the only sanction deployed, despite newspaper moral panics that often demanded imprisonment of speedsters.[7] It also resulted in chronic under-enforcement as magistrates refused to convict, and police were so unwilling to enforce speeding laws that in Britain the Home Office had to insist on police action in this regard. Speeding laws were widely regarded not as preventive criminal justice aimed at producing safety but as a form of stigmatization and taxation that targeted law-abiding people.

The emergence of risk-based law changed much of this. The post-World War II 'democratization' of driving rapidly produced a new phenomenon: 'the road toll', a term that referred to road carnage as a mass or statistical reality. By the early 1960s this had become a matter of national concern not simply in terms of the individual tragedy of 'accidents', which had existed from the start, but as a threat to the well-being of the population. It was in this 'biopolitical' context that the road deaths and injuries appeared as both a statistical phenomenon and one of national importance. And it was in this context over the ensuing decade or more that traffic safety appeared primarily in the form of aggregate risk rather than individual danger. Thus, risk assessments and legal measures that embraced and embodied these statistical realities proliferated around the road toll: drink-driving, road engineering,

[5] W Plowden, *The Motor Car and Politics 1896–1970* (1971).
[6] O'Malley, *The Currency of Justice* (cited in n 4) 99–102.
[7] O'Malley, *The Currency of Justice* (cited in n 4) 98–100.

vehicle design and equipment, and of course speeding were all transformed in a relatively short span of time around measures of aggregate risk—and mostly at a time when other aspects of crime prevention more generally were still marginal, low-status tasks assigned to superannuated police officers.

Speeding regulation was transformed into preventive justice in two principal ways. First, speeding was identified as a risk factor. That is, like blood alcohol content some years later, speed was made to appear as objectively linked to rates of traffic accidents, death, and injury. Speed in some measure began to lose its standing as a 'merely technical' offence and came instead to be seen as objectively harmful: high speed was closely correlated with high risk of death and injury. Driving well above the speed limit now attracted greater punishment not simply because it represented a greater disregard for law but at least equally because it represented a greatly elevated *scientifically* demonstrable harmful potential.[8] Travelling above a certain speed, or within a certain margin greater than the speed limit, now became a stand-alone legal criterion of dangerous driving. An equally important observation is that once speed became a precisely calculable risk factor for death and injury, it came to be associated with new enforcing technologies that operated in the name of a criminal law based in the prevention of harm. New instruments in the form of speed and red-light cameras—dubbed 'safety cameras'—now could measure crime objectively, and for that matter remotely. They could detect *and* calibrate offending, courtesy of risk's objectification of the speed-harm nexus. These apparatuses detected historically unprecedented volumes of offending.[9] Almost unnoticed by criminology, a sea change without comparison in the history of criminal justice had occurred: the creation of 'mass preventive justice'—a justice that was in part produced by risk's measurability.[10] Shortly I will turn to some of the significant consequences and characteristics of this emerging justice, and of the political and legal discourses and struggles that were rapidly to make themselves felt. But first, it is necessary to form some idea of the technological components and agents of this change.

[8] This may lead to a conclusion that mass preventive justice is a product of technological innovation. Certainly, as will be explored shortly, technological change has greatly facilitated the detection and processing of large numbers of offences and infractions. Yet even before such innovations as traffic cameras, computers, and breathalysers, important changes were in train, such as the emergence of traffic courts in the USA. There, greatly simplified procedures were developed for dealing with the exponentially growing volume of traffic disobedience. In this way it could be argued that mass preventive justice, and its technological apparatus, have both been a response to officially recognized mass disobedience on a historically unprecedented scale.

[9] O'Malley, *The Currency of Justice* (cited in n 4) 79–82.

[10] Arguments abound that speed alone is not a safety concern because risk is always an effect of other variables such as weather, road conditions, traffic density, etc. These claims will later be noted with respect to opposition to mass preventive justice. Indeed, historically such claims were often made in court, and the example of Stirling Moss mentioned above is only an unusual variant of this. The same claims were made with respect to alcohol consumption. The advantage of risk-based calculation, it will be recognized, is that all those other factors are held constant. More precisely, as the correlations are based on very large numbers of accidents, all such conditions are randomized and, whatever the conditions, the risk of accidents increases with speed and/or alcohol consumption.

## C. The technical infrastructure of mass prevention

For many years, traffic flows and safety have been technologically regulated. Traffic lights appear as one of the first of these technologies, followed in the 1930s by parking meters. Significantly both were intended to displace human labour: prevention and preventive justice alike are closely associated with economic registers of costs and benefits. But increasingly ubiquitous is an array of monitoring and recording apparatuses including red-light cameras, speed cameras, bus lane cameras, automatic number plate recognition technologies (ANPRs) that are intended not only to detect but in important ways to anticipate and prevent harms. Under a discourse of 'safety' they register and record offences and infringements, and transmit their data to central computers that, in turn, calculate and issue penalty notices or more rarely trigger pursuit and apprehension. All are connected in various degrees of directness and responsiveness to risk-based models that calculate, anticipate, and modulate flows and circulations of traffic. All actively put into effect what are held to be preventive safety measures against risky offences and offenders.

Through such technologies, in the 21st century motorists are subjected to a digitized regime governed by codes and protocols in the name of harm minimization, risk, and security. Bar-code scanners and registration plate readers passively register vehicle and driver identifiers. Radio frequency identification devices (RFIDs) actively transmit identifying codes and perform protocols that provide the identification of risky vehicles. In some instances, such devices are operated by police—or increasingly by cheaper security employees—either from moving or stationary vehicles or from roadside sites. Essentially, these instruments displace the more problematic and 'subjective' technologies involving police measuring speeds with stopwatches or by recording the speedometer reading of a pursuing police vehicle—problematic because much more prone to challenge in courts. While human-operated 'radar' technologies are retained and even have been expanded in their use, they are being joined and sometimes surpassed by instruments that in the name of safety displace enforcing subjects altogether.

Traffic monitoring cameras—alongside CCTV, access cards, and the like—are now a routine part of life. Embedded in the traffic environment, they map exactly on to Deleuze's (1995) vision of 'control societies' in which the management of distributions, flows, and circulations is prioritized over the government of individuals. While individual justice historically has been the principal concern of liberal law—and forms the basis of what many would consider to be the essential heart of criminal justice—mass preventive justice challenges this. In a double movement, individuals are being displaced by their coded identifiers, while at the same time these identifiers place them as elements of a distribution rather than as liberal subjects.[11] Although by no means as simple—or as technologically determined—as

[11] O'Malley, 'Simulated Justice' (cited in n 4).

this sounds, the basis of this claim is well understood.[12] As risk has provided both the rationale and the calculable foundation for mass preventive justice, distributions, and the shaping or modulation of them, become the primary concerns. Individuals 'matter' only as elements of risk pools, and, as already suggested, the 'inner state' of the offender motivations, understandings, and intentions becomes of lesser interest than the risk-bearing behaviour. Although I will not return to the point for some time, it is vital to recognize that this is not necessarily how the subjects of such justice view things. The very fact that drivers frequently dispute an intention to speed, or claim that they make balanced and reasonable judgements about whether it is safe to speed, is at the heart of much resistance to mass preventive justice.[13]

The relevant enforcing technologies associated with such justice register measurably 'risky' behaviours. In the era of informatics, they attach these registrations to identifying codes: the digital images of registration plates, bar codes, and so on mentioned above. These codes attach the behaviour, calibrated as an offence, to a legal subject. But that subject is not the complex subject of liberal criminal law. Mass preventive justice more or less requires a shift away from individual justice because the sheer volume of mass disobedience detected made familiar processes of trial and even summary justice unworkable in practice. As Fox has demonstrated, the mounting pressure of business forced the 'streamlining' of procedure. The 'owner' of a vehicle came to be the subject of 'on-the-spot fines' for which penalties were fixed—mitigation and aggravation practically disappeared.[14] An effective reverse-onus justice was imposed, and strong financial incentives in the form of discounted fines were put in place to discourage opting-in to court procedure. For administrative convenience, 'owners' were assumed to be the offending drivers, unless they could prove otherwise, and identified by their driver's digital licence number. Individuals only rarely—statistically speaking—appear in the operation of mass preventive justice. For the most part they remain throughout preventive justice procedures as electronically coded entities: what Deleuze refers to as 'dividuals', corresponding to drivers, owners, operators, and so on.[15] They are detected as codes, 'judged' and sentenced as codes, through coded informatics they expiate their sentence—overwhelmingly through electronic payment of a fine or cancellation of licence. For the most part, this electronically coded dividualization is what mass preventive justice relies upon in order to work.

The fact that risk can be digitized and justice thereby automated is both a cause and a consequence of the emergence of mass preventive justice. In its ideal form, we

[12] See, eg, B Castel, 'From Dangerousness to Risk' in G Burchell, C Gordon, and P Miller (eds), *The Foucault Effect. Studies in Governmentality* (1991) 281–98; M Feeley and J Simon, 'The New Penology: Notes on the Emerging Strategy of Corrections and Its Implications' (1992) 30 *Criminology* 449–74.

[13] See, eg, H Wells and D Wills, 'Individualism and identity. Resistance and speed cameras in the UK' (2009) 6 *Surveillance and Society* 259–74.

[14] Fox, *Criminal Justice on the Spot* (cited in n 4). For further details see O'Malley, 'Simulated Justice' (cited in n 4).

[15] G Deleuze, 'Postscript on control societies' in G Deleuze (ed), *Negotiations 1972–1990* (1995) 177–82.

might say, this is a system of perfect prevention. In principle the technology displaces expensive human labour and levies fines that pay for its own endless expansion. The trajectory of technological expansion, thus funded, allows for the monitoring of all traffic, everywhere and at all times. Of course, the system is in practice incomplete. At present fixed policing devices—installed on posts, gantries, and buildings—are merely scattered about the road system. As well, their whereabouts often can be predicted and their identification built into commercially available 'onboard' mapping software. So in theory it remains possible for drivers to offend at will—although still running the risks posed by mobile speed cameras. Some drivers, at least to judge by blogs posted on a multitude of websites, find the array of fixed cameras so objectionable they claim to speed elsewhere 'on principle'.[16] Every effort at risk reduction has the potential to create such new risks of offending. But in their turn control technologies do not stop still for long. 'Point-to-Point' enforcement already exists or is being introduced in many jurisdictions. Cameras record entry and exit times with respect to monitored stretches of road, allowing computers readily to calculate average speeds and thus to detect speeding over considerable distances. Even where such stretches of road involve multiple speed limits, simple algorithms are entered into the computers to allow for this.[17]

Again, human cussedness and ingenuity being what it is, online postings record various schemes for evading or disrupting the preventive potential of these apparatuses. Some drivers, for example, avow that they would enter the monitored zones and park for whatever period they calculate as necessary, before then speeding over the remaining stretch at fantasized speeds of 300 km or upward. Others advocate or market 'ghost plates' that render identification impossible for ANPR systems, or more crudely, 'hinged' number plates that can be lowered when needed.[18] Cheap devices are available to warn when a vehicle comes under radar surveillance; other technologies are available online that jam laser or radar detectors. Many such devices of all types are illegal but in wide circulation. But countering almost all such manoeuvres, Intelligent Speed Adaptation (ISA) or EVI (electronic vehicle identification) systems are being developed and implemented for generalized deployment. Already used in vehicle fleets, these come in several forms. Using active RFIDs and GPS technology embedded in the vehicle, linked to a database

[16] Examples of this and related online responses are dealt with at length in section F of the chapter.

[17] 'Point-to-Point Speed Enforcement' at <http://www.rta.nsw.gov.au/roadsafety/speedandspeedcameras/avespeedsafetycameras/index.html>.

[18] For example, on registration plate detection see <www.ghostplates.com/> and for an array of responses from disgruntled drivers see such sites as <http://www.policespeedcameras.info/Speed_Camera_News_United_Kingdom/uk_news> and its Australian parallel site <http://www.roadsense.com.au>. These sites are frequently referred to in this chapter partly because they act as collection points for postings from a great array of (largely like-minded) online sources. For this reason they offer an effective resource for readers wanting to follow up on these and related issues. But more importantly, they act as 'hubs'—connecting resisting dividuals, traditional and new media, party politics, and so on—for online information networks of the kind discussed by L Introna and A Gibbons, 'Networks and resistance. Investigating online advocacy networks as a modality for resisting state surveillance' (2009) 6 *Surveillance and Society* 238–9.

that maps speed zones, the system detects at any moment whether the driver is exceeding the speed limit.[19] They can be developed to take account of variable speed limits such as are applied in adverse weather conditions, places where there are accidents or road works, and time-variable school zones.[20]

In the 'soft' versions of such technologies, a warning device advises drivers they are exceeding the speed limit or are approaching changed traffic regulatory conditions, but there are progressively more aggressive versions. If the driver ignores warnings, data—which include calculations of the excess speed at any moment, and the distance over which such speeding occurred (which may be considered an additional risk factor and *thus* an aggravation of the offence)—can be transmitted directly to a central registry. Finally, in a move that makes the leap from perfect detection to perfect prevention, the vehicle can be disabled or speed limits can be imposed by remote modulation of the braking system or accelerator.[21] In effect this version of 'designing out crime' is only a modification of such commercial systems as 'Onstar'. For over a decade these have provided owners of luxury cars with a service that tracks their vehicle, can disable it in case of theft, or even remotely open doors and start the vehicle in cases where the owner has lost keys or fobs. Given obvious safety concerns, for example where the driver is speeding in case of an emergency, an override capability exists similar to that built into cruise control—but override is activated at the risk of prohibitive penalties for misuse.[22]

## D. The politics of mass prevention and the fantasy of control?

It is possible to imaginatively project this diagram of apparatuses and routines into a totally governed future, all in the name of risk and safety. This is even more so because, as only hinted thus far, money is a critical feature of mass preventive justice. I have developed this argument elsewhere at length.[23] The predominance of the fine as the primary sanction in mass preventive justice makes possible the funding of its almost infinite expansion. As well, the low political profile of fines, as merely money, as another price of modern life, can be regarded as minimizing opposition and resistance—especially when compared to the liberal fetish of liberty

[19] R Winnett and D Gadher, 'Goodbye speed cameras, hello a spy in every car' (2003) *Times Online* 24 August.

[20] For a brief overview of these technologies, see <http://wikipedia.org/wiki/Intelligent_speed_adaptation>.

[21] M Paine, D Paine, and I Faulks, 'Speed limiting trials in Australia' 21st Enhanced Safety of Motor Vehicles Conference, Stuttgart 15–18 June 2009. See also M Regan, 'On-road evaluation of ISA, Following Distance warning and Seat-Belt reminder systems' (2006). See also <http://www.rta.nsw.gov.au/roadsafety/2009_conference.html>.

[22] In practice, these technologies can also record the history of the vehicle—its routes, speeds, etc. While a politics is yet to develop around ISA/EVI—except in anticipation—it is argued that the RFID technology on which it is based is highly vulnerable. If the manufacturer's design protocols are known, all elements including the identification code itself can be tampered with or turned off.

[23] O'Malley, *The Currency of Justice* (cited in n 4) and O'Malley, 'Simulated Justice' (cited in n 4).

and bodily pain.[24] This is surely enhanced when it is recognized that the entire process of such justice is publicly invisible and anonymous, as detection, judgment, and punishment may all appear online. As well, liberal individuals are hardly called into being: we appear as codes. In the vast majority of cases there is no court ceremonial or public identification and humiliation. And because money is involved, the law in practice cannot and does not investigate who actually pays. It may be my employer, spouse, friend, parent. What matters is only that money is paid, not who pays it.[25] The principal sanction of criminal justice in this way appears literally rather than figuratively as a money price, fixed by a risk calibration and not negotiable, payable by anyone—not only the wrongdoer. Fines seemingly appear merely as another annoying cost of everyday life in a consumer society. And from a regulatory position, it matters only that prices modulate the supply of unwanted actions.

In this light, mass preventive justice *could* be seen as expanding exponentially at the same time that it is disappearing into the monetized welter of commodified life.[26] In his brief discussion of 'control societies', however, Deleuze makes clear that he is presenting a *diagram* of power.[27] That is, it is a model of an ideal knowledge or technology of governance and no more than this. The same needs to be recognized in relation to mass preventive justice. The danger with all such accounts is that they are projected forward into epochal visions in which a process already under way is made to appear as if it will inexorably unfold according to a technologically determined logic. It is a seduction not always resisted by some of Deleuze's most influential interpreters.[28] For Deleuze, however, the response to identifying new diagrams of power should be neither to embrace them—for example as control could be seen simply as an escape from discipline's tyranny—

[24] It may be objected that fines infringe on our liberty by reducing our freedom to choose life options. This is, of course, the case. But I would argue strongly that it is the coercive deprivation of the freedom of movement that holds a special place in liberal moral and political thought. In part, I take this to be one reason why fines are so systematically ignored by criminologists, and by comparison with imprisonment virtually absent in media debates on justice policy and practice. Marxists, of course, have long made the point that economic coercion is far less 'visible' to liberal bourgeois thought than physical coercion and regard this as one of the ideological ruses that legitimates capitalism. For further discussion see P O'Malley, *Law, Capitalism and Democracy* (1983) ch 2.

[25] Of course, there may be objections to this. Here I am commenting on what courts do rather than on possible moral debates over the rectitude of the practice. Of course, this matter has been recognized explicitly by governments, and it underlies the invention of traffic demerit points as a means of legally sanctioning any tendency to regard fines as a licence to speed.

[26] While it is tempting to suggest that such fines should not be considered part of the criminal law, overwhelmingly they are formally understood as such—available to challenge in the criminal courts and ultimately backed up by other criminal law sanctions. Rather than inventing some other category, it is probably more worthwhile to consider that criminal justice is gradually changing some of its principal forms, and also becoming less easy to distinguish from other forms of justice. The development of Criminal Infringement Notices in Australia is one example of how exactly this form of justice is being extended to deal with 'traditional' offences such as assault, minor drug offending, and public order breaches: New South Wales Law Reform Commission, *Penalty Notices* (2010). In Britain this, and a wide variety of other 'regulatory' forms of governing criminality, are discussed by A Crawford, 'Governing through Anti-Social Behaviour' (2009) 49 *British Journal of Criminology* 810–31.

[27] Deleuze, 'Postscript on control societies' (cited in n 15) 181.

[28] W Bogard, *The Simulation of Surveillance: Hypercontrol in Telematic Societies* (1996).

nor to dread them as producing an even more perfect micro-management of all life.[29] Rather we should register the emergence of lines of flight associated with these emergent diagrams—the new and unanticipated directions that are created by, through, and around them—and to identify and develop a politics that will locate and minimize the dangerous potentialities that appear.

Yet, if individuals disappear so comprehensively from mass preventive justice to be replaced by networked dividuals, then what politics can emerge? What politics will emerge in the 'reduction' of civil society to what Hardt[30] describes as 'post civil' existence, in which individual (liberal and disciplinary) identity is dissolved or fragmented into dividuality as control operates through disaggregating and governing 'identifiers'? What solidarities can form in this domain where dividuals appear as fragmented elements, categories, and identifiers that have no tradition of political action remotely comparable to class politics that was associated with disciplinary society?[31] What resistance can develop in relation to a form of government that has as its overt logic the prevention of harm, and such a seemingly defensible programme as the maximization of traffic safety? As will be seen, government websites in particular argue that the prevention of death and injury is a powerful reason to impose what are after all relatively minor restrictions on motorists. More than this, their case appears as the prevention of scientifically demonstrable harm, rather than the harms of traditional criminal law that—as critical criminologists constantly remind us—are often little more than the moralizing preferences of a dominant class or interest group.

In this light, arguably more even than with respect to most other crime prevention, traffic interventions would appear difficult to resist. How could a politics that challenges mass preventive justice be *possible*, let alone be justified? Does this imply a vanguard role for academics and their allies who somehow must bootstrap a critical politics on behalf of what Hardt and Negri refer to as 'multitude', the mass of fragmented, de-individuated consumers of preventive law?[32]

All of this may be exacerbated, as argued elsewhere,[33] by the fact that much of the control diagram operates beneath the radar of liberal rights. Extensively it governs through commodities and involvement in a world of commodities. This is particularly clear with Deleuze's example of the credit card economy, in which controls are immanent in the system—that, for example, open or close off access according to our risky status as consumers.[34] But all this is true too for traffic regulation. Arguably the most significant 'circulation' for many of us on a day-to-day basis, vehicular traffic is a regulatory domain in which much participation is

[29] Deleuze, 'Postscript on control societies' (cited in n 15) 178.

[30] M Hardt, 'The withering of civil society' in E Kaufman and K Heller (eds), *Deleuze and Guattari: New Mappings in Politics* (1998) 36.

[31] J Simon, 'The ideological effects of actuarial practices' (1988) 22 Law and Society Review 771–800; D Savat, 'Deleuze's objectile. From discipline to modulation' in M Poster and D Savat (eds), *Deleuze and New Technology* (2009) 45–62.

[32] M Hardt and A Negri, *Empire* (2000).

[33] O'Malley, 'Simulated Justice' (cited in n 4).

[34] G Deleuze, 'Postscript on control societies' (cited in n 15) 179–80.

both formally voluntary and purchased: in the form of vehicles, driving licences, vehicle registrations, access fobs and cards. These have the potential to subject us to participation and potentially perfect control in one and the same moment. They can thus be seen, as Newman argues, as eroding democratic politics even as they invest our lives. It is part of a new order in which

> the folding of the public and private sphere produces a new social space in which one is no longer a citizen with rights and liberties—this liberal paradigm applied only when there was an autonomous civil society—but rather a citizen whose movements must be continually controlled and monitored, and whose identity must be continuously verified.[35]

The governance of traffic perhaps supplies a model of this arrangement, in which the development of 'virtual justice' transforms 'justice' into an anonymous domain in which fines are levied and paid, licences cancelled and withdrawn, fees, discounts, and premiums loaded up and packaged in prices paid by anyone, and all in virtual space. The ceremonial of justice, the assertion of rights, the complexities of prosecution and defence are dissolved. No space for a politics to challenge mass preventive justice seemingly survives.

But that is not quite what has happened, nor is it the case that the onward sweep of mass preventive justice has gone unchallenged and unchecked. In fact, political critiques and new political discourses and solidarities have emerged around such developments, facilitated by the very e-media and technologies upon which the new control technologies themselves depend. In a few cases there have been challenges to law in the courts. In others, political parties have picked up these 'sectional' politics and aligned them with their programmes.[36] But perhaps more interesting are the innumerable online discussion forums, blogs, online media publications, websites, and so on that focus in part or entirely on the issue of new traffic-tracking technologies. Some of these, of course, are the government websites that promote and justify developments. A few involve much more ambivalent traditional organizations—such as the national motoring associations that have politicked related fields since the turn of the 20th century. Some are sites such as Wikileaks and Wikipedia that attract an array of anonymous contributors of various degrees of expertise. But many spring up from individuals—or more precisely anonymous dividuals often writing under pseudonyms—whose solidarities are generated rather than destroyed by the disaggregation of identity.[37] Separated from large-scale political movements, they form political groupings around single issues such as safety cameras that, as Agamben expresses it, 'form a community without affirming an identity'.[38] It is not at all, as might be feared or assumed, that control societies

[35] S Newman, 'Politics in the age of control' in Poster and Savat (eds), *Deleuze and New Technology* (2009) 114.

[36] H Wells, 'Risk and expertise in the speed limit enforcement debate: Challenges, adaptations and responses' (2011) 11 Criminology and Criminal Justice 225–41; also Introna and Gibbons, 'Networks and resistance'(cited in n 18) 233–58.

[37] For an excellent discussion and empirical examination of such processes, see Introna and Gibbons, 'Networks and resistance' (cited in n 18).

[38] G Agamben, *The Coming Community. Notes on Politics* (1993) 86.

eliminate politics by their very ordinariness, anonymity, and embeddedness in everyday life. In some degree, they *facilitate* specific forms of 'mass' resistance. As Introna and Gibbons argue,

> It is our claim that such a virtual network may be a powerful actor through the enactment of *information politics*, in particular. The success of such an information network's information politics—i.e ability to generate politically relevant information and move it by the most effective means to the place where it will have most impact at the most critical time will in part be facilitated by... how well this network connects with other relevant actors such as information and surveillance commissioner, traditional media, new media, researchers and so forth. It is our proposition that an effective enactment of information politics by the network will be an essential constitutive element of a meta-surveillance network, which in turn is an important element of resisting state surveillance practices.[39]

In short, it is not at all that we should expect some new 'pure' form of online politics to emerge—but rather (as will be seen) that this new resistant politics will hybridize, as networked sites interact with news media and party politics.

Thus it is not necessarily the case, as Newman envisaged, that subjects are transformed into 'consumers of government services' that translate disputes 'into problems to be solved by experts and technicians'.[40] Quite to the contrary. The politics that have opened up have, precisely, challenged state supportive evidence and expertise. As well, they have directly challenged the money sanctions that the magnitude of perfect detection apparently renders an indispensable (and 'invisible') sanction for mass prevention. Questions of privacy, human rights, and the impact of procedural 'economies' that have been ongoing concerns are also aired—although rather less intensely than might be anticipated. It is significant that the two domains of these 'minor' politics have been exactly those—the jurisprudence of risk and safety, and the role of money sanctions—that theoretically driven analysis regards as key *resources* of government.[41] In some ways they have also proven Achilles heels. It is to the examination of these, and of related discussions concerning the procedures of mass preventive justice and its implied and actual threats to privacy, that analysis now turns.

## E. Challenging the jurisprudence of risk

Of course, as well as being a medium for the expression of resistance, the Internet is a site where governments and their agencies promote mass preventive justice. Fairly typical is the New South Wales Road Transport Authority (RTA), that headlines its webpage on mobile speed cameras with the caption 'Capturing speedsters. Anywhere. Anytime', which is immediately justified by reference to the road toll in

[39] Introna and Gibbons, 'Networks and resistance' (cited in n 18) 238–9.
[40] Newman, 'Politics in the age of control' (cited in n 35) 115.
[41] O'Malley, 'Simulated Justice' (cited in n 4).

terms of numbers killed and injured.[42] In this light, 'mobile speed cameras have been introduced because they are recognised internationally as a best practice road safety countermeasure to reduce speeding, leading to a reduction of crashes. The introduction of mobile speed programs in Queensland and Victoria has reduced casualty rates in those states by at least 25 per cent.'[43] With respect to fixed safety cameras—which may be speed cameras, red-light cameras, or both—the RTA claims that 'the use of cameras to enforce speeding has proven road safety benefits', and points out that 'independent research found that where cameras have been installed there has been a 70 per cent reduction in speeding resulting in a 90 per cent decline in fatalities and a 23 per cent reduction in injuries'.[44] In turn, it claims that safety cameras are installed at sites determined by the number of crashes and the 'cost to the community' of these crashes. Further, it is argued that evaluations of Point-to-Point enforcement have shown a 50 per cent reduction in fatal and serious injury crashes.[45]

If these claims are taken at face value then, as noted, they justify the rolling out of more blanket coverage and more sophisticated monitoring systems. But the Internet has proven a singularly effective medium for registering and circulating contradictory evidence. The most frequent challenges involve straightforward claims that data are far more varied and unclear than police and road safety authorities admit. In Britain, for example, a good deal of such critique has arisen around decisions by (largely Conservative) local councils in 2010 to scrap the widespread use of speed cameras because of doubts as to their effectiveness.[46] In many examples cited there was no decrease in the rate of accidents after the introduction of cameras.[47] But what clearly triggered enduring and widespread concern was evidence on such activist sites as 'www.policespeedcameras.info' that British government figures 'showed for 32 speed camera sites there were an average of 48 more accidents involving death or serious injury' over the previous 12 months, while at 38 red-light camera sites there had been 'an average of 62 more accidents'.[48] The reported

[42] 'Mobile Speed cameras' at <http://www.rta.nsw.gov.au/roadsafety/speedandspeedcameras/avespeedsafetycameras/index.html>.

[43] This is available at <http://www.rta.nsw.gov.au/roadsafety/speedandspeedcameras/avespeedsafetycameras/index.html>.

[44] At <http://www.rta.nsw.gov.au/roadsafety/speedandspeedcameras/avespeedsafetycameras/index.html>.

[45] At <http://www.rta.nsw.gov.au/roadsafety/speedandspeedcameras/avespeedsafetycameras/index.html>.

[46] For an overview of this local politics and the data generated, see <http://en.wikipedia.org/wiki/Traffic_enforcement_camera>.

[47] For example, J Tozer, 'Town that scrapped "motorist tax" speed cameras sees no increase in accidents', available at <http://www.dailymail.co.uk> (24 April 2010); D Barrett, 'Speed camera switch-off sees fewer accidents', available at <http://www.telegraph.co.uk/motoring/news/7931842 07/08/2010>.

[48] D Williams, 'Speed cameras may cause accidents' (2005) *Evening Standard* (24 June) 6. The figures obviously are exaggerated, as these are total rather than average figures and news that accident levels had fallen in 730 other London sites was either passed over or implicitly queried because the data came from the London safety partnership that managed the scheme. It was also claimed that Scottish road accident statistics showed that after five years of speed cameras, road accident statistics had not improved.

increase in accidents clearly concerned most online contributors. Motoring association sites admitted being baffled and 'concerned', sometimes suggesting that there were 'individual reasons' at each site.[49] Sometimes speculations were put forward such as that by the Royal Automobile Club, that 'there could be a conflict between motorists who slow down for cameras and the growing underclass of unregistered drivers who do not'.[50] The most frequent claim was that drivers were distracted by cameras, although evidence was invariably anecdotal.[51]

In 2005, *Times Online*[52] reported that the government was blocking the installation of nearly 500 new speed cameras 'amid signs that many are beginning to doubt the effectiveness of the devices. The 38 camera partnerships which include police forces and local authorities have been ordered not to use cameras in any new sites.'[53] It is worthy of note that the Association of Chief Police Officers (ACPO) condemned the ban, saying 'it could cost lives because dangerous roads were being left unprotected by cameras'.[54] But this argument was largely ignored except in corporate media sites. At the same time it was reported that 'The Department for Transport is reviewing the rules on deploying cameras after concerns that partnerships have failed to consider alternatives such as improving junctions or erecting warnings'. Even the Parliamentary Advisory Council for Transport Safety admitted online that while it supported speed cameras, 'in some cases partnerships may have chosen to install a camera when an engineering solution may have been better'.[55] Certainly this reflected long-held views expressed online from non-official sources. It was duly noticed by such opponents that cameras represent a considerably cheaper and easier option than engineering at locations where concerns had arisen about accident rates. Indeed, the UK Road Safety Minister was widely reported online as saying that the government would cut funding because local government bodies had relied too heavily on safety cameras for too long, and the focus needed to be on other safety measures. The lines between party politics and dividual politics converged.[56]

As noted, a wide array of postings reported instances where the installation of speed cameras had *increased* accident rates. Bloggers have said that one study by a British insurance company in 2010 claimed that 28,000 road accidents have been triggered by speed cameras as drivers slowed down ahead of them and then sped up once they had passed them.[57] It was also widely posted that the introduction of

[49] Williams, 'Speed cameras may cause accidents' (cited in n 48).

[50] Available at <http://www.policespeedcameras.info/Speed_Camera_News_United_Kingdom/uk_news> (24 June 2005).

[51] At <http://www.policespeedcameras.info/Speed_Camera_News_United_Kingdom/uk_news>.

[52] At <http://www.timesonline.co.uk> (5 July 2005).

[53] P Smith, spokesperson for 'Safespeed', quoted at <http://timesonline.co.uk> (15 July2005) 1.

[54] B Webster, 'Speed camera u-turn as 500 sites rejected', available at <http://www.timesonline.co.uk> (5 July 2011).

[55] Webster, 'Speed camera u-turn' (cited in n 55).

[56] Of course, it is not imagined that the online politics is somehow a distinct sphere, any more than is the case for other media politics. Nevertheless, the form of participation is distinctive, with more or less direct participation of a multitude of voices, and it is this which lies at the basis of claims that a new form of civil society—or post civil society—may be beginning to emerge: Hardt and Negri, *Empire* (cited in n 32).

[57] Tozer, 'Town that scrapped "motorist tax" speed camera' (cited in n 47).

speed cameras and new speed limits in Australia's Northern Territory was associated with a 36 per cent increase in road deaths, and in Cumbria, England they were reported to have risen by 40 per cent after the introduction of speed cameras.[58] In particular, one 'secret' UK Ministry of Transport study (which online bloggers claimed could only be accessed after a Freedom of Information Act request) received huge Internet coverage because it showed a 55 per cent increase in injury accidents when speed cameras were used at highway work zones, and a 31 per cent increase when used on motorways where there were no road works.[59] Such data were associated with a mass demonstration on Britain's M4 motorway involving over 400 vehicles on the grounds that 'safe driving is too complex to be measured in miles per hour' and that speed cameras had distracted government from more effective interventions because of their ease of installation and other, revenue-related, advantages. Individual voices added anecdotal evidence, a typical example (from hundreds) claiming that 'speedcams make things more dangerous, not safer. You have to slow down really quickly from 70mph to 40mph and motorists slam on their brakes at the last moment'.[60] One commentator went so far as to argue that 'most accidents are caused because drivers are unable to concentrate on the road because they are looking for cameras'.[61] In short, the online politics brought together competing and conflicting expert commentaries, and to these added the experiential politics of the discontented subjects of control.

Newspaper reports were also rebroadcast online when—as for example in Melbourne in 2004—predictions that accident rates would increase when speed cameras were withdrawn proved false. Thus *The Age* newspaper was extensively quoted as arguing that this 'raises questions about the Government's strong linking of speed camera enforcement to reductions in the road toll. The police figures compare Ring Road crash and injury statistics from 2002 and 2003 with data from the first 10 months of this [2004] year.'[62] 'Between January and the end of October, there were 60 crashes causing injury on the Ring Road. The year before there were 91 injury-causing crashes and 70 in 2002.'[63]

Many online commentators highlighted the paradox that while speed cameras were attributed with reducing accidents in black spots, in practice it could often be found that overall accident rates at national or local government levels did not decline, and even that long-term declines had been turned around since the

[58] See, eg, R Cavenagh, 'Northern Territory Road toll Soars as Speed cameras take their toll', available at <http://www.roadsense.com.au.latest.html> (20 September 2008).

[59] Available at <http://www.roadsense.com.au/latest.html>. The report cited was *Safety Performance of Traffic Management* (8 May 2005).

[60] 'Speedcam doubles smashes on UK M-Way' reported at <http://www.policespeedcameras.info/Speed_Camera_News_United_Kingdom/uk_news> (5 July 2011).

[61] Brian Gregory, spokesperson for the Association of British Drivers, quoted in P Stretton, 'More councils poised to scrap speed cameras' (2008) *Daily Express* 24 October. It is typical to see an anti-speed-camera advocate quoted in the printed media and then to have that quote placed online by another anti-speed-camera organization—in this case by <http://www.roadsense.com>.

[62] 'Road toll drops while VIV speed cameras down' *The Age* (6 December 2004) 2, available at <http://www.roadsense.com.au/latest.html>.

[63] *The Age* (2 December 2004) 2.

introduction of cameras. For example, the CEO of the British Institute of Advanced Motorists, self-proclaimed as 'the largest road safety charity in the country', made the claim that speed cameras created feelings of resentment and victimization that led to a disrespect for speed limits. Thus, overall, many opponents concluded that while safety may or may not increase around cameras, crashes are driven elsewhere and this accounts for the failure of road carnage to decline.[64] Most commonly aired were observations that cameras distracted drivers, with the president of the (US) National Motorists Association taking the view that an increase in speed limits in the USA contributed to declines in accident rates because 'now motorists can coast at these faster speeds without being on the constant lookout for radar guns, speed traps and state troopers'.[65] Such 'displacement' arguments were common but rarely evidenced. But this hardly halted quite extreme opposition based on the assumption it was fact: in one of the more extreme statements, the site 'SafeSpeed' proclaimed, 'We must get these dangerous cameras off the roads right now. People are dying because of them. The term "safety cameras" will go down in history as a sick joke.'[66]

Red-light cameras have come in for an almost equal amount of criticism. Overall, even government and other official research reports indicate that their benefits are mixed, with a tendency for right-angle crashes (which are more often fatal and injurious) to decrease, but for tail-end accidents to increase significantly—largely attributed to drivers braking suddenly at camera-controlled intersections.[67] However other studies were cited, including a seven-year study of red-light cameras in the US District of Columbia, that concluded there was no evidence of reductions in accidents or injuries, and there was evidence of significant increases in certain locales. As a result of such mixed findings several US states that had installed red-light cameras abandoned the programme, including Virginia and Hawaii, while an array of others have banned their future use.[68]

Finally, claims of the success of speed cameras have been undermined by campaigns challenging them on various technical grounds. Specific conflicts have arisen around claims that individual speed cameras exaggerate recordings, resulting in unjustified prosecutions. In 2011, Alberta cancelled around 100,000 speeding tickets issued in the previous 14 months due to driver-led concerns with the accuracy of equipment.[69] The switching off of speed cameras on Melbourne's Ring Road system in 2004 was the direct consequence of an admission by the

64 Available at <http://www.policespeedcameras.info/Speed_Camera_News_United_Kingdom/uk_news> (15 June 2005).

65 'With higher speed limits American highways are getting safer', available at <http://roadsense.com.aulatest.html>.

66 Paul Smith, founder of SafeSpeed, an online organization in Britain but here quoted by another online site in Australia: 'Roads fatalities leap 39 per cent at camera sites', available at <http://www.roadsense.com.au/latest>.

67 'Red light camera', available at Wikipedia: <http://en.wikipedia.org/wiki/Red_light_camera>.

68 See, eg, Texas House of Representatives, *Red-light Cameras in Texas: A Status Report* (2006) for an overall review of data.

69 Available at <http://www.edmonton.ca/city_government/news/intersection-safetry-camera-spe.aspx>.

government that possibly thousands of drivers had been fined as a result of faulty cameras, a problem that also resulted in the 2009 switching off of the Point-to-Point cameras on that state's freeways. Again, these responses were triggered largely by protests from those who regarded themselves as victims of technical faults. By and large such difficulties were officially dismissed as teething problems. In Victoria, for example, the cameras were switched on again over parts of the freeway network within a year (although at the time of writing Point-to-Point cameras have not been reactivated). But more systematic problems were broadcast by opponents, who accessed a Victoria Police operating manual that supposedly 'outlines compelling evidence that trees, wind, billboards and even birds can cause an inaccurate reading' as well as heavy rain.[70]

It should be made clear that it is not my aim or interest to verify data or to arbitrate these disputes. Some have led to the withdrawal of cameras, others are almost laughably inaccurate. The key points are two. First, it is by no means the case that we can witness an unresisted, technologically driven roll-out of mass preventive justice in the largest field of such intervention. And secondly, a significant resource of opposition has been precisely the virtual environment. While the politics of dispute flow back and forward between arenas of traditional politics and the Internet, as should be anticipated, resistance has been extensively mobilized by and between 'dividuals' operating on single-issue politics. Contributors almost never reveal or raise class, education, gender, party political or other 'traditional' political solidarities. Their solidarity is formed around their dividuated status.

Their politics is challenging the technology of mass preventive justice rather than its purported aims of producing increased safety. These challenges to the risk-based jurisprudence and apparatus on which mass preventive justice is founded were effected by various means: by valorizing conflicting conclusions of expert studies and experiential observations that conflicted with developing preventive practices and technologies; by proposing that risk reduction may be better achieved by other techniques; and by challenging universal explanations through reference to the impact of diverse local conditions.[71] By challenging the scientific standing of the jurisprudence of risk in a key respect these online politics reveal that its strength—and thus a key strength of mass preventive justice—is also a major source of vulnerability. Perhaps precisely because its moral ground is that of safety, and because its techniques for producing safety are scientific technologies, in no other domain of justice does the regime of law appear so vulnerable to empirical critiques of ineffectiveness. This also is consistent with the fact that its moral foundation seems to rest in no other domain—in contrast, say, to much criminal justice where moral arguments other than those of safety bear at least as much weight. As may be seen by reference to the history of speeding, without the justification of physical harm minimization, simulated justice appears as a tax and thus either as inappropri-

[70] Available at <http://roadsense.com.au/latest.html> (3 June 2004).

[71] See B Wynne, 'May the sheep safely graze?' in S Lash and B Wynne (eds), *Risk, Environment and Modernity* (1996) 44–83.

ate to justice or as an implicitly illegitimate source of state revenue masquerading under a guise of security.

Necessarily, this leads to a consideration of the seemingly essential nexus between mass preventive justice and money sanctions.

## F. Money: the risky necessity?

It has already been suggested that money is one of the keys to understanding mass preventive justice. At least on the face of it, the fact that money sanctions are so cheap to administer compared to most other sanctions, linked with the fact that fines (and associated fees) produce revenues for the state, has made possible the sheer scale of traffic governance. As well, it has been suggested that the low political profile of money sanctions compared to the traditional penalties of liberal criminal law has made this expansion possible without raising insuperable barriers to the development of a form of criminal governance that governs populations not normally the target of punitive justice. Moreover, money may be directly connected to yet other facets of mass preventive justice. The (re)appearance of fines in the early 20th century was associated with the development of streamlined procedures in summary justice. The 'it's only money' effect facilitated such stripping away of procedure precisely because liberty was not directly at stake.[72]

However, the radical possibilities for this stripped-down justice assemblage were not to be realized until the late 1960s. As Fox has carefully mapped out,[73] a sequence of dramatic transformations in justice was set in motion by the fact that the huge volumes of justice business arising from traffic regulation required unprecedented innovation. Over a period of less than a decade, notices for traffic offences ranging from humble parking infringements up to serious speeding offences (short of dangerous driving) became subject to reverse onus, strict liability, and fixed penalty conditions. Opting into the judicial process rather than accepting the charge and paying the penalty ran the risk of losing sentencing discounts of up to two-thirds, and of incurring court costs. Money sanctions appeared to be absolutely critical to the viability of mass justice.

Yet money proved to be a vulnerable preventive strategy. A potentially serious issue appeared in that, given the preventive agenda, money fines appeared problematically as a purchasable licence to speed. However, this was soon resolved, at least in part, by the invention of demerit points that could be delivered as an additional sanction. (Demerit points are virtually never delivered without a fine.) This innovation had the distinct advantage of incapacitating risky drivers without raising the spectre of imprisonment. As well, demerit points proved to be available to online justice, being distributed and where necessary translated into licence

[72] S Garton, 'Bad or mad? Developments in incarceration in NSW 1880–1920' in Sydney Labour History Group (ed), *What Rough beast? The State and Social Order in Australian History* (1982) 89–110; R Freiberg and S Ross, *Sentencing Reform and Penal Change* (1999).

[73] Fox, *Criminal Justice on the Spot* (cited in n 4).

cancellation without the need for court appearances, and even being manageable online. In Australia the assemblage of fines and simulated justice survived and prospered even when for unrelated reasons it became almost impossible to imprison those offenders in default of payment. But the golden egg—the fact that preventive justice was potentially a money spinner for governments at all levels—was also the ticking time bomb. From the beginning, as mentioned, the argument that speeding offences were little more than a tax, was widely mobilized. But a century later the issue began to threaten, if certainly not the entire apparatus, nevertheless substantial elements of it.

Reflecting trends in the USA, Canada, and Australia, in Britain in 2010 a discourse emerged that had not been seen for more than a century, that of a 'war on motorists'.[74] The Conservative-Liberal Democrat coalition government began to respond to an enormous volume of complaints that despite official guidelines that prioritize accident prevention, cameras were not placed in areas of high accident risk but rather were placed where they could earn the most revenue. Such claims were commonplace on the Internet for a decade and were amplified when translated into party politics. In the USA, in particular, campaigns around this issue were prominent among factors leading to cameras being turned off in Texas as early as the 1980s, and later in Arizona, Illinois, and Alaska.[75] In 2011, the New South Wales Liberal (conservative) government banned the further roll-out of speed cameras until the results of an audit were published, triggered by claims that some of the highest-earning cameras were in areas where crashes had never been a significant problem. The government promised that where it could be shown that cameras were not proven to produce a measurable effect in increasing safety they would be removed.[76] In Britain, the 2005 roll-out ban imposed by the government had led to a host of postings repeating a *Times Online* claim that '[traffic safety] partnership staff may favour cameras over other solutions (because) they need to ensure a steady flow of income to pay their salaries'.[77] No doubt it is significant that while this report was widely aired, counterclaims from ACPO at the time, that all

[74] R Massey, 'Labour's 13-year war on the motorist is over', available at <http://www.dailymail.co.uk/news/article-1278161>.

[75] Texas House of Representatives, *Red-light Cameras in Texas* (cited in n 68).

[76] As this chapter was being completed, the results of this audit appeared. While overall arguing that data showed the cameras to be effective in reducing crashes, the report recommended the moving or replacing of 38 out of 141 cameras on the grounds that 'their primary role is revenue raising'. The change would lose the government almost AU$100 million per annum, based on the fact that between 2005/6 (when revenues were far smaller) and 2010/11 the cameras generated more than AU$347 million: *Sydney Morning Herald* (28 July 2011) 1.

[77] Reported in B Webster at <http://www.timesonline.co.uk> (15 July 2005). There were frequent references to studies that claimed to demonstrate the superiority of engineering solutions. A study originating at the University of Liverpool, for example, was quoted as arguing that 'Speed humps and cushions had a significant impact on fatal and serious accidents but cameras didn't. In 30 mph areas, humps reduced accidents at 149 sites compared to 29 per cent for other engineering changes and 22 per cent for speed cameras.' Motoring organizations such as the RAC followed up with their own views that such data showed that 'we have become hooked on speed cameras and need to think up more innovative ways of changing driver behaviour': D Williams, 'Speed cameras' effect on crashes "exaggerated"' *Evening Standard.* Reported at <http://www.policespeedcameras.info/Speed_Camera_News_United_Kingdom/uk_news> (23 May 2005).

sites submitted for approval had met official guidelines, were generally marginalized or ignored.[78]

It was not just the volumes of money generated that raised opposition—although this was the most frequently mentioned issue and generated high-profile cases. In Britain one camera became the target of a political campaign because it was reported to have earned £1.3 million over the previous decade on a strip of dual carriageway, while in NSW another was reported to have earned AU$2.2 million in the 2010–2011 financial year.[79] Some governments, such as that in the UK until 2007, dedicated the income generated to improvements in road safety, but more commonly—argued on the basis of budgetary rationality—treated fines simply as part of consolidated revenue. This, of course, makes governments vulnerable, especially as it leads to income from fines appearing in forward-planning estimates in state budgets. Equally problematic has been the widespread use of arrangements with private companies to install and operate safety cameras under contract. In models commonly used in the past the government licensed companies to install and maintain cameras, placed according to guidelines that included the requirement that the site be a high-risk zone. In exchange, the company kept a certain proportion of the revenues generated.[80] Thus in 2000 the state government of Victoria contracted with Tenix to operate cameras in freeway tunnels, allowing a bounty of AU$16 per speeding ticket issued. However, unsurprisingly this model generated very high levels of opposition online, on the grounds that it was a direct inducement to maximize fines rather than produce road safety. In most instances this practice has been curtailed. More frequently of late (although the company may often retain a small percentage of fines) the bulk of income comes from set fees paid by the relevant government. Even so, public opposition to private contractors operating speed camera systems remains high, this being a factor in the curtailments to camera operations in Arizona during 2010.[81]

Elsewhere forms of guerrilla action emerged. Some deployed humour as, for example, where signs advertising 'speed cameras' were altered to read 'greed cameras', provoking online sympathetic responses such as 'Every time I see one of these signs has been altered I have got to laugh. The government and police are making a tidy sum from these cameras.'[82] More extreme saboteurs began destroying cameras. In Britain, in Essex alone, six cameras were set on fire (with each unit costing an estimated £24,000). In one instance, websites created a social bandit out of a figure named 'Captain Gatso' (GATSOMETER is the name of a brand of speed camera) who grandly announced a struggle 'against an unjust form of taxation' and threatened 'increased operations across the country'.[83] A group called MAD (Motorists Against Detection) which reported itself as having a hard core of

[78] Webster at <http://www.timesonline.co.uk> (cited in n 77).

[79] 'Cash Cow speed cameras raise $350m' *Sydney Morning Herald* (2 June 2011) 5.

[80] Texas House of Representatives, *Red-light Cameras in Texas* (cited in n 68) 7.

[81] Texas House of Representatives, *Red-light Cameras in Texas* (cited in n 68) 7.

[82] 'Flash of wit (but police don't think it's funny)', available at <http://www.policespeedcameras.info/Speed_Camera_News_United_Kingdom/uk_news> (25 August 2006).

[83] S Khan, 'Saboteurs take out 700 speed cameras' *The Observer* (7 September 2003).

200 members, claimed responsibility for having destroyed 1000 cameras since 2000. The group claimed to use 'Internet chat forums, encrypted email and pay as you go phones to keep in touch and plan campaigns'.[84] In practice, this group—referred to insightfully in *The Observer* newspaper as 'a gang of web-surfing outlaws'—may have involved only a handful of isolated individuals, although the press estimated that some 700 cameras had been destroyed across the nation, with particularly active cells in Essex, Wales, and London.[85] The importance of such accounts is not so much the reality of the threats they posed. It was, rather, the symbolic role they appeared to occupy in an active online opposition movement mobilized primarily by the perception that money fines were an index of government agencies using the jurisprudence of risk as a cover for revenue-raising.

## G. Human rights and privacy

Perhaps, more than any single issue, it might have been predicted that privacy, and also related human rights issues, would have been the matters receiving the most attention in Internet oppositions and related politics. In practice the picture is more muted and less well articulated than are issues focused either on revenue-raising or on the effectiveness and accuracy of camera technology. For the most part, concerns are raised at the level of 'the surveillance state' and 'Big Brother' without very much more elaboration.[86] This is not to say that the matter is of low importance—as the fact of its numerically frequent appearance suggests otherwise. In the USA, such concerns have been raised as contributory concerns influencing several states (Arizona most recently) to curtail or even shut down camera systems. In part, more specific debates in the USA have been curtailed by argument (said online to stem back to the case of *Katz v United States*)[87] that the Constitution does not protect the privacy of those who are engaged in breaking the law, and that there is no privacy interest in what is routinely and regularly displayed in public.[88] Much the same argument is regularly aired in relation to a case before the European Court of Human Rights that found the Human Rights Act 1998 was not being violated where the owner of a vehicle was required to identify the driver in relation to a speeding offence.[89] Indeed, it could even be maintained that reference to such

[84] Available at <http://www.speedcam.co.uk/welcome.htm>.

[85] Available at <http://www.speedcam.co.uk/welcome.htm>.

[86] This concurs with the findings of Wells and Wills, 'Individualism' and identity (cited in n 13) 259.

[87] *Katz v United States* 389 U.S. 347 (1967).

[88] See, eg, 'Maryland Safe Zones', available at <http://safezones.maryland.gov/faqs.html>; see also the discussion by S Klein, 'Traffic cameras: Protecting our streets or invading our privacy?', available at <http://cseserv.engr.scu.edu/StudentWebPages/SKlein?researchpaper.htm>.

[89] See 'traffic enforcement camera', available at <http://en.wikipedia.org/Traffic_enforcement_camera>. I am grateful to Anthony Ashworth for pointing out that the judgment, more precisely, found that the European Convention on Human Rights and its privilege against self-incrimination were not violated in this situation: *O'Halloran v the United Kingdom* (2008) 46 European Rights Reports 407. Such drifts in meaning between original findings and Internet reports are not at all uncommon, and several examples have been noted previously.

seeming failures of privacy and human rights concerns accounts for most of the postings other than the most cursory references to Big Brother.

It is possible that much of the comparatively muted concern about this issue has been a consequence of the fact that that by and large cameras have focused only on vehicle number plates, and that photographs are taken only when tripped by a vehicle (at least arguably) breaking the law. Certainly these arguments are routinely brought up on police and government websites as FAQ issues. What is perhaps surprising is that they rarely seem to be contested—unlike the issues of accuracy and revenue-raising. There can be little doubt too that there are strategic consideration at work on the regulator's front. Thus in NSW it was reported to Parliament that the decision not to take frontal photographs was in order 'to ensure early public acceptance of the new enforcement technology by eliminating possible concerns about occupant's privacy'—an issue that had earlier been raised by the Privacy Committee.[90]

New technologies are already beginning to increase the level of online concern voiced about the privacy issue. On the one hand, Point-to-Point systems track car movements rather than simply locating cars breaking the law. In Australia, for example, concerns were raised specifically about Point-to-Point monitoring, it being argued that (in Canberra) 'the car movements of many Canberrans will be recorded on a daily basis and I think there are some genuine privacy questions that need to be ironed out'.[91] On the other hand, concerns arise out of what the technology might easily become. Thus not only do NSW police now allow frontal photography of vehicles, but the concern increasingly is being aired online that that these will involve 'full frontal images of vehicles including the driver and front passenger, that are clear enough for identification purposes and usable as evidence in court'.[92] In part, this practice has been justified as a means of stifling a growing market in trading demerit points—that is, offering to take money in exchange for falsely claiming to have been the driver of a speeding vehicle. Such a market, inter alia, clearly impacts on the safety campaigns. But given that such camera systems are already promoted by police for multiple crime-enforcement roles (for example tracking unlicensed drivers, unregistered and stolen vehicles) and would have clear advantages in national security policing, there is little doubt that this is a politics waiting to unfold. As yet, it remains an issue largely silent in online debate.

[90] See <http://www.parliament.nsw.gov.au/prod/law/qala.nsf/0/CA25708400173F6CA25704A>.

[91] See <http://www.abc.net.au?/news/stories/2010/07/212959683.htm?sire=canberra>. There are interesting questions to be worked out around the issue of how far 'privacy' is breached when the camera transmits information to a computer, and a computer transmits it to the offender. The process may remain entirely invisible to others. Perhaps this is an empirical question rather than a legal or philosophical issue alone, in the sense that some people would think this an invasion of privacy and others not. It does not appear to be a matter that has come before the courts. However, against this—as with most CCTV footage that is never viewed—such images may be *available* for viewing by other people, and hence the issue generates conventional privacy concerns.

[92] See <http://www.privacydigest.com/2008/09/28/privacy%20concerns%20speed%20cameras>.

## H. Conclusions

One suggestion underlying this chapter is that the rise of mass preventive justice is part of the monetization of justice more generally. For most of the 20th century, across most jurisdictions money sanctions have been the principal sanction in civil and criminal law, and perhaps this is true too in administrative and regulatory law more generally. Certainly this is the case if the sheer mass of traffic regulation is considered. As argued, money sanctions may have been the key to this 'massification' of justice, being cheap to administer and even providing revenues, permitting the stripping away of legal process and thus its automation, and to a degree generating less political resistance than might have arisen had traditional corporal or incarcerating sanctions been deployed routinely.

Against an overly simplistic reading of this assemblage, arguably the formation of the principal forms of opposition has primarily been through and about money. It is not simply that the revenue-earning potential of mass preventive justice has been a key issue both in its expansion and in respect of resistance to it, although this is vital. It could be suggested as well that it is money in the form of fines that drives the linked politics challenging the accuracy of the technology and its accident-reducing impact. In comparison, human rights and privacy issues are not often mentioned in online resistant discourses, and even more rarely are they the subject of elaboration. More surprising still, while demerit points are in some respects a much more serious sanction than a fine, and are the sanction next in line after fines, they too are rather rarely mentioned outside government and police websites. Quite likely this is partly because only a few lose licences compared to those fined. But equally plausible is a claim that those who lose their licences, as multiple repeat offenders or as gross offenders (that is, where very high-speed offences lead to immediate disqualification), are generally regarded as having jeopardized their claim to being everyday citizens falling victim to 'greed cameras'. Even the most rabid opponents of cameras claim to support road safety, and some of the most critical among these support the idea of cracking down on those 'hard cases' who flout speed limits rather than 'accidentally' straying. Likewise, there is little or no resistance to drink-driving versions of mass preventive justice—for which the penalty is usually both disqualification and a fine. The vast majority of opposition to mass preventive justice focuses on the speed-fine couple, and a large bulk of this—which incorporates the claims that cameras are about revenue rather than safety—queries in one way or another the link between speed and risk. This readily could lead to the conclusion that it is speed rather than money that is the principal issue. But there are other matters to consider.

It is also a characteristic of these oppositional discourses that where they do argue for alternatives to speed cameras (ie rather than simply abolishing them), they do not argue for other systems of punishment per se, but for better road engineering and driver education. If the latter is disciplinary, the former doubtless is another diagram of 'control'. It is easy to forget that road engineering immanently modulates risk, and governs circulations and distributions anonymously. Its archetype perhaps is the speed hump; its future may be immobilizing or simply 'containing' systems of electronic vehicle control that prevent vehicles speeding. The dream of prefect prevention could thus be realized and money sanctions marginalized. For this reason alone it should not be assumed that simulated justice—through remote sensing and electronically issued and expiated fines—is the future. It *may* prove to be more trouble than it's worth. And another flaw—that fines can be seen as a licence to speed—may add to this doubt. A more elaborate system of demerit points, operated just as cheaply through simulated justice, could neutralize the politics of money and direct mass preventive justice in new directions.

Even so, other lines of flight are possible and perhaps are more likely to emerge than perfect accident prevention. If developments along the lines of electronic vehicle identification and point-to-point cameras continue, and even more so if they are linked to frontal facial photography and (as is speculated) real-time video monitoring—and the technology for these already is in place—then a quantum leap may be in the offing. Police organizations have made clear the attractiveness of such systems for crime control beyond traffic offences, and the potential for linking such use with more hard-core security policing is obvious enough.[93] 'Good' circulations will remain unmolested other than for the occasional inconvenience of a fine, perhaps demerit points. But in a securitized array, where mass prevention in the name of traffic safety is linked to highly targeted prevention in the name of national security, then the discourses of simulated justice and resistance to it may morph into a new course, and a new online politics of resistance.

[93] For example Winnett and Gadher, 'Goodbye speed cameras' (cited in n 19), pointed out that the British ACPO has noted 47 different possible applications for EVI.

# Index

## *Introductory Note*

References such as '138–9' indicate (not necessarily continuous) discussion of a topic across a range of pages. Wherever possible in the case of topics with many references, these have either been divided into sub-topics or only the most significant discussions of the topic are listed. Because the entire volume is about 'prevention' and the 'criminal law', the use of these terms (and certain others occurring throughout the work) as entry points has been restricted. Information will be found under the corresponding detailed topics.

The manufacturer's authorised representative in the EU for product safety is Oxford University Press España S.A. of El Parque Empresarial San Fernando de Henares, Avenida de Castilla, 2 - 28830 Madrid (www.oup.es/en or product.safety@oup.com). OUP España S.A. also acts as importer into Spain of products made by the manufacturer.
Printed and bound by CPI Group (UK) Ltd, Croydon, CR0 4YY
14/09/2026
02216307-0012